Racism and Public Policy

Racism and Public Policy

Edited by

Yusuf Bangura
United Nations Research Institute for Social Development

and

Rodolfo Stavenhagen
El Colegio de Mexico

First published 2005 by
PALGRAVE MACMILLAN
Houndmills, Basingstoke, Hampshire RG21 6XS and
175 Fifth Avenue, New York, N.Y. 10010
Companies and representatives throughout the world

PALGRAVE MACMILLAN is the global academic imprint of the Palgrave Macmillan division of St. Martin's Press, LLC and of Palgrave Macmillan Ltd. Macmillan® is a registered trademark in the United States, United Kingdom and other countries. Palgrave is a registered trademark in the European Union and other countries.

ISBN-13: 978 1–4039–4916–5 hardback
ISBN-10: 1–4039–4916–6 hardback

This book is printed on paper suitable for recycling and made from fully managed and sustained forest sources.

A catalogue record for this book is available from the British Library.

Library of Congress Cataloging-in-Publication Data

Racism and public policy / edited by Yusuf Bangura and Rodolfo Stavenhagen.
    p. cm.
    Papers presented at a parallel conference to the World Conference against Racism, Racial
    Discrimination, and Related Intolerance that was held in Durban in 2001.
    Includes bibliographical references and index.
    ISBN 1–4039–4916–6 (hardback)
    1. Racism – Congresses. 2. Xenophobia – Congresses. 3. Race discrimination – Government policy – Congresses. 4. Minorities – Government policy – Congresses. 5. Citizenship – Congresses. 6. Social justice – Congresses. I. Bangura, Yusuf, 1950–
    II. Stavenhagen, Rodolfo.

HT1505.R37   2005
305.8 – dc22

2004056997

| 10 | 9 | 8 | 7 | 6 | 5 | 4 | 3 | 2 | 1 |
| 14 | 13 | 12 | 11 | 10 | 09 | 08 | 07 | 06 | 05 |

Printed and bound in Great Britain by
Antony Rowe Ltd, Chippenham and Eastbourne

Contents

List of Tables and Figures

List of Abbreviations and Acronyms

ASB	Amanah Saham Bumiputera
ASN	Amanah Saham Nasional
BCIC	Bumiputera Commercial and Industrial Community
BN	Barisan Nasional (Malaysian National Front coalition)
BNP	British National Party
BOP	Black Officers Forum (South Africa)
BPA	Black Police Association
CBNRM	community-based natural resources management
CETA	Comprehensive Employment and Training Act (US)
CICU	Central Information Collection Unit (Malaysia)
Congo (DR)	Democratic Republic of Congo
CPFs	community-police forums
CPI	Consumer Price Index
DAP	Democratic Action Party (Malaysia)
DF	Danish People's Party
DVU	German People's Union
EOI	export-oriented industrialization
FN	Front National (France)
4MP	*Fourth Malaysia Plan, 1981–1985*
FP	Denmark Progress Party
FPÖ	Austrian Freedom Party
FPS	Swiss Freedom Party
FrP	Norway Progress Party
GCC	Gulf Cooperation Council
Gerakan	Gerakan Rakyat Malaysia (Malaysian People's Movement)
HART	Halt All Racial Tours
ICA	Industrial Coordination Act (Malaysia)
ICD	Independent Complaints Directorate (South Africa)
ILO	International Labour Organization
ISI	import substitution industrialization
KLSE	Kuala Lumpur Stock Exchange
LAPD	Los Angeles Police Department
LN	Northern League (Italy)

ix

MCA	Malaysian Chinese Association
MIC	Malayan Indian Congress
MNCs	multinational corporations
MOOHR	Maori Organization on Human Rights
MRN	Republican National Movement (France)
MSI	Italian Social Movement
MTO	Moving to Opportunity programme (US)
MTR5MP	*Fifth Malaysia Plan, 1986–1990*, Mid-Term Review
MWWL	Maori Women's Welfare League
NDP	National Development Policy (Malaysia)
NEP	New Economic Policy (Malaysia)
NGOs	non-governmental organizations
NICs	newly-industrialized countries
NPD	National Democratic Party (Germany)
NRC	National Research Council (US)
OPP	Outline Perspective Plans (Malaysia)
ÖVP	Austrian People's Party
PAS	Parti Islam (Malaysia)
Pernas	Perbadanan Nasional (Malaysia)
PMIP	Pan Malaysian Islamic Party
PNB	Permodalan Nasional Berhad (Malaysia)
POPCRU	Police and Prisons Civil Rights Union (South Africa)
PSE	Public Service Employment programmes (US)
REP	Republican Party (Germany)
SAPS	South African Police Service
SEDCs	state economic development corporations (Malaysia)
SOEs	state-owned enterprises
SRI	Suspension Reduction Initiative (NZ)
SVP	Swiss People's Party
UDA	Urban Development Authority (Malaysia)
UDHR	Universal Declaration of Human Rights
UMNO	United Malays National Organization
UNCED	United Nations Conference on Environment and Development
VB	Flemish Bloc (Belgium)
WTO	World Trade Organization

Preface

This book is a product of UNRISD's contribution to the third *World Conference against Racism, Racial Discrimination and Related Intolerance*, which was held in Durban in 2001. The Institute invited more than 30 prominent scholars from all regions of the world to prepare papers and lead discussions in a parallel conference that focused on the research and policy dimensions of the problems of racism. High-level public figures, development policy analysts and advisers from within and outside the United Nations system chaired the ten panels. The former High Commissioner for Human Rights, Mary Robinson, opened the conference by highlighting the strong links between inequality of treatment, or racial discrimination, and inequality of outcomes as measured in terms of income, wealth, social development and power.

Racism, racial discrimination, xenophobia and intolerance are global problems. They affect the life-chances of individuals, social groups, institutions and public policies that seek to promote cohesion, equity and development. Even though the concept of race has been challenged by recent findings in genetic research, physical differences continue to influence perceptions and are an important source of prejudice in human interactions. Discussions on racism can be emotive as they often touch on issues of identity, dignity, justice and historical violations. The main value of the UNRISD conference was the neutral platform it provided to discuss the sensitive issues that world leaders were grappling with in the inter-governmental forum. It addressed the social construction of race and citizenship; the socio-economic and political forces that drive racism and inequalities; organized responses to cultural diversity; and the impact of various types of public policies on race relations.

This book discusses two important public policy issues that have been central to debates on racism. The first deals with citizenship. The history of efforts to establish accountable public sectors in multiracial societies is largely about struggles to roll back racial barriers and create a normative or legal order in which all are treated equally. Universal citizenship requires respect for cultural diversity, tolerance and accommodation. The world has certainly made progress in combating the scourge of racism and expanding the frontiers of citizenship. It is difficult to find a state that currently defines itself in racial terms or explicitly supports public policies that are racially discriminating. However, a gulf remains between theory, or law, and practice. Many individuals who work in the public sector of many countries still hold racist views and discriminate against others they consider to be different. In other words, formal equality has not translated into substantive equality. It is not surprising that institutional racism currently dominates discussions on racism. The world should not relent in its efforts to rid the public sphere of racist individuals, values and practices.

The second issue is about social justice and equitable governance. These are needed to achieve stability and consolidate the values of citizenship. However, redistributive policies are not always easy to implement since they affect people differently. Losers may resist the policies, and winners may not be strong enough to defend them. However, governments often have room for active redistributive policies. The book shows that the content, application and outcomes of redistributive policies in ethno-racial societies may vary according to whether the disadvantaged population constitutes the majority group, has attained formal citizenship long enough to defend it and has strong access to policy-making institutions; or whether beneficiaries are a minority with limited influence on government. Redistributive policies thus vary a lot in countries such as the United States, South Africa, Zimbabwe, Malaysia, Brazil and India.

We would like to thank the United Nations Department of Economic and Social Affairs for funding the conference. Thanks are also due to the governments of Denmark, Finland, Mexico, the Netherlands, Norway, Sweden, Switzerland and the United Kingdom for their core funding. Finally, we wish to thank Thomas Ansorg for helping to organize the conference and developing the conference website, and Michele Tan for formating the manuscript and checking the references.

Thandika Mkandawire
Director
United Nations Research Institute for Social
Development

Notes on the Contributors

Yusuf Bangura is Research Co-coordinator at the United Nations Research Institute for Social Development (UNRISD) for projects on Public Sector Reform and Crisis States, and Economic Policy-Making and Democratization. He received his undergraduate and doctoral degrees from the London School of Economics and Political Science in 1974 and 1978. He has taught in universities in Nigeria and Canada and worked as a visiting researcher in Sweden. He has published widely on the politics of economic relations, the African crisis, structural adjustment and livelihood strategies, democratization and ethnic conflicts. He co-coordinated the UNRISD project on Racism and Public Policy.

Hans-Georg Betz is a publicist and research associate at the Canadian Centre for German and European Studies, York University, Toronto. From 1988 to 2002, he was Professor of Comparative Politics at various North American and European universities, among them Marquette University (Milwaukee), Loyola University Rome Centre (Rome), The Paul Nitze School of Advanced International Studies (SAIS, Washington), Koc University (Istanbul) and York University (Toronto). He has held visiting positions in Japan and at New York University and Columbia University. He has published numerous works on right-wing radicalism, European politics and political culture, among them *Radical Right-Wing Populism in Western Europe*, and *Cette droite radicale en Europe: Radiographie des populismes*.

Benjamin Bowling is Professor of Criminology and Criminal Justice in the School of Law, King's College, London University and Visiting Professor at the University of the West Indies, Cave Hill, Barbados. He has a BA in Psychology from Manchester Metropolitan University and a PhD from the London School of Economics. He was formerly Senior Research Officer in the Home Office, Visiting Assistant Professor at John Jay College of Criminal Justice in New York City, and Lecturer in Criminology at Cambridge University. He contributed to the Stephen Lawrence Inquiry and has acted as a consultant to the Metropolitan Police, the Commission for Racial Equality and the United Nations. Ben Bowling's publications include *Young People and Crime* (with J. Graham),

Violent Racism and *Racism, Crime and Justice* (with C. Phillips). He is currently researching transatlantic police cooperation.

Tony N. Brown is Assistant Professor in the Department of Sociology at Vanderbilt University, USA. His primary research interest is the relationship between racism and mental health, and his approach to the issue is informed by critical race theory. He is actively involved in funded research projects that investigate the epidemiology of mental health, whites' racial attitudes, predictors of young adults' well-being and communication patterns in paediatric medical encounters.

Alexandra Campbell is Assistant Professor of Sociology at the University of New England, Maine. She received her M.Phil and PhD in Criminology from the University of Cambridge. She has researched and written on the subject of anti-racist policing and is presently completing a book on racism and 'white' racial identity on the internet.

Sheldon Danziger is Henry J. Meyer Collegiate Professor of Public Policy and Co-Director of the National Poverty Center at the Gerald R. Ford School of Public Policy, University of Michigan. He is a Fellow of the American Academy of Arts and Sciences and a member of the Macarthur Foundation Research Network on the Transition to Adulthood. His research focuses on trends in poverty and inequality and the effects of economic and demographic changes and government social programme on the disadvantaged. He is co-author of *America Unequal* (with Peter Gottschalk) and *Detroit Divided* (with Reynolds Farley and Harry Holzer), and co-editor of many books, including most recently *Securing the Future: Investing in Children* and *Understanding Poverty*.

Maria Docking is a research officer in the Crime and Policing Group, within the Research Directorate of the UK Home Office. Her main research interests are racist incidents, police–community relations, police consultation, and stop and search. She received her master's degree in Criminology and Criminal Justice from King's College, London.

Jeroen Doomernik is a researcher and project manager at the Institute for Migration and Ethnic Studies (IMES), and Lecturer at the Department of Political Science of the University of Amsterdam. On secondment from the university, he acted as senior policy adviser to the Minister for Urban Affairs and Integration and worked at the Ministry of Justice's research and documentation centre. His main interest is policy-making in the fields of integration and immigration, and the effects of such policy. His current research focuses on the perverse effects of immigration controls in general, and on human smuggling and trafficking in particular.

George M. Fredrickson is Edgar E. Robinson Professor of United States History Emeritus at Stanford University, California. His speciality is the history of racial ideologies in the United States and elsewhere. His publications include *The Black Image in the White Mind, White Supremacy, The Arrogance of Race, Black Liberation, The Comparative Imagination* and *Racism: A Short History*. He has had numerous fellowships and has been the Harmsworth Visiting Professor of American History at the University of Oxford and Fulbright Lecturer at Moscow University.

Jomo K. S. is Professor in the Applied Economics Department, University of Malaya. He serves on the Board of the United Nations Research Institute on Social Development (UNRISD) and is Founder Chair of International Development Economics Associates. Jomo has taught in Malaysia and at Harvard, Yale, Cornell and Cambridge Universities. He has written more than 35 monographs and edited more than 50 books and translated eleven volumes. Among the most recent are: *Globalization versus Development: Heterodox Perspectives, Southeast Asia's Industrialization, Manufacturing Competitiveness in Asia, Ethnic Business: Chinese Capitalism in Southeast Asia, Deforesting Malaysia: The Political Economy of Agricultural Expansion and Commercial Logging* (for UNRISD) and *M Way: Mahathir's Economic Policy Legacy*.

Ray Jureidini is Associate Professor of Sociology in the Department of Social and Behavioral Sciences at the American University of Beirut, Lebanon. He is principal editor of an introductory sociology textbook, *Sociology: Australian Connections* (now in its third edition) and has authored numerous book chapters and journal articles. Trained in industrial and economic sociology, he has published on industrial relations, manufacturing, life insurance, organ transplantation, international aid, migration, racism and ethnicity. His current research focuses on human rights and international labour migration, in particular, the dynamics of female domestic guestworkers in the Middle East.

Khoo Boo Teik is Associate Professor in the School of Social Sciences, Universiti Sains Malaysia, Penang. He is the author of *Paradoxes of Mahathirism: An Intellectual Biography of Mahathir Mohamad* and *Beyond*

Mahathir: Malaysian Politics and its Discontents. In recent years, he has collaborated with researchers from several countries in internationally funded research projects on social, economic and political change in Asia.

Tracey McIntosh is Senior Lecturer in the Sociology Department at the University of Auckland, New Zealand. Her research and teaching interests include forms of systematic violence, genocide, ethnocide, criminality and issues pertaining to Maori. She is currently developing research protocols for working with vulnerable and marginalized sectors of society, with a specific focus on indigenous groups.

Sam Moyo has more than twenty years' research experience of rural development issues with a focus on land and natural resources management, civil society organizations, capacity-building and institutional development. He has been associated with the Institute of Development Studies of the University of Zimbabwe and ZERO (a regional environment organization) in Harare. Previous publications include: *The Land Question in Zimbabwe* and *Land Reform Under Structural Adjustment in Zimbabwe.* He was Associate Professor at the Institute of Development Studies of the University of Zimbabwe and Director of the Southern African Regional Institute for Policy Studies (SARIPS) based in Harare. He currently acts as senior adviser and chair of numerous land networks, such as the Southern African Network on Land (SANL) and Land Rights Network of Southern Africa (LRNSA).

Coretta Phillips is Lecturer in the Department of Social Policy, London School of Economics and Political Science, University of London. She was formerly Principal Research Officer in the Home Office and Assistant Professor at the School of Criminal Justice, Rutgers University (USA). She has acted as a consultant to the Home Office, Loss Prevention Council and HM Prison Service. Coretta Phillips has written extensively on ethnicity, racism and criminal justice, including *Racism, Crime and Justice* (with B. Bowling). She is currently researching minority professional associations in the criminal justice field.

Deborah Reed is Director of the Population Program at the Public Policy Institute of California. She is a specialist in labour economics with research interests in labour markets, income distribution, public policy and poverty. A recipient of fellowships from the Mellon Foundation and Yale University, she has served as a consultant to the World Bank, in addition to her teaching and research activities.

Rodolfo Stavenhagen is a Professor at El Colegio de Mexico. He has carried out research on problems of development, agriculture, indigenous peoples, human rights and ethnic conflicts in the Third World. He was Assistant Director General of UNESCO, and is on the board of a number of human rights organizations. He has been a Special Rapporteur on Indigenous Peoples for the United Nations High Commissioner for Human Rights since 2001. He has published, among others, *The Ethnic Question, Ethnic Conflicts and the Nation State, Between Underdevelopment and Revolution, Social Classes in Agrarian Societies* and *Derecho Indigena y Derechos Humanos en America Latina.*

Introduction: Racism, Citizenship and Social Justice

Yusuf Bangura and Rodolfo Stavenhagen

At the beginning of the twentieth century, W. E. B. du Bois, the pre-eminent intellectual of the African-American people, foretold that it would be the century of the 'color line'. During the decades that followed, the world witnessed the rise and fall of Nazism, the Holocaust, the civil rights movement in the United States, the end of colonialism and apartheid, the emergence of indigenous peoples as political actors on the international scene, the renewal of racism in Europe and the horrendous spectacle of ethnic cleaning and genocide in Bosnia and Rwanda. A century on, the 'color line' is still with us, separating peoples and cultures, dividing the powerful from the downtrodden. Even as it binds some together in tight ethnic communities, it ties up many others in conceptual knots.

Racism exists in varying degrees in all regions of the world. Slavery, colonialism, genocide, the Holocaust and apartheid represent its most extreme form in world history; but other overt and subtle forms of racism persist in countries around the world. Racism affects social relations, influences structures of opportunities and life-chances and may provoke violence and wars. The legacy of institutionalized racism continues to weigh heavily on the development prospects of many groups and countries, constrains prospects for social cohesion, and affects implementation of public policies for equality, justice and social development.

Thinking on racism has undergone important changes since the founding of the United Nations.[1] During the first phase, racism was identified mainly with the legacy of Nazi ideology. Nazi racism was based on a carefully constructed pseudo-scientific ideology of racial purity and superiority, which has its roots in numerous strands of Western thought and found its way into the language of academic anthropology, biology, psychology and other disciplines. Today, scien-

1

tific racism no longer commands any academic recognition whatsoever, but can still be found under various guises in some scholarly institutions and publications (Barkan, 1992). The first activities of the United Nations in the struggle against racism relate to eliminating this legacy from the postwar world, and the Universal Declaration of Human Rights of 1948 well expresses this concern.[2]

The next phase relates to the struggle against colonialism and the fight of colonized peoples everywhere for freedom and national liberation as well as the fight to end apartheid. The 1950s and 1960s saw numerous former colonies achieve independence, and also witnessed the civil rights movement in the United States. Colonial racism was formally abolished, but its effects linger on in many parts of the world. The United Nations proclaimed the right to self-determination in the Declaration on the Granting of Independence to Colonial Countries and Peoples of 1960, later incorporated as Article 1 of the Human Rights Covenants adopted by the General Assembly in 1966.[3] Emphasis shifted from individual attitudes and structured racist ideologies to the rights of peoples and the building of a new, more equitable international order. The rise to prominence of the Third World framed the background for a new scenario of international inequities, later to be accentuated by the process of economic globalization.

During the 1970s and 1980s racism re-emerged in a new guise, this time in the industrial heartlands of the North, involving mainly migrant labourers from the periphery, refugees and former colonial subjects. Incidents of racist violence, including riots, increased in the urban neighbourhoods of Western Europe. Racial discrimination was reported in the areas of education, housing, employment, health services and the criminal justice system, in which the youth of racial minorities have been particularly singled out through a process of 'criminalization'. Besides Blacks, Latinos have been prominent victims of racial profiling and discrimination in the United States.[4]

A number of states began to see racism not as a series of isolated incidents, but as a patterned and structured social problem. Massive transnational migration flows provoked widespread political debates about the perceived dangers of too many foreign migrants, the need for demographic 'balance', the control of borders, and so forth. Latent racism became manifest once again, and politicians capitalized by playing the 'immigrant-racial' card. The emergence and voter appeal of extreme right-wing political parties raised the issue to new levels. Some states enacted anti-discrimination legislation and new immigration laws, others set up commissions to study racial issues, and the European

Parliament prepared reports and passed resolutions on the topic. Racism in Europe had once more become an international issue of concern.

The nature of the debate was changing, however. Few people openly advocated racial discrimination of the phenotypical variety, and in the new global environment, the very concepts of race and racial relations were undergoing transformation. As immigrant communities mushroomed in the industrial states, perceived biological distinctions meshed with recognized cultural differences. In some countries, 'race relations' became a code-word for relations between culturally differentiated communities. Human rights defenders were now no longer advocating general equality (which seemed to many to be unattainable), but a new concept: *the right to be different.* States were expected to become less assimilationist and more pluralistic. Cultural differences were not to be abolished, but respected and celebrated. The always elusive melting-pot was to be replaced by a spicy multicultural salad bowl.

This book addresses two important public policy issues that have influenced debates on racism. The first is the complex ways racial cleavages have shaped the evolution of citizenship, especially in countries marked by deep ethno-racial divisions. Much of the history of efforts to construct a responsive and accountable public sphere can be seen as struggles to demolish racial barriers and incorporate previously excluded groups into the system of rights and obligations that define citizenship. The struggle for universal citizenship underscores the need for governments, civil society groups, corporations and development agencies to respect cultural diversity and its underlying values of tolerance, accommodation and human solidarity.

The second issue is the promotion of social justice and equitable governance, which are seen as fundamental requirements for achieving stability and consolidating the values of citizenship. However, reforms that seek to promote social justice and equitable governance are often beset with difficulties because they deal with redistributive issues. They may be seen in zero-sum terms by some citizens. Those who stand to lose may resist or undermine the reforms, while those who stand to gain may not be strong enough to defend them. Concerns for fiscal prudence under conditions of liberal competitive markets may also act as a constraint on the bridging of inequalities.

The social construction of race and citizenship

It is now widely accepted that race is socially constructed, not biologically determined. The practice of classifying humans according to distinct races has been discredited by genetic research. On average, 99.9 per cent of the genetic features of humans are the same; of the remaining percentage, which accounts for variation, differences within groups are larger than between groups (Cavalli-Sforza, Menozzi and Piazza, 1996). Despite efforts to disseminate these findings, including the adoption of the International Convention against All Forms of Racial Discrimination in 1965, a gulf exists between scientific knowledge and popular beliefs about race. Trivial as physical differences may be in accounting for biological attributes, they structure perceptions and constitute a significant source of prejudice in social relations. As a social construct, the key attributes of race are fuzzy and open to multiple interpretations: different groups may use different yardsticks in different settings to define similar populations or individuals. A coloured person in South Africa may be classified as black in the United States even if he or she has more white than black grandparents, and the designation may be meaningless in West Africa or South Asia where the racial system that gave rise to the classification does not exist. Even people with roughly the same colour and physical appearance may be categorized as different races in certain contexts. This has been the experience of groups such as the Irish and European Jews in Europe and the United States.

The construction of race as identity may be linked with ethnicity, especially when variations in physical characteristics coincide with assumed cultural, linguistic and religious differences. Examples include relations between people of Indian and African origin in Guyana and Trinidad, indigenous Fijians and Indo-Fijians in Fiji, North and South Sudanese, Tutsi and Hutu in Burundi and Rwanda, and Chinese and Malays in Malaysia. In Burundi and Rwanda, despite the fact that the two groups share skin colour, language, religion and names, variations in height, body structure and nose shape are used to establish difference (Lemarchand, 1996). In some contexts, a group may identify itself as a separate race even if there are no clear physical differences between it and the groups it seeks to categorize as the 'other'. Thus we have concepts like the 'Yoruba race' in Nigeria, the 'Italian race' in Europe and the 'Chinese race' in Asia. Even when groups do not practise overt forms of discrimination, subtle differences in physical characteristics, which may not be apparent to outsiders, may be used to construct ideas about the 'other'.

Racial ideas may influence discourses on social integration or accommodation, encourage insular or xenophobic practices, and distort perceptions about rights and citizenship. Citizens are supposed to be bearers of equal rights and obligations. In polarized racial settings, however, social solidarity, the cornerstone of citizenship, may be embedded in racial – not civic – networks, affecting the way the public domain is governed. However, it is instructive to note that all communities, whether based on racial identification or ethnicity, are complex, undergo change and experience internal diversities and conflicts. Race, in other words, is not only constructed, it is also contested.

The first five chapters of this book discuss these issues as they relate to experiences in the United States, Western Europe, the Middle East and Southern Africa. In the United States, George M. Fredrickson points out in Chapter 1 that commitment towards universal human rights coexisted with a strong historical tendency to exclude non-white groups from citizenship. The American Revolution appealed to universalistic values of human rights, but the 1789 Constitution excluded African-Americans and indigenous Indians from citizenship. The immigration law of 1790 limited the right to naturalization to 'free white persons'. Throughout the 1830s, 1840s and 1850s, as the debate on slavery intensified, pseudo-scientific racist ideologies were used by defenders of black servitude to prevent blacks from enjoying equal rights with whites. It culminated in the Supreme Court's Dred Scott decision of 1857, which declared all blacks ineligible for citizenship. The civil war and use of black troops to defend the Union represented the first major effort to extend citizenship to African-Americans. However, this gain was undermined in the South during the Jim Crow era which lasted almost a century, when blacks suffered discrimination, disenfranchisement and torture. Struggles for racial equality intensified between the 1930s and 1960s, culminating in the Civil Rights Acts of 1964 and 1965, which made citizenship rights more enforceable. However, formal equality has not led to social citizenship: a substantially higher proportion of blacks than whites are likely to be unemployed, imprisoned, in poverty or destitute.

Fredrickson discusses the United States' experience in comparative perspective. In the main, the US commitment to a universal human rights tradition distinguishes it from the German tradition of ethnic nationalism, which produced the horrors of Nazi rule and the Holocaust. Also, the United States' acceptance of multiculturalism sets it apart from the culture-coded ethno-racial intolerance of France, despite the fact that the latter has not established colour bars to protect white privilege. He concluded that since race has been socially constructed it should not be seen as natural or inevitable. There is already a process of deconstruction of race in the United States, as can be seen in the demolition of legalized segregation, racially inspired voting restrictions and discriminatory immigration quotas.

South Africa is comparable to the United States in terms of its historical commitment to institutionalized racism (Magubane, 2001). Before apartheid, the subjugation of the African population took two forms: slavery and peonage. Laws devised for indentured white immigrants, free 'coloured' workers and emancipated African slaves provided the backdrop for South Africa's notorious master and servant laws, which from 1910 were transformed into segregatory laws, and from 1948 into apartheid, effectively denying the African population citizenship rights. The 1994 Constitution and the new Government of National Unity proscribed apartheid, upheld universal citizenship for all South Africans and committed itself to both racial and gender equality.

Racial discrimination has not thrived only in societies with laws, policies and practices that classify individuals according to biological differences. In Peru and other parts of Latin America, de la Cadena (2001) has argued that nation-builders rejected biological determinism and produced a notion of race based on morality and reason to defend social hierarchies. In this framework, education was vested with the power to dissolve differences based on physical appearance. It gave rise to what she has described as *silent racism*, since the bulk of the non-white indigenous population remained excluded from the transformatory benefits of education. In South Asia caste is derived not from physical appearances, but from ancient practices associated with occupations, marriage bonds, dietary habits and religious customs (Prashad, 2001). It constitutes a significant source of discrimination, which by many accounts is comparable to social practices under apartheid South Africa and racial segregation in the southern United States. The Dalits, or Untouchables, could 'touch' most things owned by the dominant *jati* or ruling groups if their labour was required, but when they worked for themselves their touch was regarded by the *jatis* as social pollution. Caste discrimination has been outlawed in India and, as in the United States and South Africa, affirmative action policies are in place to help Dalits bridge the socioeconomic gap. However, the enforcement of laws is lax, and discrimination, intolerance and caste-related violence persist.

Migration affects the construction of citizenship. Globalization is associated with the mass migration of people to countries perceived to offer opportunities for self-advancement. Immigrants may have a different physical appearance, culture, religion and language, which native populations may perceive as threatening to their values and notions of what a society should be. In Chapter 2, Ray Jureidini discusses the fate of migrant workers in the oil-rich countries of the Middle East. The

Middle East has experienced massive waves of immigrants engaged in short-term work, from household domestics to highly qualified professionals. The migration of cheap Asian and African female workers has produced a racialized and gendered secondary labour market in that region. These workers are associated with dirty, dangerous and difficult jobs, which nationals refuse to do, despite widespread poverty and unemployment. A central feature of the contract that underpins female labour recruitment for these jobs is its bondage character: workers are not free to access local labour markets without state approval and are attached to a sponsor for the duration of the contract. Conditions of slavery pertain for many female live-in domestic workers: threats of violence, restriction of movement, exploitative working conditions and widespread abuse. He calls for the introduction and enforcement of local labour laws and international conventions that will protect such workers.

Migration poses a challenge to traditional conceptions of the nation state in Western Europe. Nationalist struggles in Europe in the eighteenth and nineteenth centuries established a tight relationship between the state and the nation. Defined as a group of people with a shared history, culture, language and territory, a nation was expected to form a culturally homogeneous state. Recent trends in cultural diversity challenge such notions of nation state homogeneity. In Chapter 3, Jeroen Doomernik discusses three broad types of European response to immigration. The first stresses the importance of equality before the law for both legal long-term residents and traditional citizens and grants the former easy access to citizenship. It also acknowledges the ethnic origins of residents and, if they do not conflict with the principle of equality, supports the public display of such differences. This is the multicultural approach. The second is the republican ideal, which also stresses the principle of equality before the law for residents and citizens, but discourages the display of cultural practices that are different from the dominant native culture. The third type is the most exclusionary. It is founded on the old notion of nation state homogeneity in which only co-ethnics are entitled to citizenship. Illustrative examples of the three cases are the Netherlands, France and Germany, respectively. On issues related to employment, schooling and housing, Doomernik argues that there may not be much difference in policy approaches between countries that subscribe to different philosophies of citizenship. However, the different ways policy-makers apply these philosophies in different countries may affect social cohesion and the integration of immigrants in host societies.

Racism often needs mobilizers, organizations and a discourse to acti-vate or sustain it. In countries where liberal democracy is entrenched, it has been possible to gauge the extent of popular support enjoyed by racist, far right or xenophobic movements. In many Western democra-cies, xenophobic or far right parties are gaining electoral strength in local, regional and national elections, with some even participating in national governments or governing large cities. These parties often have strong links with neo-Nazi organizations, which attract a large number of unemployed youths immersed in a subculture of disobedience and intolerance. In addition, there has been a rise of xenophobic and racist groups in the transition economies of Eastern and Central Europe, espe-cially in countries with large gypsy or Roma populations.

In Western Europe, a new form of exclusionary populism, exempli-fied by right-wing political parties and movements, poses a threat to that region's democratic and liberal order. Hans-Georg Betz discusses these issues in Chapter 4. Right-wing populist parties are different from traditional parties in several way. They rely on charismatic leadership and a centralized party structure, scrupulously pursue a strategy of political marketing with a pronounced customer or voter orientation, and project a style of mobilization that appeals to popular anxieties, prejudices and resentment of the existing political order. They advocate a comprehensive programme of social change, which includes strong hostility towards foreigners and multiculturalism, as well as other issues relating to national identity, which tend to vary according to country experiences. They advocate a restrictive notion of citizenship in which only natives or long-standing indigenes can claim full membership and associated social benefits. In contrast to earlier racist parties, contem-porary right-wing populist parties do not advance notions of ethno-racial superiority. Their ideology is, instead, based on cultural nativism, which seeks to protect European, or 'one's own', society and way of life against outside influences and practices. The electoral base of these parties encompasses several groups, although young male voters with low to medium education tend to predominate. Far right parties have been included in governing coalitions in Austria, Italy and Switzerland. However, as Betz points out, these parties are often their own worst enemies: they tend to perform badly in office, causing their popularity ratings to diminish with time. He is confident that the institutions of Western democracy and civil society will be strong enough to meet the challenge posed by these parties.

Institutional racism is currently the most widely debated issue of racial discrimination. It refers to institutional practices that tend to place the victimized group in continuous disadvantage with respect to a majority or dominant group in society in a number of areas such as education, employment, career opportunities, housing, health care and other social services or societal goods or benefits that are thus unequally distributed along racial and/or ethnic lines. Institutional racism may not be the result of any personal racist motivation by people in positions of power, but it clearly affects the outcomes: biased recruitment patterns in jobs, unequal access to health care, limited career opportunities, lower quality of education and delivery of other social services, ghettoization and multiple other forms of segregation and exclusion. Whether it is blacks and Latinos in the United States, Caribbean youth in the United Kingdom, Arabs and Africans in France, Turks in Germany, indigenous peoples from Argentina to Alaska to Australia, Burakumin in Japan, Dalits in India, Berbers in North Africa, the *patterns of institutional racism* tend to be similar the world over. They are frequently not even formally considered as racist, and may appear in the guise of social and economic disadvantages simply suffered by lower-income sectors. This is the debate surrounding the issue of descent-based and work-based discrimination among Asia's untouchable castes.

There is much debate about whether 'equality of opportunity' should lead to 'equality of outcomes'. Some recent scholarship holds that development actually means more freedom of choice based on enhanced capabilities of the individual. A just society would allow all individuals equal opportunity to increase their capabilities, and therefore overcome traditional inequalities (Sen, 1999). But what if inequalities are persistent over decades and centuries and are related to community, religion, ethnicity, culture or racial distinctions and to a history of oppression and exploitation (Tilly, 1998)? Equality of opportunity is not universally enjoyed, not even when the legal system is open and basically fair. Too often racial and ethnic discrimination occurs in the functioning of legal institutions, in the realm of the administration of justice and particularly in the criminal justice system.

The elimination of racial discrimination requires, therefore, competent, neutral, responsive and accountable law enforcement agencies. However, police departments in multiracial societies may constitute part of the problem of racism; in many countries, their preferential treatment of individuals has been queried. Benjamin Bowling et al. discuss these issues in Chapter 5. Police abuses include excessive use of force, torture and racist language against people they perceive as different. They rely on published reports on four police agencies – the Metropolitan Police in London, the New South Wales Police in Australia, the Los

Angeles Police Department in the US and the South Africa Police Service – to illustrate their arguments. They argue that measures to eliminate abuse of power from police work may include the creation of a police force that reflects the racial diversity of the communities served; promotion of equality of opportunity and equality of service; establishment of structures that will aid legal, political and community accountability; introduction of civilian oversight and transparent and effective methods for handling complaints; development of ethnic minority staff networks; and innovative educational and training schemes. At the core of the reforms is the need to demonstrate clear and overt commitment to the implementation of what they have called *democratic policing*. In other words, police officers should be accountable to the law, the state and the community.

Inequalities and social justice

Racism and inequalities may be linked to discriminatory public policies, the way labour markets are structured and differential access to governance institutions. Labour markets may be racially segmented because of past public policies, unequal development or efforts by individuals from specific groups to protect advantages in certain lines of activity. Public policies and market segmentation may lead to physical segregation of groups, further reinforcing racial prejudice and antagonism. Racially segmented markets may provoke instability when they are bifurcated, encouraging groups to hold each other hostage.

Inequalities can also arise from the impact of development policies and practices on different groups. When 'race' overlaps with social class, inequalities may assume hierarchical race–class dimensions – of the types that breed xenophobia and violence. Such inequalities may mask other cleavages by creating a racially bifurcated society. Many forms of racial inequalities are, however, ambiguous. Individuals in an assumed racial group may, for instance, rank well in socio-economic terms but the racial group may be disadvantaged nationally. Inequalities may occur in education, health provision, housing, income, employment, infrastructure development and asset holdings, such as land. Race may become a powerful tool in the hands of elites and politicians in struggles over public offices and resources.

Rapid integration of economies into the world market, advances in information technologies and changes in production systems may alter structures of opportunity and shape the dynamics of race relations.

Where economies have experienced sustained levels of growth, as in the United States during the 1990s, employment and incomes may improve even for disadvantaged groups. However, technological change may reinforce inequalities or introduce new types of segregation – the so-called digital divide – if excluded groups are unable to access the new technologies. These issues are discussed in the chapters that look at experiences in the United States, Malaysia, Indonesia and Southern Africa. Using time-series data, Danziger, Reed and Brown in Chapter 6 examine changes in the relative economic status of 'white non-Hispanics', 'black non-Hispanics' and 'Hispanics' covering the period of the 1970s and the long economic boom of the 1990s associated with dramatic technological changes, industrial restructuring and immigration. Their data suggest that employment and incomes increased, poverty declined and inequality stopped rising for all three groups. However, the gaps between whites and blacks and between whites and Hispanics remain very large in a broad range of socio-economic indicators. Racial disparties are widest in wealth: in the 1980s, white households held twelve times the median net worth of black households in assets; in 1994 the net worth of whites had declined to 8.6 times that of blacks – US$52,994 vs. US$6,127. The performance of Hispanics in most measures has been negatively affected by large-scale immigration from Latin America. Recent migrants are less well endowed than long-term residents. Danziger et al. point out that economic growth is important but not sufficient to correct these gaps. Policy needs to focus 'both on removing the barriers to equal opportunity and to raising the relative education and skills of minority children'. They suggest four policies to achieve this: improving schools in poor neighbourhoods, moving inner-city residents to the suburbs, active labour market strategies and anti-discrimination strategies.

A number of policies exist for tackling racism, racial prejudice, discrimination, xenophobia and inequalities. Public policies range from legal instruments and socio-economic programmes, to educational policies that seek to change behaviour and promote inclusiveness. They may involve sensitivity to racial cleavages in devising economic and social policies and reforming governance institutions. Targeted programmes may be adopted to correct historical injustices or to assist excluded groups to get out of poverty and exploit opportunities. Public policies may be implemented in macro- and micro-level settings where groups compete for resources and public offices. They have differential impacts, including among targeted beneficiaries. They are also often contested by different groups, which makes it difficult to predict their overall effects on social change or draw universal lessons that may be applicable to all situations.

Public policies that promote social justice are a fundamental requirement for achieving stability and responsible citizenship. Affirmative action policies are associated with efforts to correct socio-economic disabilities, which certain groups may have suffered as a result of past discriminatory public policies. They focus on issues of employment, access to educational institutions, government contracts and broad areas of social policy. Their content and application may vary according to whether the targeted population constitutes the majority group and has strong access to policy-making institutions, or whether beneficiaries are a minority whose influence on legislators, the executive branch of government and administrators is limited. Policies are thus likely to vary between countries as different as the United States, South Africa, Malaysia and Brazil.

Affirmative action policies, as Danziger et al. point out, have come under considerable attack in the United States in recent years. Sections of the white population see them as open-ended commitments and reverse forms of discrimination that are likely to perpetuate a culture of dependency among the underprivileged minority vis-à-vis the state. It is also contended that these policies largely benefit minority elites and constitute a violation of individual rights. Minorities who benefit from affirmative action are rightly worried that the gains obtained over the past decades will quickly be eroded and that the indicators revealing unequal access by disadvantaged minorities to social benefits will rise once again. Affirmative action policies are now being dismantled or questioned by the courts (Curry, 1996). The dominant ideology that drives opposition to affirmative action is liberal individualism, which espouses a policy of colour-blindness: the practice of not using race when carrying out a policy (Loury, 2001). Colour-blindness should be distinguished from race indifference: the practice of not considering how a chosen rule might impact various racial groups. Both can ameliorate or exacerbate the social disadvantage of racial minorities. However, given the history of institutionalized racism in the US, Loury contends that struggles for racial equality may require a reordering of moral concerns: racial justice before race blindness or race indifference.

The debate in Malaysia, where the disadvantaged group has majority status, is different. Chapters 7 and 8 address these issues. In Chapter 7, Jomo K. S. assesses the extent to which the Malaysian government has been able to redistribute incomes, assets and other resources to the

Malay. Inequalities in key socio-economic indicators, such as wealth, incomes, employment and the professions, have narrowed between Malays and Chinese. Poverty rates have also radically declined, although this may be attributed to the spectacularly high growth rates enjoyed in the 1970s and 1980s. And the poor may not have benefited to the same extent as rich Malays. The growth of inter-ethnic business coalitions in which the ethnic Malay partner secures rents for gaining access to government-determined business opportunities, with the ethnic Chinese partner providing the business acumen of getting the job done, has encouraged cronyism. He argues that affirmative action policies should be applied efficiently if they are not to generate discontent and waste.

In Chapter 8, Khoo examines the social and political effects of affirmative action policies in Malaysia in light of the financial crisis of the mid-1990s which threatened social peace in South East Asia. He draws lessons from the Malaysian experience of affirmative action for Indonesia, where conditions for Malaysia-type affirmative action policies may face serious constraints. Globalization does not only offer opportunities for positive social change. It also creates economic crises and deprivation. One of the most common crises may occur in the financial sector. Financial volatility or crisis is associated with the opening of the capital accounts of developed and emerging market economies in the 1980s and 1990s. In South East Asia, the economic instability that followed the financial crisis of 1997 has ripped the social fabric of countries as jobs, incomes and welfare protection are lost or undermined.

As Khoo points out, this has provoked racial and ethnic riots, especially in Indonesia where the *Reformasi* movement ended Suharto's three-decade 'New Order' regime. However, Malaysia, which has a history of racial violence, seems to have avoided Indonesia's type of ethno-racial implosion. Instead, the pressure for change has attracted a coalition of parties and groupings drawn from diverse groups, religious affiliations and ideologies. Politicians and analysts attribute Malaysia's relative success in managing ethno-racial relations to its pre-crisis affirmative action programme – the New Economic Policy. This redistributive programme, which favours the Malays, who were perceived as disadvantaged vis-à-vis the Chinese, incorporated other objectives: high capacities for policy-making, state intervention in the economy and other modes of governance associated with East Asia's developmental state. It seems the strategy has had the overall effect of radically recomposing Malaysia's class structure, altering the balance of power between different groups and empowering the state to deliver economic and political outcomes. Divisions have opened up within the dominant ethnicity. The narrowing of socio-economic disparities between the two main ethnic groups has led to a healthier, less virulently ethnic, discourse on political transformation, despite the suspicions that remain on both sides.

In other situations, such as that of indigenous peoples in Latin America and elsewhere, compensatory measures for age-old discrimination take different forms. Here the issue is not so much the possibility of individuals obtaining greater access to the collective goods of society through existing institutions, but rather the design of institutions that will improve the life-chances and levels of welfare of disadvantaged communities and collectivities. In many parts of the world indigenous peoples have been deprived over the years of their homelands, their land and resources and the major requirements for their subsistence as peasant societies or as hunters-gatherers or pastoral nomads in fragile ecosystems. Here legal and institutional remedies to perennial discrimination include the restitution, demarcation and protection of traditional territories and homelands, agrarian reform, investment in infrastructure, and local and regional development projects of all kinds. In some countries special government agencies for indigenous affairs deal with these issues, but they are often accused of being too bureaucratic and paternalistic, when not downright authoritarian (Daes, 2001).

Increasingly, ethnic minorities and indigenous peoples are demanding some sort of regional, political or cultural autonomy. While there are many different forms of autonomic relations between a state and existing minorities, these are complex issues which often involve rethinking the traditional nationalistic concept of territorial sovereignty, and not many states are willing to relinquish what they consider an essential element of their power and legitimacy. Indigenous peoples, for example, have insisted in the United Nations, and at the World Conference Against Racism held in South Africa in September 2001, that they must be recognized *qua* peoples and that their right to self-determination (including autonomy) be respected. Some governments disagree, and that is why the draft UN Declaration on Indigenous Rights has been stalled in a working group of the Commission on Human Rights. Indigenous organizations have interpreted this resistance as yet another form of racism.[5]

Another problem that has dogged race relations is land inequality. Colonization produced sharp inequalities in land holdings between Europeans and the indigenous communities they conquered. In the Americas and Australasia, indigenous communities were almost eliminated, except in some parts of Latin America. In Southern Africa, however, the indigenous African population accounts for the overwhelming majority of the population; but as in the Americas and Australasia, land distribution is heavily skewed in favour of Europeans. In recent years, the land issue has gained much public attention as indigenous communities demand redistribution. The problem has taken a dramatic turn in Zimbabwe where, with active government support, individuals who participated in the war of liberation, and peasants have occupied white-owned farms; and an overwhelming proportion of the white community has joined a multi-ethnic opposition party in efforts to oust the government and protect advantages. In Canada, the United States and Australia, the land question has focused on monetary compensation and provision of land or reservations to indigenous groups. The debate in the latter set of countries also includes defence of the cultural rights of indigenous communities, raising questions about how to balance individual and group rights in democratic settings.

In Chapter 9, Sam Moyo discusses the political economy of land distribution and race relations in Zimbabwe, South Africa and Namibia – three states that experienced high levels of settler colonialism. In these countries, the black majority remain landless and largely excluded from development. In Zimbabwe, approximately 4,500 white farmers (0.03 per cent of the population) control 31 per cent of the land under freehold tenure, which is about 42 per cent of the agricultural land. In contrast, 1.2 million black families subsist on 41 per cent of the country's land area. In South Africa, 60,000 white farmers own almost 87 per cent of the land (85 million hectares). On the other hand, at least 12 million blacks subsist on only 17.1 million hectares, of which only 5 per cent is potentially arable. Whites own two-thirds (36.2 million hectares) of all freehold farms in Namibia, which cover 44 per cent of the total land. On the other hand, 138,000 black households subsist on only 33.5 million hectares or 41 per cent of the available land.

The independence agreements and constitutions, which protect the right to private property, ensure continued control by whites of prime lands. Under these agreements, land can be disposed of only on a willing seller–willing buyer basis. Moyo argues that several myths have acted against land redistribution in Southern Africa: the land rights held by whites are not only legally valid but socially and politically legitimate, even though these rights were acquired by forceful alienation of Africans from their land; the freehold land tenure system in which whites predominate is superior to customary tenure; land reform policies are irrational and undermine food security because they place short-term political problems of imbalances over economic stability; large-scale white farmers are more efficient ecological managers than smallholders, who are said to misuse their land; and white farmers contribute more to the economy than smallholders.

Moyo discusses the limitations of these conceptions as well as the various demands by social groups for land. He notes that most government establishments have tended to underplay the demand for land. The Zimbabwe land crisis and the surge in land occupations in peri-urban South Africa have underscored the latent, huge demand for land distribution in the region. He points out that pressure for land reform in Zimbabwe has traditionally built up just before elections. To garner votes and give content to their social delivery agenda, various political parties develop vantage points on land reform. However, Moyo observes that while the Zimbabwe opposition movements have pursued valid demands for democratization within a liberal human rights framework, those demands have limited social democratic content, especially in relation to land reform. He concludes that race relations could be improved if donors and former colonial authorities acknowledge the historical and contemporary social justice issues that underpin land distribution in the region. Former colonial powers should pay for land transfers and individual white farmers should facilitate transfers. Market-led land reform policies will not solve the problems of land inequalities.

Racial discrimination impacts on men and women differently, underscoring the need for a gendered understanding of social justice and citizenship in racially segregated societies. Tracey McIntosh pursues these issues in Chapter 10 with respect to New Zealand, where, she argues, race, gender, sexuality and class interlock. In this regard, there are dangers in imagining a universal 'female' or homogeneous ethno-racial groups in the formulation of public policies. Maori women, for instance, share with Maori men the scars and disadvantages associated with the European colonization of New Zealand: poor education and health status, low incomes and employment, inadequate housing and over-representation in crime as both victims and offenders. Maori women and men have played vital roles in improving the legal status, socio-economic well-being and political representation of the Maori in New Zealand's public institutions. However, she argues that the preservation of all aspects of Maori culture may disadvantage Maori women, who require more equity in economic and political life as well as access to resources, power and knowledge. Public policy for just social development must improve the participation of Maori women in both male-dominated Maori institutions that have evolved to redress Maori disadvantage in public life as well as in national institutions that regulate the lives of all New Zealanders.

Conclusion

Public policies regarding racism have tended to be reactive rather than proactive, remedial rather than preventive. In Western Europe, for example, state responses to racist violence have waxed and waned according to what some observers have identified as repeated waves of violence related to factors such as immigration and the political fortunes of extreme right-wing parties at election time. Affirmative action policies, particularly in education, may become popular when the social mobilization of discriminated minorities rises, and will be discarded or diminished at low levels of mobilization. Legislation on indigenous rights was introduced in Latin America in the 1980s and 1990s after the emergence of new indigenous movements. Unless the pressure is kept up, such legislation will have little effect on the daily conditions of life of millions of indigenous peoples. While formal apartheid has been abolished, the new global apartheid continues to affect the life-chances of millions of people the world over (Witte, 1996; Stavenhagen, 1998).

As economic and social transactions between distinct communities and groups continue to be 'racialised' in so many societies, the concept of race becomes socially relevant and racism becomes part of a system of power relations between racialized actors, including not only individuals, but also institutions, the state and the global economy. Blaming the 'system' in the abstract, however, is not a very constructive way to deal with the issues; it leads to the old, rather ineffective approach of saying 'we cannot do anything unless the system changes'. But who will change the system, and how? As far as racism is concerned, the locus of action has usually been the state or even lower-level units. While global approaches are necessary – and the World Conference against Racism is an example of this – national and local-level policies continue to be essential. Here we encounter a number of alternative approaches.

At the basic level of individual human rights, the struggle for equality has been a driving force throughout history. Wherever individual members of a discriminated group are disadvantaged through unequal treatment before the law or unequal access to opportunity and services of all kinds, or are politically, socially and culturally excluded from effective participation in violation of the basic principles of international human rights law, then any and all measures designed to overcome such disadvantages must be pursued. Experience shows, however, that simply removing legal barriers and proclaiming formal equality is never enough.

To remedy this situation, numerous countries, as we have seen, have adopted some form of affirmative action or preferential treatment for members of discriminated groups and such measures have proved to be fairly successful as far as they go, though they have also led to countermeasures and challenges from groups who fear for their privileges. The thrust for equality does little to address major group differences between ethnic and racial communities however, a question that has bedevilled debates on the relationship between the state and such collectivities, particularly when the latter are clearly in a subordinate position. States may face these issues by adopting various long-term strategies:

Segregation: the patent failure of this policy is clear in the history of race relations in the United States and South Africa.

Assimilation of the subordinate groups into the dominant society involving their disappearance as distinct cultural or ethnic peoples, a policy that has been implemented the world over in such disparate settings as indigenous Latin America, Berbers in North Africa, Moluccans in Indonesia and Kurds in western Asia, among others. Observers have described cases of forced assimilation as forms of cultural genocide or ethnocide. This policy may be successful at times but usually entails a high social cost and major violations of human rights.

A somewhat different situation prevails in countries that have important contingents of immigrants, where assimilation is said to be not only in the 'national interest' but also in the best interests of the immigrant groups themselves. While assimilation is often presented as a solution to the tensions and confrontations that accompany the settlement of immigrant groups, including refugees and asylum-seekers, it can also be said that the policy itself generates tensions and confrontations.

A softer position – to label it some way – involves *integration* of subordinate groups into the dominant society, which really means incorporation into the dominant model of the nation state (which is often an ethnocratic state), at the same time respecting certain features of their collective identities (maybe the use of language, freedom of religion, local forms of social organisation, etc.).

Much more contentious is the recent emphasis on *multiculturalism*. As a consequence of what some have called an 'ethnic revival', partly resulting from the universalization of the discourse of human rights, partly as an answer to the weakening of the nation state, in part as a substitute for the decline of overarching social and political ideologies, the recognition and celebration of diversity lead to a new awareness concerning the role of culture in shaping social communities and conditioning individual behaviour. Some countries, such as Canada, have adopted active policies of multiculturalism, namely the official recognition of numerous communal identities (Native Americans, linguistic communities, immigrant minorities), which has led to the adaptation of the legal system to the requirements of culturally differentiated collectivities within the federal state structure. Thus it represents a respect for the collective rights of ethnic groups, particularly those that for historical reasons occupy subordinate positions in the wider society. Within the framework of a renewed debate on the meaning of citizenship, the notion of multicultural citizenship has taken hold of public discourse and is being considered in many different contexts. To the extent that the denial of cultural identities is a form of racism, multicultural citizenship rights may be considered as an effective way of combating racism, discrimination and exclusion at the social level. It does, however, require rethinking the idea of the nation state itself. This is indeed the challenge facing a number of states in the former Soviet Union and Yugoslavia, where the long-cherished idea of the multinational policy was violently destroyed during the nationalist conflicts of the 1990s (Kymlicka, 1994).

To the extent that the reification of cultural differences may also become a form of exclusion and even racism, multiculturalism as an objective of public policy is receiving a good deal of criticism lately. It has other problems as well, such as the possibility of setting up conglomerates of legally fixed communal identities in a corporate structure that may run counter to the current world tendency towards democratic liberalism. Moreover, in so far as ethnic community structures may impinge on the individual human rights of their own members (for example, by demanding strict religious conformity or adherence to traditional marriage customs) legally sanctioned multiculturalism (in the form of autonomy, for example) may be at odds with the idea of universal human rights.

Increasingly, there is talk of *interculturality* rather than multiculturalism *per se*. This would not deny cultural diversity among groups, but rather strengthen it through flexible structures of governance and socialization, within the context of state structures that are not culturally bound to any particular model of the 'nation state'. How the idea of interculturality would play out in the fields of education, communication, social control, cultural creativity, administration of justice, political representation, and so forth is still an open question. But the debate has begun.

Notes

1. Early work on race and racism was carried under the auspices of UNESCO. See UNESCO (1956) and Kuper (1975).
2. 'Article 2. Everyone is entitled to all the rights and freedoms set forth in this Declaration, without distinction of any kind, such as race, colour, sex, language, religion, political or other opinion, national or social origin, property, birth or other status.'
3. Paragraph 2: 'All peoples have the right to self-determination, by virtue of that right they freely determine their political status and freely pursue their economic, social and cultural development.'
4. After the terrorist attacks in New York and Washington on 11 September 2001, Arabs have also become the target of racial profiling.
5. Statement by Rigoberta Menchu Tum at the World Conference Against Racism, Durban, South Africa, September 2001.

References

Barkan, E. (1992) *The Retreat of Scientific Racism*. Cambridge: Cambridge University Press.

Cavalli-Sforza, L. L., Menozzi, P. and Piazza, A. (1996) *The History and Geography of Human Genes* (abridged paperback edition). Princeton: Princeton University Press.

Curry, G. E. (ed.) (1996) *The Affirmative Action Debate*. Reading, Mass.: Addison-Wesley.

Daes, E-I. A. (2001) Indigenous Peoples and Their Relationship to Land. Final working paper presented by the Special Rapporteur. United Nations (E/CN.4/Sub.2/2001/21).

de la Cadena, M. (2001) The Racial Politics of Culture and Silent Racism in Latin America. Paper presented at the UNRISD conference on Racism and Public Policy, Durban, South Africa. 3–5 September.

Kuper, Leo (ed.) (1975) *Race, Science and Society*. Paris: UNESCO Press.

Kymlicka, W. (1994) *Multicultural Citizenship. A Liberal Theory of Minority Rights*. Oxford: Clarendon Press.

Lemarchand, R. (1996) *Burundi: Ethnic Conflict and Genocide*. UNRISD and Woodrow Wilson Centre. Cambridge: Cambridge University Press.

Loury, G. (2001) The Superficial Morality of Colour-Blindness in the United States. Paper presented at the UNRISD conference on Racism and Public Policy, Durban, South Africa. 3–5 September.

Magubane, B. (2001) The Social Construction of Race and Citizenship in South Africa. Paper presented at the UNRISD conference on Racism and Public Policy, Durban, South Africa. 3–5 September.

Prashad, V. (2001) Cataracts of Silence: Race on the Edge of Indian Thought. Paper presented at the UNRISD conference on Racism and Public Policy, Durban, South Africa. 3–5 September.

Sen, A. (1999) *Development as Freedom*. New York: Alfred A. Knopf.

Stavenhagen, R. (1998) Indigenous Peoples: Emerging International Actors. In Crawford Young (ed.), *Ethnic Diversity and Public Policy*. Basingstoke: UNRISD and Macmillan, pp. 133–52.

Tilly, C. (1998) *Durable Inequality*. Berkeley: University of California Press.

UNESCO (1956) *The Race Question in Modern Science*. Paris: Unesco Press.

Witte, R. (1996) *Racist Violence and the State*. London: Longman.

Part I
Racism, Xenophobia and Citizenship

1
The Historical Construction of Race and Citizenship in the United States

George M. Fredrickson

Nationalist ideologies have often associated membership of a nation state (existing or imagined) with primordial ethnic identities. Nations have thus been regarded as extended kin groups or communities of descent (Smith, 1984). In the context of European history, the ethnic basis for citizenship was most fully articulated in Germany during and after the process of unification and in the nations of Eastern Europe that emerged within the Austro-Hungarian empire and became independent after World War I. France and Great Britain have manifested a more complex relationship between ethnicity and citizenship. The former has combined a strong sense of its ethnocultural identity with the universalistic republicanism fostered by the revolution of 1789, and the latter has been a multinational kingdom under a relatively benign English hegemony. American identity and citizenship have not been based in any compelling and consistent way on the ethnocultural character of its population. But, more than the nations of Europe, it has made physical 'race', especially as represented by differences in skin colour, a determinant of civic and social status.

The founding document of the American republic declares: 'All men are created equal; that they are endowed by their Creator with certain unalienable rights; that among these are life, liberty, and the pursuit of happiness'. If followed literally, the Declaration of Independence of 1776 would have signalled the birth of a nation in which the only qualification for equal citizenship would have been membership in the human race. (Women were then generally subsumed under the category of 'men' or 'man'.) But the Constitution that created the federal union in 1789 condoned exclusions and inequalities based on race or colour. Although it used euphemisms to refer to the institution of slavery, the Constitution accommodated itself to the desire of the southern states to consign people of African descent to permanent servitude. For purposes of representation and taxation, each slave was to be counted as three-fifths of a free person. Other provisions had the effect of denying to the federal government the power to legislate against slavery where it existed under state law.[1]

Also significant for the future of black–white relations was the fact that the Constitution provided no definition of national citizenship that might have precluded the states from discriminating on the grounds of race. The only mention of citizenship in the Constitution is in Article IV, section 2: 'The citizens of each State shall be entitled to the privileges and immunities of citizens in the several States.' This clause gave no precise content to the rights of a citizen and appeared to make national citizenship derivative of state citizenship. The Constitution, however, did give the federal government the power to determine the qualifications for naturalization. Most Americans acquired citizenship by birth in accordance with the British tradition of *jus soli*, which was based originally on the right of the king to command the allegiance of all those who happened to be born in his domain.[2] But it was up to Congress to prescribe the conditions under which immigrants could become citizens. The Naturalization Act of 1790 provided relatively easy terms: two years' residence, 'good character' and an oath of allegiance to the Constitution. But the right to citizenship through naturalization was limited to 'free white person[s]' (Kerber, 1997: 841; Smith, 1997: 159–60). There was no prospect of Asian immigration at this time, and Indians within the nation's borders were ineligible for naturalization because the tribes to which they belonged were considered, in the words used later by Chief Justice John Marshall, 'domestic dependent nations'.[3] It is likely, therefore, that the restriction was aimed mainly at the free people of African descent who circulated within the Atlantic world.

There was no recorded debate on naturalization and the colour bar; the Congress was merely following the precedent of several states, which had earlier used the power they possessed over naturalization under the Articles of Confederation to limit the privilege to whites (Kettner, 1978: 214–16). The lack of controversy was indicative of the powerful consensus that had emerged since the first blacks had arrived in Virginia 171 years earlier that people of African descent belonged to an inferior race unqualified for the social and political rights originally associated with the status of free subjects of the British Crown and later with what was due to citizens of the American republic.[4] That assumption derived initially and primarily from the association of African ancestry with slavery or enslavability, but rationalizing and mystifying the economic incentive to take advantage of African vulnerability were the phobias and anxieties that came to be associated with physical difference and especially dark skin pigmentation (Fredrickson, 1988: 189–205).

What citizenship meant in the pre-Civil War period is revealed in Supreme Court Justice Bushrod Washington's 1823 enumeration of the rights that were implied in the privileges and immunities clause. Basic among them were 'protection by the government; the enjoyment of life and liberty, with the right to acquire and possess property of every kind, and to pursue and obtain happiness and safety, subject nevertheless to such restraints as the government may justly prescribe for the good of the whole'. A long list of more specific rights ensued, including 'the benefit of the writ of habeas corpus' and equality under the law, 'to which *may* be added the elective franchise, as regulated and established by the laws or constitution of the state in which it is to be exercised' (Kettner, 1978: 259; emphasis added). It would prove significant that access to the suffrage was viewed here as a possible concomitant of citizenship, but not as an essential one. In 1823 some states still limited the franchise to property holders and taxpayers, although such restrictions were in the process of being eliminated. White women were citizens for most purposes, but were denied the suffrage until 1920. The extension of manhood suffrage in the 1820s and 1830s was done in a blatantly racist fashion. In some states blacks with property who had previously possessed the right to vote were disfranchised at the same time that all white males were made eligible to vote. The political system that was emerging has been aptly described as a 'Herrenvolk democracy' (Fredrickson, 1987: 61–4, 90–6).

Although the right to vote was not firmly established as a prerogative of citizenship, being denied it when all other males could exercise it clearly relegated black men to an inequality of political status that made them less than full citizens. The Supreme Court's Dred Scott decision of 1857, which declared that free blacks could not be citizens of the United States, reflected the realities of the time, if not, as was claimed in Chief Justice Taney's decision, the intentions of the framers of the Constitution. The federal government discriminated against blacks in the pre-Civil War period by forbidding them from becoming naturalized citizens, carrying the mail or being issued passports for foreign travel. The states, including the northern states that had abolished slavery, added to the disabilities associated with race in antebellum America. Besides denying free blacks the right to vote, most states prohibited them from testifying in court against whites, serving on juries, attending common schools and having equal access to common public amenities or facilities. Some even forbade free blacks from other states from entering their jurisdictions (Karst, 1989: 48–9; Litwack, 1961).

As the controversy over the extension of slavery to the federal territories heated up in the 1850s and propelled the nation towards Civil War, both sides invoked white supremacist ideologies to support their positions. Southern defenders of the expansion of slavery used arguments derived from science and the Bible to maintain that the enslavement of blacks was a 'positive good' wherever it existed. Northern advocates of 'free soil' – those who would limit slavery to where it already existed under state law – sometimes contended that one of the greatest evils associated with the expansion of the South's 'peculiar institution' was that it would entail bringing blacks into regions that could otherwise be homogeneously white. To a considerable extent the southern cause in the sectional controversy of the 1850s was hierarchical biracialism and the northern one was white homogeneity, or total black exclusion. The popularity in moderate anti-slavery circles of schemes to colonize freed blacks outside the United States reflected a belief in the impossibility of equal citizenship for African Americans. One of those who most cherished the utopian vision of an America without either slavery or blacks was Abraham Lincoln (Fredrickson, 1987; 1988).

The Dred Scott decision, with its formal and categorical denial of citizenship rights to African Americans, was in effect for little more than a decade. It was overturned in the wake of a civil war which occasioned the abolition of slavery and the enlistment of blacks, including freed slaves, in the army that was fighting to preserve the Union against the Southern secessionists. Emancipation did not itself entail citizenship, as was evident from the status of antebellum 'free Negroes'. But military service did. The classical definition of citizenship in a republic, which remained an influential aspect of American republicanism before the enfranchisement of women in the twentieth century, was closely associated with the bearing of arms. He who was asked to fight for the republic also had a right to participate in the deliberations that preceded a resort to arms. According to the historian Linda Kerber, 'arms bearing for the Union was an experience that came before citizenship and helped set the terms for it. Black men risked their lives for the Union . . . and the claim that they had bought their rights with their blood suffused constitutional debate and also the discourse of Reconstruction' (Kerber, 1998: 243).

The Fourteenth Amendment to the Constitution, ratified in 1868, provided the first substantive and potentially enforceable conception of national citizenship. Its purpose was to provide legal equality for the emancipated slaves, most of whom had been loyal to the Union, in order to protect them against the oppressive designs of ex-Confederates, who, under the lenient Presidential Reconstruction of 1865–66, had passed discriminatory state laws that approximated slavery in a new guise. Section 1 of the Amendment set forth the basic terms: 'All persons born or naturalized in the United States, and subject to the jurisdiction thereof, are citizens of the United States. No State shall make or enforce any law which shall abridge the privileges and immunities of citizens of the United States; nor shall any State deprive any person of life, liberty, and property, without due process of law; nor deny to any person within its jurisdiction the equal protection of the laws.' The intention clearly was to establish a birthright citizenship that would include African Americans. The Amendment was not, however, meant to apply to Indians, whose membership in tribes who had made treaties with the United States was thought to place them beyond the direct jurisdiction of the nation and therefore not entitled to its constitutional protections. It is also noteworthy that 'equal protection of the laws' was provided to all persons, not just citizens. As a result aliens, including aliens deemed ineligible for citizenship because of racially discriminatory naturalization laws, could sometimes gain judicial relief from unfair and unequal treatment by appealing to the Amendment (McClain, 1994).

The Fourteenth Amendment did not by itself eliminate the racial qualification for naturalization, which continued to be restricted to 'free white person[s]'. Recognizing an inconsistency in its overall Reconstruction policy, in 1870 Congress amended the immigration laws by extending to immigrants of African descent the right to become naturalized citizens. By adding blacks rather than extending the right to all immigrants, Congress deliberately made Asians the only nonwhites who were 'aliens ineligible for citizenship'. Beginning at the time of the 1849 Gold Rush, Chinese immigration to California had been proceeding apace. Since these newcomers differed physically and culturally from the native white population – in addition to being nonwhite they were also non-Christian – they were the targets of a xenophobic reaction that was particularly strong on the West Coast. They were welcomed only by employers, especially railroad builders, who wished to take advantage of their services as workers who could be hired for less than whites. The discrimination and abuse that they encountered in the West did not elicit much sympathy in the East. The stereotypes of the Chinese as filthy, diseased, heathenish and willing to work for wages no white man would accept circulated nationally and created a set of negative expectations (Miller, 1969; Saxton, 1971). According to the racialized anthropology or ethnology of the mid-to-late nineteenth century, both blacks and Chinese were naturally inferior races lacking the innate capacity for self-government and democratic citizenship that all white males supposedly possessed. But because of their usefulness to the Union cause in the Civil War and to the Republican Party during Reconstruction, blacks were granted a dispensation – a temporary immunity to extreme prejudice and discrimination. The Chinese could make no such claims on influential segments of white opinion.

The period between the end of Reconstruction in 1877 and World War I saw the triumph of a broad-gauged racism that included not merely people of colour but also sub-categories of Europeans. It was the heyday of what the political scientist Rogers M. Smith has called 'ascriptive Americanism – the belief that what fully qualified someone for American citizenship was a bloodline that could be traced to northwest Europe (Smith, 1997). The process of invidious differentiation began with the Chinese Exclusion Act of 1882, the first legislation that prohibited a specific racial or ethnic group from entering the country. By the 1890s southern states were segregating African Americans by force of law, a practice that the Supreme Court in the notorious 1896 *Plessy* v. *Ferguson* decision found to be compatible with the Fourteenth Amendment. (Its supposition was that separate facilities could somehow be made equal. It was not until the 1954 decision in the case of *Brown* v. *The Board of Education* that the court recognized the falsity of this assumption.) One by one, between 1890 and 1910, southern states effectively nullified the Fifteenth Amendment passed in 1870, which prohibited denial of the right to vote 'on account of race, color, or previous condition of servitude'. They did so by establishing qualifications for the suffrage that made no mention of race, but were clearly intended to be used (and were in fact used) to deprive most southern blacks of access to the ballot box. The brutal lynching of African Americans for real and imagined crimes or simply for violations of racial etiquette became routine in many parts of the South and occurred occasionally in the North as well. By the turn of the century the power of white prejudice had made a mockery of the Fourteenth Amendment's promise of equal citizenship (Litwack, 1998).

The racialization of immigrants from Southern and Eastern Europe began in the 1890s with the rise of the immigration restriction movement and culminated in the discriminatory quota system that was implemented by the Immigration Act of 1924. It has been alleged by some historians that immigrants from Italy and parts of the Austro-Hungarian or Russian empire were not considered to be 'white' when they first arrived (Jacobson, 1998). This may be true in some cases. There were questions about whether Sicilians in southern Louisiana should go to white schools, black schools or to separate schools of their own. But in general the racism directed at the 'new immigrants' was not colour-coded. There were in fact two distinct systems of hierarchical racial classification that were operative around the turn of the century. The one that was based primarily on colour – white over black, brown and yellow – could rationalize the total exclusion or legalized segregation of the stigmatized group. The one that associated the cultural characteristics of certain European nationalities with their genetic makeup – and also at times found a physical correlative in non-chromatic features like head shape – won less popular adherence and had a more limited impact. Many nativists believed that a more or less coercive programme of assimilation could turn Italians, Greeks and Slavs into good Americans, provided that there were not many of them to deal with. Most of them did not advocate prohibition of immigration from Southern and Eastern Europe or the segregation and disfranchisement of those already in the country. They merely contended that allowing such people to enter the country in large numbers was endangering the national culture and the quality of the nation's breeding stock or gene pool. Hence their numbers should be reduced to manageable proportions. On the level of popular invective, Jews and Italians were sometimes distinguished from 'white men'. But no one seriously doubted that they were members of the same white or Caucasian 'great race' as old stock Americans. It was the importation from England and Germany of the notion that 'the little races' of Europe could be ranked – with Nordics, Teutons or Anglo-Saxons possessing characteristics superior to those of Latins or Slavs – that informed the racist ideology of the upper-class leaders of the immigration restriction movement.[5]

Anti-Semitism also reared its ugly head in the United States in the early twentieth century. Although less virulent than the variety that had emerged in France, Germany, Austria and Czarist Russia, it became acceptable in elite circles in the East and Midwest and led to at least one notorious lynching in the South.[6] The kind of racist anti-Semitism that came to hideous fruition in Nazi Germany and the Holocaust did not become politicized in the United States in the way that white supremacy did, at least in the southern states. But it did result in a pervasive pattern of discriminatory access to higher education, certain professional and business opportunities, housing, social clubs and hotels or resorts. It was not pigmentation, even in a symbolic sense, that inspired American anti-Semitism. Hostility derived from two principal factors: the traditional Christian belief that Jews were religious and cultural subversives, and resentment at the competitive success of Jews in some lines of endeavour (which led to the charge that they habitually engaged in sharp practice). Prejudice against Jews may have been more intense and durable than that directed at Italians, Greeks and Poles, but it did not approach the virulence of anti-black and anti-Asian sentiment (Higham, 1984: 95–174).

In the early twentieth century, Japanese immigration to California aroused fears that the United States faced a 'yellow peril'. As a result, the Japanese government was induced to limit voluntarily the emigration of its nationals to the United States in return for the promise of better treatment of those who were already in the country. But the 'Gentlemen's Agreement' of 1907 did not prevent the state of California from passing a law in 1912 that denied Japanese immigrants the right to buy land in the Golden State. Asian immigrants were not only denied access to naturalization but were also being deprived of the 'equal protection of the laws' supposedly guaranteed to 'all persons' by the Fourteenth Amendment. The Darwinian conception of a 'struggle for existence' among the races aroused fears that evolutionary success – 'survival of the fittest' – would go to the most prolific race rather than to the most intelligent and moral. The teeming masses of Asia were regarded as a serious threat to white hegemony throughout the world. Within the United States, once Asian immigration had been curtailed and it had been determined that the black population was not increasing faster than the white, the most pressing concern was the fact that Southern and Eastern European immigrants had larger families than old stock Americans. It was in this context that President Theodore Roosevelt warned of 'race suicide'. One solution was for the native born to have more children; another was to curtail further immigration of people of inferior stock, a goal that was accomplished in 1924.

What lay behind the multi-targeted racism and xenophobia that crested in the early twentieth century? The stresses and strains of a rapidly modernizing society would seem to provide a large part of the explanation. Anxieties and insecurities always intensify at a time of massive social and economic transformation. It was around 1900 that the United States ceased to be a predominantly agricultural and rural society and became one that was principally urban and industrial. Consequently, time-honoured ways of life, sources of authority and prestige, and even ways of making a living, were being threatened. The class and status order was being reconstructed in a way that created new winners and losers.

One of the most persuasive psychosocial explanations of intensified racism is that people who feel threatened by forces that they cannot control or even understand will scapegoat the ethnic or racial Other. The most compelling example is the way that losing World War I heightened German anti-Semitism and gave the Nazis a demonology that they could exploit in their drive for power. The nature of the sense of threat or danger to native-born white Americans from a specific group – blacks, Asians or 'new immigrants' – differed in each case, but the mechanism was the same. The Other was blamed for one's own failures and inadequacies, whether they be cultural, sex and gender-related, or simply economic. Native-born white workers, at a time of bitter and often violent conflict between labour and capital, had good reason to fear the use by employers of blacks and Asians as strike-breakers or replacement workers. But they succumbed to racism when they disdained extending the boundaries of the working class to include workers with a different skin colour and attributed their cooperation with union-busting employers to innate servility rather than to the pressure of economic circumstances (Montgomery, 1987: 25, 46, 81–7).

In the South, the increasing numbers of whites who were losing ground economically as a result of the vicissitudes of the cotton-based economy eventually turned on blacks rather than mobilizing *with* blacks against the landlords, merchants, banks and corporate enterprises that were exploiting the landless proletarians of both races. In the words of W. E. B. Du Bois, 'the white group of workers, while they received a low wage, were compensated in part by a sort of public and psychological wage. They were given public deference and titles of respect because they were white. They were admitted freely with all classes of people to public functions, public parks, and the best schools' (Du Bois, 1970: 700). The economically dominant middle and upper classes obviously benefited from encouraging divisions among the disadvantaged, but it would be simplistic to view them as nothing more than self-interested and cynical manipulators. They also saw the world in racial and ethnic, as well as class, terms, and they could imagine themselves to be philanthropists rescuing the masses of their racial compatriots from degrading associations. Elite whites in the South could afford to be more paternalistic in their treatment of blacks than the poorer whites who were competing with them economically. But this did not mean that they were less racist. Their self-image as gentry with roots in a slave-holding class required that they be surrounded by blacks who could be forced to play the role of child-like servants and dependants (Williamson, 1984). In the North, members of the old Anglo-American elite deflected the 'status anxiety' arising from new wealth onto the immigrants who were allegedly threatening their cultural hegemony as charter members of America's 'cultivated classes' (Solomon, 1956).

Such social pressures and tensions help to explain why there had to be scapegoats, but it does not fully explain why particular racial or ethnic groups were chosen to play the role. Pre-existing stereotypes, such as the image that arose before emancipation of African Americans as natural slaves or the view of the backward and heathenish Chinese sent back by missionaries before the era of immigration, helped to pre-determine their selection as targets of prejudice and discrimination. It also gave to the stereotypes the kind of content that could intensify the hostility or contempt that they aroused. The social construction of race should be viewed as a complex process in which the immediate con-texts provided by structural relationships interact with the cultural lega-cies of earlier relationships or contacts to produce a licence to hate or denigrate the Other.

The period between World War I and the 1970s saw a sustained and partially successful struggle to expand the meaning of substantive American citizenship to cover groups previously excluded and to include rights and privileges not previously extended to those born or naturalized in the United States. The achievement of women's suffrage in 1920 strengthened the connection between citizenship and suffrage. The granting of US citizenship to all American Indians in 1921 was a mainly symbolic act that had little or no practical effect on the lives of Native Americans who lived on impoverished reservations, but it did at least universalize birthright access to American nationality. After the dis-criminatory restriction of immigration in the 1920s, the status of those who had previously arrived from Eastern and Southern Europe or were the children and grandchildren of foreign-born parents gradually improved. This process has somewhat misleadingly been called 'whiten-ing'. What is undeniable is that many 'white ethnics', as they later came to be called, stressed their own pigmentation as a basis for gaining acceptance as Americans (Barrett and Roediger, 1997). The Democratic Party of the 1930s, which under the banner of the New Deal greatly enhanced the role of the federal government in social and economic affairs, appealed to the white ethnics and represented their interests as part of a coalition of minorities that constituted a new majority. It also promulgated a new concept of social citizenship by entitling most working Americans to old age pensions and unemployment benefits.

African American voters were part of the New Deal political coalition. The large numbers who migrated to the North in the 1910s and 1920s regained the right to vote, thereby creating an incentive for urban politicians to provide some favours or benefits in return for their support. Congressmen whose margins of victory might depend on the 'Negro vote' were likely to vote for federal anti-lynching legislation or against the confirmation of a notoriously racist nominee for a Supreme Court judgeship.[7] The New Deal was more responsive to black interests than any political movement since Radical Republicanism, but it fell far short of providing equal citizenship for African Americans (Sitkoff, 1978; Kirby, 1980). Because the white South was also part of the New Deal coalition, the Roosevelt administration did not openly challenge the southern pattern of segregation and disfranchisement or even support federal legislation against lynching. Furthermore, the exclusion of servants and farm labourers from the protections of social security denied to much of the black population the benefits of the new social citizenship.

Although there was not a substantial advancement in the cause of civil rights for African Americans during the 1920s and 1930s (apart from some Supreme Court decisions against the flagrant denials of equal justice), the intellectual justification for the differential treatment of racialized groups came under attack. A new school of anthropologists attributed human diversity to culture rather than genetics, and studies of human intelligence began to question the notion that there were significant differences in the intellectual endowment of various 'races' (Stocking, 1968: 195–233; Barkan, 1992). But it was not until World War II that ideological racism was challenged to such an extent that it became intellectually disreputable – a necessary precondition for an assault on legalized white supremacy. Gunnar Myrdal's classic study of the status of African Americans, *An American Dilemma*, published in 1944, won considerable acclaim for its contention that discrimination against blacks was in contradiction to 'the American creed' of equal rights and opportunities for all (Myrdal, 1944). This argument made sense only if blacks were included among the 'men' or full-scale human beings to which the Declaration of Independence applied. Those racists who viewed blacks as innately unqualified for full citizenship were put on the defensive during and immediately after World War II because of the similarity of anti-black ideology to the anti-Semitism of the Third

Reich. The NAACP's call for a double victory, over Nazism abroad and racism at home, resonated with many Americans.

Revulsion against Nazi racism was not in itself sufficient to make racial equality under the law and at the ballot box a high national priority for politicians and policy-makers. It took the Cold War and the struggle with Communism for 'the hearts and minds' of Africans and Asians to create a climate of opinion conducive to the achievement of equal legal and political rights for blacks in the United States. The initial effect of the Cold War was to retard the struggle for civil rights. During the McCarthyite 'red scare' of the late 1940s and early 1950s, progressive causes of all kinds fell under the cloud of suspicion that they were Communist-inspired. By the late 1950s and early 1960s, however, paranoid fears of domestic subversion had receded and the international rivalry of the United States and the USSR had become a struggle to gain influence over the decolonized new nations of Africa and Asia. In this context, policy-makers began to realize that the practice of Jim Crow was an enormous propaganda liability. Historians and political scientists have recently documented what was long suspected: the success of the civil rights movement in the 1960s depended heavily on 'reasons of state' as they were perceived by influential Cold Warriors. Just as the need to preserve the Union against the secessionists had made emancipation seem necessary a century earlier, the need to defend the 'free world' against Soviet Communism gave impetus to the struggle for African American legal and political equality that came to fruition in the Civil Rights Acts of 1964 and 1965.[8] Highlighting such pragmatic considerations is not meant to imply that the agency of black protesters and demonstrators was unimportant. It was when non-violent resisters confronted and exposed the hatred and injustice of the Jim Crow regime – as in Little Rock, Arkansas in 1957 or Birmingham, Alabama in 1963 – that the headlines around the world put the United States in the embarrassing position of preaching democracy but conspicuously failing to practise it.

1965 can now be seen in retrospect as a high point of racial egalitarianism in the United States. In that year the effective and enforceable Voting Rights Act made African Americans full citizens of the polity. In the same year a new immigration law was passed that abolished discriminatory national quotas. Both actions had significant results. Access to the suffrage led to a rapidly growing number of black elected officials, to the point where the proportion of blacks in the national House of Representatives approached their percentage of the total population. The end of racial and ethnic qualifications for immigration made it possible for large numbers of Asians and Afro-West Indians to come to the United States and become naturalized after five years. This influx and the legal or illegal entry of millions of Mexicans and other Latin Americans created a greater degree of racial and ethnic diversity than the nation had ever known. Some have predicted that by the mid-twenty-first century the United States will have a 'nonwhite' or non-Euro-American majority – a demographic situation that already exists in California.

Do these developments mean that the United States has achieved the egalitarian dream derived from a literal reading of the Declaration of Independence and ceased to be a society permeated with racial prejudice and discrimination? What has happened since 1965 makes it clear that formal legal and political equality does not automatically entail equal citizenship. Full citizenship requires more than extending formal rights; it should also mean that the newly included are accorded enough respect to make them feel that they truly belong to the nation. As the French revolutionaries understood, a democratic republic requires fraternity as well as legally acknowledged liberty and equality. If a minority is generally disliked or resented, it will be discriminated against in an extra-legal or *de facto* fashion unless the government acts vigorously to protect its members.

By any objective standard, African Americans continue to be greatly disadvantaged in comparison to their white compatriots. Blacks are now more residentially segregated from whites than they have ever been; they earn on the average only about three-fifths as much as whites, are twice as likely to be unemployed and have only about one eighth as much property or net worth. More than half of all the convicts in American prisons are African-Americans. They fall also far below general American standards in such indices of well-being as life expectancy, infant mortality, unwed motherhood and susceptibility to HIV/AIDS.[9]

A major reason for the disparity is, of course, the accumulated disadvantages resulting from a long history of enslavement and racial oppression. The current call for 'reparations' is based on a belief that African Americans have been the victims of a man-made historical disaster for which the entire society should assume responsibility. Clearly, enslaved blacks made an enormous contribution to the economic growth of what became the richest nation in the world, a veritable 'land of opportunity' for native and foreign-born whites. Simple justice might seem to require that the white beneficiaries of the uncompensated toil that laid the foundations for national growth and prosperity should be taxed to pay the debt. But there is little or no chance that the white majority will be willing to make the sacrifices required. Affirmative action policies in employment and education would be another way to begin to overcome the handicaps resulting from past discrimination, but the courts have held that 'racial preferences' cannot be justified on such grounds. The failure to use race-specific policies to overcome historically created inequalities could mean the indefinite perpetuation of these inequalities. Black degradation confirms the prejudices of whites without a sense of history, and encourages alienation and bitterness among blacks, who may rightly feel they lack the respect that substantive citizenship should entail.

But the current situation of blacks and other racialized minorities, such as Mexican Americans, is not merely the residue of past injustice. The partial dismantling of the welfare state is depriving the poor, who are disproportionately black and brown, of access to the social citizenship adumbrated by the New Deal. Furthermore, active discrimination in access to housing, employment, loans, medical care and education persist. The anti-discrimination laws are either inadequately enforced or fail to cover some of the more subtle ways in which racial bias is expressed. The situation of African Americans has certainly improved somewhat in the last half-century. To a much greater extent than in the past high achievers can rise to positions of power and prestige. For the growing African American bourgeoisie the privileges associated with class to some extent overcome the liabilities associated with race. But poorer blacks, confined to the inner city ghettos from which the middle class has largely fled, suffer from a double handicap of race and class that is extraordinarily difficult to overcome (Wilson 1978, 1987).

The social construction of a 'Latino' or 'Hispanic' ethno-racial category has differed in significant ways from the racialization of African Americans. Since the time that substantial numbers of Mexicans were incorporated into the United States as citizens under the terms of the treaty of Guadalupe Hidalgo in 1848, Mexican Americans have, for the most part, been officially classified as white. But the extent to which they have been discriminated against, segregated and discouraged from voting – particularly in the southwestern United States, where virtually all of them were concentrated until quite recently – belies that designation and has made them socially, if not legally, people of colour. The current census categories of 'Hispanics' and 'non-Hispanic whites' suggest that Latinos without obvious Indian or black ancestry are still white in some sense but may nevertheless be treated as Other. Difficult to determine is the extent to which the prejudice against Latinos in general, and Mexican Americans and Puerto Ricans in particular, is 'racial' (based on the phenotypic effects of varying degrees of Indian or

African, as well as Spanish, ancestry) or cultural (resulting from the fact that Latino groups have been more prone to maintain their ethnic and linguistic distinctiveness than immigrants from Europe). The 'greater' stereotype applied to Mexicans suggests revulsion at their physical appearance, but the current agitation for 'English only' laws highlights the alleged threat to Anglo-American culture from the persistence of Spanish as the lingua franca in Latino communities.

The pan-Hispanic identity affirmed by Latinos themselves is primarily cultural. (What else could it be, given the great diversity of ancestries and phenotypes?) Latino intellectuals have been in the forefront of the campaign for multiculturalism in the United States. Noting that the American concept of individual rights does not normally include the right to remain culturally distinctive, they have advocated a new 'cultural citizenship' that includes the right to be different without being denied the respect and recognition that full citizenship should entail (Flores and Benmayer, 1997). A question remains, however, as to whether the pan-Hispanic identity is the natural outgrowth of cultural commonalties or a defensive reaction against the tendency of Anglo-American society to lump all Latinos together and 'racialize' them. The differences between Mexicans, Puerto Ricans, Cubans, Dominicans, Central Americans and South Americans might seem, from an objective perspective, to outweigh a similarity based mainly on language.

In the case of Asian Americans, the racializing tendencies of American society and the group solidarities that they may evoke are even more evident. Asians or 'Mongolians' were one of the primary classifications of the racist anthropology that originated in the eighteenth century and culminated in the early twentieth. Yet the groups currently considered Asian in the United States are culturally quite diverse. They include Japanese, Chinese, Koreans, Vietnamese, but also the South Asians who were often regarded as Caucasians or Aryans by earlier generations of physical anthropologists. The killing a few years ago of a Chinese American mistaken for a Japanese by unemployed auto workers who blamed Japanese competition for their plight shows how racists can disregard ethnic or national distinctions. But pan-Asian defensive solidarity seems to be somewhat less developed or urgently advocated than the movement for pan-Hispanic identity. Anti-Asian prejudice has declined considerably since the turn of the century panic about the 'yellow peril' – most precipitously in the years since the internment of Japanese American citizens during World War II (perhaps the most blatantly racist act of the United States government since the Civil War).

Currently, Asians still suffer from subtle forms of discrimination, such as glass ceilings preventing Asian engineers employed by large corporations from moving from production to management as readily as their white counterparts. But, in comparison to African Americans and even Mexican Americans, Asian Americans appear to be on the way to being assimilated by the Euro-American majority. On the whole, they seem less insistent than Latinos that there be respect for their cultural distinctiveness. (The diversity of languages among them deprives bilingualism of its capacity to serve as a rallying point.) Furthermore, high rates of intermarriage between Asians and whites and the apparent freedom of their offspring to choose their own racial identity create the possibility that the privileged American race of the future will be of mixed European and Asian ancestry.[10] Despite the current absence of a strong trend in this direction, it is also possible to conceive of a growing tolerance of cultural diversity and an increasing acceptance of Latinos as full-fledged members of American society. Were it not for the continuation of a massive influx from South of the border, second- and third-generation Mexican Americans might currently be in a position analogous to that of Americans of Italian descent in the decades after immigration restriction. (During the period between the 1920s and the 1940s most Italian Americans inhabited a social and cultural world of their own but were nevertheless being assimilated economically and politically.)

Harder to imagine is the extending to African Americans the degree of respect and recognition that would make them full and equal citizens in substance as well as in legal forms. No other ethno-racial group was enslaved for two-and-a-half centuries in what became the United States, or, despite the attainment of *de jure* citizenship in 1868, was subjected to such an elaborate and comprehensive system of legalized discrimination and segregation. There is a long history of the incorporation of groups that initially inspired hostility and discrimination but which were able to exploit their putative whiteness to gain entry at the expense of the perennial Other – the African Americans who remain to the present day the principal 'negative reference group' against which white – or non-black – America persists in defining itself (Fredrickson, 1998).

Our understanding of the social construction of race and citizenship in the United States can be enhanced if we enrich the kind of comparative perspective that was briefly invoked at the beginning of this chapter. France and Germany are two European countries that have dealt with ethno-racial diversity in ways that are often contrasted. The

United States is often paired with France as an exemplar of 'civic nationalism', while Germany is designated as the prime exponent of 'ethnic nationalism' (Greenfield, 1992). The American pattern, as we have described it, is actually a peculiar hybrid of these two types. What is distinctive about it is the coexistence of a universalistic affirmation of human rights and a seemingly contradictory set of exclusions based on race or colour. Although the egalitarian ideals expressed in the Declaration of Independence, Abraham Lincoln's Gettysburg Address and Franklin D. Roosevelt's 'Four Freedoms' speech seem to apply to all humankind, the America that was experienced by blacks, Indians, Asians, Mexican-Americans and at times even by some categories of immigrants from Europe was often one of racialized hierarchy. One way that Americans could avoid blatant contradiction was to define the Other as subhuman or inherently childlike and thus incapable of self-government or democratic citizenship. Liberty and equality could continue to be celebrated but as the prerogative of the *Herrenvolk*, or at least its male members, rather than as a universalistic recognition of the rights of humanity.

France, the other classic example of civic nationalism, has also failed to live up to the principles set out in its charter of universal rights – '*les droits de l'homme*'. Initially, the French Revolution inspired a consistent cosmopolitanism that went to the point of making foreigners resident in France the legal and political equals of native-born inhabitants. But the wars in which the French republic become embroiled after 1793 aroused a xenophobic nationalism that resulted in the persecution of aliens and in effect made the rights of man the prerogative of a select group designated as citizens. The access to citizenship in the French Republic has not been based strictly on *jus soli*, like the English and American, but was originally based on *jus sanguinis*, like the German. What has made France much more hospitable to immigrants than Germany is that birthright citizenship was extended to the third generation in 1851 and to the second in 1889 (Brubaker, 1992; Weil, 1996).

The fact that those born in the French colonies of North Africa before independence are considered birthright citizens and that automatic citizenship comes to the children of all immigrants when they reach maturity means that contemporary France has made citizenship relatively easy to obtain. But serious proposals to make the second generation meet rigorous standards to qualify for citizenship, as well as the calls for banning immigration from non-European sources emanating from Jean-Marie Le Pen and his Front National, demonstrate a persistent French proclivity for xenophobia. But the ethnic side of French nationalism – defence of *la culture française* from alien influences – can be distinguished from American racism. No sharp colour line has been drawn in France. In fact, survey data show that the French are less prejudiced against Francophone blacks than against new arrivals from North Africa, who are distinguished from the native French by culture and religion rather than by skin colour (Horowitz, 1992).[11]

If one is willing to adopt an expansive definition of racism one could say that the French version is culture-coded, whereas the American is colour-coded. Of course the French are not completely immune from colour prejudice, and Americans have been known to have xenophobic reactions to cultural difference. But there is a significant relative difference. In general, and especially in recent times, the American 'melting pot' has been more tolerant of ethnic and religious diversity than cultural assimilation *à la française*. Exclusion in the American case has normally been based on colour or some other concept of innate 'racial' difference. The French, on the other hand, have been most antagonized by what they take to be a wilful resistance to the absorption of French culture. Haitian immigrants have been received much more hospitably in France than in the United States. But strong adherence to Islam has often been deemed by the French to be an insuperable obstacle to assimilation, a view that is shared by adherents of both the dominant tradition of secular republicanism and the minority right-wing persuasion based on Catholic traditionalism (Brubaker, 1992). Despite allegations of Arab-American support of terrorism and anti-Semitism, the rapid growth of Islam in the United States has occasioned remarkably little concern or anxiety. Imams are now serving as chaplains in the armed forces and one expects any day to hear the celebratory litany of America as the happy home of 'Protestants, Catholics and Jews' enlarged to include Muslims.

In apparent contrast to both the United States and France, German identity and citizenship have been rooted in a relatively pure and highly exclusionary form of ethnic nationalism. In France the revolutionary republican state engendered the nation, and in the United States the founding fathers created a political structure that would give meaning to American nationality in the absence of any distinctive ethnic identity. (The free population of the United States in 1789 was predominantly English in origin, but, having revolted against English rule, Americans could scarcely establish a unique identity based on cultural antecedents.) But in Germany cultural and linguistic nationalism preceded the establishment of a unified nation state. Furthermore, the German cultural nationalism that preceded the unification of 1870 derived much of its content from the romantic revulsion against the Enlightenment doctrine of universal human rights. In the German conception it was the collective soul of a people – the *Volksgeist* – that had the right to self-determination not the independent rational individuals of democratic political thought.

The German immigration law of 1913 carried the principle of *jus sanguinis* to its logical conclusion. Germans living abroad and their descendants had an automatic and perpetual claim to German citizenship, but people born in Germany who were not of German stock could not become naturalized. In the words of Roger Brubaker, 'the 1913 law severed citizenship from residence and defined the citizenry more consistently as a community of descent' (Brubaker, 1992: 149, Cesarini and Fulbrook, 1996: 88–105). During the Nazi era the concept of German citizenship became completely racialized when all those whose families had acquired citizenship in earlier times but who could not claim Aryan descent – mostly Jews and Slavs – were stripped of their German nationality.

Germany's ethno-racial conception of citizenship survived defeat in World War II. The law of 1913 remained in effect, although some very recent modifications have made citizenship through naturalization somewhat easier for non-Germanic immigrants. What has not changed at all is the eligibility for instant citizenship of those of remote German ancestry who may have lived abroad for generations – for example, the Volga Germans of Russia who left their German-speaking homelands in the eighteenth century. The children and grandchildren of Turks who came as guestworkers thirty or forty years ago are still regarded as foreigners and face many obstacles if they wish to be naturalized. In 1992 400,000 Turks who were born in Germany retained their resident alien status (Fulbrook, 1996: 78; Kastoryano, 1996: 133–57; Wilpert, 1993: 225–35).

The role of race in the construction of citizenship in Germany and the United States can be fruitfully compared. The unavoidable Enlightenment context for the creation of American nationality made racists assume that the dominant whites stood for humanity in general and were worthy of all the human rights specified by eighteenth-century philosophers. But blacks, Indians and Asians were 'races', which meant that they lacked the attributes needed for exercising the responsibilities of democratic citizenship. A narrower and more ethnic strain can also be detected at certain points in American history, namely the belief that only those of Anglo-Saxon, Germanic or Nordic ancestry were qualified to hold the reins of self-government. But the ability of immigrants from the Celtic, Latin and Slavic regions of Europe to claim whiteness and thereby distinguish themselves from blacks and Asians made these more exclusive assertions of racial priority unavailing in the long run. In the German case, the process began not so much with the racialization of the Other as with the self-racialization of the Germans. They became 'the master race', with a right to rule over other Europeans and non-Teutonic Caucasians. This vision was permeated with anti-Enlightenment particularism. Jews became the prime target of German racism because they seemed to represent everything the *Volkisch* Germans rejected – universalism, cosmopolitanism, rationalism, an aptitude for commerce and finance, artistic innovation – in short, modernity.[12]

If Jews were the scapegoats for German anti-modernism, blacks and to a lesser extent other people of colour served to buttress the American self-concept as the most modern of nations – the vanguard of human progress. The African American stereotype, in contrast to the German-Jewish, was of a people incapable of being modernized rather than of one that was too modern for its own and everyone else's good. When the United States and particularly the South evinced signs of social and economic backwardness, it was easy to put the blame on the presence of 'primitive' African Americans. When the United States became an imperial power seeking to transform the world in its own image, it was similarly easy to blame the resistance and recalcitrance that it encountered on the racial deficiencies of 'the coloured races'.

But there is some hope to be derived from an account of the social construction of race and citizenship in the United States. To contend that race has been socially constructed is also to maintain that it is not natural or inevitable. What has been constructed can also be torn down or 'deconstructed'. To some extent this has already happened with the overthrow of legalized segregation, racially motivated voting restrictions and discriminatory immigration quotas. In this chapter I have been very critical of the United States. But I am also proud of the fact that racial injustice has never been unchallenged. Sustained protest and resistance from its victims has aroused a sympathetic response from at least some of the beneficiaries of white supremacy. The national conscience – the desire to live up to the standard of human rights set forth in the Declaration of Independence – has usually needed to be supplemented by 'reasons of state' or persuasive claims that the national interest is adversely affected by racism to become efficacious. But at least it shows that white Americans are capable of recognizing priorities higher than the maintenance of racial privilege. That may be something we can build upon.

Notes

1. Such as federal responsibility to assist in the return of fugitive slaves and to come to the aid of state authorities in time of domestic insurrection.
2. On the English background of American conceptions of citizenship, see Kettner (1978: 13–61).
3. Marshall's decision in the 1831 case of *Worcester* v. *Georgia* was meant to protect the Cherokees against the extension of state law over territories assigned to them by treaties with the federal government. It was not, however, enforced by the administration of Andrew Jackson, which was committed to the removal of the Indians from the southeastern states to designated areas west of the Mississippi.
4. The standard work on the development of anti-black prejudices in early American history is Jordan (1968).
5. The classic expression in an American context of this form of racism is Grant (1916).
6. Leo Frank was lynched by a Georgia mob in 1915, after he had been accused of murdering a white Christian woman who worked in the factory that he managed.
7. In 1931 the nomination of Judge John Parker was rejected by the Senate in part because he had once declared that blacks should not have the right to vote.
8. The impact of the Cold War is demonstrated in Dudziak (2000) and Klinker with Smith (1999).
9. Valuable summaries of the current status and condition of African Americans include Hacker (1992); Massey and Denton (1993); Patterson (1997); Oliver and Shapiro (1995); and Shipler (1997).
10. For some figures on the extent of intermarriage among Asians, see Gall and Gall (1993: 144).
11. Asked which category of immigrants constituted the greatest difficulty for integration, 50 per cent of French respondents named North Africans and only 19 per cent specified black Africans.
12. The comparison made here between German and American racism is developed more fully in Fredrickson (2002).

References

Barkan, E. (1992) *The Retreat of Scientific Racism*, Cambridge: Cambridge University Press.

Barrett, J. R. and Roediger, D. (1997) 'Inbetween Peoples: Race, Nationality and the "New Immigrant" Working Class', *Journal of American Ethnic History*, 16, 3–43.

Brubaker, R. (1992) *Citizenship and Nationhood in France and Germany*, Cambridge, Mass.: Harvard University Press.

Cesarini, D. and Fulbrook, M. (eds.) (1996) *Citizenship, Nationality, and Migration in Europe*, London: Routledge.

Du Bois, W. E. B. (1970; orig. pub. 1935) *Black Reconstruction in America, 1860–1880*, New York: Atheneum.

Dudziak, M. (2000) *Cold War Civil Rights: Race and the Image of American Democracy*, Princeton, NJ: Princeton University Press.

Flores, W. V. and Benmayer, R. (eds.) (1997) *Latino Cultural Citizenship: Claiming Identity, Space, and Rights*, Boston: Beacon Press.

Fredrickson, G. M. (1987; orig. pub. 1971) *The Black Image in the White Mind: The Debate on Afro-American Character and Destiny, 1817–1914*, Middletown, Conn.: Wesleyan University Press.

Fredrickson, G. M. (1988) 'Social Origins of American Racism', in *The Arrogance of Race: Historical Perspectives on Slavery, Racism, and Social Inequality*, Middletown, Conn.: Wesleyan University Press.

Fredrickson, G. M. (1988) 'America's Diversity in Comparative Perspective', *The Journal of American History*, 85, 859–87.

Fredrickson, G. M. (2002) *Difference and Power: A Short History of Racism*, Princeton, NJ: Princeton University Press.

Gall, S. B. and Gall, T. L. (eds.) (1993) *Statistical Record of Asian Americans*, Detroit: Gale Research.

Grant, M. (1916) *The Passing of the Great Race*, New York: Charles Scribner's Sons.

Greenfeld, L. (1992) *Nationalism: Five Roads to Modernity*, Cambridge, Mass.: Harvard University Press.

Hacker, A. (1992) *Two Nations: Black and White, Separate, Hostile, Unequal*, New York: Scribners.

Higham, J. (1984 rev. edn) *Send These to Me: Immigrants in Urban America*, Baltimore, Md: Johns Hopkins University Press.

Horowitz, D. L. (1992) 'Immigration and Group Relations in France and America', in D. L. Horowitz and G. Noriel (eds.), *Immigrants in Two Democracies: The French and American Experiences*, New York: New York University Press.

Jacobson, M. F. (1998) *Whiteness of a Different Color: European Immigrants and the Alchemy of Race*, Cambridge, Mass.: Harvard University Press.

Jordan, W. (1968) *White over Black: American Attitudes toward the Negro, 1550–1812*, Chapel Hill: University of North Carolina Press.

Karst, K. L. (1989) *Belonging to America: Equal Citizenship and the Constitution*, New Haven, Conn.: Yale University Press.

Kastoryano, R. (1996) *La France, l'Allemagne, et leurs immigées; Negocier l'identité*, Paris: Armand Colin.

Kerber, L. (1997) 'The Meanings of Citizenship', *Journal of American History*, 84(3).

Kerber, L. (1998) *No Constitutional Right to be Ladies: Women and the Obligations of Citizenship*, New York: Hill and Wang.

Kettner, J. H. (1978) *Development of American Citizenship, 1608–1870*, Chapel Hill: North Carolina University Press.

Kirby, J. B. (1980) *Black Americans in the Roosevelt Era*, Knoxville: University of Tennessee Press.

Klinker, P. A. and Smith, R. M. (1999) *The Unsteady March: The Rise and Decline of Racial Equality in America*, Chicago: University of Chicago Press.

Litwack, L. F. (1961) *North of Slavery: The Negro in the Free States, 1790–1860*, Chicago: Chicago University Press.

Litwack, L. F. (1998) *Trouble in Mind: Black Southerners in the Age of Jim Crow*, New York: Alfred A. Knopf.

Massey, D. S. and Denton, N. (1993) *American Apartheid: Segregation and the Making of the Underclass*, Cambridge, Mass.: Harvard University Press.

McClain, C. J. (1994) *In Search of Equality: The Chinese Struggle against Discrimination in Nineteenth-Century America*, Berkeley: University of California Press.

Miller, S. (1969) *The Unwelcome Immigrant: The Image of the Chinese, 1775–1882*, Berkeley: University of California Press.

Montgomery, D. (1987) *The Fall of the House of Labour: The Workplace, the State, and Labor Activism, 1865–1925*, Cambridge: Cambridge University Press.

Myrdal, G. (1944) *An American Dilemma*, New York: Harper and Row.

Oliver, M. L. and Shapiro, T. M. (1995) *Black Wealth/White Wealth: A New Perspective on Racial Inequality*, New York: Routledge.

Patterson, O. (1997) *The Ordeal of Integration: Progress and Resentment in America's 'Racial' Crisis*, Washington, DC: Civitas Counterpoint.

Saxton, A. (1971) *The Indispensable Enemy: The Anti-Chinese Movement in California*, Berkeley: University of California Press.

Shipler, D. K. (1997) *A Country of Strangers: Blacks and Whites in America*, New York: Alfred A. Knopf.

Sitkoff, H. (1978) *A New Deal for Blacks: The Emergence of Civil Rights as a National Issue: The Depression Decade*, New York: Oxford University Press.

Smith, A. D. (1984) *The Ethnic Origins of Nation*, Oxford: Blackwell.

Smith, R. (1997) *Civic Ideals: Conflicting Visions of Citizenship in U.S. History*, New Haven, Conn.: Yale University Press.

Solomon, B. M. (1956) *Ancestors and Immigrants*, Chicago: University of Chicago Press.

Stocking Jr, G. W. (1968) *Race, Culture, and Evolution: Essays in the History of Anthropology*, New York: Free Press.

Weil, P. (1996) 'Nationalities and Citizenship: The Lessons of the French Experience for Germany and Europe', in D. Cesarini and M. Fulbrook (eds.) *Citizenship, Nationality and Migration in Europe*, London: Routledge.

Williamson, J. (1984) *The Crucible of Race: Black–White Relations in the American South since Emancipation*, New York: Oxford University Press.

Wilpert, C. (1993) 'Les Fondements institutionnels et idéologiques du racisme dans la Republique Fédérale d'Allemagne', in M. Wieviorka (ed.) *Racisme et Modernité*, Paris: La Découverte.

Wilson, W. J. (1978) *The Declining Significance of Race: Blacks and Changing American Institutions*, Chicago: University of Chicago Press.

Wilson, W. J. (1987) *The Truly Disadvantaged: The Inner City, the Underclass and Public Policy*, Chicago: University of Chicago Press.

2
Migrant Workers and Xenophobia in the Middle East

Ray Jureidini

Introduction

Various forms of racism and xenophobia can be found in all societies. Stemming from a fear of strangers, social groupings or cultures are generally based on features of similarity, values and beliefs which determine the binding forces of individual and social identity to the exclusion of the 'other' (see Said, 1978; Turner, 1993; Ahmed, 2000). This chapter is concerned with contemporary xenophobic elements relating to foreign migrants in the Arab countries of Lebanon, Jordan and the Gulf states in the Middle East, with particular reference to the status of foreign female domestic employees (see Jureidini, 1998).

On a terminological note, following Banton (1997: 44), it is assumed that 'racism' refers to 'any hostility based upon beliefs about inherited biological differences', while 'xenophobia' refers to hostility 'that is based upon beliefs around cultural differences' or a hostility towards foreigners. In the case of some countries, xenophobia may be translated into hostility towards immigrants. Racism can be identified in two forms. First, 'individual racism' relates to more or less isolated incidents of discriminatory or violent behaviour of individuals, such as attacking a person in the street because he or she has dark skin (Jureidini, 2000). It is often easily identified, but not easy to document if it is not officially reported. Institutional racism may occur in the form of laws that specifically discriminate against certain people such as under apartheid in South Africa. In other words, it involves 'structural relations of subordination and oppression between social groups' (Abercrombie, Hill and Turner, 1994).

It is often difficult to distinguish between racism and xenophobia. Unless there is clear evidence of racism in the form of references to biological differences such as skin colour, it is perhaps more appropriate to refer to xenophobic practices and attitudes. In Arabic, the term *Abed* is used to denote both a 'black' person and a 'slave' and it can still be heard with reference to Africans and Sri Lankans. It is in this context that African migrants and Asians are physically distinguished and often looked upon as inferior or simply ignored or dismissed. Their presence, however, is largely associated with their prevalence in positions of servility of one form or another. Anecdotes abound of African and Asian men and women who hold prestige positions (diplomats, professionals) being mistaken for servants and treated with contempt. It seems ironic that anti-Arab and anti-Muslim racism, vilification and stereotyping are widespread in many Western countries (and possibly elsewhere), while we find Arab racism or xenophobia against others in the Middle East. In this sense, no victim ethnic group can be assumed to be by definition morally pure and devoid of xenophobic elements (see Hage, 2000; Jureidini and Hage, 2001).

With regard to domestic workers in the Middle East, prior to the influx of foreign workers into Arab households, these positions were mainly filled by Arab women or girls. They were less vulnerable because even if the father visited only once a year, it was as much an act of protection as it was to collect her wages. For there was a shared culture, with an understanding that family honour was at stake. This honour enforced a certain sense of responsibility on the employing family. However, with Sri Lankan and Filipina women, their families are distant. They come from a different culture and, in the case of Sri Lankans, a different religion (mainly Buddhist). Mostly travelling alone and in a foreign country with little or no communication with the outside world, their contractual arrangements are such that they have few rights, no freedom and are kept virtual prisoners in the households in which they are employed. They cannot form or join unions, and there is no serious regard for their well-being other than from the embassies and consuls in the host countries. Given the numbers of migrant workers involved, diplomatic missions cannot keep track or monitor the many thousands of their nationals in the host countries. In addition, there is an economic interest not to undermine the labour market demand for their migrant workers, who collectively represent a major source of foreign earnings.

Historical context

The major influx of foreign workers into the Middle East began following the oil price boom in 1973 which resulted in an enormous boost of wealth for the Arab Gulf states (United Arab Emirates, Oman, Saudi Arabia, Qatar, Kuwait and Bahrain, comprising the Gulf Cooperation Council, or GCC). The Gulf countries evolved grand development plans and had the funds to pay for them, but had a totally inadequate workforce; for example, the GCC countries had a combined workforce of only 1.36 million (Abella, 1995). Initially, both skilled and unskilled workers from other Arab countries (principally Egypt, Yemen, Palestine, Jordan, Lebanon and Sudan) and from Asia (mainly Pakistan and India) almost doubled the populations of Saudi Arabia and Kuwait in the decade to 1985.

Between 1980 and 1985 the share of Asians in the foreign workforce rose to around 3.2 million, from about 30 per cent to over 63 per cent, of whom over 2 million were in Saudi Arabia. By the early 1980s an increasing number of migrants were recruited from South East Asia (Thailand, Philippines, Indonesia, South Korea). Up to the end of the 1980s nationals from these countries comprised over half the Asian migration to the Middle East. By 1990, workers from Bangladesh and Sri Lanka had increased their share of Asian migrants to over 20 per cent of the Asian workforce in the region (see Abella, 1995; also Birks and Sinclair, 1980).

In 1985 oil prices fell rapidly, prompting a cutback in infrastructure development in the Gulf states and migration from Asia dropped by almost one third. As Abella (1995: 420) point out, the 'fall would have been more severe if not for the growth in employment in the service sector (from hotels to personal services) which absorbed ever increasing numbers of workers, especially women from Sri Lanka, Bangladesh, Indonesia and the Philippines'. These women became a significant part of the feminization of international migration, travelling alone, rather than as appendages of their husbands, and had become the major breadwinners of the household, many leaving husbands and children at home (Campani, 1995).

At the same time, expatriate migrants from other Arab states were being reduced, as often for political as for economic reasons. For example, the political activities of Yemenis, Egyptians and Palestinians were considered to be potentially threatening, but they were also more expensive: 'From the economic standpoint there were advantages in hiring more Asians rather than Arabs. The Asians were reliable, their workers accepted lower wages and they did not require the same social support services as the Arabs, who were more likely to settle and bring their families' (ibid., see also McMurray, 1999).

One of the distinguishing features of the mass migration experience in the Gulf states, compared with Europe, was the idea that the diversification of nationalities would deflect the potential political encroachment by Arabs from other regions. Although of common cultural, religious and linguistic origins, non-national Arabs were a threat, 'especially those who have lived in the region since the 1960s or were born there, since they may feel they should have a stake in their country of residence' (Oxford Analytica, 2001). Thus, the diversification of nationalities to include East and West Asians was for both political and economic expediency.

Unlike the Arab sending countries, Asian governments pursued active policies for overseas employment, partly to alleviate unemployment and partly to generate foreign income (see Abella, 1995; Rosales, 1999). Their labour force had become a major export item that generated considerable earnings. Castles and Miller cite ILO figures which show that for countries with serious trade deficits, remittances from migrants can be significant. For example, 'Pakistani workers remitted over US$2 billion in 1988, which covered 30 per cent of the cost of imports. Indian workers remitted US$2.6 billion, the equivalent of 15 per cent of imports' (Castles and Miller, 1998: 148). Most of these funds came from the Middle East. On a somewhat smaller scale, remittances from the Middle East to Sri Lanka between 1980 and 1986 doubled, from US$112 million to US$264 million (Eelens et al., 1992: 4). Filipino migrants in 1997 remitted some $5 billion (KAKAMMPI, 1998). In 1999 total remittances to Sri Lanka from overseas workers totalled US$1 billion (Kannangara, 2000). This constituted around 20 per cent of foreign goods imports for the previous year and more than the trade deficit of US$0.7 billion (see also Seddon, 2001, on Nepali remittances from the Gulf). In the GCC countries, foreign workers repatriate over US$25 billion to their home countries annually (ESCWA, 2000).

As increasing numbers of 'cheap' foreign workers from Asian and African countries fulfil the demand for unskilled workers, so the particular kinds of jobs found in the secondary labour markets become racialized. That is, the dirty, dangerous and difficult jobs become associated with foreign Asian and African workers, such that nationals in these countries will refuse to undertake them, despite their high levels of poverty and unemployment. As discussed below, although the intention is to reduce the foreign labour force in the Gulf states, growth has occurred, primarily because of the demand for unskilled labour.

Xenophobic practices

Xenophobia with regard to foreign workers, and domestic workers in particular, has three aspects. First, the preference for temporary contract labour which precludes the possibility of citizenship. Second, preferential treatment is usually given to nationals, although particular kinds of menial work have now been 'allocated' to foreigners. Third, disdain and abuse towards those who are visibly 'different' (particularly Sri Lankans, Filipinas, Ethiopians and other Africans) can be observed in the kind of treatment that is meted out to them by nationals, particularly employers.

Conditions and vulnerability of temporary contract labour

The high proportion of foreign nationals working in the GCC countries is a distinguishing feature of their labour force, compared with other Arab countries. Typically, temporary foreign contract employees are the most favoured type of migrant as there are no expectations of permanent settlement or citizenship rights. None of the Middle Eastern countries covers such employees under local labour law and no UN or ILO conventions are in force and ratified which offer national or international protection, particularly for unskilled labourers (see below on international conventions). However, despite the temporary nature of such labour contracts, there remains a permanent pool of migrant workers in the receiving countries. Depending upon the numbers, ethnic community development ensues (Evans-Pritchard, 2001).

In Middle Eastern countries there are no quotas on the number of migrants allowed in; nor do local labour laws and regulations (or, indeed, international conventions) specifically cover temporary contract migrants. Domestic workers, among others, are excluded (Rbeihat, 2000; Jureidini and Moukarbel, 2001; Oxford Analytica, 2001). The characteristics of temporary contract migrants, however, are not unique to the Middle East. Many of the restrictions on this category of migrants are implemented elsewhere. Where the Middle East differs compared with most other countries though is that domestic employees mostly live in so that further limitations on freedom have become normative elements in the employer–employee relationship.

The general limitations of temporary foreign contract labour do not allow the freedom of choice to move from one employer to another in the local labour market of the host country – at least, not without the express permission of the government. They also require permission from their employer, who acts as their 'sponsor'. The expectation is that they will leave the country on the expiration of their contract unless they obtain a renewal of their work and residency permits and the contract is extended. As the nature of their stay in the host country is temporary, citizenship and citizenship rights do not apply. In this sense, temporary foreign contract labour (whether skilled or unskilled) may be seen as formally 'unfree' labour. Those who do leave their employer (or 'run away') and those who do not renew their visas and permits are rendered illegal and are at risk of arrest and deportation. Periodic crackdowns are made to find and deport illegal foreign residents. In almost all countries, thousands of people in these categories continue to live and work, although precise numbers are unknown.

Preference to nationals and racialization of labour markets

Figures which detail occupations and industries according to nationality in the Arab states are not available. None the less, some cursory data are available which indicate the proportion of migrant workers in the aggregate according to industry or occupation. For example, in Oman, in every industry sector (for 1993), with the exception of mining and quarrying, the vast majority of employed are migrant workers – for example, in agriculture, 73 per cent; manufacturing, 92 per cent; construction 96 per cent; restaurants and hotels, 93 per cent; wholesale and retail, 87 per cent; mining and quarrying, 42 per cent. In professional occupations, migrants comprise 49 per cent; administrative and managerial workers, 44 per cent; clerical and related workers, 30 per cent; sales workers, 63 per cent; service workers, 92 per cent; and production workers, transport and labourers, 64 per cent (International Labour Organization, 2001).

Briefly, the above figures indicate the predominance of migrants in secondary market jobs (in terms of absolute numbers) and a more or less equal proportion with Omani nationals in the upper end of professional, managerial and technical positions. The high proportion of locals in clerical positions reflects their privilege in the public sector. Similar figures apply to Bahrain and Kuwait, and presumably to the other GCC countries as well.

There are also migrants in the skilled categories which are encouraged, rather than reviled, although most Gulf states are articulating the need to reduce their reliance upon them in favour of their own nationals. On the other hand, in March 2001, Bahrain announced a scheme to grant citizenship to long-term foreign residents. They need to fulfil certain conditions, such as sufficient financial assets, health insurance, a knowledge of Arabic and permanent residence of at least 15 years for

Arab nationals and 25 years for non-Arabs (*Khaleej Times*, 11 June 2000; 29 March 2001). The precise number of foreign nationals who have been granted citizenship in the Gulf states is unknown.

In most cases, GCC nationals refuse to accept low-paying manual jobs that require minimum skills. Over the years, however, more and more GCC nationals have acquired the education and skills for the better-paying jobs (ESCWA, 2000: 11). Thus, as nationals increasing obtain better education and skills, they are more likely to fill primary sector jobs, leaving secondary sector jobs for foreigners.

Because of the low workforce participation rates of female nationals in the GCC countries (no more than 15–20 per cent; see ESCWA, 1999) there is a much higher proportion of foreigners represented in the workforce compared with the population. This indicates that the presence of foreigners is primarily for work rather than for settlement with family members. Foreigners fill jobs ranging from those with low remuneration and minimum skills to professionals and those requiring high technical skills. As the population growth rates for nationals of the GCC countries are among the highest in the world, averaging 3.5 per cent annually, their governments are concerned to create employment opportunities for their nationals. Another economic impetus for replacing foreigners is to reduce remittances abroad (ESCWA, 2000).

Kuwait

In Kuwait, foreign workers include approximately 295,000 Indians, 274,000 Egyptians, 157,000 Bangladeshis, 101,000 Pakistanis and 100,000 Sri Lankans. Over 90 per cent of nationals work in the public sector, where salaries and benefits are higher than in the private sector. About 300,000 foreign workers are employed as domestic helpers, around one third from India and another third from Sri Lanka (*Khaleej Times*, 30 May 2001). Measures to reduce their presence in Kuwait include freezing access to free medical and educational services and introducing a tax on foreign workers, ostensibly to create jobs for Kuwaiti nationals (Labour and Social Affairs Minister, Abdel Wahhab Al Wazzan, quoted in AFP, 'Kuwait to Tax Foreign Workers', 23 December 1999).

Oman

The number of foreign workers in Oman increased by 34 per cent in 2000 compared with the previous year (*Bahrain Tribune*, 6 June 2001). Recent statements by the Ministry of Social Affairs, Labour and

Vocational Training have called for 'Omani citizens not to exaggerate their demands for foreign workers in the agricultural sector and for domestic helpers, as there are already many foreign workers in the country' (*Khaleej Times*, 12 March 2001). The largest population of foreigners are Indians and Pakistanis, many of whom arrive with higher levels of skill and a preparedness to work for lower wages than Omanis. Filipinos are estimated at around 20,000 and Sri Lankans 35,000, the majority of them working as domestic employees. The government's main efforts to reduce the number of foreigners have been to target the many thousands whose legal status is 'irregular'. As with all the Arab countries, annual 'amnesties' are offered to those without valid documents as an enticement to leave the country without penalty. This often means that the relevant embassies are required to provide their nationals with an emergency certificate, or *laissez passer*, to facilitate their departure. Those who do not avail themselves of the amnesty (whether from fear or ignorance) become vulnerable to police crackdowns (*Gulf News*, 3 May and 7 May 2001).

Bahrain

In Bahrain there are similar concerns about reducing the foreign labour presence. It is estimated that around one per cent of foreign workers are 'runaways' from their sponsors and agencies. Urging the private sector to hire more Bahrain nationals, the Minister for Labour and Social Affairs argued it was partly to reduce the remittances sent abroad. Around US$480 million was remitted from Bahrain in 1997 (*Gulf News*, 23 April 1999; *Bahrain Tribune*, 26 May 1999). Other factors included 'unfair competition' with local labourers and the need to alleviate unemployment and poverty among the poor (*Bahrain Tribune*, 14 February 1999). To further reduce the number of illegal foreign workers, it was decided to relax transference rules to allow foreign workers to change sponsors within the country. This would release them from the need to remain with abusive and exploitative employers (*Gulf News*, 29 November 2000).

Saudi Arabia

Over the past several years in Saudi Arabia, there has been a policy of 'indigenization' in an attempt to reduce foreign labour in favour of Saudi nationals. For example, between 1994 and 1999, the share of jobs filled by nationals increased from 39.2 per cent to 44.2 per cent. This policy is to be continued as a priority in Saudi Arabia's five-year plan for 2000–5, during which time it is anticipated that around 200,000 positions currently filled by foreigners will be replaced by nationals. In September 2000 it was decreed that all establishments employing 20 or more people will be required to employ at least 25 per cent nationals (ESCWA, 2000).

United Arab Emirates

In the United Arab Emirates (UAE), foreigners are mainly from India (781,000), who comprise over half the expatriate workforce, Pakistanis (262,000) and other Asians (225,000). Some 70 per cent of Indians come from the Kerala region. Those from other Arab countries number around 155,000 (ESCWA, 2000). With a population of around 2.7 million in 2000, about 85 per cent are now foreign nationals (*Khaleej Times*, 10 February 2000). As in Kuwait, the UAE is attempting to limit the inflow of foreign unskilled workers in the country, partly by removing the indirect supports, such as free health services and free education.

In October 1999, the UAE government announced a ban on unskilled Indian and Pakistani workers as a process of 'restoring the demographic balance' within the country (*Gulf News*, 22 October 1999). However, within a month of the ban companies began replacing them with Nepalese labour, who are 'known for being cheap and reliable' (*Gulf News*, 1 September 1999). By July 2000 the number of Nepalese had risen to over 15,000 (*Dawn*, 8 July 2000; see also Seddon, 2000). In August 2000 they announced the doubling of fees for labour permits and in the following month introduced an employment visa requirement that all foreign workers have a minimum of a secondary education (*Gulf News*, 28 August 2000; *Dawn*, 27 September 2000).

Lebanon

In the case of Lebanon, the presence of Syrian workers, particularly in agriculture and construction, is an added political dimension. These workers are largely undocumented, but continue to work freely because of the Syrian political and military presence in the country. Further, Palestinian refugees who, since 1948, have been treated formally as foreigners, have been prevented from working in various occupations and professions. The discrimination against Palestinians has two justifications. First, allowing citizenship rights and naturalization is seen as contrary to the legitimate demands in terms of rights of return to Palestine; and second, the assimilation of Palestinians will mean a large influx of Sunni Muslims, which will undermine the politically sensitive demographic 'balance' of the population.

Foreign female domestic employees

Recent studies of foreign female domestic workers have been conducted in only three of the countries under consideration: Lebanon, Jordan and the UAE.

In mid-1999 some 700,000 Sri Lankan women were working abroad as housemaids (Nonis, 1999). Most of these women work in the Gulf states, mainly in Kuwait, Saudi Arabia, UAE and Oman, as well as in Lebanon and Jordan. The remainder migrate to Singapore and the Maldives (Kannagara, 1999b). Sri Lankans comprise perhaps the largest single group of women working as domestic maids throughout the world today, followed by Filipinas.

As of August 1999, Saudi Arabia was the largest labour market for Filipino workers, who numbered around 650,000 (*Gulf News*, 5 August 1999). In 1999, the number of housemaids in the UAE exceeded 200,000, constituting around 7 per cent of the population and representing around one housekeeper for every two or three nationals. There were some 75,000 Sri Lankan housemaids and another 70,000 working in other manual, unskilled positions (*Gulf News*, 2 February 1999). In 2001 in Lebanon, embassies reported there were between 80,000 and 100,000 Sri Lankans and 20,000 Filipinas, and around 5,000 Ethiopian women, almost all in domestic service (Jureidini and Moukarbel, 2001). As of August 2000, 35,000 Sri Lankans and 7,000 Filipinas were working as domestic maids in Jordan, according to the respective embassies (Rbeihat, 2000).

It may be argued that the legal, administrative and working conditions of foreign domestic workers are consistent with Bales' (1997) concept of 'contract slavery'. Bales contends that contract slavery contains three elements: 1) violence or the threat of violence; 2) restriction of physical movement; and 3) economic exploitation.

The following summary of these conditions and treatment applies to all of the countries addressed in this chapter, with some minor variations.

Violence or the threat of violence

On the issue of violence or the threat of violence (or 'abuse') foreign maids may be subjected to physical, sexual, psychological and/or emotional abuse. Demeaning or degrading treatment is a particularly insidious form of abuse. Aggressively delivered orders, shouting and constant belittling criticism contain an underlying threat of violence or may be seen as violent. Abuse may also include withholding food, not allowing the worker the freedom to prepare her own food and relying on the 'handout' of the *Madame*, which may be leftovers from the family meal. There have been cases where locks were put on refrigerators and, in one case, an alarm was installed. Employees may be belittled on a daily basis, such as by name-calling (*Hmara*, or 'donkey', is the most common term used). Sometimes, names are changed to suit the employer.

Another form of violence and threat of violence comes from recruitment agencies. An employee who is procured through these agencies is usually 'guaranteed' by the agency and will be replaced within the first three months if she is deemed unsuitable. However, it is common knowledge that if an employer returns the maid to the agency, there is a strong likelihood that she will be punished in some way as a disciplinary measure. Reports of serious physical abuse by agencies, bordering on torture, have been revealed (see below). A number of agencies now employ a Sri Lankan or Filipina to deal with employees directly who becomes the abuser.

Perhaps the major threat of abuse derives from the practice of withholding passports and other identity papers that are mostly held by the employer and sometimes by the agency. Employees cannot leave the house for fear they may be caught by the police or General Security and arrested or imprisoned because they are not carrying their identity papers. There is a tacit expectation that detention by the security forces will be accompanied by some form of physical or even sexual abuse.

Newspaper reports of individual cases of severe physical abuse by employers and agencies have been reported over the past two years in the Lebanese *Daily Star*. These included beatings, slapping, scalds from boiling coffee, broken ribs, scars, bruises and hospitalization. Many so-called suicides have been reported of Sri Lankans, Filipinas and Ethiopian women. Although the suicide rate in Sri Lanka is also high (Gamburd, 2000), these deaths are always suspicious. No arrests or criminal charges have ever been brought against an employer or agency. One agency was suspended in Lebanon after a particularly brutal assault and following a formal complaint by the Sri Lankan ambassador. 'We took her in [to the agency] and they taught her a lesson. *Taamouah atle mrattabe* [they beat her well]' (Lebanese female employer; Jureidini and Moukarbel, 2001). The daily abuse reported to researchers is almost always from the *Madame* of the house, who normally has the responsibility to manage the maid. This includes hitting, slapping, pulling or even cutting of hair, pushing around, belittling, verbally insulting, name-calling and constant criticism of their work.

Part of the dilemma in domestic work is that neither employer nor employee can assume an arm's length, rational approach to the contractual relations, for the arena is the ideologically 'natural' sphere of the female domain, with all the emotional and cultural baggage that is bound up in it. This results in a highly charged set of dynamics between the maid and her *Madame* (Tandon, 2001).

It is interesting to note that there is relatively little evidence of sexual abuse of domestic workers in Lebanon and Jordan, while there are widespread reports of rape and sexual harassment in the Gulf. Sabban (2001: 33) states that:

> most complaints of sexual abuse reported by foreign female domestic workers were against older men, either in Saudi Arabia, or in the Emirates . . . This phenomenon is one of the outcomes of the oil booms . . . Elderly males find themselves suddenly rich, but socially frustrated, and with no roles or pleasure. Their first source of pleasure is poor women, whose easier, cheaper and younger sexuality can alleviate their frustrations.

Denial of freedom of movement

Most recruitment agencies advise their clients not to allow domestic workers to leave the house unaccompanied. This, they argue, is to maintain control over her to prevent her from speaking to other maids and then demanding more wages. It is also assumed that she may engage in sexual relations, possibly getting pregnant and thus would have to be sent home (abortion is one alternative, but it has to remain clandestine). Some maids are locked in the house when the family is absent. Few are given a key. Few are allowed to make telephone calls. Constraints on freedom of movement also mean that they cannot form social relations outside the employment relationship.

The withholding of the passport is illegal by all international standards and also serves to restrict movement. Regular checks and raids are made in all countries to arrest those whose papers are irregular. Yet, it is worth noting that this practice is one which has come to be accepted as standard, not only by agencies and employers, but also by the state, foreign embassies and some human rights activists. On arrival at the airport, for example, the authorities take the migrant's passport and hand it directly to the employer/sponsor, who must be there to take her home. Withholding of the passport is seen as justified, particularly in the early weeks of employment, until trust has been established. It is a form of insurance policy against the maid absconding, for the employer has made a substantial payment in advance, which can range from

US$1,500 to US$3,000. Some view this as part of the slavery conditions, as she is virtually 'bought' from the agency.

Exploitative working conditions

Reports from studies around the world confirm that when migrant domestic workers are asked what tasks they perform, they answer 'everything'. They clean, wash, serve meals, cook or prepare food, care for children, tidy up, take out the garbage, water plants, shop, walk the dog, feed the cat, and so on. The average length of the working day is between 16 and 17 hours and they are often 'on-call' 24 hours a day, particularly if there are babies in the family. They rarely have days off. Some never have a day off. Sometimes a few hours are given on a Sunday for religious services, and even then may be accompanied by the employer. Some (such as Buddhists from Sri Lanka) may not have access to a place of worship from their own religion (Evans-Pritchard, 2001). Denial of time off and holidays is another indicator of slavery-like practices (see Wijers and Lap-Chew, 1997).

A common practice is to withhold wages. There have been cases reported where maids have worked for up to six years without being paid. Some have wanted to return home after their two- or three-year contract has expired, but could be prevented from doing so by their employer because they would have to return without any money. It is uncommon to find employers being forced to pay wages owed, although with the more recent intervention of diplomatic representation, some actions are being felt. In the UAE in 1997, for example, there were some 1,600 complaints from Sri Lankan maids ranging from non-payment to harassment lodged with the Ministry of Labour and Social Affairs. Due to a number of measures implemented by the Sri Lankan government, the number of complaints the following year halved. For example, recruitment was required to be managed only through agents registered with the Foreign Employment Bureau and employers were forced to register with the Sri Lankan diplomatic missions (*Gulf News*, 2 February 1999).

Most migrant domestic workers have live-in arrangements, and some have good living quarters, particularly in the new luxury apartments. Employers prefer that they have their own bathrooms as it is considered unseemly that they should share with family members. If she has to share a bathroom she will be required to clean it immediately after use. However, most accommodation facilities are substandard. The maids often do not have their own room and there are many cases where they sleep in the laundry on a mattress or in the living room (which means they cannot retire until the whole family has gone to bed). Alternatively, they may sleep in the kitchen or on the balcony.

Notes on the Gulf

In Bahrain, the Naim Philanthropic Fund began a programme in 1999 to replace foreign workers with poor local women as maids. The objective was poverty alleviation and to 'prevent the negative social, cultural and religious influence these house helpers have on children' (*Gulf News*, 7 February 1999; 13 July 2000). On the other hand, by late 2000, the Minister of Labour and Social Affairs issued a statement to all embassies, overseas workers' organizations and governments to:

> take action against abusive recruitment agencies and to educate workers on their rights . . . [including] . . . insurance against workplace injury, safety and security in the workplace through international safety standards, annual holiday, passage back home, repatriation and termination indemnity. (*Bahrain Tribune*, 4 October 2000)

In January 2000 in UAE, the Dubai police reported that '60 per cent of family crimes and offences involve housemaids' (*Gulf News*, 15 January 2000). According to the study, the influence of housemaids, 'many of whom do not understand local culture and traditions and are not Muslim', is creating language and behavioural problems among UAE children in elementary schools.

One third of the cases referred to the local Public Prosecution Department were cases filed by or against housemaids, an indication of the poor relations between housekeepers and their sponsors. Maids usually take out the ill-treatment that they get from their employers on the children (ibid.).

'One solution,' it was argued, 'is to hire Muslim Arab housemaids because they understand the children's language and can contribute to their religious education'. On the other hand, if mothers did not 'delegate their responsibilities to housekeepers', many of the problems would not arise (ibid.).

As in Bahrain, the UAE authorities have issued public statements showing some concern at the governmental level for the rights of foreign domestic workers. Following a number of cases filed by and against housemaids, Lt.-Col. Saleh Karwa'a of the Immigration Department recognized the 'lack of laws organizing the relationship between the housemaids and her sponsor . . . [and] . . . that recruiting agencies do not translate the employment contracts into the native language of the housemaids to enable them to understand their legal rights and responsibilities' (*Gulf News*, 4 December 1999). He went on to warn that those who do not honour their contractual responsibilities would face prosecution. Such statements are rarely heard in the region, and further research needs to be done to reveal more details about the number and types of cases which arrive in the courts.

International conventions

The following Articles from the Universal Declaration of Human Rights (adopted by the General Assembly in December 1948) are being violated against foreign domestic workers in the Middle East:

Article 5
No one shall be subjected to torture or to cruel, inhuman or degrading treatment or punishment.

Article 13
1. Everyone has the right to freedom of movement and residence within the borders of each State.
2. Everyone has the right to leave any country, including his own, and to his country.

Article 23
Everyone has the right to work, to free choice of employment, to just and favourable conditions of work and to protection against unemployment.
2. Everyone, without any discrimination, has the right to equal pay for equal work.
4. Everyone has the right to form and to join trade unions for the protection of his interests.

Article 24
Everyone has the right to rest and leisure, including reasonable limitation of working hours and periodic holidays with pay.

International Labour Organization Conventions

While there are many ILO Conventions that deal with acceptable and unacceptable standards of work and remuneration, there are no ILO Conventions that specifically deal with domestic workers. Domestic workers are defined as workers who are not members of the family or household, but who are employed to 'facilitate the running of domestic life and personal needs' (ILO, 2000: 31). Further, it is acknowledged that the large majority of domestic workers throughout the world are migrant or immigrant women. The particular category of female domestic workers with whom we are concerned are migrant women, that is, temporary migrant workers. Most ILO protective measures cover permanent immigrants or those 'who have been regularly admitted to the territory of a member State' (ILO, 2000: 74). There are no ILO Conventions that deal specifically with temporary workers.

While it is suggested that migrant workers should enjoy all the rights applied to national workers (with respect to remuneration, hours of work, overtime arrangements, paid holidays, etc.), there needs to be a recognition that migrant workers are being employed largely *because* they are not receiving the normal labour entitlements of Arab nationals; and because they are largely willing to accept less rewarding conditions of work. The willingness is there because they receive 4–5 (or more) times the income they would receive in their home countries.

The most important ILO Conventions and recommendations for the benefit of migrants are the Migration for Employment Convention 1949 (no. 97); the Migration for Employment Recommendations 1949 (no. 86); the Migrant Workers Convention 1975 (no. 143); and the Migrant Workers Recommendation (no. 151). But these Conventions have not been ratified by many countries, and 'No country in the Middle East has ratified any of the [major] ILO conventions' (Pires, 2000).

Conventions in the Arab region

According to Pires (2000) the fundamental document relating to human rights in the Arab world is the Cairo Declaration of Human Rights in Islam, which was adopted by the Organization of the Islamic Conference in 1990. It guarantees freedom from discrimination based on various grounds for all individuals. Specifically in the field of migration, the Agreement of the Council of Arab Economic Unity (1965) provides for freedom of movement, employment and residence and abolishes certain restrictions upon movement within the region. In 1968, the Arab Labour Organization developed the Arab Labour Agreement, the purpose of which is to facilitate labour movement in the region, giving priority to Arab workers. These same provisions were reiterated in the 1970s with the strengthening of measures to retain jobs for Arab workers and to remove non-Arab workers from the region. This reduction of external non-Arab migrants from the Arab labour market was particularly evident throughout the 1980s, which was part of the Strategy for Joint Arab Economic Action and the Charter of National Economic Action. It favoured Arab over non-Arab labour to 'reduce dependence on foreign labour'. In 1984 this doctrine was reiterated in the Arab

Declaration of Principles on the Movement of Manpower calling for inter-regional cooperation (Pires, 2000). During the 1990s, however, there was considerable relaxation of these principles. While a massive return migration to Asia and Africa from the Gulf states was evident just prior to and during the First Gulf War, there has been a gradual rein-troduction of cheap foreign labour into most Arab countries (see Castles and Miller, 1998). However, little in the way of regional or international human rights legislation or ratification covering Arab or non-Arab migrant workers has been forthcoming.

United Nations Conventions

It is generally accepted that the most appropriate international con-vention which covers the rights of temporary foreign workers, and foreign female domestic employees in particular, is the 1990 United Nations International Convention on the Protection of the Rights of All Migrants, Workers and Members of their Families (see de Beijl, 1997; Doomernik, 1998; Young, 2000). However, in one of the regional preparatory meetings for the World Conference against Racism held in Kathmandu, Nepal in 2001, a resolution urged the governments of Nepal, Indonesia, Bangladesh, India and Thailand to ratify this Con-vention immediately. Although passed in 1990, it has not yet come into force because it requires the signatures of 20 countries and, as of May 2001, had been ratified by only 16 states (AFP, 2001). The major dilemma facing the Lebanese government in signing this Convention is that the legal status and rights of migrants are to be recognized – a condition the Lebanese would not want to grant to the hundreds of thousands of undocumented Syrian workers in the country (see Young, 2000). However, this Convention is the most comprehensive landmark instru-ment dealing with human rights conditions of migrant workers, and the only one that clearly does not exclude temporary contract migrants. It also extends some of its provisions to undocumented migrants.

Redress mechanisms and public policy

The governments of Sri Lanka and the Philippines have made frequent visits and representations to the receiving countries of their nationals in the Middle East in attempts to ameliorate the problems faced by their migrant workers. For example, in 1999, as a clear recognition that abuse and breach of contracts were occurring, leaving runaway women stranded, vulnerable and liable to be captured and returned to their employer, or imprisoned, the Sri Lankan Foreign Employment Bureau established 'safe houses' in the embassies in Lebanon, the Gulf states and other countries to provide safety and temporary shelter for those who encounter problems with their employers (Nonis, 1999).

In March 2000 the Indian Ambassador in Kuwait announced the enforcement of a ban on the employment of Indian domestic workers in Kuwait (issued in June 1999), following reports of abuse, corrupt agents and low wages (*Gulf News*, 2 March 2000). At that time around 150 domestic workers were being housed in the embassy shelter. Similar stories of Sri Lankans fleeing their employers are rife. For example, in January 2000, 200–250 domestic workers were sheltered in the Sri Lankan embassy's 'safe house'. In 1999 some 750 Sri Lankans were repatriated because of employer harassment, including sexual assault (*Gulf News*, 21 January 2000).

Almost all the countries considered in this analysis have policies to reduce their (economic) dependence on foreign labour. ESCWA, for example, has recommended that GCC countries replace Asian workers with those from other countries in the Arab region 'in the spirit of regional economic cooperation'. They also suggest that, in replacing foreigners with nationals, they should 'consider the option of raising taxes on expatriates rather than imposing quotas to limit their numbers' (ESCWA, 2000: 20). Bans and quotas on immigration have merely stimulated an illegal trade in forged work permits and bogus sponsorships (Girgis, 2000). However, none of the policies and measures to reduce the number of foreigners in the Middle Eastern countries to date has been successful (Oxford Analytica, 2001).

Such responses from an economic perspective are normal, but preventative measures against abuse also need to be sought. For example:

1. More cases concerning illegal practices and abuse by Arab nationals should be brought before the courts. In most cases of abuse, withholding of wages or breach of contract in one form or another, the migrant women are either not prepared to press charges or cannot afford legal representation. Funds should be provided that cater for legal cases, including the accommodation and protection required in the time it takes for a case to reach the courts. These cases should have high media publicity to act as a deterrent – that is, if the judgments are made in favour of the aggrieved migrants.
2. Protective legislation in local labour law should be made which specifically covers temporary foreign contract workers and with specific reference to domestic workers.

3. Recruitment agencies should be regulated more stringently. This would include strict professional training and accreditation in the legal and ethical requirements to avoid the kinds of practices outlined above. This should be done in consultation with the sending countries.

4. Contracts should be written and explained in the migrant's own language and signed in the presence of a representative of their own country. With domestic workers, for example, they should not go to the home of their employer immediately on arrival, but pass through some form of official embassy office, or attend a seminar on the proper employment codes of practice, with their employer.

5. Government departments, companies and corporations should establish an explicit policy and set of rules and procedures for their employees with respect to 'household help', in the tradition of corporate 'best practice' (see Jureidini, 2001, regarding the model policy of the American University of Beirut).

6. In accordance with ILO policy (Convention 181 on Private Employment Agencies, 1997, Article 7, 1), private recruitment agencies should not charge any fees or charges, directly or indirectly, to the employee. The fees and charges currently being taken out of the initial salaries of migrant workers place them in a situation of 'debt bondage', which should be eliminated.

7. Finally, if there were some way of alleviating the costs to the employers in bringing workers into the country, perhaps measures, such as withholding of passports and restriction of movement, could be circumvented. The ostensible reasons given for these abuses is to prevent the migrant from absconding and the employer (and the agency) losing their investment. Ordinarily, corporations must bear the risk of employees leaving because of the principles of 'free labour', which originated in the French Evolution. However, in the arrangements between individual members of a household and domestic employees, such principles do not seem to apply in practice. In this regard, it is suggested that the sponsorship rules for temporary foreign workers should be relaxed. In other words, to allow greater freedom of workers to leave their employer for whatever reason and to seek employment elsewhere in the local labour market. Interestingly, in his recommendations for greater economic liberalization of the Gulf economies, Girgis makes the same proposal, but based on the principle of greater market freedom to 'search for the highest rates of return' (2000: 17).

While a number of these suggestions deal with formal redress mechanisms to alleviate or eliminate forms of xenophobia and slavery in Middle East countries, it should be noted that such reforms may affect the labour market in terms of the demand for foreign workers. If this is the case, governments of both receiving and sending countries may not be supportive.

Conclusion

Not all migrant workers referred to in this chapter are treated badly. Many are treated with respect and dignity, are paid on time, given time off and return to their home countries having earned up to three or four times what they could have earned if they had not migrated. As a result, their families prosper (see Massey et al., 1993; Taylor, 1999; on the economics of remittances).

How are we to explain xenophobia in the Arab Middle East? For unskilled foreign workers in the Gulf states it may simply be an issue of economics and nationalism – that is, a desire to reduce the dependency on foreign labour which results in the repatriation of billions of dollars annually in remittances to the labour-sending countries. However, when we consider foreign female domestic employees, other factors come into play. First, their position within the household or as cleaners in organizations itself is inherently and traditionally a servile one. We can surmise that layers of repression and oppression take their toll on the lower orders in the status hierarchy. A repressive government and religious regulation result in frustrations seeking release against those who are more vulnerable. Women employers' culpability in the abuse of domestic maids can be linked to the former's assumed second-class status in Arab families among other possible explanations, which cannot be discussed here.

Whether one considers the phenomenon of the rise of domestic servants as one of 'repoliticizing the private sphere' or of 'refeudalization of modern exploitation and violence', as is argued in some debates in the European context (see Lutz, 2001), in the Middle East one wonders whether it is merely a remnant or a continuity of a feudal orientation.

It is not possible to canvass all the possible explanations of the way in which racism and xenophobia play out in the Arab Middle East. It would be glib to suggest only religion or an inherent cultural brutality, for the same phenomenon may be found in many other countries, whether against Indonesians in Malaysia, Filipinas In Taiwan, Thais and

Romanians in Israel, Mexicans and Puerto Ricans in North America, Sri Lankans in Lebanon, North Africans in France or Pakistanis in England. Rather, we might focus more upon the aspects of vulnerability of domestic workers in these countries and seek to find mechanisms to reduce that vulnerability.

References

Abella, M. (1990) 'Sex Selectivity of Migration Regulations Governing International Migration in Southern and South-Eastern Asia', in *International Migration Policies and the Status of Female Migrants*, Proceedings of the United Nations Expert Group Meeting on International Migration Policies and the Status of Female Migrants, San Miniato, Italy, 28–31 March, pp. 241–52.

Abella, M. (1995) 'Asian Migrant and Contract Workers in the Middle East', in R. Cohen (ed.) *The Cambridge Survey of World Migration*, Cambridge: Cambridge University Press, pp. 418–23.

Abercrombie, N., Hill, S. and Turner, B. (1994) *Penguin Dictionary of Sociology*, Harmondsworth: Penguin Books.

AFP (2001) 'Asian Countries to Ratify UN Treaty to Protect Migrant Workers', *Daily News*, 1 May.

Ahmed, S. (2000) *Strange Encounters: Embodied Others in Post-Coloniality*, London: Routledge.

Al-Moosa, A. and McLachlan, K. (1985) *Immigrant Labour in Kuwait*, London: Croom Helm.

Amnesty International (2000) 'Saudi Arabia: Asian Workers Continue to Suffer Behind Closed Doors', *Amnesty International Index*: MDE 23/33/00, 1 May.

Anderson, B. (2000) *Doing the Dirty Work: The Global Politics of Domestic Labour*, London: Zed Books.

Ariffin, R. (2001) Domestic Work and Servitude in Malaysia. Paper presented to workshop on *Domestic Service and Mobility*, The International Institute of Social History, Amsterdam, 5–7 February.

Arnold, F. and Shah, N. (1986) *Asian Labour Migration: Pipeline to the Middle East*, London: Westview Press.

Bales, K. (1997) *Disposable People: New Slavery in the Global Economy*, Berkeley: University of California Press.

Banton, M. (1997) *Ethnic and Racial Consciousness*, London: Longman.

Barsotti, O. and Lecchini, L. (1995) 'The Experience of Filipino Female Migrants in Italy', in United Nations (ed.) *International Migration Policies and the Status of Female Migrants*, New York, pp. 153–63.

Birks, J. and Sinclair, C. (1980) *International Migration and Development in the Arab Region*, Geneva: International Labour Office.

Brochmann, G. (1993) *Middle East Avenue: Female Migration from Sri Lanka to the Gulf*, London: Westview Press.

Campani, G. (1995) 'Women Migrants: From Marginal Subjects to Social Actors', in R. Cohen (ed.) *The Cambridge Survey of World Migration*, Cambridge: Cambridge University Press, pp. 546–50.

Castles, S. and Miller, M. (1998) *The Age of Migration*, Basingstoke: Macmillan Press.

Chang, G. (2000) *Disposable Domestics: Immigrant Women Workers in the Global Economy*, Cambridge, Mass.: South End Press.

Chin, C. (1997) 'Walls of Silence and Late Twentieth-Century Representations of the Foreign Female Domestic Worker: The Case of Filipina and Indonesian Female Servants in Malaysia', in *International Migration Review*, Vol. 31, No. 2, Summer, 353–85.

Cohen, R. (1987) *The New Helots: Migrants in the International Division of Labour*, Avebury: Aldershot.

de Beijl R. (1997) Combatting Discrimination Against Migrant Workers: International Standards, National Legislation and Voluntary Measures – the Need for a Multi-pronged Strategy. Paper prepared for the Seminar on *Immigration, Racism and Racial Discrimination*, Centre for Human Rights, International Migration, International Labour Organization, Geneva.

Doomernick, J. (1998) 'Labour Immigration and Integration in Low and Middle-Income Countries: Towards and Evaluation of the Effectiveness of Migration Policies' *Conditions of Work, International Labour Migration*, Geneva: International Labour Organization.

Eelens, F., Schampers, T. and Speckmann, J. (eds) (1992) *Labour Migration to the Middle East: From Sri Lanka to the Gulf*, London: Kegan Paul International.

ESCWA [Economic and Social Commission for Western Asia] (1999) *Women and Men in the Arab Region: A Statistical Portrait 2000*, New York: United Nations.

ESCWA [Economic and Social Commission for Western Asia] (2000) *Preliminary Overview of Economic Developments in the ESCWA Region in 2000*, New York: United Nations.

Evans-Pritchard, D. (2001) Sri Lankan Community in Lebanon. Paper presented to the conference *Lebanese Presence in the World*, Lebanese American University, Beirut, 28–29 June.

Gamburd, M. (2000) *The Kitchen Spoon's Handle: Transnationalism and Sri Lanka's Migrant Housemaids*, Ithaca, NY: Cornell University Press.

Girgis, M. (2000) National Versus Migrant Workers in the GCC: Coping with Change. Paper presented at the *Third Mediterranean Development Forum*, 'Voices for Change, Partners for Prosperity', Cairo, March.

Grandea, N. and Kerr, J. (1998) 'Frustrated and Displaced: Filipina Domestic Workers in Canada', in *Gender and Development*, Vol. 6, No. 1, March, pp. 7–12.

Haddad, R. (2001) 'Sri Lanka Requests Inquiry on "Suicide"', *Daily Star*, 6 July.

Hage, G. (2000) *White Nation: Fantasies of White Supremacy in a Multicultural Society*, Sydney: Pluto Press and Routledge.

ILO (2000) *International Labour Office ABC of Women Workers' Rights and Gender Equality*, Geneva: International Labour Organization.

International Labour Organization (2001) *International Labour Migration Data Base*, http://ilm.cdtel.fr/english/ilmstat.

Jureidini, R. (1998) 'Palestinian and Foreign Labour in Israel', *Journal of Arabic, Islamic and Middle Eastern Studies*, Vol. 4, No. 2, pp. 25–46.

Jureidini, R. (2000) 'Race, Ethnicity and Immigration', in R. Jureidini and M. Poole (eds) *Sociology: Australian Connections*, Sydney: Allen & Unwin, pp. 190–215.

Jureidini, R. (2001) *Migrant Women Domestic Workers in Lebanon*. Report prepared for the International Labour Office, Beirut, Lebanon.

Jureidini, R. and Hage, G. (2001) 'The Australian Arab Council: On the Possibilities of Arab Anti-Racist Activism in Australia', in G. Hage (ed.) *Arab-Australians Today: Citizenship and Belonging*, Melbourne: Melbourne University Press.

Jureidini, R. and Moukarbel, N. (2001) Contract Slavery: the Case of Female Sri Lankan Domestic Labour in Lebanon. Paper presented to workshop on *Domestic Service and Mobility*, The International Institute of Social History, Amsterdam, 5–7 February.

KAKAMMPI (Association of Filippino Migrant Workers and Families) (1998) Insecurity in a New World Order: The Crisis of Philippine Overseas Migration. Workshop Presentation at the *Second Annual Conference on Alternative Security in Asia Pacific: Prospects and Dilemmas*, Bayview Hotel, Manila, 22–24 July.

Kannangara, A. (1999a) 'Govt seeks to ensure safety of Lankans in Saudi', *Daily News*, 28 August.

Kannangara, A. (1999b) 'Nearly 160,000 Lankans Found Employment Abroad Last Year', *Daily News*, 20 April.

Kannangara, A. (2000) 'Rs. 7 Billion Remitted By Lankans Employed Abroad', *Daily News*, 8 April.

Lutz, H. (2001) At Your Service Madame! Migrant Women as Domestic Workers in Europe. Paper presented to workshop on *Domestic Service and Mobility*, The International Institute of Social History, Amsterdam, 5–7 February.

Massey, D., Arango, J., Hugo G., Kouaouci, A., Pellegrino, A. and Taylor, J. (1993) 'Theories of International Migration: A Review and Appraisal', *Population and Development Review*, Vol. 19, No. 3, September, pp. 431–66.

McDermott, M. (1999) 'Afro-Asian Migrants in Lebanon', Report of the Committee on Pastoral Care of Afro-Asian Migrant Workers, Beirut (unpublished manuscript).

McMurray, D. (1999) 'Recent Trends in Middle Eastern Migration', *Middle East Report*, No. 211, Summer, pp. 16–19.

Nonis, A. (1999) 'Safe Houses for Sri Lankan Workers Abroad', *Sunday Observer*, 16 May.

Oxford Analytica (2001) Executive Brief: 'Non-National Workers in the Gulf States: Numbers, Origins, Status and Treatment', 4 and 5 April.

Ozyegin, G. (2001) Untidy Gender: Maids, Madams and Husbands of Domestic Service in Turkey. Paper presented to workshop on *Domestic Service and Mobility*, The International Institute of Social History, Amsterdam, 5–7 February.

Palmer, P. (1989) *Domesticity and Dirt: Housewives and Domestic Servants in the United States, 1920–1945*, Philadelphia: Temple University Press.

Pires, J. (2000) Untitled paper presented at the *Legal and Social Rights of Asian and African Migrant Workers in the Middle East Conference*, Caritas Mona Seminar, 9–12 May, Beirut.

Rajagopalan, P. (2001) Domestic Service in India: Culture of Poverty for Women. Paper presented to workshop on *Domestic Service and Mobility*, The International Institute of Social History, Amsterdam, 5–7 February.

Rbeihat, S. (2000) 'A Concept Paper on the Situation of Female Domestic Migrant Workers in Jordan', *UNIFEM Strategic Planning Workship on Female Migrant Workers in Asia*, Katmandu, Nepal, 30–31 October.

Rosales, L. (1999) 'Legislative Agenda on Filipino Migrant Workers', *Public Forum on the Philippines* Report, The Hague, The Netherlands.

Sabban, S. (2001) Foreign Female Domestic Workers in the United Arab Emirates. Paper presented at the CLARA Workshop on *Domestic Service and Mobility* at the International Institute of Social History, Amsterdam, 5–7 February.

Said, E. (1978) *Orientalism*, Harmondsworth: Penguin.

Saleem, A. (2001) Domestic Workers in Pakistan. Paper presented to workshop on *Domestic Service and Mobility*, The International Institute of Social History, Amsterdam, 5–7 February.

Sanjek, R. and Cohen, S. (eds) (1990) *At Work in Homes: Household Workers in World Perspective*, Washington: American Anthropological Association.

Seddon, D. (2001) 'From the Himalayas to the Gulf: Nepali Foreign Labour Migration and Remittances – A Case Study of Globalization'. Paper presented at the Conference on Globalisation and the Gulf. 2–4 July 2001, Institute of Arab and Islamic Studies, University of Eveter.

Shawabkeh, A. and Halaseh, I. (2001) Working Paper Presented to the ILO/UNIFEM Workshop on the Status of the Immigrant Female Worker in Jordan, Amman, 20–22 February.

Tabbara, B. (2001) 'ESCWA Region and Racism'. Unpublished manuscript, Human Development Section, ESCWA, Beirut.

Tandon, R. (2001) Between Work and Home: The Limits of Rationalized Labour: A Study of Migrant, Tribal, Women, Domestic Workers in New Delhi. Paper presented to workshop on *Domestic Service and Mobility*, The International Institute of Social History, Amsterdam, 5–7 February.

Taylor, J. (1999) 'The New Economics of Labour Migration and the Role of Remittances in the Migration Process', in *International Migration*, Vol. 37, No. 1, pp. 63–88.

Turner, B. (1993) 'Outline of a Theory of Human Rights', in Bryan Turner (ed.) *Citizenship and Social Theory*, London: Sage, pp. 162–90.

Wijers, M. and Lap-Chew, L. (1997) *Trafficking in Women, Forced Labour and Slavery-like Practices in Marriage, Domestic Labour and Prostitution*, Utrecht: Foundation Against Trafficking in Women.

Yan, S-L. (2001) Modern Slaves: Foreign Maids in Taiwan. Paper presented to workshop on *Domestic Service and Mobility*, The International Institute of Social History, Amsterdam, 5–7 February.

Young, M. (2000) *Migrant Workers in Lebanon*, Beirut: Lebanese NGO Forum.

3
Immigration, Multiculturalism and the Nation State in Western Europe

Jeroen Doomernik

Introduction

In the years following World War II, the whole of Western Europe gradually became a region of immigration. In the first instance, this concerned people displaced by the war and its aftermath (redrawn borders and policies of what later distastefully became known as 'eithnic cleansing'). Subsequently, politics induced people to leave what by then had become the Eastern Bloc. Most notably, this led to migration from the German Democratic Republic to the German Federal Republic, and emigration from Hungary (1956) and Czechoslovakia (1968). The arrival of such newcomers was never seen as immigration as such, but rather as an anomaly, a one-off phenomenon, and caused little discomfort in the countries where these people sought refuge. Moreover, these immigrants were easily absorbed in expanding labour markets. In fact, rebuilding destroyed economies induced an even greater need for labour. In the 1960s and 1970s this led to the arrival of what were euphemistically called guestworkers from the countries surrounding the Mediterranean. As the word guestworker implies, this immigration was conceived to be of a temporary nature – which it turned out not to be.

After the oil crises of the mid-1970s many guestworkers lost their employment due to economic restructuring. As they were guestworkers, it was generally assumed that they would return to their countries of origin. Some did, but many stayed and were joined by their spouses and children.

After the war, colonial states, such as Great Britain, France and the Netherlands, were faced with the arrival of many immigrants following decolonization. Their arrival too was seen as a temporary anomaly, to be accommodated but then forgotten. However, like the settled former guestworkers, family reunification and formation came in their wake. These migration flows have meanwhile largely dried up but have been replaced by asylum seekers and refugees who, on the waves of economic globalization, have found their way to Europe from many parts of the globe. Even a country that seemed immune to immigration – the Irish Republic – has witnessed in recent years the influx of many newcomers and the return of migrants who earlier left for the New World. In short, even though *de facto* immigration has taken place in most West European countries for the past four to five decades, and in considerable numbers, governments for a long time, and some even today, failed to define in proper terms what actually was happening.

This impaired perspective in most instances has led to short-term government responses. Migration pressure is not easily alleviated as its causes, though manifold, are often first and foremost of a demographic nature (Amersfoort and Doomernik, 1998). The integration of immigrants, especially of those from less developed countries, should be conceived in terms of generations rather than legislative periods.

Immigration poses a challenge not just to labour market needs but also to the welfare systems of West Europe. In most instances, all legal residents of a country are granted certain basic rights – a minimum of economic security, a roof over the head, access to the educational system for minors, and the like. Like an insurance system, it may not be a great problem if a few individuals claim compensation without having contributed premiums over a long period of time. If, however, their numbers are large, at some point the system may not be able to shoulder the burden. Now this principle in itself would validate a policy of rejecting every form of non-economically induced immigration. However – and this explains why post-guestworker immigration did take place – economic arguments are not the only ones a liberal democratic state needs in order to maintain its legitimacy. Human rights concerns are just as important, and not without reason enshrined in international treaties, including the European Convention on Human Rights. Those treaties prevent governments from closing the doors on unsolicited immigration, even though at times attempts are made to keep the chink as small as possible. In effect, immigration has become part and parcel of the modern world and will not cease until global economic integration and equality have been reached.

The dominant discourse within some states such as Germany and Austria has, nevertheless, been one of denial: '*Deutschland ist kein Einwanderungsland*' is a phrase until very recently frequently used in a country such as Germany that at one stage in the 1990s had one of the highest immigrant populations in Europe. In other countries – for instance, Sweden, Britain and the Netherlands – in contrast, policy-makers have adjusted to the reality of immigration, albeit perhaps grudgingly. In these countries, ideas have developed about what the presence of newcomers with markedly different cultural and socio-economic backgrounds from the native population might entail and whether it calls for particular types of policies. Yet another type of response can be found in France. This is a country that for more than a century considered itself to be a country of immigrants. It was a nation in which it did not matter where one's parents came from, for all citizens were treated as essentially French.

On the basis of this very broad and simplified overview, a typology of three types of immigration countries can be construed:

- immigration countries with ostrich habits;
- immigration countries that would prefer not be countries of immigration, but are willing to come to grips with reality;
- immigration countries that believe in the integrating power of their culture and nation.

Following the example of Castles and Miller (1993: 39) we can distinguish four ideal types of nationhood – a concept closely related to a state's self-perception – and thus with direct consequences for the notion of who belongs to the nation and under what conditions newcomers can become full members.

1. The *imperial* model views belonging to a nation 'in terms of being a subject of the same power or ruler' (ibid.). No modern liberal state fits this model, but the European past has seen very clear examples in the Austro-Hungarian, Russian and Ottoman empires. Until the Nationality Act of 1981 this model also applied to Britain (ibid.).

2. The *ethnic* model defines membership of a nation on the basis of common roots and destiny, reflected in use of a common language and culture, and hence belonging to the same ethnic community. This then, almost by definition, excludes newcomers with other cultural traits and different roots from becoming full members. Among the main immigration countries, Germany comes closest to this type, at least until very recently. There is a reluctance to grant citizenship to all those who are not born of at least one German parent (the prevalence of the so-called

jus sanguinis, literally 'law of the blood' but perhaps better translated as 'law of descent'). If citizenship is granted through naturalization, this is preferred to be seen as the crowning point after a process of (near) assimilation. At the same time, however, large numbers of immigrants arrive who are granted German citizenship the moment they cross the German border. These are the so-called *Aussiedler*, descendants of German colonists who moved to settle in the eastern parts of Europe in earlier centuries. This illustrates the importance of the country's 'law of descent'. The current Schroeder government, which assumed office in late 1998, while maintaining the principle of *jus sanguinis* has developed policies that are more in line with reality. Naturalization laws have been relaxed, especially for the children of immigrants (if they grow up in Germany they can opt for German citizenship), and Germany is being quite revolutionarily redefined as an immigration country. Even the opposition parties in parliament have embraced this principle.[1] This does not mean that Germany will receive many more immigrants than it does today, but the new policies should better accommodate labour market needs, especially for the highly skilled. Nevertheless, the rhetorical change is remarkable.

3. In the *republican* model, belonging to society is predominantly defined as belonging to a political community. Newcomers can become full members if they agree to live according to its political rules. Citizenship then is seen as a logical prerequisite of integration rather than, as is the case in the ethnic model, the end result of that process. In spite of some fluctuations in its policies, France can be considered a good example of a state that practises this model. This is reflected in its *jus soli*, the 'law of the soil', which grants citizenship not only to children of French descent but also to anyone born on French territory, and by the relative ease with which foreign-born immigrants can become citizens. It is further reflected in a strong belief in the assimilating capacities of the French nation and the ensuing lack of any kind of minority-based rights or minority-targeted policies.

4. The *multicultural* model is based on the idea that cultural differences within a society are normal. Differences are not necessarily problematic provided they do not hinder full participation in a society's core fields, i.e. in the educational system, in the labour and housing markets, and in democratic decision-making processes. To this end, equality before the law needs to be achieved as well and as quickly as possible. Uncomplicated citizenship rules are one instrument to achieve this, but states

practising this model may additionally grant many civil and political rights to foreign nationals, making them almost equal to nationals. The Netherlands, for example, grants local suffrage to non-European Union nationals who legally reside in the country for five years.[2] It also has policies explicitly aimed at integrating immigrants and their descendants into Dutch society. Integration is defined as having equal access to society's resources and institutions. Assimilation is not a policy goal; instead provisions are made to facilitate the institutionalization of the immigrant's culture and religion.

One might expect each of these types of countries to have different policies when it comes to issues pertaining to the integration of newcomers, or even no policies in a nation that simply fails to perceive newcomers in need of integration. This also implies that the objective position of immigrants compared to the native population might be different as a result of these different policies. To put this hypothesis to the test, we shall look at integration policies in France, Germany and the Netherlands and briefly discuss the position of immigrants in those countries. While not excluding other ethnic groups, doing so we concentrate our attention on Turkish immigrants and their descendants.[3] This choice is inspired by the fact that they arrived at around the same time and for the same original reason, i.e. as industrial workers. Moreover, immigrants from Turkey are present in considerable numbers in all three countries, though the numbers are by far the largest in Germany. In Germany, Turks, at just over two million persons, account for about 2.5 per cent of the country's population. France and the Netherlands are respectively home to slightly under and above 200,000 Turkish immigrants. These figures, it should be noted, are distorted by the fact that in France they pertain to non-nationals (many immigrants will have become French nationals) whereas Dutch statistics include every person born in Turkey, regardless of his or her nationality.

Integration

As Böhning (1995) notes, integration can refer to both a state of being and the process towards it. The state of being integrated may be defined as a situation in which immigrants and their descendants hold a position that is similar to natives with comparable and relevant characteristics, notably in terms of age, education and gender. Such a definition is not necessarily embraced by all observers, but would seem a sensible one for our present purpose. The term assimilation is then reserved for a situation in which citizens of foreign descent cannot be 'detected' in society other than perhaps by their surname, nor view themselves in any way as members of a group originating abroad.[4] The process of integration should not be seen as a one-way street. As in a chemistry experiment, social elements can be combined to form products, but they can also, by means of a catalyst, be separated. In the social sciences this process is called 'disintegration'.

Integration policies can be examined along two dimensions: the subjects and the fields aimed at. On the issue of subjects, a distinction can be made between general and targeted policies (or in Hammar's, 1985, terms: direct and indirect immigrant policies). The first type of policy addresses all persons within the population who have certain characteristics, such as being deprived or marginalized, or running the risk of becoming so. The second type of policy singles out specific categories of people, e.g. immigrants and their descendants in general or from certain countries of origin in particular.

When the focus is on the fields of integration, policies may aim at the most commonly targeted field, which is the labour market. With the possible exception of people born rich or otherwise economically well off, being integrated in the labour market determines to a considerable extent their integration in most, if not all, other spheres of society. Besides the financial aspects of being economically active, work constitutes an important element in an individual's sense of purpose and structures their life-chances. From any government's point of view, moreover, it is expensive to support people who cannot take care of themselves; under- or unemployment is a waste of human capital; and unemployment may destabilize society's social fabric.

In addition to integration policies aimed at the labour market, governments may also try to support and encourage the integration of immigrants (or other potentially or actually marginalized persons) in other fields. As pointed out, there are more or less direct links between housing, schooling and income, and governments may assume that once income is assured, integration in other fields should be an automatic consequence. In practice this link is not one-dimensional and, moreover, is not instantaneous. Place of residence, for example, may determine a person's access to employment and/or upward mobility. One need only imagine a situation where large numbers of disadvantaged people are housed together in suburban areas with no or few industries, with no or few direct transport routes to the city centre or other parts of town where employment could be found, and, as a consequence of the generally low-income situation, little retail or other economic activities within the area itself. This example is not hypothetical,[5] but more common are situations where some kind of geographical clustering of disadvantaged persons – among whom immigrants are often disproportionately found – occurs, especially in the larger cities. This then may cause governments, whether local, provincial or national, to devise measures to increase the opportunities for adequate education for second-generation immigrants[6] that might, as a result of the low income, poor education and lack of language abilities of their parents, otherwise remain beyond their reach. Another type of policy may be aimed at providing good quality housing as such or at trying to move poorly housed people into other neighbourhoods – perhaps dispersing them, in the hope of increasing their integration.

In addition to policies that address integration into the core sectors of society, governments may also seek to intervene in the fields of religion and culture. In some states (notably those based on the republican ideal) these aspects are left to the private sphere, whereas in others (those embracing the multicultural ideal) governments may perceive the need for an active (or at least facilitating) role. Examples from the Netherlands are numerous, for instance state subsidies for Islamic and Hindu public broadcasting companies and state-funded Islamic and Hindu public schools. Furthermore, local and national government see religious immigrant organizations as discussion partners on an equal footing with other types of organizations.[7]

The above shows that integration can be measured in a whole range of areas, including those associated with questions pertaining to mono- or multicultural society. Interesting as those might be, it would seem doubtful if, for instance, it is always relevant for immigrants to adopt the food preferences of their host society, and enjoy particular types of music and literature or the nationally preferred soap opera. Nor is it crucial whether they support Arsenal, Ajax, FC Bayern, Olympic Marseille or Galatasaray for the UEFA Cup. Even though anthropologists may not fully agree when we discount these types of adaptation, it can be agreed that the well-being of immigrants *and* that of the receiving society above all depends on such key issues as employment and education (see also Böhning, 1996). Employment provides an individual with the means to acquire decent housing in a desirable neighbourhood, which again determines where his or her children go to school. Whether this is a school populated with disadvantaged children, perhaps with the same ethnic background, or one with children from a diversity of backgrounds, can be crucial in determining whether a child develops its full intellectual potential. In other words, it will determine whether immigrant communities will become long-term ethnic minorities who cannot escape the poverty trap. Once integration into society's core sectors or fields has been completed, one may doubt whether the question as to whether our societies have become multicultural will still hold much interest. We may have gained a couple of new religions and a host of new tastes in food, but that would be about it. This does not mean, however, that a nation's commitment to accepting diversity is not crucial. It definitely is, but not, as shall be demonstrated, in the way often thought. Catering for cultural and social diversity will more quickly and easily result in a society with a high level of social cohesion than policies explicitly aiming at cultural uniformity and assimilation.

France

Policies towards legal immigrants basically are inclusive and based upon the republican ideal of *liberté, égalité et fraternité*. For the century or so preceding the 1970s this stance was complemented with a liberal immigration regime. As to integrating newcomers, two main strategies have until this day been employed: easy access to all political rights by an active naturalization policy towards legally residing foreigners, and a firm belief in the assimilationist capacities of the French nation. This belief remained unchallenged until about the 1970s when the immigrant population began to change in character. Previously, immigrants had predominantly come from surrounding countries (Italy, Spain and Portugal) and their integration into the labour market had posed few problems. This was different with subsequent immigration from North Africa, and also, though the numbers were smaller, from Turkey. The oil crises had substantially limited the need for unskilled and semi-skilled workers, making the economic integration of those newcomers problematic. An additional 'problem' was that their religion (Islam) and other cultural properties set them aside from mainstream society more than had been the case with the Southern European immigrants, who predominantly had been Roman Catholics, like the native French population. The republican model under those circumstances could not assimilate these newcomers as easily as it had in earlier eras.

From the viewpoint of the immigrants, the assimilationist tradition collided with their desire to retain and build on their religion, a desire doubtlessly reinforced by their lagging economic integration. This mismatch between the expectations of the French state towards immigrants and their own ambitions and needs has for the past decades remained a large source of contention. Especially among young people, usually born and bred in France, dissatisfaction has become evident. The fact that French urban areas exhibit a high level of geographical segregation (Thave, 1999) whereby immigrants and their descendants are often found in high-rise suburbs – the *banlieux* – exacerbates dissatisfaction. Periods of unrest and clashes with the police (sometimes culminating in fatal casualties) are not unknown. But also the wearing of the hijab by schoolgirls meets with strong reactions on the part of the French authorities. The Front National's electoral appeal also seems by and large to lie in its anti-Islamic and anti-immigrant rhetoric.

The policy response has been to improve living conditions in the *banlieux* and to invest in schools in deprived areas and youth schemes. Those policies are of a general nature and, as a result of ethnic segregation, benefit immigrants and their descendants to a much larger extent than native French people.

In addition to cultural 'distance' between the French native population and Muslim newcomers the labour market position of many immigrants, and not just of the Turks,[8] has remained precarious until this day. Unemployment among Turkish immigrants (according to the 1995 figures) stands at close to 30 per cent for men and 45 per cent for women. Among natives the employment rate is 12 per cent (INSEE, 1997). Figures for 1999 do not differentiate sufficiently between countries of origin to follow up on the unemployment rate for Turkish immigrants but do show a wide discrepancy between immigrants (i.e. foreign-born persons) and French native-born workers. Just over 20 per cent of all immigrants were unemployed, and among these Moroccans stand out with 32 per cent unemployment for males and approximately 44 per cent for females.[9]

The fact that French statistics provide only a crude indicator of the position of members of ethnic communities in economic or other terms is an excellent illustration of French traditions. The term immigrant is, in both the statistics and in policy-making, and etymologically correctly, reserved for persons who are born abroad. As far as this principle stresses equality before the law, few will argue against that. However, it ignores cultural differences between individuals and communities and the objective fact that some or even many persons, though equal before the law, do not enjoy the same opportunities to participate fully in society. In other words, by emphasizing the presumed assimilationist character of French society, the interests of immigrants and especially their descendants and others who do not want to assimilate into mainstream French society or, perhaps more seriously, are not equipped to do so, remain out of reach of official policies.

In short, economic integration in France remains a problem and social cohesion is at risk due to the state's inability (or perhaps unwillingness) to accommodate cultural difference.

Germany

We have seen that German political discourse on immigration has been based for a very long time on a strict denial of the reality of immigration. The effect of a policy myth is not likely to disappear as quickly as the Schroeder government's (and opposition's) radical change in policy rhetoric. It would be too simple, however, to conclude that the German government did not intervene in the past when it comes to the integration of immigrants.

National policies[10] on integration have always been strictly related to economic participation, the proposed immigration legislation being no different. After the ban on recruitment following the economic downturn of the early 1970s, many Turkish immigrants returned home, either because they lost their jobs and residence permits, or wanted to return on their own initiative, or because they were included in a remigration scheme (with financial incentives). Even today, being unemployed for a prolonged period of time puts the residence status of non-European Union immigrants who have not yet attained an establishment permit at risk. This applies to 26 per cent of Turks (Groenendijk et al., 1998), and excludes foreigners, such as refugees, who have been admitted under international obligations. Naturalization has for a long time been very difficult to achieve because the German government believed that it should be the end product of a completed integration, or in effect even assimilation, process and not, as in France, the beginning of a more complete integration. At least partly due to this prolonged exclusion in legal terms, the unemployment rate among Turks in Germany is comparatively low, though very clearly on the increase (from 14.5 per cent in 1986 to 22.5 per cent in 1996 while for the labour force as a whole it is 11.2 per cent). Simply put, an immigrant either accepts any employment, however dirty, dangerous and poorly paid, or returns home. German policies have thus succeeded in 'exporting' potential unemployment to Turkey.

Policies on integration are, not surprisingly, aimed at the labour market. Unemployed immigrants are included on a non-discriminatory basis in schemes to reintegrate them into the labour market. Yet, they are also, time and again, reminded of the possibility of returning to their country of origin. Even among young people this principle seems to create unrest, or as the German Commissioner for Foreigners Affairs puts it:

> Whereas the numbers of young people who want to return decreased between 1979 and 1989 from 29.6% to 5.6%, the numbers of young-sters who are not yet sure increased: those without plans or with the intention to stay on for a couple of years are more than 60% of the respondents. *This is extraordinary because many of those are born and bred here.* (Beauftragte der Bundesregierung, 1995: 74; emphasis added)

In the field of cultural diversity the German government prefers to keep itself aloof for the country is fundamentally German and should not become multicultural. Islam is not generally recognized on the same basis as the 'native' religions, Roman Catholicism and Protestantism. Institutions representing those latter two are granted – by the country's constitution – substantial influence in many spheres of society: the state collects their taxes, they have a voice on the boards of the public broadcasting services, can organize their own schools, etc. Similar claims from Islamic organizations have always been rejected with the argument that they qualify for similar recognition only once they have formed a church-like institution (Doomernik, 1995). For a religion distinguished by its lack of hierarchy, this is nearly impossible to fulfil, which is a source of serious frustration among German Muslims who are predominantly of Turkish origin.

During the early 1990s the annual number of immigrants (non-nationals) stood at about one million. If you include ethnic Germans (*Aussiedler*) that number increases by another 200,000. Today the number of immigrants is still considerable (in 2000 they were about 700,000).[11] In effect, Germany is one of the most significant immigration countries in the world. The official denial of this fact has, at least in my view, done much to incite the unrest and race-centred violence among (small) parts of the native population, images of which were published around the globe. If governments proclaim a 'truth' that everyone can easily falsify, its legitimacy as the representative of the public interest is seriously undermined. Neo-Nazis and other racists are given the opportunity to claim that their violent actions merely put into practice the words spoken by mainstream politicians.

In short, German migration policies have long been able to keep the incidence of unemployment among Turkish immigrants low, but disintegration in the labour market has become evident. Perhaps much clearer and more relevant in this context is that a repeated denial of the facts has put a serious burden on social cohesion.

The Netherlands

After the oil crises, the Dutch government held the view that further immigration should be as minimal as possible. At the same time it came to the conclusion that migrants who would like to return home should be assisted whereas those who preferred to stay should be integrated as far as possible. There were no serious attempts to curtail the immigration of family members of those who stayed and settled. In due course, the immigration policies came to resemble those of France: an establishment permit after five years of legal residence (regardless of whether a person is employed or not) and relatively easy access to citizenship (about half of all former Turkish nationals now hold a Dutch passport) in order to encourage the migrants to participate in all spheres of society. Unlike in France, cultural diversity is extolled. The Dutch government officially considers the country to have become multicultural. This is less surprising than it may seem as the Netherlands has a tradition of managing cultural differences as a consociational democracy – a system akin to the parallel inclusion of minority groups but with a joint roof (parliament) where those decisions affecting all are made (Lijphart, 1977).

Decision-making has always required compromises as no party (each representing one of the minorities: liberal and conservative Protestants, Roman Catholics, Liberals and Social Democrats) is large enough to dominate all the others. This means that if the state is required to fund a particular kind of institution for one minority, the others demanded parity. Especially during the first half of the twentieth century this principle resulted, for instance, in large numbers of Catholic and Protestant hospitals, schools (even at the university level the consequences could be seen) and later equal broadcasting time on state radio and television. Even though cultural differences among the native population have lost much of their relevance, especially within politics, the legal framework intended to accommodate such differences is still in place. As a result the Netherlands today has a large number of Islamic, and some Hindu, primary schools and an Islamic and a Hindu broadcasting corporation, all of which is paid for by the state. Neither the French nor the German government would contemplate such institutionalization.

Catering for cultural difference can be considered to have been the spearhead of Dutch integration policies during the 1980s. However, during the past decade or so, policies have moved in the direction of general ones aimed at assisting all members of society who are disadvantaged or are at risk of becoming so. These policies are matched by a strong advocacy for full participation for *all*, the right to be different and the value this adds to society. The term currently employed is 'citizenship' (*burgerschap*), not in its legal sense but to stress the rights and obligations all legally resident persons have towards each other and to society at large.[12] In addition, anti-discrimination policies are well developed, not just in legal terms but also by stimulating local initiatives and public relations campaigns. Whether this is an effect of those policies or a particular trait of Dutch society is difficult to establish. It is nevertheless important to note that ethnically motivated violence is very rare in the Netherlands, especially compared to France or Germany.

Looking at the labour market, however, disintegration has long been evident, probably even to a larger extent than in France and most certainly in Germany. In 1994 the unemployment rate among Turks[13] stood at 30 per cent and their net participation rate was very low, whereas unemployment among natives was 7 per cent. Due to high levels of economic growth, the past few years have seen a steady decline in unemployment rates (in 1999 it had dropped to 13 per cent among Turks and 3 per cent among natives) and a gradual increase in net participation rates among members of ethnic minority groups can be observed (figures from CBS, 2000). Whether this represents a genuine reversal of the disintegration trend or is largely the result of near full employment can be established with some certainty only when the next economic downturn sets in.

In the field of labour market integration the policy reaction has been defined not only in general but also in specific terms. From the 1970s onwards, national and other public authorities have pursued preferential hiring practices (including for women). In order to stimulate similar practices among other employers, during the 1990s two laws were passed (the second being a revision of the first law) basically requiring employers to monitor the ethnic composition of their labour force and make them sensitive to the need for it to be diverse.[14] Although evaluation of these policies is pending, it is safe to assume that their impact is relatively small.

In short, the Netherlands has developed a policy aimed at inclusion of those who have legally settled,[15] even at great economic cost, and of accommodating differences. Policy responses are of a general nature, yet based upon the multicultural ideal, unless these are seen to be insufficiently effective. Nevertheless, among Turks and most other immigrant groups unemployment is still rather high.

Summary and conclusions

One main difference between the three countries discussed used to lie in the realm of immigration policies, i.e. those by which a government defines who can find legal residence within its borders, for what duration and to what end. Yet convergence is evident, especially in the German government's fundamental policy changes. This convergence is likely to develop further with the continued integration of the European Union, not least while the intention has been formulated to arrive at uniform immigration policies in the foreseeable future. However, what would seem at least as important are not government policies but how they are discussed in public. It is, for instance, important to realize that now that Germany has officially become an immigration country, it is unlikely to have much more immigration than it previously did. Yet, if a country's elite time and again stresses the fact that immigrants are basically unwelcome, this sets a fundamentally different tone compared to when a government sends more moderate signals or goes as far as to welcome the arrival of newcomers and new cultures.

Contrary to our assumption, we found few differences in active integration policies: in all cases the labour market and – something we have not addressed – the education system are central. In those fields general policies are the rule in all three countries. But, as we have seen, there are major differences between states in the ways they take account of cultural diversity, with France and Germany on the one hand, and the Netherlands on the other. Those differences seem to be first and foremost the consequences of tradition and hardly of long-term, proactive thinking. Nevertheless they may show us the direction in which such thinking should move.

For the time being in all three countries we are witnessing trends of disintegration. For the first generation of Turkish immigrants labour market disintegration, though at varying rates, is marked. Yet the labour market position of Turks in Germany is considerably better than that of their compatriots in France and, until very recently, in the Netherlands.

If we look for possible explanations for this trend, the most obvious one is a mismatch between labour market needs and labour supply. Many of the jobs the guestworker generation came to fill have disappeared. This is especially the case in the Netherlands where the economy has moved away from labour-intensive production towards the service industries. Only few of the former guestworkers were able to find new jobs in these new industries due to a lack of skills and language deficiencies. As a result, many became long-term unemployed or left the labour market altogether. Turkish immigrants of a later date did to some extent manage to find employment in the service sector, but again did not have the skills that qualified them for management positions. For those who were educated in the Netherlands, the story is different, provided, of course, their educational levels match those of their native peer group.

Yet, this does not mean that we can reduce the trends we have observed to a mere sum of economic needs and labour supply. Time and again it has been empirically established, for instance through situation testing commissioned by the International Labour Office's migration branch in Germany (Goldberg et al., 1995), the Netherlands (Bovenkerk et al., 1995), Belgium (Arrijn et al., 1998) and Spain (Colectivo IOE, 1996), that discrimination may seriously impede the labour market access of members of minority groups and immigrants. Analyses of secondary sources for the United States (Bendick, 1996) and the United Kingdom (Wrench and Madood, 2001), including the results from situation testing, led to the same conclusion. The methodology used in this type of testing is basically very simple: have two candidates apply for a job (or an apartment) whose objective properties differ in only one respect: their ethnic origin. If the candidate with the native background is significantly more often hired (or given the tenancy) than the other candidate, discrimination is in evidence. Of course, the hiring stage is usually left out of the testing and a first positive or negative reaction on the side of an employer (or landlord) is used as benchmark. What emerges from all these experiments unequivocally is that discrimination is a feature of our societies. It should be pointed out though that the same extent of discrimination could not be established in all cases: some ethnic groups are more likely to be viewed negatively than others. In the Netherlands, for instance, Moroccans suffer more discrimination than Turks or people from the former Dutch colonies.

Another factor one should keep in mind when looking at unemployment statistics is continued immigration. It is not easy to establish who the unemployed are – recently arrived newcomers with few language skills or permanently marginalized long-established migrants? Put differently, a constant stream of newcomers who need to be integrated economically keeps unemployment high if there is no immediate labour market need on their arrival.

On the one hand, the impact of continuing immigration could be construed as an argument for restrictive policies. On the other hand, we should not be so certain. If we compare German and Dutch policies, we find a paradox. In Germany the government appears to have been able to keep unemployment among Turks low by tying residence permits to being in employment, forcing migrants either to return to Turkey or accept any job offered to them, however unpleasant, unhealthy or poorly paid. In the Netherlands secure residence status is fairly easy to attain, and as a rule not dependent on one's economic position. This is part of Dutch policy aimed at inclusion. The German policy has always been aimed at long-term exclusion except of those who are considered to be German (like the so-called *Aussiedler*) or, under certain conditions, those who aspire to assimilate. It does not seem far-fetched to assume a direct link here between those policies and the extent to which ethnic violence occurs: in Germany this is a common feature of everyday life, in the Netherlands such violence is extremely rare. In other words, exclusionary policies may well be beneficial in short-term economic terms but undermine social cohesion in the longer run, whereas inclusionary policies are beneficial for society's cohesion but economically expensive in the short and medium run.

A last important aspect we should consider is the effect of levels of learning, especially those of the first generation. One should bear in mind that many of the original immigrants enjoyed little education. In fact, especially among Moroccan immigrants, a large number were illiterate. Among Turkish immigrants illiteracy is less common, yet levels of education are generally low (i.e. restricted to primary education). It is perhaps not surprising that their children do not participate in higher education. But then, the emancipation of the native working classes did not come about in a single generation. As mentioned in the introduction, cultural difference should not be discounted, but the conclusion seems justified that class differences are by far the most important factor determining the present and future position of immigrants and their descendants.

Now if the above is true, what types of policies would be most likely to facilitate intergenerational mobility? Obviously, there are those policies that reduce or remove obstacles. These are located not just in the realm of integration policies, but also in the field of what we would call immigration policies that are about access and settlement. And they are about the allocation of rights. In Scandinavia and the Netherlands we usually agree on the principle that a settled immigrant should basically have the same rights as citizens, with the exception of full suffrage. This is different in many other countries and for this reason we will spell them out.

1. A secure residence status after a relative brief period of time (say 3–5 years) which means protection against the threat of expulsion, regardless of whether one is employed or not.
2. The right to family reunification with no discriminatory provisions (i.e. provisions that are reserved for aliens) and no limits as to the duration of legal residence within which reunification should take place. This principle is cemented in the European Convention on Human Rights, but governments in the past have sought to be as conservative as possible in their interpretation of this basic right.
3. The right to vote in local elections for holders of a permanent establishment permit.
4. The right to acquire citizenship once the immigrant is in possession of a permanent establishment permit.

It is typically societies that call themselves multicultural that have policies granting those rights. Admittedly, France comes near in its immigration practice but evidently not in the domain of integration or the discourse surrounding it. Germany very clearly until very recently did not.

And then there are some rights currently not bestowed on foreigners, whether in multicultural or assimilationist states, that one might also want to address:

- The extension of the rights of free movement within the European Union currently reserved for citizens of member states to those immigrants who hold a permanent establishment permit. The European Union's Tampere summit of Autumn 1999 did address the topic, but consensus on the matter seems to be as remote as it has been for years.
- The right for those who want to return to their country of origin or to a third country to retain an establishment permit (and hence the option to return) for a meaningful period of time.

Both these rights would greatly increase the mobility of migrants not just within Europe, but also between Europe and the countries of origin.

For the restrictions we have now in place first and foremost put a premium on staying, regardless of whether this is beneficial to the migrant or the state where he or she has settled.

Furthermore, governments should in every way possible combat irrational discrimination in all areas of society. The necessary basis for this has to be provided for by means of a comprehensive body of legal provisions, both in civil and in penal law.[16] This has to be backed by sufficient and suitable means by which to implement these provisions, e.g. low thresholds for complainants to claim their right to equal treatment and effective law enforcement. This is not difficult to defend in multicultural societies, though it should be mentioned that a number of countries have not yet implemented anti-discrimination legislation in full. France and Germany have no specific legislation against racial discrimination.

Lastly, it pays governments to be as open as possible when it comes to accommodating ethnic or cultural differences. Provided governments manage to state this unequivocally as a policy aim, for instance, by defining the country as multicultural, such a stance will greatly increase the well-being of immigrant communities and, when managed carefully, not alienate the native population. The paradoxical outcome could well be that such a policy change would lead, to a large extent, to assimilation. Stressing the need for assimilation, in contrast, may well have the opposite effect.

The interesting thing about all the policy elements listed is that they incur virtually no costs and basically require no more than a change in attitude and legislation. Perhaps one should be cautious to demand of states that they bring about the integration of newcomers by financial means. Obviously, making available language courses, professional training and the like is necessary, but removing those obstacles that unduly hinder individuals in the development of their full potential needs to take priority. And this, by the way, does not just pertain to immigrants.

Notes

1. The present opposition consists, among others, of the Christian Democrats and the Liberals who, between 1982 and 1998, constituted the German government. It was this government that maintained that Germany is not a country of immigration making this sudden change in stance rather remarkable.
2. The right to vote and stand as a candidate for provincial and national elections remains the privilege of nationals.
3. Many of the data presented here are also found, and in much greater detail, in Doomernik (1998).

4. Good examples are found in Germany where a surname ending in –ski signifies Polish roots; and in the Netherlands where French names are not uncommon, denoting descent from the Huguenots who settled there during the seventeenth century.
5. The suburbs around many of the main French cities and the housing estates around the larger Scottish cities are some examples that spring to mind.
6. It is at times a confusing and inaccurate term. The second generation may be considered to consist of people born in the country where their parents have settled and therefore are strictly speaking not immigrants. Furthermore, in many instances these children are citizens of the receiving state and not foreigners. Depending on the definition, second-generation immigrants may also be the children born abroad of the original immigrants but immigrating as minors and not on their own initiative.
7. Each nationality has its own advisory council to the government, in which various types of organizations (labour, religion, sports, etc.) work together.
8. Many North Africans are, or always have been, French nationals and therefore not statistically traceable.
9. Deducted from Thave (2000, graph 3).
10. The individual states that together constitute the Federal Republic have a considerable amount of autonomy when it comes to policies regarding cultural issues. This is something that is not considered in this overview.
11. The number of departing foreigners is considerable too, putting net migration at a much lower level (see Walwei, 2001).
12. Recent newcomers are, wherever relevant, under a legal obligation to follow integration courses (language classes but also in order to learn the basic facts about Dutch society). These are called *inburgeringscursus*.
13. Persons born in Turkey or in the Netherlands but having at least one Turkish-born parent.
14. Establishing ethnicity is on the basis of the employee's self-definition.
15. At the same time migrants who have not been granted the right to settle are vigorously excluded from all claims to public resources by means of the 1998 *Koppelingswet*, which requires all service providers to check every client's residence status. This law has sparked many discussions and some municipalities have refused to withdraw the social security benefits of illegal residents.
16. The burden of proof in civil law lies considerably lower than in penal law and hence often is a more useful tool for combating everyday types of racial/ethnic discrimination.

References

Amersfoort, H. van and Doomernik, J. (eds.) (1998) *International Migration. Processes and Interventions*, Amsterdam: Het Spinhuis.

Arrijn, P., Feld, S. and Nayer, A. (1998) *Discrimination in Access to Employment on Grounds of Foreign Origin: the Case of Belgium*, Geneva: International Labour Office.

Beauftragter der Bundesregierung für die Belange der Ausländer (1995) *Bericht der Beauftragten der Bundesregierung für die Belange der Ausländer über die Lage der Ausländer in der Bundersrepubliek Deutschland*, Bonn/Berlin, December.

Bendick, Jr, M. (1996) *Discrimination against Racial/Ethnic Minorities in Access to Employment in the United States: Empirical Findings from Situation Testing*, Geneva: International Labour Office.

Böhning, W. R. (1995) 'Labour Market Integration in Western and Northern Europe: Which Way Are We Heading?', in W. R. Böhning and R. Zegers de Beijl (eds.) *The Integration of Migrant Workers in the Labour Market: Policies and Their Impact*. Geneva: International Labour Office, pp. 1–21.

Böhning, W. R. (1996) 'Melting Pot' or 'Salad Bowl' – Socio-economic Integration Matters Most! Paper presented at the Migration Dialogue conference on immigration issues and integration policy, Chicago, 25–28 April.

Bovenkerk, F., Gras, M. J. I. and Ramsoedh, D. with the assistance of Dankoor, M. and Havelaar, A. (1994) *Discrimination against Migrant Workers and Ethnic Minorities in Access to Employment in The Netherlands*, Geneva: International Labour Office.

Castles, S. and Miller, M. J. (1993) *The Age of Migration. International Population Movements in the Modern World*. Basingstoke and London: Macmillan.

Centraal Bureau voor de Statistiek (CBS) (2000) *Allochtonen in Nederland 2000*, Voorburg/Heerlen: CBS.

Colectivo IOE: Angle de Prada, M., Actis, W., Pereda, C. and Pérez Molina, R. (1996) *Labour Market Discrimination against Migrant Workers in Spain*, Geneva: International Labour Office.

Doomernik, J. (1995) 'The Institutionalization of Turkish Islam in Germany and the Netherlands: a Comparison', *Ethnic and Racial Studies*, Vol. 18 (1), pp. 46–63.

Doomernik, J. (1998) *The Effectiveness of Integration Policies towards Immigrants and their Descendants in France, Germany and The Netherlands*, Geneva: International Labour Office.

Goldberg, A., Mourinho, D. and Kulke, U. (1995) *Arbeitsmarkt-Diskriminierung gegenüber ausländischen Arbeitnehmern in Deutschland*, Geneva: International Labour Office.

Groenendijk, K., Guild, E. and Dogan, H. (1998) *Security of Residence of Long-Term Migrants. A Comparative Study of Law and Practice in European Countries*, Strasbourg: Council of Europe (CDMG).

Hammar, T. (ed.) (1985) *European Immigration Policy: a Comparative Study*, Cambridge: Cambridge University Press.

Institut National de la Statistique et des Études Économiques (INSEE) (1997) *Les Immigrés en France*. Paris: INSEE.

Lijphart, A. (1997) *Democracy in Plural Societies: a Comparative Exploration*, New Haven and London: Yale University Press.

Thave, S. (1999) 'Les étrangés et leurs logements', *INSEE Première*, No. 689, December.

Thave, S. (2000) 'L'emploi des immigrés en 1999', *INSEE Première*, No. 717, May.

Walwei, W. (2001) 'Arbeitsmarktbedingte Zuwanderung und bedenkenswerte Alternative – Strategien zur Erschliessung von Personalreserven', *IAB Werkstattbericht*, Nr. 4/21.3.

Wrench, J. and Madood, T. (2001) *The Effectiveness of Employment Equality Policies in Relation to Immigrants and Ethnic Minorities in the UK*, Geneva: International Labour Office.

4
Exclusionary Populism in Western Europe in the 1990s: Electoral Success and Political Impact

Hans-Georg Betz

Introduction

Since the late 1980s, a new type of right-wing party and movement has made considerable electoral gains in a number of liberal democracies in Western Europe. Among the most successful of these parties have been the Austrian Freedom Party (FPÖ), the Swiss People's Party (SVP), the Belgian Flemish Bloc (VB) and the Norwegian Progress Party (FrP). Other significant parties are the Italian Northern League (LN), the Danish People's Party (DF) and the two rival movements in France: Jean-Marie Le Pen's Front National (FN) and Bruno Mégret's Republican National Movement (MRN). Finally, there are several marginal parties such as the German Republicans (REP), the German People's Union (DVU), the Danish Progress Party (FP) and the Swiss Freedom Party (FPS) (for an overview, see Betz and Immerfall, 1998; Decker, 2000; Hainsworth, 2000; Perrineau, 2001).

Several characteristics distinguish these parties and movements from the more traditional parties: reliance on charismatic leadership and centralized and hierarchical party structure; the scrupulous pursuit of a populist strategy of political marketing; and, perhaps most importantly, a style of political mobilization that appeals primarily to popular anxieties, prejudices and resentments, particularly against the political establishment. Ideologically, these parties and movements espouse a political doctrine of exclusionary populism. Its main characteristic is a restrictive notion of citizenship, which holds that genuine democracy is based on a culturally, if not ethnically, homogeneous community; that only long-standing citizens are full members of civil society; and that society's benefits should accrue only to those members of society who, either as citizens or at least as taxpayers, have made a substantial contribution to society. The spirit of this doctrine is reflected in the notion of 'own people first' and the call for 'national preference', which are core demands of right-wing populist parties in the current debate on immigration in Western Europe. In recent years, exclusionary populism has gone beyond xenophobia, turning into a new 'post-racist' form of cultural nativism. The new populist cultural nativism, rather than promoting notions of ethnocultural superiority, aims at protecting 'the own' society, culture and way of life against what is seen as alien intrusion, contamination and subversion, whether under the guise of American popular culture or Islamic religious practices and a religiously inspired lifestyle.

Despite the re-emergence of blatantly nativist ideas in Western Europe, openly neo-Nazi and neo-fascist parties have seen themselves even more marginalized than they already were before the rise of the populist right. Although they still exist on the fringes of the political system – the most prominent examples are the National Democratic Party of Germany (NPD); the British National Party (BNP); and the re-founded Italian Social Movement (MSI) – these parties have not much of a social base and even less success at the polls (see, for example, Eatwell, 1998: 143–55). At the same time, however, their importance as way-stations for neo-Nazis and skinheads as well as disseminators of racist, anti-Semitic and Holocaust negationist literature should not be underestimated. However, compared to exclusionary populism, their impact has been relatively limited, in part because of their insistence to hold on to an ideology that has been totally discredited in Western Europe. As a result, the extreme right has largely failed to capitalize on the emergence of immigration as an important political issue and has had to leave the field to the right-wing populist parties.

Unlike the radical and extreme right during much of the postwar period in Western Europe, the contemporary populist right is no longer confined to the margins of the democratic system. In fact, in a growing number of cases, right-wing populist parties have assumed positions of significant political influence, be it on the local, regional or even national level. The most recent example has been the inclusion of the Northern League in the Berlusconi government, where it holds three portfolios, among them the Ministry of Justice. Other parties holding positions of national responsibility are the FPÖ in the Austrian coalition government, and the SVP, which has been part of Switzerland's grand coalition government (*Bunderat*) since before World War II. With these developments, exclusionary populism has moved to centre stage, much to the consternation of the established parties, which all too often have been at a loss of how to respond to the populist challenge.

Electoral progress in the 1990s

For a new party family trying to establish itself firmly in the West European party system, the 1990s proved to be an exceptional decade for the populist right. Electorally, the radical right made dramatic gains in a number of countries, in the process launching a serious challenge to the established parties. Programmatically, the radical right increasingly set part of the agenda, forcing the traditional parties to adopt not only its exclusionary populist rhetoric but also much of its xenophobic programme. Strategically, the radical right made great strides in their attempt to be taken seriously as potential coalition partners.

The radical right's electoral gains in the 1990s were particularly dramatic in Austria and Switzerland. They were considerable in France, Belgium, Norway and Northern Italy, and quite significant in Denmark. However, in Germany and Sweden the populist right has remained a marginal factor, and other democracies, such as Britain, have not had a genuinely populist radical right party.

In Austria, under the leadership of Jörg Haider, the FPÖ went from 9.7 per cent in 1986 to 22.5 per cent of the votes within eight years. In the most recent election (1999) the party gained 26.9 per cent of the vote, enough to surpass the conservative Austrian People's Party (ÖVP) as the second largest party in the country, albeit by only a handful of votes. In Austria's parliament, the FPÖ increased its representation from 18 seats in 1986 to 52 seats in 1999.

In Switzerland, in the 1990s, the SVP more than doubled its electoral support, which traditionally had been around 10 per cent in national elections. In 1991, the SVP received 11.9 per cent of the vote; four years later it gained 14.9 per cent of the vote – which at the time was considered a political earthquake; finally, in 1999, the party gained 22.5 per cent of the vote. This means that within less than a decade, the SVP moved from being the smallest to being the largest of the major parties in Switzerland, increasing its seats in the parliament from 25 in 1991 to 44 in 1999. In the process, the SVP all but destroyed its main competitor on the populist right, the Freedom Party of Switzerland (formerly the Automobile Party), which in 1999 lost all its seats in parliament (it had gained seven in 1995) and most of its constituency to the SVP.

In France, the FN saw a slight gain in its electoral support between the two parliamentary elections of 1993 and 1997. In 1993, the party took 12.4 per cent of the vote; in 1997, it was 14.9 per cent. This almost matched Jean-Marie Le Pen's score in the 1995 presidential election, when he won 15 per cent of the vote, indicating that the FN had solidified its support. Because of France's electoral system, the party managed to fill only one seat in the National Assembly in 1997. At the same time, however, because of its progression in a considerable number of electoral districts, which allowed many of its candidates to advance to the decisive second round, the party played a significant role in determining the outcome of the election.

In Belgium, in the 1990s, the VB established itself as a major political force in Flemish politics. In national elections, the VB's gains increased from 6.6 per cent of the vote (10.3 per cent in Flanders) in 1991, to 7.8 per cent (12.2 in Flanders) in 1995, and 9.9 per cent (15.4 in Flanders) in 1999. By the end of the 1990s, the VB was the third largest party in Flanders, holding 15 seats in the national parliament and 22 in the Flemish parliament. However, the party's progress was most dramatic in Belgium's second largest and most prosperous city, Antwerp, where the VB gained 33 per cent of the vote in the 2000 local elections, up 5 per cent from 1994.

In Norway, the Progress Party, after experiencing a significant decline in the early 1990s which saw its level of support drop to 6.3 per cent of the vote in the general election of 1993 (from 13 per cent in 1989), made a dramatic comeback in the late 1990s. In the parliamentary election of 1997 the party obtained its best result ever. With 15.3 per cent of the vote, which translated into 25 seats in parliament, the FrP emerged as the second largest party in the country.

In Northern Italy, the LN (Northern League) rose within a few years to become the region's most prominent party. Although the party campaigned almost exclusively in the northern part of the country and although its strongholds were concentrated in a relatively small area along the foot of the Alps, the LN managed to gain 8.4 per cent of the vote in 1994 and a bit more than 10 per cent of the vote in 1996. Because of the idiosyncrasies of the Italian electoral rules, the Lega gained 118 seats in 1994, but only 59 seats in 1996.

Finally, in Denmark, the DF (Danish People's Party) gained 7.4 per cent of the vote in the general election of 1998, which translated into 13 seats. The DF is the main successor to the Danish Progress Party, which, under the leadership of Pia Kjærsgaard, in the early 1990s had won around 6 per cent of the vote. The Progress Party split in the mid-

1990s. Subsequently, Kjærsgaard founded the DF and turned it into a major force in Danish politics. However, after winning 2.4 per cent and four seats in 1998, the Progress Party virtually collapsed when its four members of parliament decided to leave the party in the autumn of 1999.

The situation was similar in Sweden. There, New Democracy, after gaining 6.7 per cent of the vote in the first election it contested in 1991, all but disappeared from the political scene after its two leaders resigned from politics before the 1994 election. In 1994, the party garnered a mere 1.2 per cent of the vote, and in 1998, 0.2 per cent of the vote. The radical right fared little better in Germany. In none of the national elections in the 1990s did the German radical right gain enough votes to overcome Germany's 5 per cent hurdle. In the first all-German election of 1990, the REP attracted 2.1 per cent of the vote, in 1994, 1.9 per cent, and in 1998, 1.8 per cent. In the last election, the DVU gained an additional 1.2 per cent of the vote, which brought the united right-wing support (including 0.3 per cent for the NPD) to 3.3 per cent of the vote. The German radical right did make significant gains in some regional elections. Thus in Baden-Württemberg, the REP gained 10.9 per cent in 1992 and 9.1 per cent in 1996; the DVU 12.9 per cent in 1998 in Sachsen-Anhalt, and 5.3 per cent in 1999 in Brandenburg. But despite these noteworthy successes, the radical right in post-unification Germany has largely remained a marginal political factor.

Resentment amidst affluence

Although open hostility towards foreigners, strong opposition to immigration and vocal objection to the emergence of multiculturalism in general are central characteristics of all new right-wing populist parties in Europe, most of these parties are not single-issue protest parties. On the contrary, in the majority of cases, they promote a more or less comprehensive programme of socioeconomic, sociocultural and sociopolitical change, whose implementation would have far-reaching consequences. Thus both the Northern League in Italy and the Flemish Bloc in Belgium have, on occasion, been vocal proponents of the breakup of their respective nation states; the Austrian Freedom Party has marketed itself as an anti-system party working towards the creation of a Third Republic; and the Swiss People's Party has called for an end to Switzerland's consociational institutional system.

Generally, the new right-wing populist parties have rarely hesitated to adopt new issues, as long as these promised to mobilize popular resentments. Often the choice and appeal of these issues can be explained only in the individual national context. Examples are the vocal defence of Switzerland's role during World War II by Christoph Blocher, leader of the SVP's influential Zurich branch; the Lega Nord's appeal to Northern Italian resentments against the *mezzogiorno* and 'Rome, the Big Thief' (the caption of a famous Lega poster) in general; the VB's attempts to exploit diffuse Flemish resentments against the Walloons and particularly the transfer of funds from the affluent north to the struggling south; Jörg Haider's assault on the pillars of Austria's postwar national identity and self-understanding; and calls by Carl Hagen, the leader of the Progress Party, on the Norwegian government to spend some of the huge surplus oil funds to improve the socioeconomic situation of the elderly and particularly their health care. This suggests that in many cases the electoral appeal of right-wing populist parties in Western Europe has been as much a result of their ability to appeal to country-specific issues and grievances as it has been a result of their readiness to exploit popular misgivings about questions related to immigration and multiculturalism.

A case in point was the dramatic upsurge of the SVP under the leadership of Christoph Blocher in the mid-1990s. It is hardly a coincidence that Blocher's rise to national and international prominence occurred at a time when Switzerland was coming under increasing pressure to deal with its less than unblemished record during World War II. As soon as Switzerland's war-time role came under closer scrutiny in the mid-1990s, Blocher rose in defence of his country, defiantly expressing his sympathies for those of his fellow citizens whose patriotic feelings had been offended and whose achievements had been questioned (Blocher, 1997). Charging that the Swiss were neither ashamed of their history nor could be blackmailed, Blocher launched a fierce attack against Switzerland's domestic and foreign critics, focusing particularly on the role of the Jewish World Congress as 'the leader of the campaign against Switzerland of the past and the present' as well as other Jewish organizations, 'which are demanding money' while pretending they were not interested in the money. Blocher went so far as to compare the call made be some Jewish organizations for a boycott of Swiss products with the Nazi boycott of Jewish businesses in the 1930s, which 'initiated the atrocious extermination of the Jewish people'.[1] To guarantee a broad dissemination of his views, Blocher had copies of his major speech on 'Switzerland and the Second World War' distributed to several hundred thousand Swiss households and also made available on his website.

With his intervention Blocher established himself as a strong defender of Swiss national interests and an advocate of the ordinary Swiss citizen. This impression was strengthened further when, a few days before the 1999 election, his detractors published a letter in a widely read newspaper, which Blocher had sent to a Jürgen Graf, the author of a pamphlet deploring the 'demise of Swiss freedom', in which he stated that the author was right (Graf, 1997; for an account of the affair by the book's author, see http://www.ety.com/tell/books/jglife/01.htm). While in the letter Blocher expressed agreement with the general premise of the argument, nothing suggested that he had actually read the pamphlet. As it happened, the author was a notorious Holocaust denier, who used this pamphlet to rant how 'political correctness, Holocaust ideology, Jewish Terror, a corrupt justice system, left wing politics, a close connection to the EU and Maastricht can and will ruin a country' (see http://www.ostara.org/graf). The publication of the letter so close to the election was clearly designed to discredit Blocher as a right-wing extremist and thus diminish the SVP's chances. Blocher immediately rejected the charge and swiftly went on the counterattack, charging the media with conspiring against him in a blatant attempt to influence the outcome of the election (see *Neue Züricher Zeitung*, 1999: 13). In this way, Blocher presented himself not only as a victim of a campaign of character assassination, but also as a tough fighter against media bias and political correctness.

Blocher's style reminded many observers of Jörg Haider, who marketed himself in the 1990s very successfully with the catchphrase, 'He says what you think'. More than any other right-wing populist leader in Western Europe, Haider owes his rise to political prominence to a calculated strategy of assaulting elite values, political conventions and the tenets of Western European political correctness. For one of Austria's most astute observers, Haider is 'the personified antithesis to political correctness' who constantly breaks with Austria's postwar language code, challenging its taboos. As a result, Haider represented for many voters 'a symbolic liberation' (Burger, 2000a: 8; 2000b: 391). The most notorious examples – which are also the ones that have cost him most dearly – of this strategy were his provocative references to the Nazi period, the older generation's role in the Nazi dictatorship and the atrocities committed by the regime. In the process, Haider sought not only to exonerate his parents and their generation of involvement in a genocidal regime; he also consciously assaulted the hypocrisy of the official version of Austria's postwar identity grounded in the victimology of 'Austria – Hitler's first victim', which had very little to do with historical reality. In the process he implicitly attacked the established parties, which tarnished Haider with the Nazi brush while conveniently forgetting that they had allowed many former Nazis 'to recycle themselves and become prominent postwar Austrian politicians' (Cohen, 2000: 57). Thus Haider not only publicly dismissed the notion of the Austrian nation as an 'ideological miscarriage', he also was one of the first major politicians to reject the notion of Austria as Hitler's first victim. At the same time, he went so far as to state that the Third Reich was 'the most horrible criminal regime' responsible for 'mass extermination' and that there was no justification for these crimes (see, for instance, Wolffsohn, 1995: 114). Ironically enough, given Austrian unwillingness to confront the past, even these statements represented a provocation of the official language code, whose characteristic is silence.[2]

The extent to which Haider's political strategy was dominated by appeal to resentment became obvious once again shortly before a regional election in Vienna. A few days before the election, in which the FPÖ was expected to incur major losses, Haider made a short pun during a speech at the party's traditional Ash Wednesday meeting. Referring to Ariel Muzikant, the president of the Jewish cultural community in Vienna, Haider remarked that he did not understand how somebody whose name is Ariel (the brand name of a popular washing detergent) 'can have so much dirt sticking to him'. Haider's 'joke' immediately drew charges of anti-Semitism, which allowed Haider to counterattack, lashing out against political correctness and hypocrisy and those among the intellectual elite promoting them. Asking who decided what was a permissible critique of 'a member of the Jewish religious community' he charged Muzikant with having tried to discredit the newly formed coalition government at home and particularly abroad. Reminding his audience that Muzikant and his family had come to Austria as immigrants, he concluded: 'From an Austrian citizen one can expect patriotism and decency when his country is being slandered from abroad. For Mr. Muzikant, the applause of Austria's enemies was more important' (Haider, 2001).

These two brief examples suggest that the radical populist right's appeal cannot be reduced to the question of immigration and multiculturalism. Rather, at least in part, Blocher, Haider and other prominent right-wing populist politicians have been so successful because they have consciously promoted themselves as advocates of ordinary citizens, as spokesmen for their unarticulated opinions and sentiments ('what most people really think'), who are capable of giving them voice and, in the words of a well-known FN slogan, of 'rendering the word to the people'. This suggests that right-wing populist mobilization in Western Europe in the 1990s was primarily based on opposition to the political and intellectual establishment and their values, similar to populist mobilization elsewhere (Mayer, 1996a: 210, 212). From this perspective, the gains of the populist right in the 1990s were above all a reflection and expression of growing voter disenchantment with the political establishment, general alienation from the political process and rising dissatisfaction with representative democracy.

A number of empirical studies have demonstrated that there is a strong association between political disenchantment and support for the populist right. Nonna Mayer, in her analysis of the 1995 presidential election in France, characterized the typical FN voter as somebody highly dissatisfied with the functioning of democracy and highly critical of the political establishment. In fact, at the time of the election, more than 60 per cent of Le Pen's supporters thought that democracy in France was dysfunctional (Mayer, 1996: 210, 212). Similarly, Peter Ulram and Fritz Plasser have shown for Austria that the rise in support for Haider and the FPÖ in the late 1980s and throughout the 1990s was largely driven by anti-establishment motives, namely the desire on the part of a growing number of voters to exact revenge on the two major parties via the ballot box (Plasser and Ulram, 2000: 225–41). Marc Swyngedouw, in an analysis of the 1995 parliamentary election in Belgium, suggests that anti-political sentiments and feelings of political powerlessness are important motivating factors behind VB support. A growing number of voters, who 'object to the political methods of the established parties (clientelism, ideological blurring, etc.) and the corruption (scandals) in which they are involved' hope, by voting VB, to rejuvenate the Belgian political system (Swyngedouw, 2001: 238). Finally, Jørgen Goul Andersen and Tor Bjørklund argue that disenchantment with the established parties and political cynicism account to a large degree for the success of the Scandinavian Progress parties in the 1980s and 1990s. In the mid-1990s, the voters of the two Progress parties displayed by far the highest level of political distrust of all voters in the two countries. The same was true for the supporters of the short-lived party in Sweden in the early 1990s (Andersen and Bjørklund, 2000: 207–9). Comparative studies based on aggregate survey data come to similar conclusions that suggest that the voters of right-wing populist parties generally tend to display a significant level of dissatisfaction with democracy and the political process, and that dissatisfaction with democracy, in turn, tends to increase the likelihood of supporting right-wing populist parties (Falter and Klein, 1996; Knigge, 1998; Ivaldi, 2001).

What these studies suggest is that the populist right's appeal in the 1990s was primarily a result of widespread political disaffection and disenchantment – symptoms of a larger crisis in the democratic process and of political legitimacy in general. Right-wing populist parties derived much of their success from their ability to present themselves as representatives of a new 'politics of anti-politics' – direct, close to the people and their interests, and, above all, outside the mechanisms of traditional parliamentary politics (see Ivaldi, 1999: 226–9). Surveys suggest that right-wing populist voters in the 1990s were not only deeply disenchanted with the established political parties, but also increasingly disenchanted with representative democracy. Thus in the mid-1990s, in France, 85 per cent of those voters sympathizing with Jean-Marie Le Pen and his ideas, and in Italy, 71 per cent of those who supported the LN, thought that what the country needed was a strong man who would sort things out (Mayer, 1996b; Diamanti, 1997). This suggests that the radical right had attained at least one of its main objectives: to discredit and delegitimize the political establishment in the eyes of a growing segment of the electorate as a first step towards a more fundamental transformation of the existing system.[3]

Exclusionary populism

Within the populist right's strategy of delegitimation, in the 1990s, the question of migration and multiculturalism gradually assumed a central position, in terms of both political marketing and the political programme. As a result, right-wing populist parties increasingly marketed themselves – and were seen – primarily as anti-foreigner, or, perhaps more precisely, anti-foreignization parties. Although all right-wing populist parties object to the continued influx of non-Western European migrants to Western Europe, migration itself is only one among a range of issues related to the presence of foreigners on the exclusionary populist agenda. Others include questions of internal security, national and cultural identity, the allocation of social benefits, public education and citizenship. In general, these parties have promoted a panoply of policies, including calls to reduce the number of immigrants to zero while gradually expelling and repatriating the resident non-European foreign population to their countries of origin, demands for a halt to all new immigration, and the introduction of strong, state-sponsored measures to integrate the resident foreigners into society using methods that border on forced assimilation.

The populist right's exclusionary agenda is informed by post-racist notions of ethno-pluralism, adopted from the French New Right (*nouvelle droite*). This is a new form of cultural nativism, whose central characteristics are its 'differentialist' line of argumentation and its appeal to rights. In the process the populist right abandoned the traditional right-wing extremist recourse to notions of inherent inequality and natural hierarchy asserting instead 'the incommensurability of different cultures' as justification for their attempt 'to preserve collective identities (and inter-communitarian differences' at all costs) (Taguieff, 1993/4: 101). At the same time, the populist right started to promote a language of rights – rights of the indigenous people, rights to the preservation of one's own culture and language and a right to individual safety – designed, as Roger Griffin has put it, to respond to 'deepseated and understandable fears about the erosion of identity and tradition by the globalizing (but only partially homogenizing) forces of modernity' (Griffin, 2000: 173).

As a result, right-wing populist opposition to immigration and multiculturalism was increasingly driven as much by questions of national and cultural identity as by more practical, interest-based considerations, although the latter continued to figure more prominently in the parties' programmes and policy statements. The essence of these considerations found expression in the well-known FN call for 'national preference' (*préférence nationale*), which the party tried to put into effect in the four cities of which the FN gained control in the late 1990s. As Paul Hainsworth has put it, national preference means, in practice, 'propagating the idea of reserving or prioritizing state-provided goods and benefits (such as jobs, housing and social payments) for nationals, on the basis of a distinctly restrictive citizenship, rather than to the population at large, on the basis of equity' (Hainsworth, 2000: 10). In more cases, calls for national preference have been advanced particularly to discourage the influx of refugees seeking asylum in the affluent welfare states of Western Europe, which became the central issue on the exclusionary populist agenda in the 1990s.

In Austria, the FPÖ has appealed to a range of prejudices and resentments against new labour migrants, refugees and non-West European foreigners residing in the country. As early as 1993, Haider wrote in his programmatic book *Die Freiheit, die ich meine* that there was 'a fundamental right to *Heimat*, but none whatsoever to immigration'. At the same time he charged that the 'experiment of multicultural society' had failed to 'work anywhere' and become a nightmare for many citizens, warning that with increasing numbers of immigrants there was a growing threat to society as a result of 'incompatible norms' clashing in a narrow space (Haider, 1993). While initially adopting the call for 'zero immigration', the party modified its position for the 1996 election by adding that this policy would be in force as long as there were Austrian citizens without work and/or a home. Finally, for the 1999 election the party used the country's already high population density, topography and limited resources to justify its anti-immigration stance. At the same time, however, the party tried to use the question of immigration in support of its strategy to discredit the left-wing parties. Thus in 1999, the FPÖ distributed leaflets in Vienna that charged the left, among other things, with doing nothing to prevent 'black African asylum seekers' from dealing in drugs and with ignoring the needs of Austrian families with children since there were thousands of foreign families waiting on Austria's borders.

Similarly, for the 2001 regional election in Vienna, the party made 'foreigners' the central issue of its campaign strategy, which was consciously designed to appeal to people's grievances and anxieties. The party's list was headed by Helene Partik-Pablé, a member of parliament and the party's expert on immigration issues, who had gained notoriety in 1999 when she remarked during a parliamentary debate that the 'black African drug dealers are particularly aggressive, which obviously lies in the nature of these people' (http://www.parlinkom.gv.at). Given her background, it was hardly surprising that the party's anti-foreigner campaign focused almost exclusively on problems increasingly seen as being associated with immigrants, such as drug trafficking and crime in general. Most of the party's policy proposals focused on halting the influx of migrants, expelling illegal immigrants and making it easier to identify foreigners. At the same time, the party emphasized its rejection of multiculturalism, calling instead for the complete integration of foreigners into Austrian society and particularly their adaptation of the 'indigenous value catalogue' (FPÖ, 2001: 8–13).

Similar to the FPÖ, in Switzerland the SVP presented itself in the late 1990s increasingly as defenders of Swiss culture and identity against the threat of 'foreignization'. This was in part an attempt to attract the supporters of smaller far-right parties like the Swiss Democrats and particularly the Freedom Party of Switzerland, which in the early 1990s had made the 'struggle against *Überfremdung* [foreignization]' the centre of its marketing campaigns. In part it also reflected the growing importance of Christoph Blocher who, at the beginning of the 1990s, as head of the Campaign for an Independent and Neutral Switzerland (AUNS) had gained political prominence by leading the ultimately successful opposition to Switzerland's membership of the European Economic Community. Before the most recent national election, the SVP spent much energy on questions of immigration and especially asylum. In 1998, it issued a lengthy position paper on migration policy. This was followed, in 2001, by a detailed paper on integration policy (SVP, 1998, 2001). Both papers stressed reducing the influx of migrants and making every effort to ensure that foreign residents integrated themselves into Swiss society, even if the SVP, unlike what the FPÖ seemed to demand, acknowledged that foreigners could not be expected to assimilate completely by abandoning their own culture and traditions. At the same time, the SVP launched a signature campaign against 'the abuse of the right to asylum'. By the end of 2000 the campaign had secured more than 100,000 signatures, the required number for a popular initiative (see http://www.admin.ch/ch/d/pore/vi/vi296.html; http://www.svp.ch/Deutsch/Asylinitiative/zustandegekommen.htm). However, when far-right parties launched their own campaign, designed to reduce the number of foreign residents in Switzerland from 25 to 18 per cent of the total population, most of the party leadership, including Blocher, came out against the initiative, obviously fearing economic repercussions. This, however, did not prevent the party's grassroots representatives, at a stormy party meeting, overriding the leadership and voting overwhelmingly in favour of the initiative.

Like other right-wing populist parties, the SVP was particularly adamant in its rejection of multiculturalism. As Thomas Meier, an SVP *Kantonsrat* from Zurich, put it in a leading right-wing paper, multiculturalism is a 'dangerous experiment, doomed to failure', which, at the end, means nothing less than 'the demise of culture' (Meier, 2000). Not surprisingly, the SVP in Zurich, the city with the highest number of foreign residents, made the struggle against the evolution of a multicultural society the focal point of its *Ausländerkonzept*. Arguing that multiculturalism threatened Swiss culture with destruction while furthering hostility towards foreigners, the Zurich SVP concluded that 'the model of the "multicultural society" is an ideal, which cannot be squared with reality' (SVP, 1998).

The preservation of cultural identity, reflected in the strict rejection of multiculturalism, is central to the cultural nativism and 'reactionary tribalism' represented by the contemporary populist right. For instance, as the LN in Italy started to lose support at the polls in the 1990s, it adopted an increasingly shrill rhetoric of difference and cultural preservation in the face of what the party considered 'uncontrolled immigration'. Initially, the party focused on the growing problem of illegal immigration and particularly rising crime rates, which it associated with '*i clandestini*'. Thus, in the late 1990s, the party's official daily newspaper, *La Padania*, published a series of articles on northern Italian cities allegedly overrun and besieged by immigrants. At the same time, the party came out strongly against the evolution of a 'multiracial society'. Umberto Bossi, in a speech in 2000, declared not only that the LN stood above all 'for the diversity of the peoples, starting from our own peoples, and from their right to freedom', but also that the party was strictly opposed to what he called 'the absolutism of racism', based on 'indirect violence' characterized by the 'denial of any difference' (Bossi, 2000).

In recent years, right-wing populist cultural nativism and reactionary tribalism have increasingly focused on the challenge posed by the growing presence of Muslims in Western Europe. For the radical right, the social and cultural order promoted by Islam is fundamentally opposed to Western values. As Haider put it in the early 1990s: 'Human rights and democracy are as incompatible with the Muslim religious doctrine as is the equality of women. In Islam, the individual and his free will count for nothing, faith and religious struggle – *jihad*, the holy war – everything' (Haider, 1993: 93). Even more drastic is the German Republikaner, for whom Islam represents 'the greatest threat to the Western world and its values' (http//garbsener-buergerschaft/de/islam.htm). By the late 1990s, most right-wing populist parties were habitually promoting anti-Muslim sentiments to appeal for votes. Hostility towards Muslims was particularly pronounced among the FN, and, after the split, especially in Bruno Mégret's MRN, the REP and the VB, of which the VB produced some of the most vicious, openly racist cartoons explicitly directed against Muslims. The central charges were always the same: Islam is a religion of intolerance, its culture fundamentally incompatible with European values and secular laws. The growing presence of Muslims in Western Europe was nothing short of an invasion, with the objective of taking advantage of Western Europe's liberal and democratic laws in order to establish an Islamic order. This was seen as a new colonialism in reverse, which would inevitably lead to a fundamental clash of civilizations and identities, with terrible consequences (see, for example, Mégret, 1999).

In the late 1990s, anti-Islamic sentiments were increasingly also expressed – albeit less overtly – by the more moderately xenophobic parties, such as the Scandinavian Progress parties and the SVP. Thus in its statement on foreigners, the Zurich SVP charged 'certain immigrant groups' with 'cultural intolerance' which made 'living together with them on a multicultural basis simply unthinkable'. Further on in the text, the party made it clear which groups it meant:

Islam is increasingly becoming the main obstacle to integration. And yet, the proportion of immigrants from Islamic countries is continuously increasing. In Europe, we fought for centuries for liberal and democratic values, for the separation of state and church and gender equality. It is a particular irony of history that the same left-wing and liberal forces, who led this fight, are today the most eager advocates of generous immigration policies – policies, which threaten the basic Occidental values. (SPV 1998)

The LN tried to regain its position by promoting itself as the defender of Western values and even Christianity (see Guolo 2000: 890–901). The most spectacular action was a demonstration against the planned construction of a mosque in the outskirts of Lodi, which featured slogans such as 'Padania Christian, never Muslim'. At the same time, the party used its official newspaper to warn its readers of the fundamental danger posed by Islam, which was hanging over Europe like 'Damocles' sword' (del Valle, 1999).

In the 1990s, the populist right in Western Europe made questions of immigration and multiculturalism the centre of their electoral appeal. Even those parties that initially had promoted themselves primarily as a force for fundamental political renewal increasingly focused on immigration (see, for example, Andersen and Bjørklund, 2000). There is a number of reasons for this turn. First, immigration promised to remain a major political problem for which there was no easy solution. In addition, immigration, more than most other issues, could be used against the political establishment, whose ambiguous and often contradictory positions and actions provoked public anger and resentment, given the widespread negative sentiments with regard to the issue among Western European populations. This was particularly the case with respect to questions of cultural diversity and integration. This might partly explain the radical right's increasing focus on identity politics in the late 1990s, which could easily be framed in the larger context of globalization, thus appealing to diffuse anxieties and resentments generated by global change. This, at least, was the advice given by Franz Schönhuber, ex-REP leader and still a highly influential figure on the radical right with strong ties especially to the FN, who suggested that the radical right focus more on the religious and cultural aspects of globalization, which in his view were of 'essential importance for the whole European right' (Schönhuber, 1999). Finally, immigration was a concrete enough experience for many West Europeans, and could therefore easily be used as an explanation for a number of societal ills, ranging from rising crime rates to the growing fiscal crisis of Western Europe's comprehensive welfare state.

Immigration has also been the one issue where the populist right has had the most significant impact on the official political discourse. In the 1990s, virtually all the major centre-right and centre-left parties in Western Europe adopted a more or less restrictive stance on immigration, residence and citizenship. The most recent example was Tony Blair who a few weeks before the 2001 general election reminded the British voters that during the previous three years, 'Britain's asylum rules [had] been significantly strengthened not weakened' to the point that some criticized them as 'unnecessarily draconian' (Blair, 2001). As a result, right-wing populist parties ran the danger of being outflanked by the established parties. This might partly explain the declining appeal of some of these parties; and it might be an additional reason why the radical right in the late 1990s turned to the relatively new issues of culture and identity. However, the radical right did not have a monopoly on this issue.[4] In any case, the argument does not explain why some right-wing parties have done well despite the increasingly restrictive official line on immigration. One explanation is that voters, seeing the impact of the populist right on the established parties, continue to vote for the radical right to prevent the established parties from once again relaxing immigration policies. A second possible explanation is that the voters of the populist right support far more stringent policies on immigration than the established parties have so far adopted – for example, a complete halt to making transfer payments to asylum seekers, or severe benefit cuts for aliens (see Betz, 2004).

Whatever the motives, there can be no doubt that a large proportion of those supporting the radical right in the 1990s did so particularly because of these parties' restrictive position on immigration. This is hardly surprising in the case of overtly nativist parties such as the FN, the REP and the VB; but it has increasingly also been true for the initially less overly xenophobic parties. Andersen and Bjørklund, for instance, have demonstrated that even the voters of the Scandinavian Progress parties 'are strongly opposed to immigration, which is seen as a threat to national identity, and a huge majority favour cuts in foreign aid' (Andersen and Bjørklund, 2000: 211). These results are compounded by studies based on an analysis of comparative survey data, which generally show a high correlation between support for right-wing populist parties and highly negative attitudes towards various aspects of immigration and multiculturalism (Gibson, 1995; Knigge, 1998: 262–7).

The social basis of exclusionary populism

Right-wing radical and extremist parties have traditionally been most successful during periods when social and economic turmoil gives rise to popular insecurities, dissatisfaction and resentment. Not surprisingly, the radical right's rhetoric resonated particularly among those social groups that were objectively most affected by socio-economic problems and change, or at least subjectively felt their future prospects to be affected negatively by them. In the current debate on right-wing radicalism, this argument is captured by the 'modernization loser' thesis. The thesis holds that the rise of right-wing populism in the 1980s and 1990s has to be seen in the context of a combination of large-scale socio-economic changes, captured by notions of the end of mass production, the transition to post-industrialism, the information (technology) revolution and of globalization. Each of these developments contributed to the undermining of the postwar Western European model of 'organized (welfare) capitalism' while furthering tendencies of individualization and – potentially – 'de-solidarization'.

The modernization loser thesis is informed by the idea that large-scale socio-economic and socio-structural change, induced by the impact of the information revolution, globalization and the end of organized capitalism, produces winners and losers. In the current environment, an individual's ability to cope with large-scale change depends crucially on the amount of his or her cultural capital, i.e. education and skills. The argument is that those groups that have relatively low amounts of cultural capital are most likely to see significant diminutions of their life-chances, giving rise to anxiety and resentment, which in turn makes them particularly receptive to the radical right's resentment-based appeal. (For a more elaborate discussion, see Betz, 2001: 413–18.) Therefore, the individuals and groups most likely to support the radical right are persons with low levels of education, below-average skills and particularly those unemployed or facing the threat of unemployment.

One important trend that seems to support the modernization loser thesis is the increasing 'proletarianization' of the social base of right-wing populist parties in Western Europe in the 1990s. In fact, during the 1990s, many of these parties turned into a new type of working-class party. This was particularly so in the case of the most pronounced xenophobic parties, such as the REP, the VB and particularly the FN (resulting in what Nonna Mayer has called *ouvriéro-lepénisme* and Pascal Perrineau *gaucho-lepénisme*) (Mayer, 1999: 85–91; Perrineau, 1995: 243–61). Thus in 1995, VB support among blue-collar voters was twice as high (at about 17 per cent) as among other occupational groups (at about 9 per cent) (Swyngedouw, 1998: 71).[5] One example is the LN, which in the early 1990s had attracted a cross-section of the northern Italian electorate. By the mid-1990s, its core constituency had 'shifted to a group primarily composed of workers and artisans living in small towns and working for the myriad of small and medium-sized factories located throughout Lombardy and the northeast. In fact, during the 1996 elections the League became [northern] Italy's largest working-class party given the characteristics of its supporters' (Beirich and Woods, 2000: 132). Whereas in the early 1990s only one out of six northern Italian workers voted LN (16.6 per cent), by 1996, the party was attracting almost a third (31.2 per cent) (Biorcio, 2001: 255–6). The majority of these were industrial workers from the private sector.[6] The FPÖ experienced a similar development. Between 1990 and 1999, the percentage of Austrian workers voting FPÖ increased from 21 to 47 per cent. Among younger male workers, the FPÖ gained an absolute majority (57 per cent) in 1999 (Plasser and Ulram, 2000: 232–4; Ulram, 2001: 217). The same was true for the Scandinavian Progress parties, which in the 1990s had also become working-class parties. In fact, in the 1990s, the two Progress parties 'obtained a higher proportion of workers among their electorate than any other party, including the Social Democrats' (Andersen and Bjørklund, 2000: 216–18).

It would be tempting to interpret the proletarianization of the right-wing populist electoral base as a revolt against globalization and modernity in general. However, this is not entirely persuasive. For one, in the 1990s, the radical right did particularly well in countries and regions that distinguished themselves by high levels of affluence and relatively low levels of unemployment. In fact, Austria, Northern Italy, Norway and Switzerland have some of the lowest levels of unemployment in Western Europe. Equally significant, studies show that unemployment is much less directly associated with support for the radical right than might be expected (see, particularly, Knigge, 1998: 266–7). This may be due to high levels of unemployment benefits and the growing importance of active labour market measures adopted by most West European welfare states. This suggests that the dramatic increase in working-class support for right-wing radical parties in the 1990s might have been less a direct response to structural change than an indirect response to the established (especially left-wing) parties' political response to structural change, in particular the traditional left's gradual adoption of free-market doctrines, programmes and policies in the course of the 1990s, which appear to have left many working-class voters disenchanted.

While right-wing radical parties have increasingly turned into pre-dominantly working-class parties, workers are hardly the only signifi-cant social group supporting these parties. Generally, the radical right has been particularly attractive to younger, particularly first-time voters. At the same time, there has been a significant gender dimension, with women, independent of age, much less likely to vote for the radical right than male voters. Although the gender gap has been one of the most fascinating aspects of the right-wing populist vote, little effort has been made to advance a detailed and convincing explanation that goes beyond the speculative and anecdotal (see, for example, Givens, 2000). Finally, the radical right has also attracted a significant number of white-collar voters, professionals and other segments of the self-employed – groups that generally are more likely to profit than to suffer from struc-tural change. In the most recent election in Switzerland, for instance, the SPV did disproportionately well among these groups. The same was true for the FPÖ, despite growing proletarianization tendencies (see Longchamp 2000: 406; Plasser and Ulram 2000: 232) Again, this sug-gests that support for the radical right has primarily political reasons; in this case perhaps disenchantment with the relative slowness with which governments have responded to global change, thus raising fears of loss of competitiveness or of falling behind.

The right-wing populist dilemma and its challenge

Contemporary right-wing populist parties have presented themselves as a new political force, beyond the antagonisms and cleavages that have traditionally defined left and right. Appealing to and promoting popular resentments, they have pretended that these antagonisms are no longer relevant for politics. However, the composition of their electoral base suggests that the radical right is faced with fundamentally contradic-tory and potentially irreconcilable interests and expectations, which are likely to become increasingly virulent. The FPÖ's recent losses in Vienna are a strong indication of the likely consequences of this process. As the party itself acknowledged after the election, the FPÖ's losses reflected widespread voter disaffection with a party which had promoted itself as the advocate of the 'ordinary man on the street' and his interests, while pursuing a policy of fiscal austerity once it came to power. Ironically, the outcome of the Vienna election was above all an expression of protest against the FPÖ. This was reflected in the fact that the party lost a considerable number of its 1999 voters to the growing pool of nonvoters.[7] As one observer put it, frustration over the government's consolidation measures weighed more heavily with the ordinary man in the street than anti-foreigner slogans (Linsinger, 2001). It is hardly a coincidence that immediately after the election, Haider launched a full attack on the government and particularly its (FPÖ) finance minister, Karl-Heinz Grasser, who was held responsible for the government's austerity programme, and publicly called on the FPÖ to pursue what he called a new 'politics with heart' (*Profil*, 2000). Given growing electoral volatility, it is debatable whether this strategy will be enough for the party to recapture lost voters.

More generally, the recent dramatic losses incurred by the populist right in Austria and Northern Italy suggest that the radical right is hardly less politically vulnerable than the traditional parties. Unlike the traditional parties, populist parties derive much of their success from the skills of charismatic leaders to appeal to a wide range of voters and from their ability to convince voters that a vote for them will force the established parties to pursue policies they would not have pursued otherwise (especially with regard to immigration). This might explain in part the hierarchical organizational structure and highly authoritarian internal climate characteristic of most of these parties, which guarantee a measure of cohesion. At the same time, hierarchical structures and an authoritarian climate tend to provoke dissent resulting in defection and splits, which, in turn, severely threaten the image these parties seek to portray of themselves. The drastic decline in support for the French radical right following the FN's split into two rival parties is a case in point – even if the gains of the Danish People's Party after its split from the Progress Party show that decline is not always inevitable.

Finally, the radical right, like other new parties such as environmental/Green parties, are always faced with the problem of 'issue theft' by the established parties. One reason the radical right in Germany (and also in Great Britain) remain marginalized is that the traditional centre-right adopts a highly restrictive line on immigration. However, this argument should not be pushed too far. In most cases, this strategy has failed to reverse the radical right's electoral fortunes, especially when the radical right manages to present itself as relatively flexible with respect to new issues while at the same time maintaining a strong anti-establishment stance.

Despite the existence of a number of obstacles to new political parties in Western European democracies, the radical right has become a significant and relatively influential political force. Against expectations, most right-wing populist parties have remained a viable political factor that represents a major challenge to democracy and its fundamental values. This is not to say that the radical right poses a threat to the rules of the game of democracy, which all the relevant parties discussed in this chapter have accepted. Unlike in the past, in contemporary Western Europe, what is at stake is not the democratic consensus. Rather, what is at stake is something more fundamental, namely the future of Western European identity and basic values. It is hardly a coincidence that the rise of the populist right has occurred at a time when Western Europe is trying to define itself in terms of a community of values 'formed by the spiritual and political history of the continent', which can legitimately claim to have universal appeal.[8] The populist right, with its aggressive promotion of ethnocentric nationalism, cultural nativism and exclusionary populism, advances a notion of Western European identity that is diametrically opposed to the moral founda-tions of a community of values based on the achievements of the Euro-pean historical experience. With the populist right's gains in recent years, there is a danger that European identity might become little more than 'a white bourgeois populism defined in opposition to the Muslim world and the Third World' instead of a basis for diversity and integra-tion (Delanty, 1995: 155). Although at the present time there is no reason for alarmism, it certainly is necessary to remain vigilant.

Notes

1. 'Demands made under threat of boycott must be rejected with utmost deter-mination. Let us not forget: It was the boycott of Jewish business in Germany that initiated the atrocious extermination of the Jewish people. Whoever averts boycotts by complying with demands, whoever gives in to blackmail, will be repeatedly exposed to blackmail and subject to new boycotts' (Blocher, 1997).
2. There are good reasons to believe that Haider's strategy was motivated in part by his personal grievances and resentment. For a detailed discussion of these questions, see Betz (forthcoming). What John Keegan has written about David Irving holds true for Haider: Like Irving, Haider 'lets insecurities, imagined slights and youthful resentments bubble up from within him to cloud his mind. It is as if he becomes possessed by the desire to shock and confound the respectable ranks of academe, to write the unprintable and to speak the unutterable' (Keegan, 2000).
3. Surveys suggest that the LN was particularly successful in shaping the (negative) attitudes of its supporters towards Italy's institutional structure (Diamanti, 1996).
4. In Italy, for instance, the Muslim threat was evoked by some high figures in the Catholic Church as well as the well-known political scientist, Giovanni

Sartori (see http://www.quotidiano.net/art/2000/09/13/1292048; *El Pais* 2001, http://www.elpais.es/suplementos/domingo/20010408/entrevista.htm).
5. Multivariate analysis confirms the statistical significance of the working-class variable (see Lubbers et al., 2001).
6. In 1996, the proportion of private sector industrial sector workers among its electorate was twice as high (20 per cent on a national basis) as its overall result (10 per cent) (Maraffi and Segatti, 1997: 40).
7. According to one analysis, more than a quarter of its 1999 voters stayed at home in 2001 (*Der standard*, 2001).
8. For a list, see Havel (2001: 61–2).

References

Andersen, J. G. and Bjørklund, T. (2000) 'Radical Right-Wing Populism in Scandinavia: From Tax Revolt to Neo-Liberalism and Xenophobia', in P. Hainsworth (ed.), *The Politics of the Extreme Right*, London and New York: Pinter.

Beirich, H. and Woods, D. (2000) 'Globalisation, Workers and the Northern League', *West European Politics*, vol. 23, no. 1.

Betz, H. G. (2001) 'Entre succès et échec: l'extrême droite à la fin des années quatre-vingt dix', in P. Perrineau (ed.), *Les Croisés de la société fermé*, Paris: Editions de l'Aube.

Betz, H. G. (2002) 'Haider's Revolution or The Future Has Only Just Begun', in G. Bischof, A. Relinka and M. Gehler (eds.) *Austria in the European Union*. Contemporary Austrian Studies, vol. 10, New Brunswick; Transaction Publishers.

Betz, H. G. (2004) *La droite populiste on Europe: extrême et démocrate*, Paris: Autremont.

Betz, H. G. and Immerfall, S. (eds.) (1998) *The New Politics of the Right*, New York: St. Martin's Press.

Biorcio, R. (2001) 'Separatistischer Regionalismus in einer reichen Region: die Lega Nord', in D. Loch and W. Heitmeyer (eds.), *Schattenseiten der Globalisierung*, Frankfurt: Suhrkamp.

Blair, T. (2001) 'Immigrants are Seeking Asylum in Outdated Law', *The Times*, 4 May.

Blocher, C. (1997) *Switzerland and the Second World War: A Clarification*, http://www.cins.ch/second.htm; and *Switzerland and the Eizenstat Report*, http://www.cins.ch/eiz.htm.

Bossi, U. (2000) Pontida speech, http://www.leganord.org/politica/comunicati/2000/giugno/pontida.htm (15 June).

Burger, R. (2000a) 'Romantisches Österreich', *Leviathan*, vol. 28, no. 1, p. 8.

Burger, R. (2000b) 'Austromainie oder der antiaschistische Karneval', *Merkur*, vol. 54, no. 5, p. 91.

Cohen, R. (2000) 'A Haider in Their Future', *New York Times Magazine*, 30 April, p. 57.

Decker, F. (2000) *Parteien unter Druck*, Opladen: Leske & Budrich.

Delanty, G. (1995) *Inventing Europe: Idea, Identity, Reality*, New York: St. Martin's Press.

del Valle, A. (1999) 'Una Spada di Damocle incombe sull'Europa', *La Padania*, 23 July.

Der Standard (2001) SORA analysis results, 26 March.

Diamanti, I. (1996) *Il male del Nord*, Rome: Donzelli.

Diamanti, I. (1997) 'Divisi su Fisco, garanzie e federalismo', *Il Sole 24 Ore*, 18 July.

Eatwell, R. (1998) 'The BNP and the Problem of Legitimacy', in H. G. Betz and S. Immerfall (eds.), *The New Politics of the Right*, New York: St. Martin's Press, pp. 143–55.

El Pais (2001) Interview with Giovanni Sartori, 'La inmigración sin límites es una amenaza', 8 April, http://www.elpais.es/suplementos/domingo/20010408/entrevista.html.

Falter, J. and Klein, M. (1996) 'The Mass Basis of the Extreme Right in Contemporary Europe in a Comparative Perspective', *Research on Democracy and Society*, vol. 3, pp. 55–9.

FPÖ (2001), *Programm für Wien*, pp. 8–13.

Gibson, R. (1995) 'Ant-Immigrant Parties: The Roots of Their Sucess', *International Issues*, vol. 38, no. 2, pp. 119–30.

Givens, T. E. (2000) *Gender Differences in Support for Radical Right, Anti-Immigrant Political Parties*, The Center for Comparative Immigration Studies, University of California-San Diego, Working Paper no. 6, 21 March.

Goot, M. and Watson, I. (forthcoming) 'One Nation's Electoral Support: Where Does it Come From, What Makes it Different and How Does it Fit?' *Australian Journal of Politics and History*.

Graf, J. (1997) *Vom Untergang der schweizerischen Freiheit*, http://www.ety.com/tell/books/jglife/01.htm. http://www.ostara.org/graf.

Griffin, R. (2000) 'Interregnum or Endgame? Radical Right Thought in the Post-fascist Era', *Journal of Political Ideologies*, vol. 5, no. 2, p. 173.

Guolo, R. (2000) 'I nuovi crociati: la Lega a l'Islam', *Il Mulino*, vol. 49, pp. 890–901.

Haider, J. (1993) *Die Freiheit, die ich meine*, Frankfurt: Ullstein.

Haider, J. (2001) 'Der Aufstand der "Gutmenschen"', *Die Presse*, 17 March.

Hainsworth, P. (2000) 'Introduction: The Extreme Right', in P. Hainsworth (ed.), *The Politics of the Extreme Right*, London and New York: Pinter.

Hainsworth, P. (ed.) (2000) *The Politics of the Extreme Right*, London: Pinter.

Havel, V. (2001) 'Fact or Fiction?', *Index of Censorship*, vol. 30, no. 2, pp. 61–2.

Ivaldi, G. (1999) 'L'extrême droite ou la crise des systèmes de parties', *Revue Internationale de Politique Comparée*, vol. 6, no. 1, pp. 226–9.

Ivaldi, G. (2001) 'L'analyse comparée des soutiens électoraux du national-populisme en Europe occidentale. Apport et limites des grands programmes d'enquêtes transnationales (1990–1998)', in Pascal Perrineau (ed.), *Les croisés de la société fermée*, Paris: Editions de l'aube, pp. 57–9.

Keegan, J. (2000) 'A Good Historian, A Terrible Thinker', *National Post*, 14 April.

Knigge, P. (1998) 'The Ecological Correlates of Right-Wing Extremism in Western Europe', *European Journal of Political Research*, vol. 34, pp. 262, 271.

Linsinger, E. (2001) 'Ressentiment zog nicht', *Der Standard*, 26 March.

Longchamp, C. (2000) 'Die nationalkonservative Revolte in der Gestalt der SVP. Eine Analyse der Nationalratswahlen 1999 in der Schweiz', in F. Plasser, P. Ulram and F. Sommer (eds.), *Das österreichische Wahlverhalten*, Vienna: Signum.

Lubbers, M., Scheepers, P. and Billiet, J. (2001) *Multilevel Modelling of Vlaams Blok Voting: Individual and Contextual Characteristics of the Vlaams Blok Vote*, unpublished paper, Department of Sociology, University of Nijmegen.

Maraffi, M. and Segatti, P. (1997) 'Partiti ed elettori dal 94 al 96', *Italian Politics & Society*, no. 47.

Mayer, N. (1996a) 'The National Front Vote and Right-Wing Extremism, 1988–1995', in *Extremism Protost, Social Movements and Democracy Research on Democracy and Society*, vol. 3, ed. F. Weil, Greenwich, CT: JAI Press.

Mayer, N. (1996b) 'Rechtsextremismus in Frankreich: Die Wähler des Front national', in J. Falter, H. G. Jaschke and J. R. Winkler (eds.), *Rechtsextremismus: Ergebnisse und Perspektiven der Forschung*, (PVS-Sonderheft 27), Opladen: Westdeutscher Verlag, pp. 388–405.

Mayer, N. (1999) *Ces français qui votent FN*, Paris: Flammarion.

Mégret, B. (1999) http://www.m-n-r.com/discourswagram.htm, 16 November.

Meier, T. (2000) 'Irrweg "Multikulturelle Gesellschaft"', *Schweizerzeit*, 3 March.

Neue Züricher Zeitung (1999) 'Unfreiwillige Wahlhelfer: Ein Brief, die "Briefaffäre" und der Erfolg der SVP', 10 October, p. 13.

Perrineau, P. (1995) 'La dynamique du vote Le Pen. Le poids du "gaucholepénisme"', in P. Perrineau and C. Ysmal (eds.), *Le Vote de crise: L'élection présidentielle de 1995*, Paris: Presses de Sciences Po, pp. 243–61.

Perrineau, P. (ed.) (2001), *Les Croisés de la société fermée*, Paris: Éditions de l'Aube.

Plasser, F. and Ulram, P. A. (2000) 'Rechtspopulistische Resonanzen: Die Wählerschaft der FPÖ', in F. Plasser, P. A. Ulram and F. Sommer (eds.), *Das österreichische Wahlverhalten*, Vienna: Signum, pp. 225–41.

Profil (2000) 'Haiders Kampf gegen Haiders Regierung', 2 April.

Schönhuber, F. (1999) 'Der Islam und die europäische Rechte', *Nation & Europa*, nos. 11/12. http://www.schoenhuber-franz.de/kolumnen/NE_2000_1999/derislamunddieeuropaeischerechte.htm.

Stenographisches Protokoll, 168 (1999). Sitzung des Nationalrates der Republik Österreich, XX. Gesetzgebungsperiode, 10 May, http://www.parlinkom.gv.at (14 June).

SVP Stadt Zürich (1998), 'Ausländerkonzept', http://www.svp-stadt-zuerich.ch/Konzept9812/Default.htm (15 June).

SVP (1998) 'Migrationspolitik glaubwürdig und zukunftsorientiert', March; 'Geld allein garantiert keine Integaration', January 2001. Both papers can be ordered as email attachments from the party's website. http://www.svp.ch/Deutsch/Asylinitiative/zustandegekommen.htm.

Swyngedouw M. (1998) 'The Extreme Right in Belgium: Of a Non-existent Front National and an Omnipresent Vlaams Blok', in H. G. Betz and S. Immerfall (eds.), *The New Politics of the Right*, New York: St. Martin's Press.

Swyngedouw, M. (2001) 'The Subjective Cognitive and Affective Map of Extreme Right Voters: Using Open-ended Questions in Exit Polls', *Electoral Studies*, vol. 20, no. 2, p. 238.

Taguieff, P. A. (1993/94) 'From Race to Culture: The New Right's View of European Identity', *Telos*, nos. 98–9, p. 101.

Ulram, P. (2001) 'Sozialprofil und Wahlmotive der FPÖ-Wähler: Zur Modernität des Rechtspopulismus am Beispiel des Phänomens Haider', in D. Loch and W. Heitmeyer (eds.), *Schattenseiten der Globalisierung*, Frankfurt a.M.: Suhrkamp.

Wolffsohn, M. (1995) Interview with Haider, '. . . Und morgen Haider', *Bunte*, 14 December, p. 114.

'Morganland contra Abendland: Zwei Welten prallen aufeinander . . .' http://garbsener-buergerschaft/de/islam.htm.

Il monito di Biffi (2000) 'Immigrati sìm ma solo cattolici', *quotidiona.net*, 13, September http://www.quotidiano.net/art/2000/09/13/1292048; http://www.admin.ch/ch/d/pore/vi/vi296.html.

5
Policing and Human Rights

Benjamin Bowling, Coretta Phillips, Alexandra Campbell and Maria Docking

Racial discrimination, xenophobia, intolerance and the abuse power are problems in police forces in many parts of the world.[1] In recent years, allegations of racism and racial discrimination have led to public inquiries into many police agencies, including the Metropolitan Police (Bowling, 1999; Macpherson, 1999; Bowling and Phillips, 2002) in London, the New South Wales Police (Human Rights and Equal Opportunities Commission, 1991; Johnston, 1991; Chan, 1997; Royal Commission into the New South Wales Police Service, 1997) in Australia, the Los Angeles Police Department (Christopher 1991; Human Rights Watch 1998) in the USA, and the South Africa Police Service (Brogden and Shearing, 1993; Cawthra, 1993, 1997; Brewer, 1994; Truth and Reconciliation Committee, 1998; Melville, 1999). In each of these places, evidence has been gathered relating to individual cases and the broader organizational context. Although these are among the best documented examples, the problems of racism, discrimination and the abuse of power have also been identified in many police agencies elsewhere.

This chapter attempts to draw general lessons from the published literature in the field with specific reference to the police agencies mentioned above. Limited space makes it impossible to provide detailed discussion of individual cases or extensive documentation in each of the four contexts. It has not been possible to conduct a fully comparative analysis of the abuse of police power, or the similarities and differences in the historical, political, socio-economic and cultural context in each locality. None the less, it is contended that there are sufficient similarities among the four contexts discussed to draw some general lessons.

Because the nature of the police mandate and the tools available to achieve it are similar across the globe, the nature and contexts surrounding abusive policing are also similar. Hence, almost identical explanations have been developed by police researchers around the world to account for the abuse of power, whether this relates to some characteristic of the individual abuser, the culture of police organizations or the larger structures of society in which they operate. As the diagnoses share similarities from one place to the next, the range of policy solutions and the problems faced in implementing them are also similar. The goal of this chapter is to explore the ways in which principles have been applied in practice and with what results.

The focus of this chapter is on the 'public police', those accountable to local or national governments and are given a 'general right to use coercive force by the state within the state's domestic territory' (Klockars, 1985). Concentrating on public police agencies, which lie at the centre of debates about securing human rights, excludes the areas of 'private policing' and 'informal policing'. The private security industry dwarfs public policing, in terms of both employees and budgets.[2] It is also often heavily armed and is afflicted by many of the problems described in this report. Although this chapter touches on the role of policing in crime reduction, an extended discussion of the effectiveness of various methods of crime prevention and maintaining community safety is beyond its scope.

This chapter is, by virtue of its subject matter, critical of the police. However, it should be remembered that the central ethic of police forces around the world is to provide protection for, and service to, the community and that many police officers join the service with the specific intention of helping communities to be safer and more peaceful places. It is to that end that this chapter is written.

Conceptualizing the uses and abuses of police power

The police service is one of the most important and powerful institutions of government. Its officers hold coercive powers second only to the military, but in contrast to soldiers, police are both a visible manifestation of state power and one with which civil society has extensive day-to-day interaction. The police (together with the army in some circumstances) hold the monopoly on the state-sanctioned use of violence against citizens. They are authorized to bear arms and, in certain circumstances, to shoot to kill. Police officers routinely detain by force, conduct intimate searches and conduct covert surveillance on those suspected of criminal involvement or intent. Clearly, the possession and use of these powers require justification. Analysts of policing have suggested two models of policing that can broadly be defined as the military/colonial model and the civil/consensual model (see Bowling and Foster, 2002: Table 1).

The paramilitary model of policing

The 'paramilitary' or 'colonial' model grows out of the direct relationship between government, army and the police, and emphasizes the use of force to control specific sections of the population. In the US, the 'military model' emphasizes a 'we/they world-view' and promotes the idea of police officers as a close-knit, distinct group and citizens as outsiders and enemies (Kappeler et al., 1994: 105–6). In this model, the police are seen as agents of central or local government rather than agents of the law (Brewer, 1994: 6).[3] Social control is based on coercion rather than consent, and force is resorted to readily, sometimes as a first resort. The police are under the direct control of governments and are partisan in enforcing the rule of a specific political regime including those that enshrine discrimination. Policing in this model requires selective enforcement in favour of the dominant group, the criminalization of minority activities and suppressing the right to protest (Jones and Newburn, 1996: 3–4). 'Policing by strangers' tends to require that recruitment not be from among locals. Where the indigenous population is employed, the bulk of the 'troops' and all the senior command are from the 'metropolitan or settler group' and do not reflect society at large (Brewer, 1994).

The community model of policing

The community model[4] is the antithesis of the military model. The community model emphasizes the deployment of a decentralized civilian force with a membership that broadly represents the population being policed resting on the axiom that the police officer is merely a 'citizen in uniform'. Policing in this model is intended to be seen as legitimate by the majority of the community, including those 'policed *against*' and is based on the principle of consent (Reiner, 2000). In this consensual model, the police are servants of the law rather than of government and are seen as 'apolitical'. This model emphasizes internal democracy and the idea that the police service should reflect the demographic and social characteristics of the communities served (Jones and Newburn, 1996). The idea of accountability is central to the community model since responsiveness and answerability to law, state and the public provide the basis for police legitimacy. The problem of crime – or more generally interpersonal violence and conflicts between citizens – requires some form of state-sanctioned force to impose binding solutions and therefore the possession of intrusive and coercive powers remains central to the definition of policing in the consensual model. In contrast to the military model, the community model sees the use of force as a last resort which, when employed, should be restricted to the minimum. It is axiomatic that in a democratic society the use of these powers can be justified only to the extent that they are lawful, necessary, proportionate, accountable and used fairly.

The two models sketched above must be seen as 'ideal types' that exist nowhere in a 'pure form'. The 'community' model has been central to attempts at police reform that have occurred in the Los Angeles Police Department, the London Metropolitan Police Service, the New South Wales Police Service and the South African Police Service over the past two decades. In Britain, the *Scarman Report*, produced in the aftermath of the widespread disorders in 1981, can be seen as a restatement of the community model of policing.[5] It has been argued that *Scarman* has been an influential basis for currently acceptable international standards in policing, particularly in Australia (Chan, 1997) and South Africa (Marks, 1999) where police chiefs have committed themselves to 'community policing', emphasizing the principles set out above. Nevertheless, it is clear that the military/colonial model still remains a powerful force within each organization. Sometimes paramilitary policing is deployed under certain 'special conditions' (e.g. to police instances of public disorder). It is also a common pattern that community policing is reserved for middle-class, suburban, white populations while paramilitary police are deployed in poor, urban, black and ethnic minority neighbourhoods.

To be effective, the police need public consent and the support of those being policed. Paramilitary policing on its own does not work, and account should be taken of the evidence with respect to policing and crime reduction initiatives (see Miller et al., 2000; Bowling and Foster, 2002: Table 4). Although such evidence is equivocal, it is desirable that the police should focus on problem-solving rather than using force, since it is the former (and not the latter) which is considered to be 'a hallmark of good policing' (see Bayley, 1998; Reiner, 2000; Bowling and Foster, 2002).

Community policing and paramilitary policing in practice

Although London is usually cited as the origin of the Peelian 'community' model of policing, it has been argued that authoritarian policing has been employed in the 'domestic colonies', the inner city areas of the metropolis where ethnic minority communities are concentrated. Certainly, the experience of 'over-policing' has been consistently illustrated by empirical research (Skogan, 1990, 1994; Fitzgerald and Sibbitt, 1997) and community experiences. Studies have found widespread personal experiences of police harassment or brutality, either directly or through families and friends (see, for example, Institute of Race Relations, 1987). Communities have complained of oppressive police tactics such as mass stop-and-search operations, coordinated raids, the use of riot squads using paramilitary equipment and continuous surveillance. Researchers have documented the pervasive, ongoing targeting that appeared to regard black areas as intrinsically criminal and black people a potential threat to public disorder (Institute of Race Relations, 1987; Keith, 1993).

In Australia, policing must be set in the context of colonization, xenophobia and racism among white Australians. The police played an important role in the legal system that facilitated the dispossession of Aborigines of their own land, suppressed Aboriginal resistance to European settlement and enforced segregation. In the contemporary period, the 1991 National Inquiry into Racist Violence reported numerous incidents of 'intrusive and intimidatory' policing, including some examples of an extreme nature (Chan, 1997). This included unwarranted entry into households, physical abuse and discriminatory policing in public places and private functions. The Inquiry was also presented with 'overwhelming evidence' of maltreatment of Aboriginal women, such as racist and sexist verbal and physical abuse, including allegations of sexual abuse and rape while in police custody (Chan, 1997: 23–5).

Modern policing in South Africa grew out of the military units responsible for the conquest and subjugation of the black population. Policing based on the Peelian model was applied to the white population, but Africans were subjected to authoritarian policing (Cawthra, 1993: 8). The notorious pass laws, restricting movement of the African population, were enforced by the police, and between 1916 and 1981, more than 17 million people were arrested for pass violations. During the apartheid era, the police were central to the state apparatus for maintaining white domination. The police were a quasi-military, racially segregated force whose primary responsibility was the enforcement of repressive and restrictive legislation. In the SAP, police brutality, torture and abuse of criminal suspects were 'routine'. In the latter years of apartheid, the police were responsible for the deliberate promotion of political violence intended to destabilize black communities.

In 1991, the Christopher Commission concluded that 'there is a significant number of officers in the LAPD who repetitively use excessive force against the public, which is 'aggravated by racism and bias' within the LAPD (Christopher, 1991; Human Rights Watch, 1998). More than one quarter of 650 officers responding to a survey said 'an officer's prejudice towards the suspect's race may lead to the use of excessive force'. Unsurprisingly, surveys also indicate that minority residents believe that white officers are aggressive and abusive in minority communities. Witnesses to the Commission reported consistently that officers verbally harassed minorities, detained African-American and Latino men who fit certain general descriptions of suspects and employed unnecessarily invasive or humiliating tactics in minority neighbourhoods such as requiring suspects to 'lie prone' while being searched.

Routine police practices: stop, search and arrest

In many jurisdictions, ethnic and cultural minorities are disproportionately subject to intrusive and coercive police powers such as 'stop and search', 'on-street interrogation' and arrest. In recent years, increasing concern has been expressed about 'racial profiling' in many police agencies across the US, including the LAPD (Harris, 1999). Racial profiling occurs when the police target someone for investigation on the basis of their race, national origin or ethnicity. In some cases, race is used to determine which drivers to stop for minor traffic violations (sometimes referred to as 'driving while black') and to determine which motorists or pedestrians to search for contraband. Racism has been identified as a chief motivating factor in police suspicion, investigation and stops and searches in the LAPD (Christopher Commission, 1991; see also Skolnick and Fyfe 1993; Ogletree et al., 1995; Human Rights Watch 1998; Williams 2001). A study in New South Wales in 1985–6 found that Aborigines were more than three times as likely to be arrested as would be expected from their numbers; they comprised 15 per cent of the population but 47 per cent of those arrested (Chan, 1997: 23). A more recent study found that Aborigines were over-represented among the population held in police cells by a factor of 19 (McDonald and Biles, 1991; cited by Chan, 1997). The use of stop-and-search powers has also been found to be discriminatory in the London Metropolitan Police. Early studies indicated that police used colour as a 'criterion for stops' (Smith and Gray, 1985) and this has persisted until the present day. UK official statistics show that black[6] people are about five times as likely as their 'white' counterparts to be stopped and searched by the Metropolitan Police (Home Office, 2000) and are also more likely to be subjected to repeated stops and more intrusive searches (Skogan, 1994). A Home Office report found that being black was a predictor of being stopped by the police, even once all other factors had been accounted for (Skogan, 1990), indicating that the pattern is explained by direct discrimination and stereotyping. Another Home Office report argued that the police contributed to the large ethnic differences in stop and search because of a 'pervasive and deeply entrenched' suspiciousness of black people (Fitzgerald and Sibbitt, 1997: 66; Bland et al., 2000; Quinton et al., 2000; Stone and Pettigrew, 2000; see also Bowling and Phillips, 2002: 138–40).

The response of police agencies is usually to argue that stop-and-search statistics simply reflect differences in patterns of involvement in crime. Some commentators draw attention to the 'skilful use of the tabloid press to convey the police view to the wider public' (Institute of Race Relations, 1987; Kappeler et al., 1994). It is true that in the places studied, criminal statistics, such as arrests and imprisonment rates, show marked over-representation of minority groups. However, the weight of evidence suggests that the disproportionate use of police powers is, at least in part, the product of discrimination. The evidence from a number of contexts suggests that the abuse of power is most discriminatory where autonomy and discretion are greatest.[7]

Death in custody and as a result of police action

In the US, the weight of evidence suggests that African-Americans are far more likely to be victims of police shootings and abuse of force than would be expected on the basis of representation in the population even once arrest rates are taken into account (Skolnick and Fyfe, 1993: 146–64; Chevigny, 1995: 48–9; see also Reiner, 2000: 130). The police force in South Africa has always had a rather militaristic nature and for many years it remained a 'policing style characterised by the use of crude maximum force' (Van der Spuy, 1990). However, it is only in recent years that reliable figures have been produced on deaths in police custody or as a result of police action. In the period April 1998–March 1999, 756 people died in police custody (Manby, 2000: 207–8) and the majority were of African origin.

In Australia, the 1991 Royal Commission on Aboriginal Deaths in Custody drew attention to the extent to which Aboriginal people had died due to the abuse of force, neglect or suicide in police cells (Johnston, 1991). Australia-wide Aboriginals accounted for 29 per cent of those in custody and 32 per cent of the deaths. The report concluded that the disproportionate number of deaths was not due to the rate at which Aboriginals were dying in custody, but the rate at which they were being taken into custody. On an Australia-wide basis an Aboriginal was 27 times more likely to be in police custody than a non-Aboriginal. A study that followed the Royal Commission (Williams, 2001) found a reduction in the number of deaths in police custody, but a significant increase in the number of deaths in prison custody.[8]

In recent years in the UK, deaths in custody have more frequently involved people from ethnic minority communities both in comparison to their numbers in the general population and in comparison to the number of people arrested (Deaths in Custody Working Group of Community Police Consultative Group for Lambeth, 1996). For the UK as a whole, in 1996/7, 57 people died in police custody or 'otherwise in the hands of the police', an increase of 14 per cent on the previous year. African/Caribbean people were six times more likely to have died in the custody of the police than would be expected from their numbers in the population. More recent figures for 1998/9 indicate an increase in numbers of deaths in custody to 68, but a lower proportion of deaths of ethnic minorities in custody relative to their representation in both the arrested and general populations (see Home Office, 2000).

Deaths in police custody provide the harshest example of unequal treatment before the law. More troubling still is the tendency to obscure information about what has happened and to create 'official misinformation' that explains the deaths as accidental or a misadventure, or even the fault of the victim (Institute of Race Relations, 1991). Police officers are in a unique position to lend 'official' credibility into their misrepresentation and sometimes even fabrications (Kappeler et al., 1994: 161). Characterization of citizens as drug abusers and criminals carries advantages to police officers in justifying the use of force. It supports the inference that force was needed to subdue the citizen (since drug users are thought of as having a tendency towards violence), it discredits the victim's account (since drug use clouds judgement and perception) and suggests that the victim is likely to be deceitful. In the process, attention is deflected away from police deviance towards questions of the victim's deviance (ibid.).

Policing styles: law enforcement or peace-keeping

Arguably, the most important reform is the reformulation of policing from the military to the community model. Community-led policing cannot merely be an augmentation of traditional policing but requires a complete reorientation of the policing role. It requires supportive management, open communications and an emphasis on social rather than physical skills. Policing conceived of as being community-controlled would be directly controlled by, and responsible to, people at a local level, be concerned with peace-keeping and problem-solving, as opposed to the dominant ethos of 'crime fighting' and 'bandit catching'. This means that the conventional state-centred conception of policing must be turned on its head. The new form of policing must give expression to a 'bottom-heavy' system, where the state police are combined with other sources located within the institutions of civil society (which could be extended to groups and individuals of society), to a situation of 'self-policing', with an emphasis on peace-keeping.

Personnel, equality of opportunity and equality of service

In a society divided by ethnic, racial, class and sectarian differences, it is to be expected that the police service will itself be affected by such divisions. If police officers share widely held beliefs that individuals from ethnic minority communities are inferior, if they share stereotypes about ethnicity and criminality, then this is bound to affect the ways in which police officers from different backgrounds relate to one another. Moreover, in many jurisdictions, there have been specific restrictions on the employment of minority communities that have shaped the contemporary context. A police service which more closely reflects the population it serves is important as a goal in its own right, but also contributes towards other ends. For example, it may increase ethnic minority communities' 'confidence and trust' in policing and also contribute towards improving service delivery.[9]

Representation and equality of opportunity in policing

The first three police officers from visible ethnic minority groups in England and Wales were recruited in 1996. Despite the increase in the proportion of serving police officers from ethnic minorities in 1986 from 0.7 per cent to 2 per cent of the police service as at 31 March 2000 (Home Office, 2000), minority groups remain considerably under-represented relative to around 7 per cent of the economically active population. This is due to a shortfall in applications and fewer being successful at the recruitment stage. Practical efforts to encourage local people from ethnic minority backgrounds to join the police service, such as conducting targeted recruitment campaigns together with community organizations, running familiarization and access courses, and providing application forms in minority languages, are all positive ways forward. However, these efforts are hindered by the fact that ethnic minority applicants will carefully consider their likely negative experiences of racism and discrimination and this will impact on the capacity of police forces to recruit ethnic minority police officers (Wilson et al., 1984).

Despite a long reform process, it is evident that the Metropolitan Police occupational culture is based on masculine and Anglocentric norms, which permeate all aspects of police work and shape the experiences of ethnic minority officers. Research evidence shows that African, Caribbean and Asian police officers find racist comments and jokes were routinely part of officers' conversations and have adopted coping strategies to deal with this (Holdaway, 1996). Until recently, neither supervisory nor senior officers appeared to be concerned with challenging this aspect of the police culture (see Her Majesty's Inspectorate of Constabulary Reports, 1995, 1997, 2000). Some officers have brought cases of racial discrimination to industrial tribunals and have received compensation. Black and Asian officers may also be marginalized from work and social networks because they do not accept negative representations of ethnic minorities, or where in the case of some Asian officers, religious observance prevents socialization that revolves around drinking alcohol.

Although African American officers have been involved in US policing since the nineteenth century, their progress was blocked by legally enforced segregation.[10] The employment of black police officers was facilitated by Title VII of the Civil Rights Act 1964, which forbade discrimination on the basis of race, sex, religion and national origin. Furthermore, the Equal Employment Opportunity Act 1972 authorized the Justice Department to bring local and state governments to court to challenge their hiring practices. Quotas successfully increased minority representation, but also led to lawsuits by white-dominated police unions. Despite gains since the 1960s, there remains significant under-representation of African American and other ethnic minorities in US police departments.

Testing and selection

If demographic composition of the police service is to better represent the community served, in most cases, the police need to recruit more black and ethnic minority officers. One way to achieve this is to evaluate selection and testing procedures for cultural bias (The Rotterdam

Charter, 1996). An obvious example is dispensing with the minimum height requirement, which placed women and Asian people at a particular disadvantage. Beyond this, however, is recruitment that attracts more minority groups, including women and non-visible sexual minorities (Chan, 1997). This would not mean lowering standards, but *changing standards*. Such skills as the ability to interpret and translate should be criteria for selection. Arguably, policing in the nineteenth-century 'military model' required qualities such as strength and bravery. However, contemporary policing requires general analytic, communication and other 'knowledge work' skills. Shifting from the axiom of crime fighting to that of 'peace-keeping' also requires social skills in conflict-resolution and skills in maintenance of order by peaceful means rather than the resort to force.

Recruitment targets

Positive or affirmative action schemes aim to achieve equality of representation in a given time. They have symbolic value, which demonstrates that society regards discrimination as a serious issue and diversity as an important goal. It also enables different communities to throw up talented individuals who may act as role models. To avoid a backlash among those officers whose dominance is threatened, the Rotterdam Charter[11] suggests that there should be public statements to explain why such action is necessary and that such action is not 'favouritism', but stems from a requirement that the police should reflect the community they serve. There is also the danger of disadvantaging relatively underprivileged members of advantaged groups (e.g. working-class white women) and miss their real targets by benefiting only relatively privileged members of disadvantaged groups (e.g. middle-class men from minority communities).

In South Africa there are affirmative action programmes to 'level the playing field' in recruitment to the South Africa Police Service (Cawthra, 1993), but despite efforts to recruit more women and black officers, it is 'an institution that remains largely unaltered in terms of personnel' (Marks, 1999). In South Africa, the police are often not drawn from the community that they serve and so this makes it more difficult for them to build up good community relationships. It therefore seems logical that more of an effort should be made to recruit new officers from the areas they will eventually serve, although this might risk creating policing enclaves.

The US experience suggests that there is a risk that ethnic minority police officers may be 'ghettoized' by being assigned to predominantly minority neighbourhoods (Dulaney, 1996; Walker et al., 1996). Specifically using ethnic minority officers to police areas of high ethnic minority settlement may disadvantage them if they do not receive the necessary breadth of experience required to be promoted. It can also perpetuate stereotypes that only ethnic minority officers can police ethnic minority communities. In South Africa, black police were given responsibility for policing black populations only. Black police officers were treated worse than their white counterparts and were instructed to leave the European population alone. A significant aspect of this is the importance of having officers who can understand the language of the community they are serving so perhaps incentives should be given to those who show an interest in learning the language of those groups that are likely to fall under their jurisdiction.

In Britain in 1998, the Home Secretary published local and national targets for the increased recruitment, retention, career progression and senior level representation of ethnic minority operational and non-operational staff in the Home Office, police, prisons and probation services (Home Office, 2000). The first progress report on meeting these ten-year employment targets revealed problems in recruiting, retaining and promoting ethnic minorities to meet the targets set in the police service; levels of senior representation still remain low (Home Office, 2000).

Retention

In the light of their experiences on the job, it is not surprising that the 'retention rate' for ethnic minority police officers is lower than for white police officers. In the UK, rates for resignation and dismissal from the police service were much higher among ethnic minorities than white officers in 1997/8. Holdaway and Barron's study of the reasons for resignation among black and Asian former police officers found that it is the unchallenged racist 'banter' within the police force that has turned away many officers (Holdaway, 1991; Holdaway and Barron, 1997; Stone and Tuffin, 2000). There needs to be, therefore, positive stances towards policies to deal with discrimination to confront cultural and behavioural issues (Her Majesty's Inspectorate of Constabulary, 1997) through legal remedies, for example.

As in the US, in the UK, ethnic minority-run professional organizations, such as the Black Police Association's (BPA), have been set up to provide support and a forum for ethnic minority officers, and to campaign and lobby for reform. The National Black Police Association, established in November 1998, has assisted in setting up more than 20 black police associations across the UK, representing the views of black police officers and civilians. These developments have been given support from the police inspectorate, who have recommended that police forces have mentoring, informal networking and welfare support as part and parcel of their retention policies (Her Majesty's Inspectorate of Constabulary, 1997).

There are two main groups in South Africa which have been formed to try to ensure equality of opportunity for officers once recruited into the force: the Police and Prisons Civil Rights Union (POPCRU) and the Black Officers Forum (BOF). Police unionism in South Africa has provided a real challenge to the SAPS to speed up the transformation process. The POPCRU is important for two reasons: it helped place democratization of the police into the forum for debate and it showed the public that some of the police did care about human rights issues. Three high-ranking black officers launched the BOF in June 1998. It is primarily concerned with transforming the SAPS and represents those who are in positions of management and can therefore initiate changes from the top down. Both organizations are positive initiatives as they represent useful internal watchdogs to ensure a positive commitment to reform is adhered to (see Marks, 2000).

Promotion

Racism and other barriers to the promotion of black officers in the SAPS has remained. There is also the breakdown of police management where the number of black high-ranking officers are in short supply (Marks, 2000). In August 1992, black police were for the first time promoted to the rank of general; with the integration of the former 'homeland' police forces in April 1994, the situation changed dramatically as 26,000 black police, many of them officers, and including 20 generals, were incorporated into the SAP. By 1995, the SAPS was 35 per cent white, 54 per cent African, 8 per cent coloured and 3 per cent Asian, with women constituting 19 per cent of the force (Cawthra, 1997). Ongoing concerns about racism, the abuse power and corruption in the SAPS led the National Head of Equity in the SAPS to conclude that transformation has not yet occurred in the South Africa Police Service (Marks, 2000).

In March 2000, in England and Wales, only 14 per cent of ethnic minority officers were in promoted ranks within the police service compared to 23 per cent of white officers. Bland et al.'s (1999) career profiling of a matched sample of white and ethnic minority police officers showed that the latter take an average of around 12 months longer to be promoted to the rank of sergeant (five months longer for Asian officers and 18 months for African/Caribbean officers). In recognition of the very serious under-representation of minority officers in the more senior ranks, the Metropolitan Police Service response has been to create a Senior Officer Development Programme for minority officers (Her Majesty's Inspectorate of Constabulary, 2000). Reforming police executives have also used legislative changes and other measures to create fairer recruitment and promotion practices and to end formal segregation within police departments. Black police officers are among the most respected police reformers and have been credited with regulating police use of deadly force, creating community policing programmes and opportunities for women and minority officers, as well as developing innovative programmes to reduce police–black conflict (Dulaney, 1996).

Linking equality of opportunity and equality of service

Developing a police service that more closely reflects the society that it serves has been proposed as a means to making services more appropriate, relevant and accessible to all members of the community. The literature on the criminal justice professions highlights the importance of the relationship between equality of opportunity for employees *within* a service and the quality of service that it provides to the public. Clearly, if a police service cannot treat its own members fairly, it has little chance of treating the public it serves fairly. Perhaps ethnic minority police officers will not operate with the same working stereotypes as white officers and that understanding and respect for ethnic minority citizens will prevent the kind of oppressive policing that has occurred in contexts where local officers are predominantly, or exclusively, white.

Including groups previously excluded can have the effect of transforming the organization. Arguably, just by 'being there' women and ethnic minorities will bring different perspectives and become catalysts for change within the organizational culture (Brown, 1997). To have any real effect on service provision, minority workers must be able to contribute to decision-making. The counter-argument is that recruiting women and members of marginalized social groups does not initiate change and that in fact the new recruits 'assume a commitment to the institution . . . and absorb the "working personality" of the other officers' (Brogden and Shearing, 1993). Changes in recruitment policy are unlikely to have an effect on the police work unless they are complemented 'by significant structural changes in the character of the police organisation related to the normative handing of police–public encounters' (Brogden and Shearing, 1993).

Training

For there to be a real change towards a more democratic police force, ongoing training and development are required. Brewer states that 'training in race awareness must successfully relate the concept to the reality of policing, depoliticise it, and show its practical usefulness rather than present it as a moral crusade' (Brewer, 1994). In 1992, the University of Witwatersrand in South Africa carried out a comprehensive survey of police training colleges (Cawthra, 1993). It argued for a training curriculum highlighting the need for policing based on respect for human rights and community policing, and recommended that training should continue in police stations throughout an officer's career. Although training is clearly important for implementing change, it can be superficial and there are questions about its effectiveness. To be of real value, the skills and knowledge learned have to be implemented on the ground. Sometimes the structures of policing and perceived 'reality on the ground' make it difficult to implement new skills (Marks, 1999).

Brogden and Shearing (1993) argue that the legitimacy of a new policing system in South Africa rests in part on the commitment of state officers to recognize social inequality, and seek to compensate for it by positive action. The first step towards such a goal must be located in innovative training programmes, which should make officers reflective of their own attitudes whilst promoting positive images of minorities. As the Rotterdam Charter argues, training should help to ensure that officers' personal attitudes are consistent with professional ethics.

To assure that officers possess the necessary skills to police a plural society it is crucial that the content of the training provided is of a high quality. Before such a goal can be realized, some critics have suggested a review of teacher training methods that encourages trainers to acknowledge their own prejudices and attitudes. The essential function of training for cultural diversity, then, is to remove ignorance and the dogmatism that springs from it. This may be achieved by involving communities, non-governmental organizations and such institutions as schools and universities. However, it is critical to realize that racism gains its strengths from too many quarters simply to be taught out of existence; training is only part of the solution to a complex problem.

Human rights, policing and anti-discrimination

The role of the police lies at the centre of debates about means by which states endeavour to meet their obligations of protecting the rights and freedoms of the people.[12] Human rights derive from the inherent dignity and worth of the human person and are universal and indivisible. These rights, enshrined in international instruments, go to the heart of crime prevention and policing as they protect the rights to life, liberty and security of the person and protect against torture, cruel or degrading treatment and unnecessary or arbitrary deprivation of liberty. These instruments also establish that those deprived of their liberty should be treated with humanity, respect and dignity.

Human rights protections impose both positive and negative require-ments on police. The *positive requirement* is for the police to keep people safe or guard their security. This is recognized in the provisions of Article 28 of the Universal Declaration of Human Rights, which states that 'everyone is entitled to a social and international order in which [human] rights and freedoms . . . can be fully realised'. The *negative requirement* is for the police to guard the liberty of the people through the imposition of constraints on the excessive use of state power. Article 29 of the Universal Declaration of Human Rights (UDHR) states that in exercising rights and freedoms, 'everyone shall be subject to only such limitations as are determined by law solely for the purposes of securing due recognition and respect for the rights and freedoms of others and of meeting the requirements of morality, public order and the general welfare in a democratic society'.

The use of force is central to police work and this carries the risk that the police will interfere with the right to life[13] by causing death or serious injury. Two international instruments protect the public against the arbitrary deprivation of the right to life and give guidance to the police on the use of force (Crawshaw et al., 1998: 26). The 'Principles on the Effective Prevention and Investigation of Extra-Legal, Arbitrary and Summary Executions'[14] and the 'Basic Principles on the Use of Force and Firearms by Law Enforcement Officials'[15] restrict the use of force to that which is objectively reasonable, necessary and proportionate[16] in the prevailing circumstances.[17]

The right to liberty of the person[18] is also affected by police powers to arrest and detain, and this right is protected by Article 9 of the UDHR, which prohibits arbitrary arrest and detention. All these rights are given force in the International Convention on Civil and Political Rights. People in detention are vulnerable to ill-treatment and torture, a gross violation of human rights. The right to a fair trial, the presumption of innocence[19] and the prevention of arbitrary interference with privacy[20] are all at risk during the investigation of crime due to such practices as the searching of clothing, homes, vehicles and personal possessions, the interviewing of suspects and the taking of intimate samples.

As we have seen, policing frequently bears most heavily on communities defined by their 'race', ethnic origin or other spurious grounds, and therefore international instruments protecting against discrimination are also of crucial relevance to the governance of policing.[21] The International Convention on the Elimination of All Forms of Racial Discrimination (1965) prohibits 'any distinction, exclusion, restriction or preference based on race, colour, descent, or national or ethnic origin which has the purpose or effect of nullifying or impairing the recognition, enjoyment, exercise, on an equal footing, of human rights and fundamental freedoms in the political, economic, social, cultural or any other field of public life' and requires states to guarantee full and equal enjoyment of fundamental rights and freedoms for all.[22] Article 2 requires states to eliminate all forms of racial discrimination to *amend, rescind or nullify any laws* and regulations (local or national) which have the *effect of creating or perpetuating* racial discrimination wherever it exists (Banton, 1996). The police thus have a responsibility to avoid discriminating and also to avoid practices that sustain, perpetuate or compound injustice in other spheres such as housing, employment, etc. The implications of human rights standards in this field is that the police should go beyond avoiding discrimination and work actively towards eliminating racism and promoting social justice.

In spite of the fact that police officers are cited as human rights abusers who are frequently used as an instrument for control and repression, the positive function of the police must be remembered. They have the roles of creating social order within which everyone has an equal right to enjoy a range of fundamental freedoms, actively protect the lives and property of all irrespective of 'race' and ethnic (and other) minorities from discrimination. The Rotterdam Charter enjoins the police to be 'gatekeepers of equality, integration and cohesion' and must therefore be 'active and reliable . . . guardians of anti-discrimination legislation' (The Rotterdam Charter, 1996: 10).

International human rights instruments set minimum standards for the provision of anti-discriminatory and democratic policing. These international norms have been widely ratified and in many places are enshrined in parallel domestic law. In order for any such instruments to be practically effective, there is a need for robust mechanisms of accountability to ensure compliance.

Accountability

The extent to which the police are accountable to the public they serve has been described as being 'the measure of a society's freedom' (Institute of Race Relations, 1987: vii). Yet the procedures that should guarantee accountability are often seriously flawed and extremely resistant to change. It is when there are *actual* abuses of police power that issues of police accountability come to the fore. However, it goes much further than this, encompassing accountability for the routine contacts between the police and members of the public. Police accountability requires those who hold coercive and instrusive powers to explain what actions they take, for what reasons and with what consequences. These can then be tested against agreed standards and norms of conduct. Where errors and abuses occur, systems of accountability provide the opportunity for redress for injured parties and to learn from past mistakes. Systems of accountability are also one of the key mechanisms that have been proposed for reducing the extent of discrimination and for developing a greater respect for fundamental human rights and freedoms in policing.

Accountability to the law

It is a central plank of orthodox legal theory that the police are, first and foremost, accountable to the law rather than being based on allegiance to a political or social group. Gilroy and Sim (1987) argue that law, police and court action cannot be separated. Rather than being directly accountable to the law, discretion in policing means that the law is permissive (see Skolnick, 1996; Lustgarten, 1986; Grimshaw and Jefferson, 1987). The law defines when a police officer *may* act, but cannot direct a police officer to act, or act in a particular way in a given instance (Lustgarten, 1986). In practice, the law is frequently used as a resource by the police to achieve police-defined goals (Gilroy and Sim, 1987; Holdaway, 1996). For example, although the police may stop and search someone only if they have 'reasonable suspicion' or 'probable cause to believe' that an offence has been committed, these concepts are so permissive that, *in practice*, the police can stop and search anyone in almost any circumstance. Hence, some of the abusive practices described above have been facilitated by the law, rather than prevented by it.

Accountability to the state

In an open and democratic society, accountability to the state provides some measure of protection against the abuse of power. In some contexts[23] procedures connecting the state police to the wider society served to facilitate, not prevent, police discrimination and abuse of power. None the less, the police should be directly accountable to a democratically elected political authority and, to avoid possible abuses by the government, decisions and activities should be made as transparent as possible, through lay monitoring (Brewer 1990; Brogden and Shearing, 1993). It is important that power over the police is not concentrated in the hands of a small number of centrally located people, but should be distributed widely through, for example, committees of political representatives and nominated lay people, responsible to the elected government (Brewer, 1990). This is problematic in contexts where the majority population is happy for the police to oppress minorities.[24]

In Britain where a 'tripartite structure of accountability' diffuses power',[25] the doctrine of constabulary independence gives a great deal of autonomy and wide operational discretion to the Chief Officer and indeed to officers on the street. In recent years, Britain has seen a shift away from political accountability towards 'financial' and 'managerial' accountability (Jones and Newburn, 1997: 12). Managerialist reforms emphasize effectiveness and efficiency and defines participation in terms of consumers purchasing services. As Jones and Newburn suggest, policing in this formulation is incorrectly presented as a politically-neutral 'technical exercise', the output of which can be measured and thus its performance judged (Jones and Newburn, 1997: 15). Less emphasis is placed on responsiveness to elected bodies, direct participation or equity. Thus, formal democratic institutions play an even more limited role in the development of policy or changing criminal justice practice (ibid.; see also Chan, 1997, on the potential for managerial reform).

Accountability to the community

It has been argued that structures of police governance should reflect the demographic characteristics of the community. However, in each of the places studied, black and ethnic minority communities are under-represented among senior police officers and in police authorities. The idea of policing by consent is compromised if systems of accountability fail to reflect the ethnic diversity of the population. This 'democratic deficit' has long been recognized and attempts have been made to increase the responsiveness of the police to minority communities through the introduction of 'consultative committees' such as those recommended by *Scarman*. Independent monitoring is important because it offers the opportunity to provide transparency, openness and accountability in policing.

In practice, however, such processes face great challenges to their effectiveness. In many instances, consultative arrangements have offered few opportunities for local communities to exert any control over the police organization because consultation does not amount to accountability. Reviews of such mechanisms in England have concluded that they are of marginal importance to the principal areas of police activity (see, for example, Morgan, 1989; Commission for Racial Equality, 1991: 3). Even the more effective of such consultation mechanisms have found that the police often act without informing or consulting the community. The deficit in legal and political accountability is not fully redressed by the creation of new systems of 'consultation'.

Along the same lines, Community Consultative Committees were formed in New South Wales in 1987 for a limited number of ethnic minority and Aboriginal communities (Chan, 1997: 198). However, the literature on these mechanisms shows mixed results. Some spent hours talking about trivia and had little monitoring of their effectiveness. The members of the committee were not truly representative of the community, often representing business and middle-class interests and excluding young people; in some places it was clear that the members of the group were 'chosen for their compliance'. In general, the committees lacked influence in the determination and review of operational policing and were seen by the police as predominantly vehicles to disseminate information to the community. In other cases, however, senior managers were prepared to discuss operational issues raised by lay members, including the way in which police questioned suspects and were also willing to admit that the methods used by some police officers were unsatisfactory (Bul and Strata, 1994, cited by Chan, 1997: 203).

In South Africa the importance of civilian oversight is therefore of the highest importance in creating a force which has the trust of the community it serves. Studies of policing in South Africa conclude that a more community-oriented and less militarized police force is required which concentrates on a problem-solving style of policing. The National Peace Accord established Local and Regional Dispute Resolution Committee (Brogden and Shearing, 1993) and Community Police Forums were set up in the early 1990s, with varying degrees of effectiveness depending on the levels of violence in the area (Cawthra, 1997). Since 1993 there have been pilot projects setting up community visiting schemes, which are closely connected to the community–police forums (CPFs) and allow community members to observe and comment on conditions and treatment of suspects detained in police stations (Nel and Bezuidenhout, 1995).

Diana Gordon describes the development of community–police forums that were intended as the mechanisms for implementing community policing in South Africa. After a promising start, Gordon argues that the influence of CPFs has waned, the range of activities has narrowed and participation has dwindled (Gordon, 2001: 134), leading Gordon to the conclusion that 'opportunities for civilian participation in police decision-making are no longer seen as important in the vision for democratic policing' (Gordon, 2001: 135). Thus the mechanism that was intended to make citizen scrutiny of police activity a routine aspect of democracy in South Africa has 'largely fallen by the wayside' (ibid.). Crucially, in 1998 a white paper shifted the CPF functions from 'oversight' of the police to that of 'assistance'. In South Africa, the police resisted CPF criticism and were hostile to intrusion into their discretionary domain. The committees were not seen as fully representative of the community and often based on party loyalties; early CPF leaders moved into local politics or were 'hived away' without strong replacements; and the CPFs were sometimes seen as spies for the police. Although there is little agreement on what counts as 'success' in this context, Gordon concludes that there is little evidence of much impact on police accountability. She warns that there is a risk that without the CPFs or some other mechanism for deepening democracy in law enforcement, the police may regress to unresponsiveness and routine violence (Gordon, 2001: 174).

Despite the sometimes disappointing experience of mechanisms to facilitate police accountability to the community, we are of the view that this is one of the most important spheres for future work. In the UK, independent monitoring groups have historically been thought of as obstructive and unhelpful by the police. However, in recent years senior police officers have become increasingly conscious that such organizations provide information about crime and policing that can be gained from no other source. Such organizations are, therefore, of great benefit in both crime reduction and oversight of the police. Independent advisory groups, if they can work to overcome some of the problems set out above, can also play a role in creating a greater visibility of policing practices (by using the media and public meetings, for example), a challenge to stereotypical and narrow and discriminatory thinking among police officers.

Accountability for wrongdoing: complaint investigation and civilian oversight

The process by which the public can formally complain about instances of error and misconduct is the 'touchstone' of police accountability. It is through this process that the police may be called upon to account for allegations of misconduct and, where necessary, provide redress for injury arising from the abuse of force. Research shows that a higher success rate for complainants, greater empathy for those alleging discrimination and more effective remedies will enhance the credibility of the law in the eyes of ethnic minorities both within and outside of the force (The Rotterdam Charter, 1996). In the UK, the way that complaints by African, Caribbean and Asian people against the police have been handled has been subject to much criticism. Since 1990, The Police Complaints Authority of Britain has collected figures for complaints of racially discriminatory behaviour by police officers. In the first full year of recording (1991), there were 49 such complaints; in 2000 this had risen steeply to 579 (Police Complaints Authority, 2000: 19).

The police complaints system in South Africa has also been unsatisfactory, as complaints were generally handled internally and destruction of evidence was a major problem. However, under the new Constitution, the police can be held criminally liable for any violations of citizens' rights (Nel and Bezuidehout, 1995). The Independent Complaints Directorate (ICD), established in 1997, employs non-police investigators to investigate serious criminal complaints and has the power to launch its own investigation. The requirement that all deaths in custody be referred to it and investigated by it is an important development (Melville, 1999). Despite the fact that ICD's formal powers go well beyond those in most other jurisdictions, there are serious limitations on the operation of the process in practice.

The ICD has reported 'passive obstruction' and 'pockets of resistance' to its work. Sometimes there are significant delays in referral and the Directorate is not able to compel officers to be interviewed, nor can it initiate its own prosecutions. There appears to be hostility from the public towards the investigation process – on one side from those who think that it is not fully independent, and from the other by those who think that the police should be unfettered in the 'fight against crime'. Perhaps the most significant problem, however, is a lack of resources;

the ICD has 37 investigators responsible for examining the circumstances of at least 800 'police involved' deaths.

Civil litigation

Perceived and actual ineffectiveness of the police complaints procedure
and 'fear of themselves being criminalised' (Institute of Race Relations,
1987) have led victims of alleged police misconduct to forgo the official complaints procedure and pursue civil court proceedings for
damages. Legal action makes explicit the problems faced, highlights the
plight of a group and acts as a stimulus for employers to comply. The
use of the civil courts has increased dramatically over the past two
decades in London. In 1979, only seven cases against the Metropolitan
Police were heard, resulting in damages of only £1,991 being paid. By
1996/7 this had soared to 1,000 threatened actions (Metropolitan Police,
1997: 83), while damage payments have escalated to £3.9 million in
1999/2000 (Metropolitan Police, 2001).

While the extent of injury settlements suggest that complainants are
at least getting redress for the abuse of police powers, one should be
hesitant about calling this a success since it would be far better to spend
related costs on measures to improve public protection. Only a minority of instances of abuse and complaint result in the award of compensation, leaving many complainants dissatisfied and without redress.
Finally, the evidence that punitive damages are having the effect of
improving police practices or restraining the abuse of police powers
is equivocal. Civil remedies must always be available, but they cannot
substitute for robust mechanisms for complaint, investigation and
accountability.

Conclusion

Discrimination, xenophobia, intolerance and the abuse of power in
police work have wide-ranging consequences. Abusive practices lead to
unnecessary deaths, physical and psychological injuries as well as disaffection and frustration. Abusive policing strikes at the very core of the
idea of democratic policing. The police are not only guardians of liberty,
but also the gatekeepers of the criminal process. Consequently, discriminatory policing can be the first step towards criminalization, especially in contexts where prejudice and discrimination in the criminal
justice process support or compound police decision-making. While it
is tempting to resort to the 'military model' of policing practice in the
face of rising crime and violence, the evidence suggests that this is likely

not only to undermine fundamental human rights, but most likely to be counterproductive. Paramilitary policing is part of a vicious circle that contributes to the criminalization of marginalized communities, undermines state legitimacy and voluntary compliance with the rule of law, and adds to the escalation of violence in the community.

We have examined the various mechanisms through which policing reform has been implemented. The starting point must be a clear and overt commitment to the implementation of democratic policing, based on responsiveness and accountability to the community and adherence to internationally recognized human rights standards. Building on these principles, mechanisms to ensure that the axioms of policing are based on the maintenance of peace and the protection of the rights to life, liberty and security of the person; that the police force is internally democratic, demographically representative and accountable to the communities served. The road to reform is by no means straightforward and there are powerful forces pushing the police back towards militarism. National and local governments, international observers, academics and, most importantly, progressive police officers from senior managers to the officer on patrol, will need to work hard to translate a stated commitment to policing for human rights into effective and fair practices on the street.

Notes

1. Police abuse of force also occurs in countries where social divisions are based not on 'race', but on class and political affiliation (e.g. Jamaica), religious sectarianism (e.g. Northern Ireland) and tribal heritage (e.g. Rwanda).
2. In South Africa, Cawthra (1997: 98–9) estimates that the private security industry workforce outnumbers that of the public police by a figure of around three or four to one.
3. In relation to the US, most of the worst abuses have been committed by local forces under the influence of local political machines and local democracy.
4. The 'community' model has also been referred to as the 'consensual', 'civil', 'democratic' and 'liberal' model.
5. It is worth noting that *Scarman* did not ultimately reject the military model. In fact, his recommendations, including the development of public order training, have been followed by the creation of a considerable paramilitary capacity within many British police forces, including the Metropolitan Police.
6. In the British context this is usually used to describe people whose origins lie in Africa or the Caribbean.
7. Empirical evidence supports the intuitive position that greater discretion leads to greater discrimination. See Bowling and Phillips (2002: 163, 169) and also Phillips and Brown (1998).

8. Almost three times as many indigenous persons died in prison custody in the decade 1990–99 (93) than in the decade 1980–89 (39) (Williams, 2001).
9. The evidence for this is equivocal; see McLaughlin (1991) and Skolnick and Bayley (1986: 246).
10. Attempts in the United States to transform the police service into one which reflects the community served is described in Dulaney's concise but comprehensive history of *Black Police in America* (1996) (see also Cashmore, 1991; Leinen, 1977; Nicholas, 1969).
11. The Rotterdam Charter (1996) was produced by the foundation 'Policing for a Multi-ethnic Society'. It has no official status as an international document but is a model of 'best practice' for police organizations in their response to ethnic diversity arising from the initiative based in Rotterdam.
12. The relevant international instruments relating to Human Rights, policing and anti-discrimination include the following: The Universal Declaration of Human Rights (1948); The International Covenant on Economic, Social and Cultural Rights; The International Convention on the Elimination of All Forms of Racial Discrimination (1965); The International Convention on Civil and Political Rights (ICPR, 1966); The Convention against Torture and Other Cruel, Inhuman or Degrading Treatment or Punishment; Principles on the Effective Prevention and Investigation of Extra-legal, Arbitrary and Summary Executions; Code of Conduct for Law Enforcement Officials (1979); United Nations Basic Principles on the Use of Force and Firearms by Law Enforcement Officials (1990). (See Crawshaw et al., 1998; Human Rights Watch, 1998: 111–22 and appendices D–H; Hoffman, 2000.)
13. UDHR, Art.3.
14. Adopted by the United Nations Economic and Social Council, 24 May 1989.
15. It was adopted by the Eighth United Nations Congress on the Prevention of Crime and Treatment of Offenders, 1990.
16. UN Basic Principles on the Use of Force and Firearms by Law Enforcement Officials.
17. Article 3 of the UN Code of Conduct for Law Enforcement Officials.
18. Article 3 of the Universal Declaration of Human Rights.
19. Articles 10 and 11, ibid.
20. Article 12, ibid.
21. ICCPR, Article 26 asserts that all persons are equal before the law and are entitled without discrimination to equal protection of the law.
22. Article 1.4.
23. The apartheid regime in South Africa is the best example of this.
24. The notorious Frank Rizzo was repeatedly re-elected as Mayor of Philadelphia on an explicit platform of oppressive policing of which ethnic minorities were the principal victims. See Skolnick and Fyfe (1993).
25. In Britain, territorial-based policing is governed by 'the tripartite structure' of the Chief Officer, the Home Secretary and the local police authority (comprised of a mixture of elected local representatives, magistrates and government appointees).

References

Banton, M. (1996) *International Action against Racial Discrimination*, Oxford: Clarendon Press.

Bayley, D. H. (1985) *Patterns of Policing: A Comparative International Analysis*, New Brunswick, NJ: Rutgers University Press.

Bayley, D. H. (1998) *What Works in Policing*, New York: Oxford University Press.

Bland, N., Miller, J. and Quinton, P. (2000) *Upping the PACE? An Evaluation of the Recommendations of the Stephen Lawrence Inquiry on Stops and Searches*, Police Research Series Paper 128. London: Home Office.

Bland, N., Mundy, G., Russell, J. and Tuffin, R. (1999) *Career Progression of Ethnic Minority Police Officers*. Home Office Police Research Paper 107, London: Research, Development and Statistics Directorate, London: Home Office.

Bowling, B. (1999) *Violent Racism: Victimization, Policing and Social Context*, Oxford: Oxford University Press.

Bowling, B. and Foster, J. (2002) 'Policing and the Police', in M. Maguire, R. Morgan and R. Reiner (eds.), *The Oxford Handbook of Criminology*, 3rd edition, Oxford: Oxford University Press

Bowling, B. and Phillips, C. (2002) *Racism, Crime and Justice*, London: Longman.

Brewer, J. (1990) *Black and Blue: Policing in South Africa*, Oxford: Oxford University Press.

Brogden, M. and Shearing, C. (1993) *Policing for a New South Africa*, London: Routledge.

Brown, J. (1997) 'Equal Opportunities and the Police in England and Wales Past, Present and Future Possibilities', in P. Francis, P. Davies and V. Jupp (eds.) *Policing Futures: The Police, Law Enforcement and the 21st Century*. Basingstoke: Macmillan.

Cashmore, E. (1991) 'Black Cops Inc.', in E. Cashmore and E. McLaughlin (eds.) *Out of Order*, London: Routledge.

Cawthra, G. (1993) *Policing South Africa: The South African Police and the Transition from Apartheid*, London and New Jersey: Zed Books.

Cawthra, G. (1997) *Securing South Africa's Democracy: Defence, Development and Security in Transition*, Basingstoke: Macmillan.

Chan, J. (1997) *Changing Police Culture: Policing in a Multicultural Society*, Cambridge: Cambridge University Press.

Chevigny, P. (1995) *Edge of the Knife*, New York: The New Press.

Christopher, W. (1991) *Report of the Independent Commission on the Los Angeles Police Department (Christopher Commission)*, Los Angeles: City of Los Angeles.

Commission for Racial Equality (1991) *The Point of Order: A Study of Consultative Arrangements under Section 106 of the Police and Criminal Evidence Act*, London: Commission for Racial Equality.

Crawshaw, R., Devlin, B. and Williamson, T. (1998) *Human Rights and Policing: Standards for Good Behaviour and a Strategy for Change*, The Hague: Kluwer.

Deaths in Custody Working Group of the Community–Police Consultative Group for Lambeth (1996) *Lessons from Tragedies: Deaths in Custody in the Metropolitan Police District 1986–95*, London: Community–Police Consultative Group for Lambeth.

Dulaney, M. W. (1996) *Black Police in America*, Bloomington: Indiana University Press.

FitzGerald, M. and Sibbitt, R. (1997) *Ethnic Monitoring in Police Forces: A Beginning*, Home Office Research Study. London: HMSO.

Gilroy, P. and Sim, J. (1987) 'Law, Order and the State of the Left', in P. Scraton (ed.) *Law, Order and the Authoritarian State*, Milton Keynes: Open University Press.

Gordon, D. (2001) 'Democratic Consolidation and Community Policing: Conflicting Imperatives in South Africa', *Policing and Society*, Vol. 11, No. 2, pp. 121–50.

Grimshaw, R. and Jefferson, R. (1987) *Interpreting Policework*, London: Allen and Unwin.

Harris, D. A. (1999) *Driving while Black: Racial Profiling On Our Nation's Highways*, University of Toledo College of Law/American Civil Liberties Union, June 1999.

Her Majesty's Inspectorate of Constabulary (1995) *Developing Diversity in the Police Service*, Equal Opportunities Inspection Report 1995. London: Home Office.

Her Majesty's Inspectorate of Constabulary (1997) *Winning the Race: Policing Plural Communities*, HMIC Thematic Inspection Report on Police Community and Race Relations 1996/7. London: Home Office.

Her Majesty's Inspectorate of Constabulary (2000) *Winning the Race: Embracing Diversity*, Consolidation Inspection of Police Community and Race Relations 2000. London: Home Office.

Hoffman, P. (2000) 'International Human Rights Law and Police Reform', in A. McArdle and T. Erzen, *Zero Tolerance: Quality of Life and the New Police Brutality in New York City*, New York: New York University Press.

Holdaway, S. (1991) *Recruiting a Multi-Ethnic Police Force*, London: Home Office.

Holdaway, S. (1996) *The Racialisation of British Policing*, London: Macmillan.

Holdaway, S. and Barron, A. (1997) *Resigners? The Experience of Black and Asian Police Officers*, Basingstoke: Macmillan.

Home Office (2000) *Statistics on Race and the Criminal Justice System 2000*, A Home Office publication under section 95 of the Criminal Justice Act 1991. London: Home Office.

Human Rights and Equal Opportunities Commission (1991) *Racist Violence: Report of the National Inquiry into Racist Violence in Australia*, Canberra: AGPS.

Human Rights Watch (1998) *Shielded from Justice: Police Brutality and Accountability in the United States*, New York: Human Rights Watch.

Institute of Race Relations (1987) *Policing against Black People*, London: Institute of Race Relations.

Institute of Race Relations (1991) *Deadly Silence: Black Deaths in Custody*, London: Institute of Race Relations.

Johnston, E. (1991) *Royal Commission into Aboriginal Deaths in Custody: National Report: Overview and Recommendations*, Canberra: Australian Government Publishing Service.

Jones, T. and Newburn, T. (1996) *Policing and Disaffected Communities: a Review of the Literature*, A Report to the Standing Advisory Committee on Human Rights. London: Policy Studies Institute.

Jones, T. and Newburn, T. (1997) *Policing after the Act*, London: Policy Studies Institute.

Kappeler, V., Sluder, R. and Alpert, G. (1994) *Forces of Deviance: Understanding the Dark Side of Policing*, Prospect Heights, Illinois: Waveland Press.

Keith, M. (1993) *Race Riots and Policing: Lore and Disorder in a Multi-Racist Society*, London: Home Office.

Klockars, C. (1985) *The Idea of Police*, Beverly Hills: Sage.

Leinen, S. (1977) *Black Police, White Society*, New York: New York University Press.

Lustgarten, L. (1986) *The Governance of the Police*, London: Sweet & Maxwell.

Macpherson, W. (1999) *The Stephen Lawrence Inquiry*. Report of an Inquiry by Sir William Macpherson of Cluny, Advised by Tom Cook, The Right Reverend Dr John Sentamu and Dr. Richard Stone. Cm 4262-1. London: Home Office.

Manby, B. (2000) 'The South African Independent Complaints Directorate', in A. Goldsmith and C. Lewis (eds.) *Civilian Oversight of Policing*, Oxford: Hart.

Marks, M. (1999) 'Changing Dilemmas and Dilemmas of Change: Transforming the Public Order Police Unit in Durban', *Policing and Society*, Vol. 9, pp. 157–79.

Marks, M. (2000) 'Transforming Police Organisations from Within: Police Dissident Groupings in South Africa', *British Journal of Criminology*, Vol. 49, pp. 557–73.

McLaughlin, E. (1991) 'Police Accountability and Black People: Into the 1990s', in E. Cashmore and E. McLaughlin (eds.) *Out of Order*, London: Routledge.

Melville, N. (1999) *The Taming of the Blue: Regulating Police Misconduct in South Africa*, Pretoria: Human Sciences Research Council.

Metropolitan Police (1997) *Annual Report*, London: Metropolitan Police.

Metropolitan Police (2001) *Annual Report*, London: Metropolitan Police.

Miller, J., Bland, N. and Quinton, P. (2000) *The Impact of Stops and Searches on Crime and the Community*, Police Research Series Paper 127. London: Home Office.

Morgan, R. (1989) 'Policing by Consent: Legitimating the Doctrine', in R. Morgan and D. Smith (eds.), *Coming to Terms with Policing*, London: Routledge.

Nel, F. and Bezuidenhout, J. (1995) *Human Rights for the Police*, South Africa: Juta.

Nicholas, N. (1969) *Black in Blue*, New York: Meredith Corporation.

Ogletree, C. J. et al. (1995) *Beyond the Rodney King Story: An Investigation of Police Conduct in Minority Communities*, Criminal Justice Institute at Harvard Law School for the National Association for the Advancement of Colored People. Boston: Northeastern University Press.

Phillips, C. and Brown, D. (1998) *Entry into the Criminal Justice System: A Survey of Police Arrests and Their Outcomes*, Home Office Research Study 185. London: Home Office.

Police Complaints Authority (2000) *Annual Report*, London: Police Complaints Authority.

Quinton, P., Bland, N. and Miller, J. (2000) *Police Stops, Decision-making and Practice*, Police Research Series Paper 130. London: Home Office.

Reiner, R. (2000) *The Politics of the Police*, 3rd edition, Oxford: Oxford University Press.

The Rotterdam Charter (1996) *Policing for a Multi-Ethnic Society*, Rotterdam: Rotterdam Conference.

Royal Commission into the New South Wales Police Service (1997), in J. Chan, *Changing Police Culture: Policing in a Multicultural Society*, Cambridge: Cambridge University Press.

Skogan, W. (1990) *The Police and Public in England and Wales: A British Crime Survey Report*, Home Office Research Study 117. London: Home Office.

Skogan, W. (1994) *Contacts Between Police and Public: Findings from the 1992 British Crime Survey*, Home Office Research Study 134. London: Home Office.

Skolnick (1966) *Justice without Trial: Law Enforcement in Democratic Society*, London: Wiley.

Skolnick, J. H. and Bayley, D. H. (1986) *The New Blue Line: Police Innovation in Six American Cities*, New York: Free Press.

Skolnick, J. H. and Fyfe, J. J. (1993) *Above the Law: Police and the Excessive Use of Force*, New York: Free Press.

Smith, D. and Gray, J. (1985) *Police and People in London*, London: Policy Studies Institute/Gower.

Stone, V. and Pettigrew, N. (2000) *The Views of the Public on Stops and Searches*, Police Research Series Paper 136. London: Home Office.

Stone, V. and Tuffin, R. (2000) *Attitudes of People from Minority Ethnic Communities Towards a Career in the Police Service*, Police Research Series Paper 136. London: Home Office.

Truth and Reconciliation Committee (1998) *Report of the Truth and Reconciliation Committee*, South Africa.

United Nations (1948) *The Universal Declaration of Human Rights*, G. A. res. 217A (III), U.N. Doc A/810 at 71.

United Nations (1965) *The International Convention on the Elimination of All Forms of Racial Discrimination*, 660 U.N.T.S. 195.

United Nations (1966) *International Covenant on Economic, Social and Cultural Rights*, G.A. res. 2200A (XXI), 21 U.N.GAOR Supp. (No. 16) at 49, U.N. Doc. A/6316 (1966), 993 U.N.T.S.

United Nations (1966) *The International Convention of Civil and Political Rights*. G.A. res. 2200A (XXI), 21 U.N.GAOR Supp. (No.16) at 49, U.N. Doc. A/6316 (1966), 993 U.N.T.S. 3.

United Nations (1979) *Code of Conduct for Law Enforcement Officials*, Adopted by General Assembly resolution 34/169 of 17 December.

United Nations (1985) *Convention against Torture and Other Cruel, Inhuman or Degrading Treatment or Punishment*, G.A. res. 39/46 [annex, 39 U.N. GAOR Supp. (No. 51) at 197, U.N. Doc. A/39/51 (1984)].

United Nations (1990) *Basic Principles on the Use of Force and Firearms by Law Enforcement Officials*. Eighth United Nations Congress on the Prevention of Crime and the Treatment of Offenders, Havana, 27 August to 7 September 1990, U.N. Doc. A/CONF.144/28/Rev.1 at 112.

Van der Spuy', E. (1990) 'Political Discourse and the History of the South African Police', in D. Hanson and D. Van zyl Smit (eds.) *Towards Justice? Crime Control in South Africa*, Oxford: Oxford University Press.

Walker, S., Spohn, C. and DeLone, M. (1996) *The Colour of Justice: Race, Ethnicity and Crime in America*, Nebraska, Omaha: Walker Books.

Williams, P. (2001) *Deaths in Custody: Ten Years on From the Royal Commission*, Australian Institute of Criminology Trends and Issues in Crime and Justice Paper 203. Australia: Institute of Criminology.

Wilson, D. and Holdaway, S. and Spencer, C. (1984) 'Black Police in the United Kingdom', *Policing*, Vol. 1, No. 1, pp. 20–30.

Part II
Racism and Social Justice

6

Poverty and Prosperity: Prospects for Reducing Racial/Ethnic Economic Disparities in the United States

Sheldon Danziger, Deborah Reed and Tony N. Brown

Almost 15 years ago, the Committee on the Status of Black Americans, appointed by the National Research Council, issued a report, *A Common Destiny: Blacks and American Society* (Jaynes and Williams, 1989). The report presented a comprehensive review of changes in the social, economic and political status of black Americans between 1940 and the mid-1980s. The first paragraph of the preface concisely summarizes the Committee's conclusions:

> This report documents the unfinished agenda of a nation still struggling to come to terms with the consequences of its history of relations between black and white Americans. In many ways this history has left a legacy of pain, and the report would be remiss if it did not emphasize that fact. In the pages that follow, we describe many improvements in the economic, political and social position of black Americans. We also describe the continuance of conditions of poverty, segregation, discrimination, and social fragmentation of the most serious proportion. (p. ix)

When the Committee was deliberating, data on the relative economic status of African Americans and whites were available up to the mid-1980s. The US economy had performed poorly during the period from the mid-1970s to the mid-1980s, as unemployment and inflation rates had been high and earnings and income inequalities within both the white and black populations had increased. Against this background of slow economic growth and rising inequality, the report's conclusions were rather pessimistic:

Barring unforeseen events or changes in present conditions – that is, no changes in educational policies and opportunities, no increased income and employment opportunities, and no major national programs to deal directly with the problems of economic dependency – our findings imply several negative developments for blacks in the near future . . . (p. 26)

In this chapter, we revisit issues related to the relative economic status of racial and ethnic minorities in the United States after the 'unforeseen' long economic boom of the 1990s. We analyse the same time-series the Committee analysed, but update the data through to the end of the century, and we expand the analysis by focusing on the relative economic status of white non-Hispanics, black non-Hispanics and Hispanics.[1] We show how the economic boom of the 1990s with its low unemployment and inflation rates altered the relative economic status of the three largest sub-populations in the United States.

We document that there was much economic progress in the 1990s for all population subgroups – employment and incomes increased, poverty fell and income inequality stopped rising. However, the gaps between whites and blacks and between whites and Hispanics remain so large that (borrowing the key phrase from the Committee), 'barring unforeseen events or changes in present conditions', economic parity remains decades in the future. The Committee's key policy implications remain as true today as they were in the late 1980s and as true as they have been since the height of the civil rights struggles of the 1960s:

Macroeconomic growth and reduced joblessness create favorable conditions, but they do not remove some crucial barriers that exist for blacks. Improvement depends also on active promotion and vigorous enforcement of antidiscrimination laws and administrative measures to reduce discrimination in employment, education and housing. . . . Both the removal of barriers and compensatory programs are needed for full equality of opportunity. (p. 29)

Our analysis documents that economic growth on its own is necessary, but not sufficient, for reducing the persistent between-group economic disparities that characterize the US economy. If the large gaps between the white non-Hispanic majority and other racial/ethnic groups are to be narrowed, increased policy attention will have to be focused on removing barriers to equal opportunity and to raising the relative education and skills of minority children. In addition, there is a need for 'race-neutral' policies focused on all less-educated workers, as the extent of poverty and inequality within the white population is also high in comparison to the poverty rates and inequality levels of other industrialized countries.

In the context of this volume, our restatement of the need to remove barriers to equal opportunity and to adopt compensatory programmes in education and employment can be applied in South Africa and the many other nations in which one racial/ethnic group has historically controlled the economy and society and has discriminated against other groups. Glenn Loury (2004) emphasizes a similar point. He suggests that the elimination of 'reward bias', defined as 'unfair treatment of persons in formal economic transactions based on racial identity', is necessary, but not sufficient to achieve racial justice. He provides a rich discussion of the policy issues that are raised when a liberal society considers whether or not and how to pursue compensatory programmes. Our chapter merely documents that the need for such programmes is not likely to be resolved by economic growth on its own.

Trends in economic well-being

Economic conditions in the United States in 1999 (the latest year for which data were available when the chapter was prepared) were excellent. Inflation and unemployment were low (2.2 per cent and 4.2 per cent, respectively), and the budget was in surplus (about 2 per cent of GDP). Wage rates, adjusted for inflation, increased as the labour market tightened in the 1990s; however, they remained below levels achieved a quarter-century earlier. Average hourly earnings (in 1999 constant dollars) in private industry were $13.57 in December 1999, 6.4 per cent above their December 1992 level, but still 7.5 per cent below the December 1973 level of $14.61. A similar pattern holds for the official Census Bureau poverty rate (an absolute measure).[2] It fell from the mid- to the late 1990s, but was about as high in 1999, 11.8 per cent, as it had been in 1972, even though real per capita income almost doubled over this period.

Relative to most other advanced economies, the US has a high median living standard and an unemployment rate that has been lower than elsewhere for most of the past 15 years. However, the US poverty rate for all persons remains much higher than that of most other industrialized countries.[3] The 1999 official poverty rates for blacks and Hispanics (23.6 and 22.8 per cent, respectively), were higher than the rate for whites four decades earlier (18.1 per cent in 1959).

We now review trends in the relative economic well-being of the three largest race/ethnic groups in the US, utilizing 30 years of data from the Census Bureau's annual Current Population Survey (CPS). The analysis begins in 1970, the first year that allows us to produce comparable time-series. The reader should note that the 1960s was a period of rapid economic growth for all persons and a period during which the economic status of African Americans relative to that of whites improved (Jaynes and Williams, 1989). Thus, if we could have produced consistent time-series data for 1960 to 1999, they would have shown more progress for African Americans relative to whites and more absolute progress for all race/ethnic groups.

Trends in poverty, affluence and median family income

Figure 6.1 shows the trend in poverty from 1970 to 1999.[4] At the beginning of this period, poverty for African Americans was about four times that of whites (35 vs. 9 per cent in 1970); for Hispanics, about three times that of whites (25 vs. 9 per cent). Poverty changed little for any of the groups between the early 1970s and the early 1990s. During the economic boom of the 1990s, the most rapid percentage reduction in poverty was a 32 per cent drop for African Americans, from 31 to 21 per cent, between 1992 and 1999; poverty declined by 26 per cent for Hispanics, from 27 to 20 per cent, and by 22 per cent for whites, from 9 to 7 per cent. The last time there was this much relative economic progress for minorities was during the economic boom of the 1960s. By

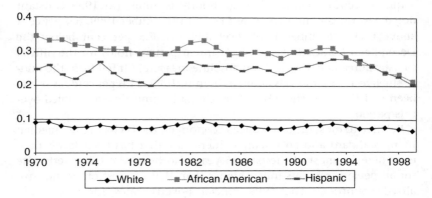

Figure 6.1   Percentage of Persons Living in Poverty, 1970–1999

Note: The official US poverty line for a family of four persons in 1999 was $17,029.

1999, the black and Latino poverty rates were about three times the rate for non-Hispanic whites and at about the level of the white poverty rate in the mid-1960s, a level that led President Johnson to declare War on Poverty.

Whereas the National Academy Committee was writing against a backdrop of economic pessimism, we offer an optimistic forecast for the poverty rate in the near future based on the positive economic experiences of the 1990s. Our projections are 'too optimistic' for several reasons. First, we ignore the statistical fact that it becomes harder to achieve the same percentage reduction in poverty from economic growth as the poverty rate falls (Freeman, 2002). Second, we assume that the economy continues to grow at the rapid pace of 1992–9 for another 14 years, even though a recession began in the US in early 2001 and is expected to continue through most of 2002. Third, we assume that the percentage reduction in poverty for each sub-group will continue at the rate of the 1992–9 period, even though African American economic progress tends to be rapid only when labour markets are very tight. Our resulting 'estimate' is that the African American poverty rate in 2013 *ceteris paribus* would fall to about 10 per cent, the Hispanic rate to about 11 per cent and the white rate to about 4 per cent. This optimistic scenario reinforces the point that economic growth can substantially reduce poverty, but, on its own, will have a limited impact on closing the between-group gaps in poverty. As we discuss below, an effective policy for reducing majority/minority differences in economic status would be to close the educational attainment and labour force skills gaps between the groups.

Figure 6.2 shows a dramatic increase for all groups in the percentage of persons living in affluence, which we define as persons residing in families that have annual incomes greater than seven times the official poverty line (see Danziger and Gottschalk, 1995, for a discussion of this measure). In 1999, a family of four was considered affluent if its annual money income from all family members was about $120,000 or more; median income for all families in 1999 was about $53,000.

Affluence has increased much more rapidly than poverty has fallen, reflecting the increased inequality of the past three decades. In 1970, 5 per cent of whites were affluent, compared to only 1 per cent each of African Americans and Hispanics. By 1999, 20 per cent of whites were affluent, compared to 8 per cent of African Americans and 5 per cent of Hispanics. The rate of affluence for African Americans doubled during the economic boom of the 1990s, from 4 to 8 per cent between 1992 and 1999. However, the extent of affluence for African Americans in

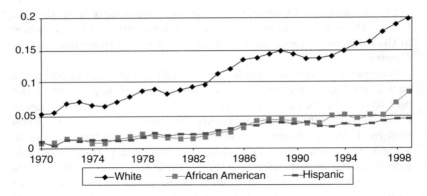

Figure 6.2   Percentage of Persons Living in Affluence, 1970–1999
Note: Affluence is defined as family income at least seven times the poverty line.

1999 was the same as that for whites in 1977; the rate for Hispanics in 1999, the same as the rate for whites in 1970. In 1999, for whites, there were about three times as many affluent persons as poor persons (20 vs. 7 per cent); for blacks (8 vs. 21 per cent) and Hispanics (5 vs. 20 per cent), the number of affluent persons was only a small portion of the number of poor persons.

Figure 6.3 shows the trend in median family income adjusted for family size in constant 1999 dollars for the 1970–9 period.[5] Incomes rose substantially up to 1973 for each group, then growth slowed. After the recessions of the late 1970s and early 1980s, median incomes were about the same in 1983 as they had been in 1973. After the economy recovered from the severe recession of the early 1980s, incomes grew for the rest of the 1980s, declined during a mild recession in the early 1990s, and then increased substantially in the late 1990s.

Income growth for Hispanics has been slower than for the other groups. The median size-adjusted income for Hispanic families in 1992 ($27,353) was about the same as it had been in 1973 ($28,428); it grew by 14 per cent for both African Americans (from $24,112 to $27,416) and whites (from $47,579 to $54,226) over these two decades. Between 1992 and 1999, median family income grew most rapidly, by 31 per cent, for African Americans (to $35,999); it rose by 13 per cent for whites (to $61,284) and by 14 per cent for Hispanics (to $31,062). As a result, the ratio of the African American median family income to the white median, which was 0.51 in both 1970 and 1992 increased to 0.59 by 1999; this ratio for Hispanics was 0.59 in 1970, 0.50 in 1992 and 0.51

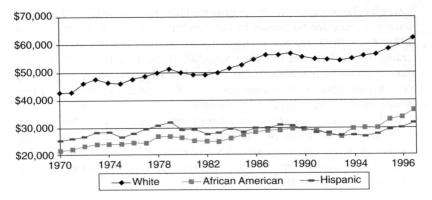

Figure 6.3 Median Family Income, 1970–1999 (1999$)

in 1999. As with the other measures of economic status, the economic boom of the 1990s was particularly beneficial for African Americans, but large racial gaps remain.

We realize that racial/ethnic differences in family structure play an important role in determining family economic resources and hence account for some part of the economic disparities shown in Figures 6.1–6.3. For example, among all families the median income in 1999 was just over $53,000. For families headed by single mothers the median was less than $23,000. African Americans have the highest share of persons living in single-mother families at 29 per cent, followed by Hispanics at 16 per cent and whites at 7 per cent. Thus, a comparison of racial/ethnic differences in median family income that adjusted for family structure differences (data not shown here) shows a higher ratio of median family income for African Americans relative to whites and higher ratio for the Hispanic median relative to that of whites (see Cancian and Reed, 2002, for a further discussion of family structure and poverty).

Part of the reason that the economic well-being of Hispanics has lagged that of both whites and African Americans in recent years is because of increasing immigration (see Smith, 2001). In 1970, 29 per cent of Hispanics were foreign-born; by 1999, the share of foreign-born had increased to 43 per cent. Because Hispanic immigrants tend to have low incomes when they arrive in the US, in part because they have much lower educational attainment than the native-born population, an increase in their share contributed to a higher poverty rate and a lower level of median family income for Hispanics. For example, median family income for Hispanics in families with a US-born head was over $38,000 in 1999; for those Hispanics in families headed by an immigrant, the median was less than $28,000. Thus, if we had restricted our data analysis to native-born Hispanics, the white-Hispanic gap in any year would have been smaller and economic trends during the 1990s boom would have been more positive.

Racial gaps in economic status stem from a number of factors. In the next section, we focus on changes in the functioning of the labour market over the past three decades and present trends in employment and earnings for workers in each race/ethnic group, holding gender, age and education constant.

Labour market trends and changes in employment and earnings

The most important determinant of poverty, affluence and family income is how individuals fare in the labour market, as earnings are the largest component of family income. Most economists agree that the main source of the stagnation in incomes and wages between the early 1970s and early 1990s was the difficulty less skilled workers faced in a changing, globalizing labour market. In 1970, for example, the mean hourly wage for full-time, white male earners between the ages of 25 and 54 who had at least a college degree was 56 per cent higher than the wage for similar men with a high school diploma or less. By 1999, the more educated group had an 82 per cent wage advantage.

There is some disagreement over the relative importance of various factors that have contributed to this rising skill differential. Labour-saving technological changes have simultaneously increased the demand for skilled workers who can run sophisticated equipment and reduced the demand for less skilled workers, many of whom have been displaced by automation. Global competition has increased worldwide demand for the goods and services produced in the US by skilled workers in high-tech industries and financial services. Lower skilled workers in US manufacturing industries increasingly compete with and are displaced by lower-paid production workers in developing countries. Immigration has increased the size of the low-wage workforce and the competition for low-skilled jobs that remain in the US. Institutional changes, such as the decline in the real value of the minimum wage and shrinking unionization rates, also moved the economy in the direction of lower real wages for the least skilled workers and higher earnings inequality. (For further discussion of labour market changes and their causes, see Danziger and Gottschalk, 1995: Chapters 6 and 7.)

Because African American and Hispanic workers have lower educational attainment than whites, the twist in the labour market against less educated workers would have had a larger negative effect on the relative employment and earnings of minority workers, even if there were no changes in the propensity of employers to hire workers of different races.[6] For example, in 2000, among men between the ages of 25 and 54, only about 7 per cent of white non-Hispanics, but 14 per cent of African Americans and 41 per cent of Hispanics had not completed a high school degree. If one defines the less educated as having a high school degree or less, then about 40 per cent of whites, 53 per cent of African Americans and 70 per cent of Hispanics were in this category in 2000.

Figure 6.4 shows the percentage of males, between the ages of 25 and 54, with a high school degree or less, who held a job during the week before the March Current Population Survey.[7] In 1970, 92 per cent of whites, and 85 per cent of African Americans and Hispanics were working. By 1992, this employment rate had fallen by 10 percentage points for whites (to 82 per cent) by 8 points for Hispanics (to 77 per cent), but by 20 percentage points for African Americans (to 65 per cent).

William Julius Wilson (1987, 1996) has written extensively about the disproportionate effects of labour market changes from the early 1970s to the early 1990s on African American men. He recognizes the importance of the race-neutral, structural changes that have led to the declines in employment for all less educated males (i.e. technological changes,

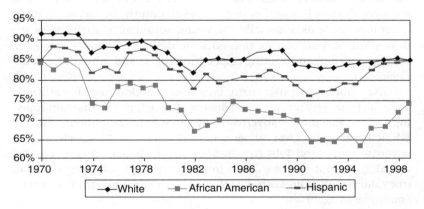

Figure 6.4 Percentage of Males, ages 25–54, with a High School Education or less with a Job Last Week, 1970–1999

globalization, etc.). But he incorporates other factors to explain the much larger employment decline for African American men than for whites and Hispanics. Wilson is critical of both conservative and liberal scholars. The former tend to assume that jobs are available to anyone who is willing to work and that the higher rate of black joblessness is due primarily to differences in motivation and cultural factors, expressed via attitudes and behaviours that are not conducive to employment in the changing labour market. Liberals, on the other hand, tend to assume that joblessness is due primarily to unequal opportunities in the public school system, which limit the development of marketable skills and persisting prejudice and discrimination in the housing and labour markets, which make employment less accessible and less attainable for African Americans relative to whites and other ethnic groups.

Wilson challenges both sides of the political spectrum. He writes that 'Although race is clearly a significant variable in the social outcomes of inner-city blacks' (1996: xiv), it is not the only factor; others include culture, social psychology and structural conditions. He does not deny the existence of negative 'ghetto-related' behaviours that make some inner-city residents unattractive job applicants for some employers. Rather, his research on the lives of inner-city residents suggests that most adhere to mainstream values and behaviours. Many of those who deviate from the mainstream labour market are reacting primarily to their environment, especially their difficulty finding jobs. The 'decline in legitimate employment opportunities among inner-city residents has increased incentives to sell drugs' (1996: 21), and the increase in crime and drug-dealing has further negative effects on the behaviour of other inner-city residents, especially the young who may 'come to view the possession of weapons as necessary or desirable for self-protection, settling disputes, and gaining respect from peers and other individuals' (1996: 21).

Wilson documents that many employers develop negative attitudes about all inner-city residents and discourage black applicants from applying for available jobs by advertising only in selected neighbourhood and ethnic newspapers. Over 40 per cent of the firms in his sample did not advertise entry-level jobs in Chicago's major dailies. Others reported that they did not recruit workers from the Chicago public high schools (they did recruit from Catholic schools) or welfare programmes or state employment agencies.

Regardless of which came first – the attitudes of residents and a lack of labour force skills due to poor schooling opportunities or the employer's prejudices and concerns about worker honesty and dependability – the result is a high rate of joblessness and distrust. 'Inner-city black men grow bitter and resentful in the face of their employment prospects and often manifest or express these feelings in their harsh, often dehumanizing, low-wage work settings' (1996: 114). This leads employers to make 'assumptions about the inner-city black workers *in general* and reach decisions based on those assumptions before they have had a chance to review systematically the qualifications of an individual applicant' (1996: 137). As a result, many qualified 'black inner-city applicants are never given the chance to prove their qualifications on an individual level because they are systematically screened out by the selective recruitment process' (1996: 137).

The 'reappearance' of some jobs in the inner cities during the economic boom of the 1990s led to increased employment for all men, including men with a high school degree or less. The employment rate for this group for African Americans and Hispanics increased by about 9 percentage points, compared to 3 percentage points for whites (see Figure 6.4). In 1999, about 85 per cent of these less educated white and Hispanic men between the ages of 25 and 54 had a job in the week prior to the March survey, compared to 74 per cent for African Americans. Again, one can conclude that economic growth is necessary for absolute and relative progress for minorities, but not sufficient to eliminate the black/white gap. The race-specific factors articulated by Wilson remain salient, as there was even a 5 percentage point employment gap in 1999 between white and African American men with a college degree or more (95 vs. 90 per cent, data for college graduates not shown).

Figure 6.5 plots the percentage of women with a high school degree of less, between the ages of 25 and 54, who had a job in the survey week over the 1970–9 period. A comparison of Figures 6.4 and 6.5 reveals that the trends for women differ dramatically from those for men. (For greater detail on labour market trends among women by race/ethnicity see Conrad, 2001.) Whereas the percentage of less educated men with a job fell between 1970 and 1999 by 6 percentage points for whites, 10 percentage points for African Americans and remained constant for Hispanics, employment for women in this age/education group increased rapidly for all three groups. Employment increased by 25 percentage points for white women (from 45 to 70 per cent), by 13 points for African American women (from 54 to 67 per cent) and by 20 points for Hispanic women (from 37 to 57 per cent). The gender gap in employment between white men and women in this education group fell from 47 percentage points in 1970 (92 vs. 45 per cent) to 15 points in 1999

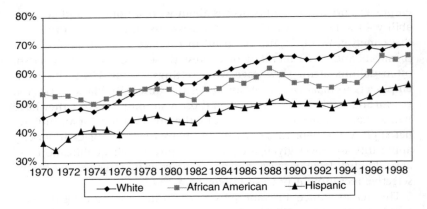

Figure 6.5   Percentage of Females, ages 25–54, with a High School Education or Less with a Job Last Week, 1970–1999

(85 vs. 70 per cent); for African Americans the gender gap fell from 21 to 7 points; for Hispanics, from 48 to 28 points. The increased employment of women is part of the reason why median family income grew over most of the past three decades even though inflation-adjusted male earnings (discussed next) were declining. (For a discussion of the contribution of women's earnings to family income, see Cancian and Reed, 2002.)

Figure 6.6 shows trends in real annual earnings for male workers between the ages of 25 and 54 who have a high school education or less; men who did not work at all during the year are not included in these calculations. The past three decades have been difficult ones for less-educated male workers of all race/ethnic groups. Real annual earnings were lower in 1999 than they were in 1970, falling in most of the years between 1973 and 1993 and then rising after that. Between 1973 and 1993, annual earnings fell by 22, 15 and 27 per cent, respectively for whites, African Americans and Hispanics. Between 1993 and 1999, they rose by 10, 24 and 14 per cent respectively, with minorities having the more rapid gain in earnings. Mean real earnings (in constant 1999 dollars) were lower in 1999 than they were in 1970 for these less-educated white men ($33,389 vs. $35,373) and for Hispanics ($23,051 vs. $25,543), but were higher for African Americans ($26,761 vs. $23.070).

In 1970, the ratio of the mean earnings for minority men with a high school degree or less relative to those of similar white male workers was 0.65 for African Americans and 0.72 for Hispanics; by 1999, it had

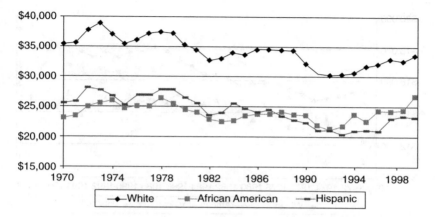

Figure 6.6 Mean Earnings for Male Workers, ages 25–54, with a High School Education or Less, 1970–1999

increased to 0.80 for African Americans, but had fallen to 0.69 for Hispanics. Similar patterns are revealed when one compares earnings trends for male workers with higher education levels (data not shown). However, the relative progress of African Americans would be less if one compared all men in this age/education category, instead of only men with earnings as is done in Figure 6.6, because of the lower employment rate of African American men discussed above.

Figure 6.7 shows trends in mean annual earnings for female workers with a high school degree or less. Again, the trend differs dramatically by gender – the real annual earnings of female workers increased steadily, whereas those for male workers declined. Earnings rose by 35 per cent between 1970 and 1999 for white working women (from $14,245 to $19,209), by 41 per cent for African American working women (from $11,950 to $16,834); and by 22 per cent for Hispanic working women (from $12,865 to $15,742). In 1999, the ratio of the annual earnings of African American women workers in this age/education class to those of similar white women was 0.88; the ratio for Hispanics was 0.82.

We have presented evidence on trends in five dimensions of economic well-being – poverty and affluence for all persons, median family income for all families, and the employment rate and annual inflation-adjusted mean earning of working men and women between the ages of 25 and 54 with a high school degree or less. In each dimension, there

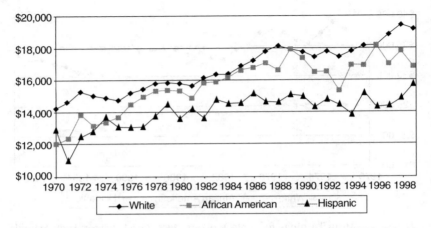

Figure 6.7   Mean Earnings for Female Workers, ages 25–54, with a High School Education or Less, 1970–1999

was substantial improvement during the economic boom of the 1990s in terms of the absolute economic status of each group and in terms of the well-being of African Americans relative to that of whites. However, large disparities remain that are unlikely to be substantially diminished soon by economic growth on its own. And, in some of these dimensions, particularly the employment rate and real earnings of male workers, there was little or no progress over the three decades.

Beyond economic trends: racism, social psychology and identity

Economists tend to focus only on trends in relative economic well-being. However, sociologists and psychologists also call attention to the social psychological consequences of the racial/ethnic differences in income employment and earnings that we have just reviewed. We focus in this section on four areas in which persisting racial inequalities affect life chances and lifestyles: (1) racial disparities in wealth; (2) perceptions of racial inequalities and emotional well-being; (3) the perceptions of racial discrimination and rational attitudes; and (4) the interrelationships among racial integration, parity and harmony. Our analysis addresses African Americans and whites, as that has been the focus of most of the research on these topics.

Racial disparities in wealth

The current employment and annual income and earnings data presented above tend to underestimate the extent of racial economic disparities in any year because they do not account for differences in assets. For example, Oliver and Shapiro (1995) show that, in the late 1980s, white households had nearly 12 times the median net worth of black households. In an update, Oliver and Shapiro (2001) document that in 1994 the median net worth of whites had fallen to 8.6 times that of blacks – $52,994 vs. $6,127. Even after they statistically controlled for differences in income, education, occupation and family structure, the wealth of African Americans remained a small proportion of that of whites. Additionally, Oliver and Shapiro (2001) note that racial differences in holdings of financial assets, which are more readily converted into cash during times of emergency than are other assets, are even greater. In 1994 the median white household held about $7,400 in net financial assets, whereas the median black household had only $100; and about three-fifths of black households compared to only about one-quarter of whites held zero dollars or less in net financial assets. Other analyses also suggest that, despite the economic boom of the 1990s, the racial wealth gap remains very large (Wolff, 1998; Panel Study of Income Dynamics, 2000).

These asset differences mean that blacks and whites with the same income tend to have different levels of economic security. Oliver and Shapiro (1995: 92) caution that wealth differences cause the 'economic footing' of many blacks who have achieved middle-class incomes to remain 'precarious'.

Perceptions of racial inequalities and emotional well-being

African American families not only have lower levels of wealth and economic security, they also have low expectations about their prospects for attaining racial equality in economic well-being. In a national survey, Blendon et al. (1995) reported that 46 per cent of black adults believed that racial problems would not be solved in their children's lifetime; nearly one in four doubted that racial equality would ever be achieved. After the 1992 riots in Los Angeles, a New York Times/CBS News poll indicated that 65 per cent of blacks expected that race riots would still be happening 25 years from that point (Smith and Seltzer, 2000). A recent poll of Californians found that, when asked to look ahead to 2020, 46 per cent of blacks, compared to 36 per cent of whites, responded that race and ethnic relations were more likely to get worse than to improve (Hajnal and Baldassare, 2001: 12).

Given the trends in income and employment discussed above, one might predict that economically disadvantaged African Americans would be more likely to be pessimistic about the future than their middle-class counterparts. The data indicate, however, that more affluent blacks express the most frustration with racial stratification (Essed, 1991; Cose, 1993; Feagin and Sikes, 1994; Jackson et al., 1995). Those who are relatively well off seem more willing than poorer blacks to cite race as having played a role in unfair events that have occurred on the job and elsewhere, and less likely to attribute these events to lack of effort or some other personal attribute.

According to Hochschild (1995: 73), 'Well-off African Americans see *more* racial discrimination than do poor blacks, see less decline in discrimination, expect less improvement in the future, and claim to have experienced more in their own lives'. This is a reversal of historical patterns. For example, she cites several surveys that asked 'Do whites want to keep blacks down?' In 1966, 43 per cent of poor blacks and 29 per cent of middle-class blacks responded affirmatively. But, by 1991, the percentage of poor blacks responding 'yes' had declined by about half to 22 per cent, whereas for middle-class blacks the per cent responding 'yes' increased to 33 per cent. Thus, at the time of the civil rights movement, the black middle class was less likely to think that whites wanted to keep blacks down, but by the 1990s, they were more likely to think this.

The psychological consequences of racial stratification are significant. Self-perceived experiences of racial discrimination are associated with increased psychiatric symptoms, clinical disorder and lowered levels of subjective well-being (Landrine and Klonoff, 1996; Thompson, 1996; Broman, 1997; Brown et al., 1999). For example, blacks who accept negative characterizations of blacks as a group tended to report higher levels of psychiatric symptoms and lower levels of well-being (Taylor, 1990; Taylor and Jackson, 1990). Rumbaut (1994) found that the expectation of racial or ethnic discrimination in adulthood was linked to increased depressive symptoms and reduced self-esteem among black adolescents. Brown et al. (2001) found that black adolescents who worried about race relations or were pessimistic about progress towards racial harmony reported lower levels of happiness and diminished satisfaction with their lives. The frequency of discriminatory experiences and the persistence of racial inequalities undermine blacks' ability to protect their emotional health and to be optimistic.

Racial discrimination and racial attitudes

Racial stratification has negative effects on racial/ethnic minorities regardless of their socio-economic status. For example, a large proportion of African Americans in recent surveys report discriminatory experiences, such as being embarrassed, harassed, ignored, fired, followed, ridiculed, singled out or otherwise assaulted because of their race or ethnic heritage (Landrum-Brown, 1990; Essed, 1991; Sigelman and Welch, 1991; Landrine and Klonoff, 1996). Even wealthy blacks report many experiences of racial discrimination, such as tokenism, racial slurs, marginalization and loyalty tests (Landrum-Brown, 1990; Jackson et al., 1995; Collins, 1997).

How might one interpret the continuing experiences of discrimination almost 40 years after the Civil Rights Act and against the background of modest improvements in the relative economic standing of African Americans? One explanation might be that whites may continue to discriminate or express racial hostility in interactions with members of minority groups because they perceive successful minorities as having taken jobs or positions in selective universities that previously they might have had. However, this does not seem to be the case. When whites and blacks in the Detroit metropolitan area were asked in 1992, 'Have you ever felt at any time in the past that you were refused a job because of your race or ethnicity?' only 7 per cent of whites but 40 per cent of African Americans responded 'yes' (Farley et al., 2000: 233–4).

Even if they have not personally felt themselves to have experienced discrimination, whites tend to be unsympathetic to affirmative action policies. A recent California poll found that only 27 per cent of whites, but 66 per cent of Latinos and 78 per cent of blacks agreed that 'affirmative action programs be continued for the foreseeable future' and that 46 per cent of whites, but only 21 per cent of Latinos and 13 per cent of blacks, 'opposed employers and colleges using outreach programs to hire minority workers and find minority students' (Hajnal and Baldassare, 2001: 15).

Additionally, whites are much less likely than racial/ethnic minorities to report that the extent of current discrimination has negative economic consequences. Kluegel and Bobo (2001) report the results of a mid-1990s survey conducted in four metropolitan areas. Respondents were asked, 'In general, how much discrimination is there that hurts the chances of a "specific group" to get good paying jobs? Do you think that there is a lot, some, only a little, or none at all?' In Atlanta, 46 per cent of whites chose 'none' or 'a little' when asked about African Americans; in Boston, Detroit and Los Angeles, about one quarter of whites chose these categories. The modal response among blacks in these areas was 'a lot' with the percentages choosing this category ranging from 57 to 69 per cent. Whites were also asked about discrimination against Hispanics in Boston and Los Angeles, and 27 and 29 per cent, respectively, selected 'none' or 'a little'. In contrast, 49 per cent of Hispanics in Boston and 59 per cent in L.A. chose 'a lot'.

Racial integration, racial parity or racial harmony

According to the 1996 General Social Survey (GSS), 65 per cent of whites believed that conditions of blacks had improved in recent years, whereas only 36 per cent of blacks concurred (Smith and Seltzer, 2000). In part, perceptual estrangement between racial groups can be attributed to an ambiguous operational definition of the 'problem' (Sigelman and Welch, 1991; Cose, 1993; Smith and Seltzer, 2000). That is, 'What is the race problem? Do blacks and whites disagree about potential policy solutions because they conceive of the problem differently?'

Small (1991) theorizes that three major facets define the contemporary race problem: racial integration, racial parity and racial harmony. Racial integration focuses on bringing members of each race into close proximity, based on the view that distance breeds ignorance, whereas contact breeds acceptance. Racial parity focuses on the goal of equalizing the distributions of outcomes for comparable whites and blacks in domains such as education, occupational status, incomes, life expectancy, infant mortality, etc. Racial harmony reflects a situation in which antagonism is low and positive effect is high.

Progress along one of these dimensions does not guarantee progress along the others. For example, black children can be integrated into the same schools that white children attend, yet be tracked away from college-preparatory classes, with little effect on racial parity in college attendance. Blacks and whites can attend the same college classes, but have minimal social contacts, with little effect on racial harmony. Similarly, an increase in the percentage of affluent African Americans may have little effect on residential integration, given persisting housing market practices and the tendency of whites to move out of neighbourhoods once the black population increases beyond a certain low percentage (Farley et al., 2000: Chapter 7).

Our intent in this section was to suggest that policy analysts and policy-makers should pay attention to the social psychological consequences of racial disparities. Hochschild (1995) points out that even if measured racial gaps in economic well-being have narrowed over the past 40 years, that perceptions of this progress differ dramatically by race. She points out that, 'African Americans increasingly believe that racial discrimination is worsening and that it inhibits their race's ability to participate in the American dream; whites increasingly believe that discrimination is lessening and that blacks have the same chance to participate in the dream as whites' (p. 56) and that 'Whites are angry that blacks refuse to see the fairness and openness of the system; blacks are angry that whites refuse to see the biases and blockages of the system' (p. 68).

We now turn to a discussion of some public policy options that, if successful, might reduce perceived, as well as measured, racial differences in economic well-being.

A policy agenda to reduce racial/ethnic economic disparities[8]

A realistic assessment of the future economic status of racial/ethnic minorities must confront several constraints imposed by the social and economic history of the United States. First, there are constraints linked to decisions made long ago about the location of plants, offices and residences. A large proportion of the nation's poor, especially poor racial/ethnic minorities, live in inner cities that have an older housing stock, are losing population and have infrastructure and tax base problems.[9] In contrast, in the outer suburban ring, open land is still available for residential, commercial and industrial developments. Most population growth and most of the new jobs in recent decades have occurred in these mostly white, higher income areas. The combination of high levels of residential segregation and the concentration of minorities in the urban core and the deconcentration of employment adds a spatial component to socio-economic disparities and policies designed to reduce them (Wilson, 1987, 1996; Yinger, 1995, 2002).

Second, there is the industrial legacy. Many less-educated workers, especially racial and ethnic minority men, achieved middle-class incomes during the post-World War II economic boom by working in well-paid, unionized manufacturing jobs. Since the early 1970s, however, these jobs have disappeared at a rapid rate. American manufacturing has successfully restructured over the last 15 years primarily by becoming more skill-intensive and more capital-intensive. For example, by the early 1990s, there were more jobs in the temporary help industry than in the motor vehicles and equipment and steel industry combined (Danziger and Gottschalk, 1995: 147–8). Productivity in the latter industries increased rapidly enough that greater output could be produced with many fewer production workers.

The third constraint is continuing white distrust of blacks and black distrust of whites. Although racial attitudes improved after World War II and especially after the civil rights movement, such that almost everyone now endorses principles of equal opportunity, many whites still endorse the stereotypes that blacks tend to work less diligently than whites, tend to be less intelligent and tend to be harder to get along with (Farley et al., 2000: chapter 8; Bobo, 2001; Kluegel and Bobo, 2001). And, discriminatory practices, especially in the housing market, continue to be widespread (Yinger, 2002).

The history of racial conflict and distrust helps explain why some employers are reluctant to hire black workers and why whites generally avoid neighbourhoods with more than token numbers of black neighbours. African-Americans consistently report that the playing field is far from level, and that they expect discrimination when they search for a job or buy a home. Many African Americans view the US as a colour-coded society, with whites holding most of the decision-making power and using it to favour other whites for good jobs and good homes. This racial distrust affects political and economic decisions, such as ones about the placement of bus routes and subway stops, funding for public schools, the placement of power plants, etc. Each race distrusts the other and tends to see a zero-sum game in which advances for once race come at the expense of the other.

In addition to historical constraints, the future of racial/ethnic disparities depends upon the nation's economic progress, changes in governmental policies and in the civic values that Americans hold. As we documented above, a high rate of economic growth is crucial for improving the living standards of all citizens, especially those of racial and ethnic minorities. However, periods of robust economic growth and declining racial disparities have not been the norm. They occurred in the 1960s and the 1990s, but the years from the mid-1970s to the late 1980s were ones of slow economic growth during which some racial/ethnic economic disparities widened.

Unfortunately, there has been no counterpart to the economic boom of the 1990s in the realm of governmental policies. The economic boom of the 1960s was accompanied by a 'policy boom' that substantially increased federal spending on a variety of social policies designed to reduce racial/ethnic and poor/non-poor disparities. There was, in response to the War on Poverty and the civil rights movement, a public and Congressional willingness to move the nation in the direction of equal opportunities in the hope that equal outcomes would follow. The Office of Federal Contract Compliance and the Equal Employment Opportunities Commission pressured large employers to hire women and minority workers; the federal courts upheld affirmative action programmes that sought to increase both employment and the occupational advancement of blacks and women.

In recent years, in contrast, government efforts in most areas of social policy, including enforcement of anti-discrimination efforts, are less vigorous than they were from the mid-1960s to the mid-1970s. Some programmes providing opportunities for minorities remain in place, but there has been a substantial reduction in the amount and scope of federal efforts, especially with regard to employment and training programmes for disadvantaged workers. Although there is still a set-aside of federal and some local construction funds to minority contractors, many similar programmes were overturned in the courts and then eliminated. Affirmative action is also currently under attack; its future rests in decisions that the US Supreme Court will render in the next few years.

While the economic boom of the 1990s was not expected by the authors of *A Common Destiny*, there have been no unforeseen policy actions trying to reduce racial/ethnic disparities. President Clinton, in 1997, did attempt to begin a national conversation about race, but it seems to have had little lasting effect. The report that was produced by his task force, *America Becoming: Racial Trends and Their Consequences* (Smelser et al., 2001), in contrast to *A Common Destiny*, did not offer any policy recommendations or provide a summary consensus of the volumes' chapters. Although the Clinton administration supported many policy initiatives that would have raised the incomes of all of the poor, and hence disproportionately helped racial/ethnic minorities (such as additional increases in the minimum wage or the provision of national health insurance), it was unable to gain Congressional approval for them.

In 2001, the Bush administration adopted as its highest priority a very large personal income tax cut that primarily benefited the highest income families. As a result, it provided proportionately less tax relief to racial/ethnic minorities than to whites. Given the tax cut, the fact that the economy slipped into recession in early 2001, and the increased spending on defence and domestic security in response to the attacks of 11 September 2001, the federal surplus quickly disappeared. This leaves the current administration and Congress, even if they had the political inclination to move forward, little in the way of federal funds to launch major policy initiatives to reduce poverty in general, or ones designed to reduce racial/ethnic disparities in particular. Recessions tend to increase the economic gap between African Americans and other groups because their unemployment rates are more responsive to the business cycle. Thus, the data presented above may represent a peak in their economic status relative to that of whites.[10]

In the long run, there may be some prospects for a civil public discussion of racial/ethnic disparities. The population is more highly educated than ever, implying a greater understanding of the nation's confrontational racial history and of the country's ideals. The nation is experiencing a dramatic racial/ethnic change as the Latino and Asian populations grow rapidly while the white and black populations increase slowly. Although it is difficult now to imagine widespread support for innovative civil rights laws or for affirmative action programmes, it may be possible for some political leader to open a dialogue on what equal opportunity means and what must be done to facilitate the removal of barriers to opportunity. If such a dialogue were successful, race might lose some of its importance as a determinant of economic status in the United States. Against this background, we now put forward a few public policy proposals that could reduce economic and racial disparities. A major goal of such policies would be to generate positive interactions across a variety of policy domains. For example, consider the following scenario, in which a positive labour market trend leads to positive population flows and favourable changes in racial attitudes.

We would begin by trying to reverse the adverse effects of labour market changes by implementing policies that both enhance the skills of job-seekers, thereby increasing their employment prospects, and increase the demand for workers with moderate skills and for those without college training, thereby raising their earnings so that poverty is reduced. If these labour market policies were successful, poverty and unemployment would fall. Higher family incomes would contribute to increased demand for housing and other goods, further stimulating economic activity. Increased employment and earnings would promote housing renovation and retail activity in poor areas, thus raising the local tax base and tax revenues.

Assume also that another set of policies, using these additional revenues, could be successfully put into place to upgrade the quality of urban public services, especially with regards to police protection, infrastructure and public schools. The resulting improvement might then discourage the continuing flight of most whites and the black middle class from central cities. Given the reduced poverty, increased employment and improvement of public services, some suburban residents might even move back to the central cities, thereby reducing racial segregation and diminishing racial stereotypes.

Of course, hopes for this kind of urban revival have been discussed for the past 40 years. And this hypothetical set of positive externalities is based on many optimistic assumptions, the most important being favourable macro-economic trends and the assumed implementation of successful labour market policies. Successful urban revitalization has been an elusive goal, with the policies that have been tried thus far yielding disappointing results (Ferguson, 2002). When one compares almost any American suburb with its central city, one still finds a series of persisting inequalities: white/black, economically comfortable/poor, low unemployment/high unemployment, schools with strong reputations/schools with bad reputations, low crime rates/high crime rates. We are not so naive as to think that the policy options we advocate could quickly eliminate these persistent divisions and inequalities; we simply think that they can be reduced.

Two additional public policy mechanisms for addressing the employment problems of racial/ethnic minorities are (a) enhanced anti-discrimination enforcement in the housing market (e.g. rental, sales and mortgage practices) to facilitate racial residential integration, and hence integration of the local public schools, and (b) enhanced anti-discrimination enforcement in the labour market (e.g. employer recruiting, hiring and promotion practices) to improve employment opportunities for minorities. Stepped-up enforcement of anti-discrimination laws, given the attitudes of whites discussed above, however, tends to exacerbate racial tensions and makes it more difficult to gain acceptance for other needed public policies. This is one reason why Wilson (1996) proposed a 'comprehensive race-neutral initiative to address economic and social inequality' (p. 205) that did not emphasize race-specific policies, such as affirmative action. The key components of Wilson's policy proposals have the same primary goals as our proposals – improvements of public schools to increase labour force skills and raise earnings of the next generation and policies to supplement low earnings of today's workers and the provision of public jobs of last resort to the persistently unemployed.

As discussed earlier, the major source of economic problems for most less educated workers are 'race-neutral' labour market changes that began in the early 1970s – especially the spread of labour-saving technological innovations and declines in the percentage of employment accounted for by manufacturing industries. These changes have reduced the employment and earnings prospects for the less educated, especially African Americans, because their economic gains in the quarter-century following World War II were largely based on high-wage manufacturing jobs. Responding to these labour market changes requires policies (1) to increase the rewards to work for low-skill workers; (2) to raise the educational attainment and skills of the young so that they will have higher wages when they enter the labour force; and (3) to provide public jobs of last resort for the most disadvantaged whom employers are not inclined to hire, even when unemployment rates are low.

What is missing are not good policy options, but the political will to take bold actions to confront the multiple economic and social problems relating to racial/ethnic disparities. Given political reality, we do not expect that describing some promising policies will lead to their adoption. These policy options tend to require a substantial infusion of public funds. Yet, as long as 'no new taxes' remains the dominant political mantra in the US, it is unlikely that these initiatives will soon be implemented. We group the policy options we favour into four categories – labour market supply-side strategies, mobility strategies, labour market demand-side strategies, and anti-discrimination strategies – and highlight a single exemplary policy in each.

Labour market supply-side strategies

Over the long run, improving educational attainment and labour market skills offer the best prospects for raising employment and earnings and closing racial/ethnic gaps in socio-economic status. In the late 1960s, if a young man graduated from high school, he had an excellent chance of finding a job that provided good wages and benefits. In the early twenty-first century, however, many high school graduates do not earn enough on their own to raise a family above the poverty line. It is critical that investments in young people be increased, with goals of reducing the high rates of school dropout in the inner city, raising the skills of high school graduates, and increasing enrolment of youth from low-income families in junior and four-year colleges.

Unfortunately, the skills and abilities and achievements needed to succeed in today's labour market are not being learned by low-income students in many troubled schools, especially those schools that are highly segregated. Compared to suburban school districts, central city schools have older buildings that require more maintenance, enrol more disadvantaged students who require additional attention and services, and have difficulty recruiting and retaining qualified teachers. Thus, to achieve the same educational outcomes as suburban schools, central city schools would need greater funding per student and higher quality teachers.

Apart from finances, central city school districts have been plagued by bureaucratic inefficiencies and other administrative impediments. Such schools would have great difficulty delivering the educational services needed to prepare their students for the demands of today's workplace even if they received additional funding. Although there is agreement on the need to improve schools, there are few models for achieving success on a large scale. There are promising results in early education programmes and after-school mentoring programmes that have raised school performance and attendance, but these programmes have been small and have operated outside of the public education system (Karoly, 2002).

Moving central city residents to the suburbs

Mobility strategies, like supply-side strategies, have been widely discussed over the past 40 years. As with public education reforms, there are fewer success stories than there are disappointments. We mention one promising strategy – 'opening up' the suburbs. Access to less skilled jobs, especially those in small firms and those located away from public transportation routes, would be increased if greater numbers of low-income, especially minority, central city residents could obtain affordable housing in the suburbs.

Residential relocation policies seek to raise employment and earnings prospects for two generations. Commuting costs are reduced and information about and access to job vacancies increase for parents. If these programmes are successful, adults will have better labour market outcomes. Even if earnings gains to parents are modest, however, the children will attend higher quality suburban schools, with likely increases in their educational performance and attainment.

The Gautreaux programme has documented such gains for both parents and children. The programme resulted from a 1976 Supreme Court consent decree in a lawsuit brought by Chicago public housing residents against the US Department of Housing and Urban Development. The residents charged that city and federal policies deliberately and unconstitutionally concentrated the black poor in public housing projects (see Rosenbaum, 1995). The settlement gave more than 5,000 public housing residents and those on waiting lists in 1981 housing vouchers that they could use to rent units outside the projects, either in the city of Chicago or its suburbs.

Rosenbaum evaluated the programme's 'quasi-experimental design'. That is, some former housing project residents used the subsidies to rent apartments in inner-city neighbourhoods, while others rented in suburban neighbourhoods where few minorities lived. He found modest gains in employment for the parents who moved from the projects to the suburbs compared to those who moved from the projects to other areas in the city of Chicago, but significant educational gains for the children. For example, 20 per cent of the interviewed children who attended city schools dropped out before completing a high school degree, whereas only 5 per cent of those attending suburban schools dropped out; and 54 per cent of the suburban high school graduates enrolled in higher education, compared to only 21 per cent of the city high school graduates.

The Clinton administration implemented a ten-year demonstration programme modelled on the Gautreaux programme and designed to test the hypothesis that poor families will be better off in a variety of economic and educational domains if they move out of neighbourhoods of concentrated poverty. The Moving to Opportunity (MTO) programme began to operate in five metropolitan areas (Baltimore, Boston, Chicago, Los Angeles and New York) in the early 1990s. MTO aims to move low-income families with children from high poverty areas (census tracts with a poverty rate of 40 per cent or more) to low poverty areas (with rates of 10 per cent or less). It provides housing vouchers for participating families, as well as assistance in housing search and counselling about housing options (Goering and Feins, 1997). Early evaluations of MTO have been promising for both the parents and the children (Katz et al., 2001).

Unfortunately, the programme expansion to other metro areas sought by the Clinton administration was not passed by Congress, in part, because of vocal opposition from white suburban residents who objected to the prospects of even small numbers of poor and minority families moving into their neighbourhoods (Yinger, 1995: 235–6). This is yet another example of the negative effects of hostile racial attitudes on public policies designed to break down the spatial concentration of poverty.

Labour market demand-side strategies

Despite a robust economic boom in the 1990s, the employment prospects and earnings levels of less educated workers remain tenuous. Through no fault of their own, they face much bleaker labour market prospects than did their counterparts in the years from the late 1940s through to the early 1970s when the economy was booming for workers of all skill levels. Many of the poor want to work and are willing to take minimum wage jobs, but do not have the skills that firms now demand. Hence, we advocate experimentation with public service jobs of last resort (for further discussion, see Danziger and Gottschalk, 1995: Chapter 8). Public service employment (PSE) programmes have a long history in the United States, but have not been politically popular since the Great Depression of the 1930s. President Reagan terminated the last large PSE programme when he eliminated the Comprehensive Employment and Training Act (CETA) in the early 1980s.

We propose that the federal government subsidize transitional low-wage jobs of last resort to the poor, about three-quarters of whom are members of racial/ethnic minorities. The federal government, for example, might pay 80 per cent of the total costs – but the positions would be administered by non-profit or community-based organizations or by local governmental agencies, which would have to fund the remainder. The goal would be to have the workers perform tasks that are socially beneficial, but for which there is little effective labour demand. We envisage workers providing labour-intensive public services that would be valued in poor communities and which are generally provided in more affluent communities – monitoring of playgrounds, neighbourhood maintenance and assisting the elderly, for example.

Graduated job ladders would provide rewards to workers who succeeded in the PSE position, but wages would be lower than the worker would receive in the private sector, thereby providing an incentive to take any available job. Employees who failed to meet performance standards would be dismissed. Those hired might be limited to a year to two years of PSE, after which they should have acquired the experience and skills needed to get a private sector job.

The jobs would provide a social safety net to poor persons who want to work, but cannot find a regular private sector or public sector job. They are particularly needed now because welfare reform has placed time limits on the cash social safety net and some welfare recipients, despite great pressure to do so, cannot find and/or maintain a job (Danziger, 2000; Danziger et al., 2000).

Anti-discrimination strategies

Although Federal and state laws ban racial discrimination in all areas of public life, enforcement is difficult and often lax; hence, the playing field is still not level when it comes to race. Because the government has been reluctant to enforce the laws vigorously, there are opportunities for private organizations to conduct audits for racial/ethnic and gender discrimination in the labour and housing markets.

Blatant racial discrimination, widespread prior to the 1960s, is now infrequent. Indeed, many employers note their commitment to non-discrimination in job advertisements, and most real estate brokers' offices post statements about their dedication to equal opportunities. However, less obvious types of racial discrimination continue and contribute to persisting high levels of racial segregation.[11] Some brokers still will not show black and white home seekers the same housing, some underwriters still do not provide home insurance to units located in minority neighbourhoods, and some police officers stop black drivers much more frequently than those who are white.

The hiring patterns documented by employer surveys (e.g. Holzer, 1996) suggest that establishments located in the suburbs, particularly small establishments serving mostly white customers, continue to prefer white applicants over African Americans. Thus, enforcement of existing equal employment laws needs to be enhanced to ensure that all establishments abide by them. Indeed, there is a complementarity between 'mobility' policies designed to improve the access of inner city residents to suburban establishments, and anti-discrimination enforcement that ensures that applicants are treated fairly once they apply for these jobs.

One way to promote fair housing and fair employment practices is to conduct frequent audit studies under the auspices of civil rights and civic organizations. Employers and landlords would be less likely to discriminate if they thought an applicant might be a participant in an audit study and that their practices would be exposed in the press and subject to lawsuits in federal courts.

Summary

Despite much progress over the past 40 years, the United States remains divided along racial and class lines. As one analyst of racial attitudes and race relations recently noted, 'We have high ideals, but cannot agree on the depth of the remaining problem – we are open to integration, but in very limited terms and only in specific areas. There is political stagnation over some types of affirmative action and persistent negative stereotyping of racial minorities; and a wide gulf in perceptions regarding the importance of racial discrimination remains' (Bobo, 2001: 294).

Although African American and Hispanic economic elites have emerged in the post-civil rights era, racial/ethnic economic disparities remain very large on all the economic measures reviewed. The policies we propose, if successfully implemented, could reduce inequalities in educational attainment, employment, occupational achievement and earnings. Without a comprehensive public policy strategy, however, it is likely that the divisions we have described will continue and, if macro-economic trends turn unfavourable, will worsen.

Notes

1. The data for Hispanics presented here should be interpreted with caution because of the dramatic increase in Hispanic immigration over the past several decades. Immigrants have below-average education and hence lower levels of economic well-being. Our analysis utilizes annual data for the years from 1970 through to 1999. However, the Census Bureau began asking about an individual's nativity only in 1994. Thus, we cannot distinguish between trends for US-born as compared to foreign-born Hispanics. It is likely that trends for the native-born are more favourable than the trends shown here for all Hispanics. See Smith (2001) for further discussion of the effects of immigration on measured economic well-being.

   The Census Bureau interviews about 60,000 households per year. Until the late 1980s, the samples were not drawn in such a way as to produce statistically reliable estimates of economic well-being for Asian-Americans, Native-Americans or for distinct sub-groups of Hispanics (e.g. Puerto Ricans). Economic well-being for more detailed race/ethnic groups and for persons classified by US-born or foreign-born are available in the Decennial Censuses. However, the micro-data from the 2000 Census were not available until 2003.
2. In 1999, the official poverty line was $16,895 for a family of four with two related children and about half that for one person living on her own. The Census reports pre-tax money income and thus does not include non-cash income or tax credits and does not exclude taxes paid. The poverty line varies with family size and has been increased since the mid-1960s only to correct for inflation.
3. Using a relative poverty measure (40 per cent of each country's median adjusted disposable personal income), Smeeding et al. (2002) show that the US rate in the late 1990s was the highest of 17 countries in the Luxembourg Income Study. Eleven of the 17 had rates that were half or less than the US rate.
4. Our poverty rates, median family incomes and mean earnings differ from those published by the Census Bureau because we use a consistent consumer price index, the CPI-U-X1, to correct for inflation throughout the period. The Census switched to this index in the early 1980s, but did not go back and recompute poverty, median income, etc. using this index for earlier years. Many economists believe that the official price index overstates inflation, and hence overstates poverty and understates growth in income and earnings. Our view is that these biases are relatively small. More importantly, they do not affect comparisons across racial/ethnic groups because the progress of each group would change by the same amount if an alternative price index were used.

5. Because a family with more members requires more income to attain the same level of economic well-being as a smaller household, we present size-adjusted medians in Figure 6.3. We first divide the income of each family by its poverty line to correct for differences in family size. Then we compute the median of this ratio and multiply it by the poverty line for a family of four of two adults and two children. This corrects for both family size changes over time and differences in family size across each of the race/ethnic subgroups. The medians reported here differ from published Census Bureau medians, which do not adjust for family size.

6. See Holzer (2001) and Smith (2001) for further discussion. Smith concludes, 'Because minority workers' skills place them in the lower part of the wage distribution, increasing wage dispersion across skill levels will decrease their wages more than those of majority workers. The last 20 years were actually a time during which slowly evolving historical forces continued to close the wage gap of Black and White male workers. These forces were simply overwhelmed by the structural shift of rising wage dispersion' (p. 95).

7. The data in Figures 6.4–6.7 are 'age-adjusted', that is, they were reweighted to match the distribution of the total population in 2000. As a result, differential changes in age for the race/ethnic groups do not affect the trends.

8. This section draws on Farley et al. (2000: Chapter 9).

9. These local infrastructure and tax base problems have more negative implications for the poor in the US than the poor in other industrialized countries because of the greater extent of governmental decentralization in the US. For example, many public services, most importantly, primary and secondary education, are paid for by funds raised by state and local governments, as opposed to the federal government.

10. Between December 2000 and March 2002, the civilian unemployment rate for all males 16 years of age and older increased from 3.5 to 5.0 per cent for whites, from 5.8 to 7.3 per cent for Hispanics, and from 7.5 to 10.7 per cent for African Americans.

11. Segregation levels have fallen modestly in most urban areas over the last 40 years, but on average remain higher when African Americans and whites are compared than they are for Hispanics and whites, or Asian Americans and whites.

References

Blendon, R. J., Scheck, A. C., Donelan, K., Hill, C. A., Smith, M., Beatrice, D. and Altman, D. (1995) 'How White and African Americans View Their Health and Social Problems: Different Experiences, Different Expectations', *Journal of the American Medical Association* 273(4): 341–6.

Bobo, L. D. (2001) 'Racial Attitudes and Relations at the Close of the Twentieth Century'. In N. J. Smelser, W. J. Wilson and F. Mitchell (eds.) *America Becoming: Racial Trends and Their Consequences*, Washington, DC: National Academy Press, Vol. I: 264–301.

Broman, C. (1997) 'Race-Related Factors and Life Satisfaction among African Americans', *Journal of Black Psychology* 23(1): 36–49.

Brown, T. N., Williams, D. R., Jackson, J. S., Neighbors, H., Sellers, S., Torres, M. and Brown, K. (1999) ' "Being Black and Feeling Blue": Mental Health Consequences of Racial Discrimination', *Race and Society* 2(2): 117–31.

Brown, T. N., Wallace Jr, J. M. and Williams, D. R. (2001) 'Race-Related Correlates of Young Adults' Subjective Well-Being', *Social Indicators* 53(1): 97–116.

Cancian, M. and Reed, D. (2002) 'Changes in Family Structure: Implications for Poverty and Related Policy'. In S. H. Danziger and R. H. Haveman (eds.) *Understanding Poverty*, Cambridge, Mass.: Harvard University Press, pp. 69–96.

Collins, S. M. (1997) *Black Corporate Executives: The Making and Breaking of a Black Middle Class*. Philadelphia: Temple University Press.

Conrad, C. A. (2001) 'Racial Trends in Labor Market Access and Wages: Women'. In N. J. Smelser, W. J. Wilson and F. Mitchell (eds.) *America Becoming: Racial Trends and Their Consequences*, Washington, DC: National Academy Press, Vol. II: 124–51.

Cose, E. (1993) *The Rage of a Privileged Class*, New York: HarperCollins.

Danziger, S. (2000) 'Approaching the Limit: Early National Lessons from Welfare Reform', Ann Arbor, MI: University of Michigan. www.ssw.umich.edu/poverty/pubs.html.

Danziger, S. and Gottschalk, P. (1995) *America Unequal*, New York and Cambridge, Mass.: Russell Sage Foundation and Harvard University Press.

Danziger, S. K. et al. (2000) 'Barriers to the Employment of Welfare Recipients'. In R. Cherry and W. Rodgers (eds.) *The Impact of Tight Labor Markets on Black Employment Problems*, New York: Russell Sage Foundation, pp. 245–78.

Essed, P. (1991) *Understanding Everyday Racism: An Interdisciplinary Theory*. Newbury Park: Sage Publications.

Farley, R., Danziger, S. and Holzer, H. (2000) *Detroit Divided*, New York: Russell Sage Foundation.

Feagin, J. R. and Sikes, M. P. (1994) *Living with Racism: The Black Middle-class Experience*, Boston, Mass.: Beacon Press.

Ferguson, R. (2002) 'Community Revitalization, Jobs and the Well-Being of the Inner-City Poor'. In S. H. Danziger and R. H. Haveman (eds.) *Understanding Poverty*, Cambridge, Mass.: Harvard University Press, pp. 417–43.

Freeman, R. (2002) 'The Rising Tide Lifts . . . ?' In S. H. Danziger and R. H. Haveman (eds.) *Understanding Poverty*, Cambridge, Mass.: Harvard University Press, pp. 97–126.

Goering, J. and Feins, J. (1997) 'The Moving to Opportunity Social "Experiment": Early Stages of Implementation and Research Plans', *Poverty Research News* 1(2): 4–6.

Hajnal, Z. and Baldassare, M. (2001) *Finding Common Ground: Racial and Ethnic Attitudes in California*, San Francisco: Public Policy Institute of California. www.ppic.org.

Hochschild, J. (1995) *Facing up to the American Dream: Race, Class and the Soul of the Nation*, Princeton, NJ: Princeton University Press.

Holzer, H. J. (1996) *What Employers Want: Job Prospects for Less-Educated Workers*, New York: Russell Sage Foundation.

Holzer, H. J. (2001) 'Racial Differences in Labor Market Outcomes among Men'. In J. Smelser, W. J. Wilson and F. Mitchell (eds.) *America Becoming: Racial Trends and Their Consequences*, Washington, DC: National Academy Press, Vol. II: 124–51.

Jackson, P. B., Thoits, P. A. and Taylor, H. F. (1995) 'Composition of the Workplace and Psychological Well-being: The Effects of Tokenism on America's Black Elite', *Social Forces* 74: 543–57.

Jaynes, G. D. and Williams, Jr. R. M. (1989) *A Common Destiny: Blacks and American Society*, Washington, DC: National Academy Press.

Karoly, L. (2002) 'Investing in the Future: Reducing Poverty Through Human Capital Investments'. In S. H. Danziger and R. H. Haveman (eds.) *Understanding Poverty*, Cambridge, Mass.: Harvard University Press, pp. 314–56.

Katz, L., Kling, J. and Liebman, J. (2001) 'Moving to Opportunity in Boston: Early Impacts of a Randomized Mobility Experiment', *Quarterly Journal of Economics* CXVI: 607–54.

Kluegel, J. R. and Bobo, L. D. (2001) 'Perceived Group Discrimination and Policy Attitudes'. In A. O'Connor, C. Tilly and L. D. Bobo (eds.) *Urban Inequality: Evidence from Four Cities*, New York: Russell Sage Foundation, pp. 163–213.

Landrine, H. and Klonoff, E. A. (1996) 'The Schedule of Racist Events: A Measure of Racial Discrimination and a Study of its Negative Physical and Mental Health Consequences', *Journal of Black Psychology* 22(2): 144–6.

Landrum-Brown, J. (1990) 'Black Mental Health and Racial Oppression'. In D. Ruiz and J. Comer (eds.) *Handbook of Mental Health and Mental Disorder Among Black Americans*, New York: Greenwood Press, pp. 113–32.

Loury, G. C. (2004) 'Racial Justice: The Superficial Morality of Colour-Blindness in the United States'. Geneva: United Nations Research Institute for Social Development. Programme Paper – Identities, Conflict and Cohesion, No. 5.

Oliver, M. L. and Shapiro, T. M. (1995) *Black Wealth, White Wealth: A New Perspective on Racial Inequality*. New York: Routledge.

Oliver, M. L. and Shapiro, T. M. (2001) 'Wealth and Racial Stratification'. In N. J. Smelser, W. J. Wilson and F. Mitchell (eds.) *America Becoming: Racial Trends and Their Consequences*, Washington, DC: National Academy Press, Vol. II: 222–51.

Panel Study of Income Dynamics (2000) Cross-sectional Wealth and Financial Wealth-Tables. Ann Arbor, MI: University of Michigan. www.isr.umich.edu/src/psid/whatsnew.html.

Rosenbaum, J. (1995) 'Changing the Geography of Opportunity by Expanding Residential Choice: Lessons from the Gautreaux Program', *Housing Policy Debate* 6(1): 231–69.

Rumbaut, R. G. (1994) 'The Crucible Within: Ethnic Identity, Self-Esteem, and Segmented Assimilation Among Children of Immigrants', *International Migration Review* 28(4): 748–94.

Sigelman, L. and Welch, S. (1991) *Black Americans' Views of Racial Inequality: The Dream Deferred*. New York: Cambridge University Press.

Small, Stephen (1991) *Racialised Barriers: The Black Experience in the United States and England in the 1980s*. London: Routledge.

Smith, J. P. (2001) 'Race and Ethnicity in the Labor Market: Trends Over the Short and Long Term'. In N. J. Smelser, W. J. Wilson and F. Mitchell (eds.) *America Becoming: Racial Trends and Their Consequences*, Washington, DC: National Academy Press, Vol. II: 52–97.

Smith, R. C. and Seltzer, R. (2000) *Contemporary Controversies and the American Racial Divide*. New York: Rowman and Littlefield Publishers.

Smeeding, T., Rainwater, L. and Burtless, G. (2002) 'Poverty in a Cross-national Context'. In S. H. Danziger and R. H. Haveman (eds.) *Understanding Poverty*, Cambridge, Mass.: Harvard University Press, pp. 162–89.

Smelser, N. J., Wilson, W. J. and Mitchell, F. (eds.) (2001) *America Becoming: Racial Trends and Their Consequences*, Washington, DC: National Academy Press.

Taylor, J. (1990) 'Relationship Between Internalized Racism and Marital Satisfaction', *Journal of Black Psychology* 16: 45–53.

Taylor, J. and Jackson, B. B. (1990) 'Evaluation of a Holistic Model of Mental Health Symptoms in Black American Women', *Journal of Black Psychology* 18(1): 19–45.

Thompson, V. T. S. (1996) 'Perceived Experiences of Racism as Stressful Life Events', *Community Mental Health Journal* 32: 223–33.

Wilson, W. J. (1987) *The Truly Disadvantaged: The Inner City, the Underclass, and Public Policy*, Chicago: University of Chicago Press.

Wilson, W. J. (1996) *When Work Disappears: The World of the New Urban Poor*. New York: Alfred A. Knopf.

Wolff, E. (1998) 'Recent Trends in the Size Distribution of Household Wealth', *Journal of Economic Perspectives* 12(3): 131–50.

Yinger, J. (1995) *Closed Doors, Opportunities Lost: The Continuing Costs of Housing Discrimination*, New York: Russell Sage Foundation.

Yinger, J. (2002) 'Housing Discrimination and Residential Segregation as Causes of Poverty'. In S. H. Danziger and R. H. Haveman (eds.) *Understanding Poverty*, Cambridge, Mass.: Harvard University Press, pp. 359–91.

7
Malaysia's New Economic Policy and 'National Unity'

Jomo K. S.

Malaysia's New Economic Policy (NEP) was announced in 1970 as part of a package of measures introduced after the political crisis of May 1969. It sought to 'eradicate poverty' and 'restructure society to eliminate the identification of race with economic function' in order to create the conditions for national unity. Since then, poverty in Malaysia has gone down tremendously, as in neighbouring Thailand and Indonesia, which did not have comparable commitments to poverty reduction, but also experienced rapid economic growth and structural transformation. Not surprisingly, the NEP has been principally associated with 'restructuring', i.e. efforts to reduce inter-ethnic economic disparities between Bumiputera indigenes and the non-Bumiputera, especially between ethnic Malays and Chinese. Hence, 'restructuring' has come to be associated with 'positive discrimination' or 'affirmative action' on behalf of the mainly Malay Bumiputeras. Such state interventions have resulted in significantly greater Bumiputera wealth ownership, business participation, education opportunities, public sector employment and promotion, as well as representation among professionals and managers/administrators.

However, these measures have also resulted in greater resentment by those who feel deprived by such policies, resulting at various times in emigration, capital flight and ethnic mobilization. Resentment is arguably greatest among the middle classes where ethnic rivalry is perceived to be greatest. Hence, while it is doubtful that the NEP has created the conditions for national unity, it has probably mitigated Bumiputera resentment of non-Bumiputera domination of business and the professions. Rapid economic growth over the last three decades, some economic and educational liberalization since the mid-1980s, as well as greater recognition of external challenges, have also served to mitigate greater inter-ethnic resentment. It is useful to begin a more careful consideration of the Malaysian experience with a brief review of the background to the NEP.

Background

Malaya achieved independence in 1957 and formed Malaysia including the Borneo states of Sabah and Sarawak in 1963 (Singapore joined in 1963, but seceded in 1965). About half the population of the peninsula then comprised ethnic Malays, with almost 40 per cent Chinese and 10 per cent Indians. In Sabah and Sarawak, there were almost no Indians, with Chinese numbering over a third. Of the indigenous Bumiputera population, Muslims and non-Muslims were almost evenly balanced in Sabah, while less than a quarter of the population of Sarawak was Muslim.

During the 1960s, economic development not only maintained, but apparently even increased, income inequalities, including the income gaps within each major ethnic group in Peninsular Malaysia. Income distribution in Peninsular Malaysia apparently worsened between 1957 and 1970, with the rich becoming richer and the poor getting poorer in all ethnic groups, especially among the Malays. While the commanding heights of the economy were still British-dominated from the colonial period, mainly Chinese businesses were ubiquitous. While most Indians and many Chinese comprised the working class, the vast majority of smallholder farmers in the peninsula were Malays. In Sabah and Sarawak, there were fewer wage earners and more working the land.

The ruling Alliance coalition in the 1960s was essentially a coalition of mainly ethnic-based parties led by the United Malays National Organization (UMNO). After the virtual elimination of the legal left in the mid- and late 1960s, essentially racialist or communal political ideologies faced little competition. Consequently, the deteriorating socioeconomic and political situation in the 1960s came to be seen and interpreted primarily in ethnic terms. Many Malays believed Chinese economic hegemony to be responsible for Malay economic underdevelopment, though in the late 1960s, the Malaysian economy was still primarily dominated by foreign investors. On the other hand, many non-Malays believed the UMNO-led Malay-dominated Alliance government to be responsible for official government discrimination against them. Most businessmen were Chinese and most government officials were Malays. Hence, Chinese capitalist, together with the Malay administrative-political elite, enjoyed most of the fruits of rapid economic growth in the 1960s.

In the third federal elections held then, the ruling Alliance coalition retained a reduced parliamentary majority despite securing less than half the popular vote with the help of gerrymandered constituency delineations. In the May 1969 election, half the Malays and the majority of non-Malays voted against the Alliance government. Though undoubtedly manipulated by certain politicians, the post-election race riots were easily triggered in the federal capital of Kuala Lumpur. As noted above, tensions had been brewing before the elections due to ethnically perceived frustrations reflecting underlying class relations. After the elections, race riots broke apparently due to culturally offensive behaviour by jubilant opposition party supporters as well as armed mobilization by youthful supporters of an incumbent chief minister who had not secured a majority in his state legislative assembly.

After the 1969 election results and the subsequent riots, the prime minister, Tunku Abdul Rahman, was gradually eased out by the late Tun Abdul Razak. Razak, the deputy leader of the ruling party and coalition, is believed to have staged a 'palace coup' – with a greater military-police role in response to the race riots – to take over political leadership with the support of party critics of Tunku, the incumbent party leader and prime minister. Thus, the replacement of the old UMNO leadership also reflected the ascendancy of the so-called Young Turks within UMNO, who had challenged Tunku's leadership from the late 1960s. After the traumatic events of May 1969, UMNO dominance of the ruling coalition became more pronounced as it co-opted most opposition parties, who were also largely ethnic-based, although they mobilized less explicitly on ethnic bases, unlike the parties in the ruling coalition. It is generally agreed that Malaysian economic policy-making changed rather drastically in the aftermath of the race riots and the UMNO palace coup associated with 13 May 1969.

While government policy before the NEP was generally considered to be basically *laissez faire* in approach, and responsive to as well as supportive of both foreign and domestic (predominantly Chinese) private sector interests, the 1970s was characterized by growing state intervention, primarily in favour of the emerging Malay elite. While such intervention generally did not threaten property rights *per se*, particular business interests – usually Chinese or foreign – have felt threatened at various times. Seen against this background then, Mahathir's economic policies of the 1980s suggest efforts to retreat from the excesses of 1970s-type state interventionism, e.g. through privatization, 'Malaysia Incorporated', deregulation and 'flexibility in NEP implementation'.

The NEP was announced after the 13 May 1969 events as one of several efforts to achieve national unity in view of the socio-economic inequality inherited from the colonial period and consolidated in the post-Independence years. The NEP was ostensibly announced to create the socio-economic conditions for achieving 'national unity' through redistributive policies. The NEP had two objectives, namely to 'eradicate poverty' regardless of race and to 'restructure society' to eliminate the identification of race with economic function. An Outline Perspective Plan (OPP) for 1971–90 identified medium- and long-term targets en route to 1990 for both NEP objectives.

The OPP included specific targets for poverty reduction and Bumiputera wealth ownership in particular. It is often forgotten that these distributional goals assumed an average annual growth rate of 8 per cent over the OPP period. Initially, the NEP was widely accepted across ethnic lines, especially after the traumatic May 1969 events. Subsequent political developments enhanced UMNO and Malay political hegemony as several opposition parties joined the newly broadened National Front or Barisan Nasional (BN) ruling coalition.

The next section will examine to what extent the NEP's declared aims have been achieved. This survey is seriously constrained by the nature of publicly available official statistics, which improved briefly in the late 1980s, only to be reduced again from the 1990s. Most older Malaysians seem to think that inter-ethnic relations deteriorated in the 1970s and 1980s, and many were inclined to attribute this – at least partly – to the implementation of the NEP. On the other hand, there has undoubtedly been considerable success in achieving specific NEP objectives as the following review will show. According to available government statistics on NEP implementation, it appears that the OPP targets had, by and large, been achieved by 1990, except for a shortfall in Malay corporate wealth ownership. The final section will examine some implications of the legacy of the primacy of the ethnic divide in the public's imaginations. This has had a tremendous constraining effect on political as well as economic options, and shapes likely political mobilization as well as coalition-building and economic policy packages.

NEP targets, expenditure and achievement

Poverty reduction

The OPP forecast that the official poverty level should be reduced from 49 per cent in Peninsular Malaysia in 1969 to 16 per cent in 1990. According to official government plan documents, the poverty rate had

Table 7.1   Malaysia: Incidence of Poverty, 1970–1999

	1970	1980	1990	1997	1999
Total	49.3	29.2	16.5	6.1	7.5
Rural	58.6	37.7	21.1	10.9	12.4
Urban	24.6	12.6	7.1	2.1	3.4
Hard-core Poor			3.9	1.4	1.4

Sources: Malaysia Plan documents.

Table 7.2   Malaysia: Incidence of Poverty (%) by State, 1970–1999

	1970	1976	1984	1987	1990	1995	1997	1999
Johor	45.7	29.0	12.2	11.1	10.1	4.2	1.6	2.5
Melaka	34.1	32.4	15.8	11.7	12.4	3.2	3.6	5.7
NegriSembilan	50.5	33.0	13.0	21.5	9.5	5.3	4.5	2.5
Selangor	42.7	22.9	8.6	8.9	7.8	2.2	1.3	2.0
Perak	52.2	43.0	20.3	19.9	19.3	4.9	4.5	9.5
Pulau Pinang	52.7	32.4	13.4	12.9	8.9	9.1	1.6	2.7
Perlis	63.2	59.8	33.7	29.1	17.2	11.8	10.6	13.3
Kedah	61.0	61.0	36.6	31.3	30.0	12.2	11.5	13.2
Kelantan	74.1	67.1	39.2	31.6	29.9	22.9	19.5	18.7
Trengganu	65.1	60.3	28.9	36.1	31.2	23.7	17.3	14.9
Pahang	56.1	28.9	15.7	12.3	10.3	6.8	4.1	2.7
Sabah	–	58.3	33.1	35.3	34.3	26.2	22.1	20.1
Sarawak	–	56.5	31.9	24.7	21.0	10.0	7.5	6.7
Kuala Lumpur	–	–	–	–	–	9.5	0.1	2.3
Malaysia	56.7*	37.7	20.7	19.3	17.1	8.7	6.8	7.5

*For Peninsular Malaysia only.
Sources: *Fifth Malaysia Plan, 1986–1990* (5MP), *Mid-Term Review of the Fifth Malaysia Plan, 1986–1990* (MTR5MP), *Second Outline Perspective Plan, 1991–2000* (OPP2), *Mid-Term Review of the Seventh Malaysia Plan, 1996–2000* (MTR7MP), *Eighth Malaysia Plan, 2001–2005* (8MP).

been reduced to 18 per cent by 1984 and 17 per cent by 1987 from 40 per cent in 1970. Tables 7.1 and 7.2 summarize official data on the incidence of poverty in Peninsular Malaysia by sector for various years since 1970. They suggest an overall reduction of poverty incidence from 49.3 per cent (official estimate) or 56.7 per cent (Anand, 1983, estimate) in 1970 to 39.6 per cent in 1976, 18.4 per cent in 1984 and 17.3 per cent in 1987 in Peninsular Malaysia alone. In absolute terms, the number of poor households dropped from 791,800 in 1970 to 764,400 in 1976 and further to 483,300 in 1984, before rising slightly to 485,800 in 1987.

Poverty incidence for all of Malaysia, i.e. including Sabah and Sarawak, fell to 6.1 per cent in 1997 and 7.5 per cent in 1999.

Official statistics suggest very impressive reductions of poverty in the 1970s and early 1980s, especially in Peninsular Malaysia. Although there are many legitimate reservations about the quality and nature of these data, there are few observers who would doubt that poverty, as officially defined, has been significantly reduced, even though part of the decline in poverty may have been due to a lowering of the poverty line. In view of the generally rapid growth of the Malaysian economy in most of the 1970s and part of the 1980s, poverty – as defined by the government – could have been further reduced, if more just and effective redistributive policies had been implemented, government waste minimized and government allocations ostensibly for poverty eradication used effectively for reducing poverty instead of enriching politicians and contractors securing rural development projects. More significantly, it appears that per capita income levels have generally risen with growth.

However, the significance, consistency and credibility of these data have been challenged on several grounds.[1] There is much doubt as to whether the definitions of income used in the various surveys concerned have been consistent, e.g. with regard to the valuation of services provided by the government, how these have been calculated in determining household incomes and actual measurement and estimation of poverty.[2] Other problems in using an income-based determination of economic welfare have also not been given adequate attention. While incomes undoubtedly influence economic welfare, it would be wrong to presume that welfare reflects expenditure, which is in turn largely determined by income. Another problem involves the estimation of income, and hence poverty, on a household basis rather than on a per capita basis. The *Mid-Term Review of the Fifth Malaysia Plan, 1986–1990* suggests that if per capita income – instead of household income – is used, the official poverty rate in Peninsular Malaysia would go down fairly significantly. While this is quite plausible and even likely, the plan document did not elaborate on why this would happen.

It also seems likely that some methods of measurement may have changed. For example, the *Fifth Malaysia Plan, 1986–1990* (p. 83) explicitly favoured a more comprehensive concept of income, which 'takes into account the imputed values for own produce consumed at home and owner-occupied housing' as well as 'the full value of public services enjoyed by households, either free or at subsidized rate (including) health, education, transport and utilities, and the various subsidies granted by the Government'. There are, of course, merits in the income concept proposed, especially as a measure of living standards or economic welfare, but reducing poverty incidence by broadening the income concept, or by comparing essentially incomparable data, raises serious doubts about the actual extent of poverty reduction.

Nevertheless, for want of more acceptable alternative data sources, official figures will be used. The prevailing official poverty measures have used a household, rather than a per capita poverty line income yardstick.[3] According to the *Mid-Term Review of the Fifth Malaysia Plan, 1986–1990* (p. 45), the poverty line income[4] (PLI) has been defined as the minimum expenditure level to secure a certain standard of living, and 'updated annually using the Consumer Price Index (CPI) to reflect changes in price levels'. The PLI should be adjusted to reflect changes in the costs of specific items making up the PLI, as their relative weights differ from the breakdown of the CPI. Also, per capita consumption expenditure is probably a far better proxy for economic welfare than household income.

The current PLI approach to poverty measurement is based on a notion of absolute poverty. There seems to be less official interest in and concern about relative poverty, i.e. inequality and income distribution. There should be closer monitoring of distributional trends in economic welfare, expenditure, income and wealth to provide a more comprehensive and accurate picture of the welfare of the Malaysian population in relation to economic growth generally, and as a consequence of implementation of the NEP – and successor policies – specifically. It is quite possible that such statistics would show relatively greater increases in incomes of poorer groups in all ethnic communities as well as a significant reduction in differences among the average incomes of the major ethnic communities – trends which the Malaysian government could well be proud of. Available income data and the basket of goods and services constituting the PLI should also be made publicly available to facilitate meaningful public scrutiny of income and poverty reduction trends.

Under the NEP, there was no official commitment to reducing income inequality except between ethnic groups, particularly between the Bumiputeras and non-Bumiputeras. Since poverty is officially conceived in absolute, rather than in relative terms in relation to a poverty line income, income inequality can grow as the poverty rate declines if economic growth is sufficiently high. Income distribution trends do provide important indications of the welfare implications of economic growth and recession, especially as they affect inter-ethnic spatial and other income inequalities.

Tables 7.3 and 7.4 show income distribution trends in Malaysia, especially Peninsular Malaysia, since independence and especially after the NEP began. Between 1957 and 1970, income inequality apparently grew, with the rich getting richer and the poor getting poorer, though serious doubts (Anand, 1983) have been raised about the comparability of the data involved. Some evidence since then points to growing income inequality during the 1970s, i.e. from 1970, through 1973 and 1976, to 1979, but other data suggest otherwise. For example, in the 1970s, the average real income of the bottom 40 per cent increased, according to the *Fourth Malaysia Plan, 1981–1985 (4MP)* (p. 37). These trends suggest that rising incomes and poverty reduction in the 1970s may have been accompanied by growing income inequality, but there is other evidence to suggest that income inequality declined during the 1970s and 1980s, and has not changed much since then. Average inter-ethnic income disparities also declined during the NEP period, but appear to have risen in the 1990s.

The first official Household Income Survey in 1984 and 1987 suggest declining overall income inequalities in the 1980s. Inequalities between Bumiputeras and non-Bumiputeras as well as those between town and country appear to have declined fairly steadily from the 1970s in Peninsular Malaysia. The 1985–6 recession apparently reduced all major income disparities by more adversely affecting the relatively better-off, while leaving the worse-off relatively less affected. Evidence for Sabah and Sarawak, available only for 1984 and 1987, suggests greater inequality there as well as similar disparity-reducing consequences of the mid-1980s recession.

The government probably has a success story to tell with its data, and the credibility of the story would be enhanced only by better public access to it. It may also be useful to reconsider the composition of the PLI and to compare it with detailed consumer price trends to make more accurate inflation adjustments to the original PLI, and also to determine a more meaningful PLI with the benefit of hindsight and the experience of the last two decades of NEP implementation. Needless to say, significant regional and locational variations in living costs (e.g. between urban and rural areas and perhaps even some of the major metropolitan centres, such as Kelang Valley and Johor Baru) should be taken into consideration.

Despite the ostensible official concern about poverty, it is quite remarkable that after more than three decades of the NEP, there is still relatively little detailed information about the characteristics of the poor, which could help ascertain the reasons and causes of poverty, as

Table 7.3   Peninsular Malaysia: Mean Monthly Household Incomes By Ethnic Group and Stratum, 1970–1999

	1970	1973	1976	1979	1984	1987	1990	1995	1999
All	423	502	566	669	792	760	1,167	2,020	2,472
Bumiputera (B)	276	335	380	475	616	614	940	1,604	1,984
Chinese (C)	632	739	866	906	1,086	1,012	1,631	2,890	3,456
Indian (I)	478	565	592	730	791	771	1,209	2,140	2,702
Others	1,304	1,798	1,395	1,816	1,775	2,043	955	1,284	1,371
Urban (U)	687	789	913	942	1,114	1,039	1,617	2,589	3,103
Rural (R)	321	374	431	531	596	604	951	1,326	1,718
Disparity ratio (C/B)	2.30	2.21	2.28	1.91	1.76	1.65	1.74	1.80	1.74
Disparity ratio (I/B)	1.73	1.69	1.56	1.54	1.28	1.26	1.30	1.33	1.36
Disparity ratio (U/R)	2.14	2.11	2.12	1.77	1.87	1.72	1.70	1.95	1.81

Note: Figures for 1970–87 in constant 1978 prices; figures for 1990–99 are constant 1990 prices.
Sources: Fourth Malaysia Plan, 1981–85, Mid-Term Review of the Fifth Malaysia Plan, 1986–90, Seventh Malaysia Plan, 1996–2000, Eighgth Malaysia Plan, 2001–2005.

Table 7.4 Malaysia: Income Shares by Income Group, 1970–1999

	1970	1973	1976	1979	1984	1987	1990	1999
Total								
Top 20%	55.9	53.7	61.9	54.7	53.2	51.2	50.0	50.5
Middle 40%	32.5	34.0	27.8	34.4	34.0	35.0	35.5	35.5
Bottom 40%	11.6	12.3	10.3	10.9	12.8	13.8	14.5	14.0
Urban								
Top 20%	55.0	–	–	–	52.1	50.8		48.9
Middle 40%	32.8	–	–	–	34.5	35.0		36.7
Bottom 40%	12.2	–	–	–	13.4	14.3		14.9
Rural								
Top 20%	51.0	–	–	–	49.5	48.3		48.0
Middle 40%	35.9	–	–	–	36.4	36.7		36.7
Bottom 40%	13.1	–	–	–	14.1	15.0		15.6
Gini Index	0.50	0.50	0.57	0.49	–	–	0.44	0.44
Theil Index	0.48	0.43	0.71	0.42	–	–		

Note: The published figures for urban and rural Malaysia in 1990 and 1999 do not add up to 100.0 per cent, but only the 1990 calculations are omitted because of the much greater disparities involved.
Sources: Malaysia Plan documents.

well as appropriate, effective and efficient measures and efforts to overcome poverty. Such detailed analytical poverty profiles are especially urgent in view of the increasingly recognized phenomenon of 'hardcore poverty', said to be relatively unaffected by existing poverty eradication policies.

The absence of a clearer understanding of the poverty phenomenon has allowed policies to go on, regardless of their efficacy in poverty eradication. Of course, once certain policies are implemented, interest groups benefiting from them tend to ensure their continuation regardless of their effectiveness in terms of their ostensible aims. This has led to the suspicion that such policies are maintained to facilitate patronage by the ruling political coalition and for the benefit of certain rural interest groups and among contractors and other business interests, rather than for the purpose of poverty reduction, as claimed.

A great deal of what is officially categorized as poverty eradication actually refers to expenditure for rural and agricultural development, much of which is certainly not for the benefit of the poor. Hence, it is crucial that expenditure for poverty eradication is provided in meaningful detail in order to ascertain to what extent such expenditure actually benefits the poor. Such evaluation is crucial in order to minimize abuses in the name of poverty eradication. Careful comparative studies can ascertain how and to what extent poverty eradication expenditure actually contributes to relieving poverty.

The evidence so far seems to suggest that poverty reduction has been largely due to rising incomes. In the rural areas, especially among the peasantry, it seems to be largely attributable to increasing productivity. However, rising productivity mainly benefits those who own their own economic resources, especially land. Inequality in resource allocation, in terms of both ownership and access, has therefore meant that such productivity gains have tended to benefit the well-to-do more than others. Hence, it is very likely that expenditure ostensibly for poverty eradication has actually brought greater benefits to the relatively well endowed, i.e. those other than the poor.

The demographic factor also needs greater consideration for several reasons. One other important factor which has reduced poverty among some of the 'target groups' has been the reduction in the population involved, e.g. in rice cultivation, small-scale rubber growing, fishing and plantation labour. Hence, despite continued population growth, there have not been corresponding increases in the number and population shares involved in these activities. On the contrary, there may well have been significant declines at least in some rural occupations.

With the ageing of the rural population as a consequence of urban migration, especially by the young, it appears that the economically active proportion of the population involved in agriculture has declined, exacerbating the phenomenon of idle agricultural land, also due to the uneconomic size of the farm land involved. With the average Malay fertility rate about double the Chinese rate at the end of the 1980s, and with the Indian rate slightly above the Chinese rate, it is also quite possible that per capita Malay income levels will continue to remain low, and poverty correspondingly high, due simply to larger household sizes.

The official focus on Malay peasant poverty has emphasized productivity-increasing efforts for self-employed rural producers at the expense of other measures to reduce poverty, consequently, adversely affecting other poverty groups. Even among the Malay peasant population, those with less access to economic resources, especially land, are ignored by the main thrust of poverty eradication efforts. Hence, peasant agricultural labourers have little to thank the NEP for. If their conditions have improved, it has been for other extraneous reasons, e.g.

full employment or productivity increases raising their wages, rather than as a consequence of NEP poverty eradication measures.

Similarly, other rural labourers – such as estate workers, mine workers and public works and land development contract labourers – have been ignored by the NEP. The importance of immigrant and contract labour for some of these jobs has served only to worsen general working conditions and lower wage rates for these occupations, rendering them even more unattractive to Malaysians, and also depressing wage rates more generally in the labour market, especially for unskilled labour.

The current approach has also tended to ignore the poor other than the main poor target groups, namely the rice farmers, rubber smallholders, coconut smallholders and fishermen. Hence, the majority of the poor in Sabah and Sarawak are largely unaffected by poverty eradication measures, while some – e.g. shifting cultivators as well as hunter-gatherers – feel their interests threatened by the logging, land development and other trends that go by the name of development. Those in the towns also feel ignored by poverty eradication measures that they perceive to be primarily, if not exclusively, rural in orientation.

However, while there are many poor groups who have been bypassed by official poverty eradication measures, they may feel less neglected by official development efforts. Since 'development', particularly the provision of infrastructure and social services, is intimately connected with government and party patronage, these poor communities – especially the Bumiputeras, and particularly the Malays – do not necessarily feel themselves ignored by government development efforts generally, although they have not benefited from the government's poverty eradication measures.

'Restructuring society'

Despite the popular rhetorical commitment by politicians to poverty eradication, the 1970s and early 1980s saw growing emphasis on the NEP's other pronounced objective to 'restructure society': to abolish the identification of ethnicity with economic function, especially to create, expand and consolidate the Malay capitalist and middle classes. As officially interpreted, 'restructuring' is not meant to abolish or change socio-economic relations between classes or economic interest groups; in practice, it mainly seeks to increase Bumiputera capital ownership and personnel shares in the more attractive – mainly professional – occupations.

In practice, restructuring efforts have been largely aimed at increasing the share of Bumiputera capital as well as the number of Bumiputera businessmen and professionals in the context of continued open capitalist development by using the public sector and state intervention extensively. The NEP's restructuring prong mainly involves redistribution of corporate stock ownership, employment and education, with the latter two sometimes considered together. There is particular interest in ownership of the modern corporate sector, though only a small minority of the population is actually involved, reflecting the dominance of capitalist interests in defining supposedly ethnic or communal interests.

Wealth distribution

However, wealth restructuring – particularly the 30 per cent target for Bumiputera share ownership by 1990 – remains the main obsession in most discussions about the NEP. Table 7.5 reflects the distribution of ownership of the corporate sector by ethnicity and residence between 1969 and 2000. The Bumiputera share rose sharply from 1.5 per cent in 1969 and 2.4 per cent in 1970 during the 1970s until the mid-1980s. While the original *Mid-Term Review of the Second Malaysia Plan, 1971–1975* target (p. 84, Table 4.8) of 9.0 per cent Bumiputera ownership by 1975 was surpassed, only 12.5 per cent of the corporate sector was in Bumiputera hands by 1980 (instead of the projected 16.0 per cent) and 19.1 per cent in 1985 (instead of the 23.0 per cent expected). Instead of the 30.0 per cent targeted for 1990, the Bumiputera share has hovered around 19.4 per cent in 1988, 19.3 per cent in 1990, 20.6 per cent in 1995 and 19.3 per cent in 1999.

Meanwhile, the share of foreign residents fell from 63.4 per cent in 1970 to 42.9 per cent in 1980, 33.6 per cent in 1983, 26.0 per cent in 1985 and 24.6 per cent in 1988, before rising to 25.4 per cent in 1990, 27.7 per cent in 1995 and 32.7 per cent in 1999. Meanwhile, the Chinese share rose from 22.8 per cent in 1969 to 45.5 per cent in 1990[5] (when ethnically anonymous ownership of locally controlled companies was largely assigned to Chinese), before declining sharply to 40.9 per cent in 1995 and 37.9 per cent in 1999. Meanwhile, the Indian share rose slightly from 0.9 per cent in 1969 to 1.2 per cent in 1985 and 1988, and 1.5 per cent in 1995 and 1999.

The most often cited government statistics mislead by exaggerating the shortfall from the 30 per cent target (originally for 1990), with Bumiputera ownership[6] hovering above 18 per cent since 1983. It is likely that Bumiputera share ownership is much higher than suggested by such government statistics.[7] All the percentages cited earlier probably underestimate their respective proportions of share ownership. If we put aside the share capital held through nominee companies and locally controlled companies of unknown ethnic ownership identity, then the total Bumiputera share of ethnically and residentially identified equity in 1988 was 24.7 per cent, with the foreign resident and Chinese shares rising to 31.2 per cent and 41.4 per cent respectively. It has been variously argued that the Bumiputera and foreign shares would be even higher if shares held through nominee companies and locally controlled companies are taken into account, though there is no empirical basis for ascertaining the veracity of such claims.

The share of 'other Malaysian residents' – often wrongly equated with the non-Bumiputera Malaysian share – rose from 34.3 per cent in 1970 to 37.5 per cent in 1975, 44.6 per cent in 1980 and 49.7 per cent in 1982, slipping to 47.7 per cent in 1983, before rising to 54.9 per cent in 1985 and 56.0 per cent in 1988, and then declining to 46.8 per cent in 1990, 51.7 per cent in 1995 and 48.2 per cent in 1999. This category includes the ethnically unidentifiable residual share of 'other, nominee companies and locally controlled companies', that could not be assigned to specific ethnic groups, which had grown from 12.2 per cent in 1969 to 20.3 per cent in 1985 and 21.2 per cent in 1988.

Ownership of locally controlled companies was presumed to belong exclusively to non-Bumiputera Malaysians from 1991, whereas such shares could also have been owned by Bumiputeras as well as foreign residents. Some would argue that they are more likely to be owned by Bumiputera individuals, especially politicians, who wish to obscure their business interests. But if we assume that these shares are divided according to the known ethnic proportions, then the Bumiputera share would rise to at least 22 per cent.

All such official figures consider only nominal share values, whereas estimates of the distribution of wealth held in shares should consider share prices, though there are many problems in estimating such market values. Since Bumiputera and foreign share ownership tends to be concentrated in the larger, more successful firms, which have been able to restructure to meet government guidelines, it is likely that the actual market value of shares held by non-Bumiputera residents is correspondingly less than nominal share ownership, whereas Bumiputera and foreign wealth would be considerably higher. Hence, it is quite possible that the 30 per cent Bumiputera wealth ownership target has been achieved. While the 1997–8 financial crisis undoubtedly affected wealth, there is little evidence of its ethnic implications except for

Table 7.5   Malaysia: Ownership of Share Capital (at par value) of Limited Companies,[a] 1969, 1970, 1975, 1980, 1983, 1985, 1990, 1995, 1999, 2002

Ownership Group	1969 RM m.	%	1970 RM m.	%	1975 RM m.	%	1980[b] RM m.	%	1983 RM m.
Malaysian residents	1,767.7	37.9	1,952.1	36.7*	7,047.2	46.7	18,493.4	57.1	33,010.5
Bumiputeras	70.6	1.5	125.6	2.4	1,394.0	9.2	4,050.5	12.5	9,274.6
Bumiputera individuals[c]	49.3	1.0	84.4	1.6	549.8	3.6	1,880.1	5.8	3,762.2
Trust agencies[d]	21.3	0.5	41.2	0.8	844.2	5.6	2,170.4	6.7	5,512.4
Other Malaysian residents[e]	1,697.1	36.4	1,826.5	34.3	5,653.2	37.5	14,442.9	44.6	23,735.9
Chinese	1,064.8	22.8	1,450.5	27.2	–	–	–	–	–
Indians	41.0	0.9	55.9	1.1	–	–	–	–	–
Others	–	–	–	–	–	–	–	–	–
Nominee companies	98.9	2.1	320.1	6.0	–	–	–	–	–
Locally-controlled companies	471.0	10.1	–	–	–	–	–	–	–
Federal and state governments	21.4	0.5	–	–	–	–	–	–	–
Foreign residents	2,909.8	62.1	3,377.1	63.4	8,037.2	53.3	13,927.0	42.9	16,697.6
Share in Malaysian companies	1,235.9	26.4	–	–	4,722.8	31.3	7,791.2	24.0	9,054.3
Foreign controlled companies	282.3	6.0	–	–	–	–	–	–	–
Net assets of local branches[f]	1,391.6	29.7	–	–	3,314.4	22.0	6,135.8	18.9	7,643.3
Total[g]	4,677.5	100.0	5,329.2	100.0	15,084.4	100.0	32,420.4	100.0	49,708.1

Notes:

[a] The classification of ownership of share capital (at par value as adopted by the *Ownership Survey of Limited Companies*) was based upon the residential address of the shareholders and not on citizenship. Residents are persons, companies, or institutions that live in or are located in Peninsular Malaysia, Sabah and Sarawak. The definition, therefore, also includes foreign citizens residing in Malaysia.

[b] Figures for 1980 are based on the *Ownership Survey of Limited Companies* cited in Malaysian government plan documents.

[c] Includes institutions channelling funds of individual *bumiputeras* such as the Muslim Pilgrim Saving and Management Authority (LUTH), MARA Unit Trust Scheme, co-operatives and the ASN scheme.

[d] Shares held through institutions classified as trust agencies such as the National Equity Corporation (PNB), National Corporation (PERNAS), The Council of Trust for Indigenous People (MARA), state economic development corporation (SEDCs), Development Bank of Malaysia (BPMB), Urban Development Authority (UDA), Bank Bumiputera Malaysia Berhad, Kompleks Kewangan Malaysia Berhad (KKMB), and Food Industries of Malaysia (FIMA). It also includes the amount of equity owned by the Government through other agencies and companies that have been identified under the Transfer Scheme of Government Equity to Bumiputeras.

%	1985 RM m.	%	1990 RM m.	%	1995 RM m.	%	1999 RM m.	%	2002 RM m.	%
66.4	57,666.6	74.0	80,851.9	74.6	129,999.5	72.3	208,797.2	67.3	278,094.0	71
18.7	14,883.4	19.1	20,877.5	19.3	36,981.2	20.6	59,394.4	19.1	73,161.8	18
7.6	9,103.4	11.7	15,322.0	14.2	33,353.2	18.6	54,046.0	17.4	66,746.0	17
11.1	5,780.0	7.4	5,555.5	5.1	3,628.0	2.0	5,348.4	1.7	6.415.8	1
47.7	42,783.2	54.9	59,974.4	55.3	93,018.3	51.7	149,402.8	48.2	204,932.2	52
–	26,033.3	33.4	49,296.5	45.5	73,552.7	40.9	117,372.4	37.9	159,806.9	40
–	927.9	1.2	1,068.0	1.0	2,723.1	1.5	4,752.9	1.5	5,951.1	1
–	987.2	1.3	389.5	0.3	1,751.1	1.0	2,888.0	0.9	3,204.7	0
–	5,585.1	7.2	9,220.4	8.5	14,991.4	8.3	24,389.5	7.9	35,969.5	9
–	9,249.7	11.8	–	–	–	–	–	–	–	
–	–	–	–	–	–	–	–	–	–	
33.6	20,297.8	26.0	27,525.5	25.4	49,792.7	27.7	101,279.2	32.7	112,727.6	28
18.2	12,672.8	16.2	–	–	–	–	–	–	–	
–	–	–	–	–	–	–	–	–	–	
15.4	7,625.0	9.8	–	–	–	–	–	–	–	
100.0	77,964.4	100.0	108,377.4	100.0	179,792.2	100.0	310,076.4	100.0	390,821.6	100

e Includes shares held by nominees and locally controlled companies (LCC). LCC records the total value of share capital of limited companies whose ownership could not be disaggregated further and assigned beyond the second level of ownership, to specific ethnic groups. Nominee shareholding was estimated to account for 5.7 per cent of the total corporate shares in 1985 or about RM4,400 million. Shares held under the LCC amounted to about RM8,100 million or 10.7 per cent of the total share capital of limited companies in 1985.

f This refers to the difference between the total assets in Malaysia and total liabilities in Malaysia of the companies incorporated abroad. This approach had to be used for Malaysia branches of companies incorporated abroad as the criteria on equity share capital could not be applied to these companies.

g Excludes Government holdings other than through trust agencies, except for 1969.

Sources: Malaysia (1971: 40; 1976: 184; 1981: 62; 1984: 101; 1986: 107; 1989; 1996: 86; 2001: 64; 2003).

evidence that government interventions have tended to favour those best connected politically.

If market values are considered instead of nominal or par values, the proportion of publicly listed foreign and Bumiputera shares would probably rise rather significantly, at the expense of the Chinese share. According to data from the Kuala Lumpur Stock Exchange (KLSE) *Annual Handbook*, incorporating information up to September 1988, 29.4 per cent of equity by nominal value was owned by Bumiputeras, with 41.9 per cent owned by 'other Malaysians' and 28.7 per cent owned by foreigners. However, when market values based on closing prices at the KLSE on 1 March 1989 are considered, the Bumiputera and foreign shares rose to 34.5 per cent and 32.2 per cent respectively, with the share of 'other Malaysians' falling to 33.3 per cent. Not surprisingly, this suggests that Bumiputera shares are generally more highly valued in the market than those held by foreigners, and especially those belonging to other Malaysians.

The official figures for distribution of share ownership do not take into account share ownership in private limited companies, which are generally smaller, but sometimes more lucrative. The distribution of share ownership does not accurately reflect wealth ownership in Malaysia, especially of non-corporate wealth held by private companies. It could also reasonably be argued that 'net tangible assets' would provide a more accurate reflection of corporate wealth distribution than par values, or even market values. Also, share capital represents only a portion of economic wealth, albeit an important one.

Similarly, the assets of foreign branches and subsidiaries in Malaysia have been ignored by such calculations. Hence, it is likely that foreign wealth and wealth-generating capacity in Malaysia has been significantly underestimated by government statistics. A fuller picture of wealth distribution and economic power has to consider other tangible assets, such as real property and agricultural land, as well as other sources of economic power, including access to rent-seeking opportunities as well as corporate control, as distinct from ownership. Hence, the Bumiputera percentage does not include shares owned by those who use nominee companies and other such devices that obscure the identity of the owner.

Not much is known about the trust agencies ostensibly set up to advance Bumiputera share ownership, entrepreneurial and managerial capability. However, in the public eye, these trust agencies have been associated with the growth of the public sector under the NEP. During the heady early years of NEP implementation, public enterprises of

various types proliferated. By the early 1980s, federal government officials were no longer quite sure how many such enterprises had been
established, not only by the federal and state governments, but also by
the various statutory bodies, regional development agencies and other
such public sector bodies. The fiscal and foreign debt crises of the early
1980s led to the introduction of structural adjustment.

In the mid-1980s, the government established a Central Information
Collection Unit (CICU), run by Permodalan Nasional Berhad (PNB).
1987 accounts revealed that almost half the 1,148 enterprises – mostly
subsidiaries and associated companies of state enterprises – were still in
the red, involving a net loss of RM1.9 bn. Some 562 companies had
losses totalling RM7.5 bn, while another 446 had profits of RM5.6 bn,
with the remainder inactive or in the process of closing down. Total
public sector investments in the 1,148 companies came to RM15.3 bn,
or about 71 per cent of the total paid-up capital of RM21.5 bn, with the
state holding at least half the equity in 813 of these companies (*South
East Asia Digest*, 21 July 1989).

The *Third Malaysia Plan, 1976–1980* projections (p. 86, Table 4.16) for
the 30 per cent Malay share of the corporate sector in 1990 anticipated
7.4 per cent for 'Malay individuals' and 22.6 per cent for 'Malay
interests'. The *Fourth Malaysia Plan, 1981–1985*, however, reduced the
share for Bumiputera individuals to 5.2 per cent (or 17.3 per cent of
total Bumiputera ownership) and raised the share for 'Bumiputera
trust agencies' to 24.8 per cent (or 82.7 per cent). However, since
then, far greater emphasis has been given to Bumiputera personal
wealth acquisition. The share of Bumiputera individuals rose significantly from 7.6 per cent in 1983 to 14.2 per cent in 1990, 18.6 per
cent in 1995 and 17.4 per cent in 1999. Meanwhile, the Bumiputera
trust agencies' share declined from 11.1 per cent in 1983 to 5.1 per
cent in 1990 and 1.7 per cent in 1999. Individuals accounted for 73.4
per cent of total Bumiputera ownership in 1990 and 91.0 per cent in
1999.

The share for Bumiputera trust agencies correspondingly fell to 9.0
per cent in 1999 – a very dramatic reversal in a relatively short space of
time, with important implications for the composition and nature of
Malay capital as well as the character and role of state intervention and
the public sector in Malaysia. Clearly, wealth accumulation by the state
on behalf of the entire Bumiputera community has been abandoned in
favour of private accumulation by individual Bumiputeras. Although for
private aggrandisement, much of such accumulation has been heavily
reliant on government dispensation. Hence, capital accumulation has

increasingly been determined by 'know-who' (political connections or influence), rather than 'know-how' (entrepreneurial ability or capabilities). While this might be more pronounced among Bumiputera businessmen, it has also been true for others who have made their fortunes contingent on opportunities involving government dispensation (Gomez and Jomo, 1999).

In fact, the issue of wealth ownership – whether of shares or other wealth – involves only the interests of a small elite. The high concentration of share capital ownership within each ethnic community was almost definitely understated in the case of the Amanah Saham Nasional (ASN). The ASN – superseded by Amanah Saham Bumiputera (ASB) from 1991 – scheme provides some indication of the degree of wealth concentration in Malaysia. The ASN and ASB schemes have had unusually high rates of participation owing to the government's efforts to maximize Bumiputera participation.

Such concentration is even more pronounced in the rest of the economy in view of government efforts to promote widespread participation in the ASN and its successor ASB schemes and the previous RM50,000 (now RM200,000) ownership limit on share units per Bumiputera. The level of concentration was also limited by the RM50,000 share ceiling for individual ownership. The ASN's and ASB's tax-free rates of return to investment has consistently been well above prevailing savings and fixed deposit interest rates. No other share ownership scheme in the country, and probably in the world, has been able to attract such widespread nominal participation. Yet, although well over two million Bumiputeras were involved by the late 1980s, the vast majority had invested RM500 or less, while about 1.3 per cent of all eligible Bumiputeras owned 75 per cent of all ASN shares!

Ethnicity in employment and the professions

Government occupational statistics also suggest that employment restructuring has, generally speaking, been achieved. In fact, Bumiputera employment in the public sector and agriculture greatly exceeds their overall demographic share. According to the World Bank, government remuneration is, on average, about 25 per cent higher than in the private sector. However, Bumiputeras are still under-represented in some of the most lucrative professions, such as medicine, accountancy and architecture, though much of this is temporary and will decline as the population ages. Nevertheless, as Table 7.6 shows, for the vast majority of the population, employment restructuring goals had, by and large, been achieved by 1990.

Table 7.6(a) Malaysia: Employment by Occupation and Race, 1970 (per cent)

Occupation	Bumiputera	Chinese	Indian	Others
Professional and technical	47.0	39.5	10.8	2.7
Administrative and managerial	24.1	62.9	7.8	5.2
Clerical and related workers	35.4	45.9	17.2	1.5
Sales and related workers	26.7	61.7	11.1	0.4
Service workers	44.3	39.6	14.6	1.5
Agricultural workers	72.0	17.3	9.7	1.0
Pr., transport and other workers	34.2	55.9	9.6	0.3
Total	51.8	36.6	10.6	1.0
Ethnic proportions	52.7	35.8	10.7	0.8

Table 7.6(b) Malaysia: Proportional Equality Index of Employment by Occupation

Occupation	Bumiputera	Chinese	Indian	Others
Professional and technical	0.89	1.10	1.01	3.38
Administrative and managerial	0.46	1.76	0.73	6.50
Clerical and related workers	0.67	1.28	1.61	1.88
Sales and related workers	0.51	1.72	1.04	0.50
Service workers	0.84	1.11	1.36	1.88
Agricultural workers	1.37	0.48	0.91	1.25
Pr., transport and other workers	0.65	1.56	0.90	0.38
Total	0.98	1.02	0.99	1.25

Note: The proportional equality index is derived by dividing the percentage of employment of each ethnic group in each sector/occupation by the percentage share in population.
Sources: Malaysia, *Fourth Malaysia Plan, 1981–1985*.

As far as occupational restructuring is concerned, by 1990 and 2000, Bumiputeras were significantly under-represented (i.e. less than 45 per cent) only at the 'administrative and managerial' level (28.4 per cent) and in sales-related occupations (36.5 per cent). Nevertheless, the Malay proportions in these occupations have greatly increased since independence, and especially under the NEP, though the Chinese proportions – 66.0 per cent and 57.5 per cent respectively – still significantly exceed their population share.

Otherwise, occupational restructuring has largely been achieved, especially in low-income employment. Rather, the main sources of tension over employment restructuring involve access to business opportunities and the more lucrative occupations. This mainly affects and concerns the middle class. Tertiary education as well as related employment and promotion opportunities are the main concerns and primary sources of inter-ethnic resentment and conflict, especially among the middle class, who correctly see these as determining their life-chances. Both sides have been very morally self-righteous about their interests and claims. On the one hand, many Bumiputeras invoke indigenous or 'native rights' and the need for 'positive discrimination' and 'affirmative action' to overcome historical disadvantage under colonialism. On the other hand, many non-Bumiputeras protest 'ethnic discrimination', 'cultural oppression' and the official undermining of meritocracy.

Ethnic percentages in professional and technical occupations broadly reflect demographic proportions in the Peninsular Malaysian population, though Bumiputera under-representation in the more lucrative and prestigious professions has been highlighted by the Malay middle class, politicians and the government. Nevertheless, as Table 7.7 shows, the Bumiputera proportion of the eight prized professions rose from 4.9 per cent in 1970 to 29.0 per cent in 1990 and 33.1 per cent in 1995 and 32.0 per cent in 1997, before measurement changes reduced the number of professionals by 45.5 per cent in 1997 and the Bumiputera share to 27.3 per cent in 1997 and 28.9 per cent in 1999. There may also be some underestimation of the Bumiputera proportion as far as those in government service (e.g. the legal and judicial service) are concerned. Perhaps more importantly, recent Bumiputera advances into the professions mainly involve the younger age cohorts. Hence, the Bumiputera proportion will continue to increase as the population ages, even if the current proportions remain unchanged. Malay professionals also seem to earn proportionately more, suggesting a likely ethnic premium in their professional charges.

As far as tertiary education more generally is concerned, the Bumiputera population in government-accredited local universities and university colleges was 67 per cent in 1985 (*5MP*, 1986: 490–1), up from 40 per cent in 1970 (*MTR2MP*, 1973: 193). The ratio was supposed to be 60 per cent from the early 1980s, as part of a 'compromise' resolution of the Merdeka University issue from the late 1970s. The controversy over ethnic quotas for public university admissions has continued to the present. The vast majority of students in private tertiary institutions have been non-Bumiputera. Most of the thousands of Bumiputera students abroad are believed to be government-funded, compared to only a small proportion of non-Bumiputeras.

Evidence on 'restructuring society' also suggests considerable success in terms of changing ethnic proportions in various lucrative

Table 7.7 Malaysia: Registered Professionals[a] by Ethnic Group, 1970–1999

	Bumiputera		Chinese		Indians		Others		Total	
1970[b]	225	(4.9%)	2,793	(61.0%)	1,066	(23.3%)	492	(10.8%)	4,576	(100%)
1975[c]	537	(6.7%)	5,131	(64.1%)	1,764	(22.1%)	572	(7.1%)	8,004	(100%)
1979	1,237	(11.0%)	7,154	(63.5%)	2,375	(21.1%)	496	(4.4%)	11,262	(100%)
1980	2,534	(14.9%)	10,812	(63.5%)	2,963	(17.4%)	708	(4.2%)	17,017	(100%)
1983	4,496	(18.9%)	14,933	(62.9%)	3,638	(15.3%)	699	(2.9%)	23,766	(100%)
1984	5,473	(21.0%)	16,154	(61.9%)	3,779	(14.5%)	675	(2.6%)	26,081	(100%)
1985	6,318	(22.2%)	17,407	(61.2%)	3,946	(13.9%)	773	(2.7%)	28,444	(100%)
1988	8,571	(25.1%)	19,985	(58.4%)	4,878	(14.3%)	762	(2.2%)	34,196	(100%)
1990	11,753	(29.0%)	22,641	(55.9%)	5,363	(13.2%)	750	(1.9%)	40,507	(100%)
1995	19,344	(33.1%)	30,636	(52.4%)	7,542	(12.9%)	939	(1.6%)	58,461	(100%)
1997[d]	22,866	(32.0%)	37,278	(52.1%)	9,389	(13.1%)	1,950	(2.7%)	71,843	(100%)
1997[d]	10,659	(27.3%)	21,298	(54.4%)	6,653	(17.0%)	515	(1.3%)	39,125	(100%)
1999	15,321	(28.9%)	28,565	(53.9%)	8,183	(15.5%)	884	(1.7%)	52,953	(100%)

Note:
[a] Architects, accountants, engineers, dentists, doctors, veterinary surgeons, surveyors, lawyers.
[b] Excluding surveyors and lawyers.
[c] Excluding surveyors.
[d] There appears to have been a significant change in the counting of professionals between 1999 (*Mid-Term Review of the Seventh Malaysia Plan, 1996–2000*) and 2001 (*Eighth Malaysia Plan, 2001–2005*), with the total number of professionals and the Bumiputra share dropping drastically.
Sources: Malaysian plan documents.

professional occupations and by sectoral employment as well as wealth ownership. Official concern appears to have moved away from school enrolment ratios, where Bumiputeras are now actually 'over-represented' owing to the generally larger size of Bumiputera families as well as the higher enrolment of non-Bumiputra children in private institutions. Even interest in enrolment at the tertiary level has declined with the considerable Bumiputera advances since the 1970s and the growing phenomenon of graduate unemployment since the mid-1980s. Instead, the focus is now primarily on the lucrative professions, where Bumiputeras are still relatively under-represented despite rapid progress, especially since the 1980s.

It is very likely that tertiary education, and especially access to these professions, will continue to preoccupy the middle class, who feel they stand to gain or lose most in this regard. For obvious reasons, focus on the lucrative professions is likely to remain. Such ethnic preoccupations previously constrained state approval of private initiatives in human resource development and domestic tertiary education development, despite the considerable foreign exchange savings that have since accrued. However, the situation has changed significantly since the mid-1980s as businesses have successfully invested in providing tertiary educational credentials. Continued regulation has provided lucrative opportunities for rentier marketing of such degrees. Such preoccupations as well as the regime's obsession with controlling campus dissent have stood in the way of the urgent need to reform higher education in order to prepare the Malaysian population better for rapid cultural and technological changes.

Expenditure

After the NEP's inception, the state's commitment and priorities – as reflected by NEP expenditure allocations – increasingly shifted away from poverty eradication towards restructuring until the *5MP*. The ratio of allocations for restructuring, compared with poverty eradication, rose steadily from 22 per cent under the *2MP* to 37 per cent under the *3MP* and 47 per cent under the *4MP*. According to the *5MP*, the *4MP* allocation ratio was later revised upward to 57 per cent, while the ratio for actual expenditure was estimated at 59 per cent (*5MP*, 1986: 231, Table 7.3). However, this ratio was revised downward for 1986–90 to 33 per cent under the *5MP*, and then further down to 26 per cent, and then 20 per cent with the *MTR5MP*. Only a small percentage of the Bumiputera population benefits significantly from restructuring expenditure, compared with the far greater proportion of the Malay population

(23.8 per cent in Peninsular Malaysia in 1987) still officially considered poor. Subsequent Malaysian five-year plan documents no longer provide the information necessary for analysis of subsequent trends.

There is considerable evidence that only a fraction of poverty eradication funds actually benefits the poor, considering the huge bureaucracy and other expenses involved. 'Of the revised allocation for poverty eradication, about 40 per cent was directly channelled to the poor through programmes such as input subsidies and basic amenities, 31.8 per cent for indirect programmes such as purchase of equipment, credit facilities and training, while the rest was essentially for supporting programmes which included the construction of related office buildings and associated management costs' (*MTR5MP*, 1989: 60). The nature of poverty eradication expenditure also provide greater benefits to the non-poor, e.g. the rice price support programme primarily benefits big farmers with large marketable surpluses of grain. Also, shifting the emphasis from poverty eradication to restructuring society probably tended to increase inequality within the Malay community, while the mid-1980s shift in the opposite direction may partly account for the reduction in Malay income inequality during 1984–7.

To improve the effectiveness and efficiency of public expenditure, including poverty eradication efforts, strict 'performance evaluation' has to be developed. Such comparative evaluation can help identify to what extent each poverty eradication measure is effective in reducing poverty or increasing incomes and economic welfare among target groups, among those who are poor as well as among others who are not poor. Such evaluation would be useful in identifying the most effective measures for eradicating poverty in the future as they would have to take into account the efficacy of specific poverty reduction measures.

Summary and conclusion

Malaysia's New Economic Policy (NEP) was first announced in 1970 as the principal policy response to the post-election race riots of May 1969, which also resulted in a significant regime change. This chapter suggests that the events of May 1969 also involved a widespread popular rejection of the ruling Alliance coalition as well as a 'palace coup' within the ruling UMNO as the 'Young Turks' supporting then Deputy Prime Minister Razak sidelined Prime Minister Rahman, who had led UMNO from 1951 and the country to independence in August 1957. The Rahman regime was seen by the new Razak regime as having been too conciliatory with the ubiquitous Chinese business community. The new

Razak NEP regime was, therefore, committed to increased ethnic affirmative action or positive discrimination policies on behalf of the ethnic Malays.

The NEP had two prongs, namely 'poverty eradication regardless of race' and 'restructuring society to eliminate the identification of race with economic function'. The NEP was supposed to create the conditions for national unity by reducing inter-ethnic resentment due to socio-economic disparities. In practice, the NEP policies were seen as pro-Bumiputera (indigene), or more specifically, pro-Malay, referring to the largest indigenous ethnic community. Poverty reduction efforts have been seen as primarily rural and Malay, with policies principally oriented to the rural Malay (peasants). As poverty reduction efforts had been uncontroversial and had declined in significance over time, the NEP came to be increasingly identified with 'restructuring society' efforts to reduce inter-ethnic disparities, especially between ethnic Malay and ethnic Chinese Malaysians.

The NEP has been associated with the first Outline Perspective Plan (OPP) for 1971–90. The OPP sought to reduce poverty from 49 per cent in Peninsular Malaysia in 1970 to 16 per cent in 1990. The actual poverty rate in the peninsular in 1990 was 17 per cent, while the national rate was slightly higher. The NEP's main restructuring target was to raise the Bumiputera share of corporate stock ownership from 1.5 per cent in 1969 to 30 per cent in 1990. The government's data suggest that Bumiputera ownership rose to about 18 per cent in 1990 and slightly over 20 per cent in 2000. Although the government originally envisaged that much of the Bumiputera corporate wealth would be held by trust agencies, private individual Bumiputera ownership has risen from less than a third to over 90 per cent. Much of the measurement of NEP achievement has been subjected to dispute. This has been exacerbated by the lack of transparency on socio-economic data deemed sensitive.

The NEP has since ostensibly been replaced by the National Development Policy (NDP) associated with the *Second Outline Perspective Plan* (OPP2) for 1991–2000, and then by the National Vision Policy linked to the *Third Outline Perspective Plan* (OPP3) for 2001–2010. Although the new policies have put far greater emphasis on achieving rapid growth, industrialization and structural change, there is the widespread perception that public policy is still primarily influenced by the NEP's policies of restructuring society.

These policies are believed to be especially important in terms of how public policies affect corporate wealth ownership as well as other areas, notably education and employment opportunities. In other words, ethnic discrimination primarily involves the business community and the middle class, where inter-ethnic tension is most acute. Inter-ethnic business coalitions have become increasingly important over time, often with the ethnic Malay partner securing rents for gaining access to government-determined business opportunities, and the ethnic Chinese partner with business acumen getting the job done. Such 'Ali Baba' arrangements have generated considerable resentment, especially among those denied access to such business opportunities.

With privatization opportunities from the mid-1980s largely decided on a discretionary basis by the government leadership, there has been growing resentment and criticism of 'rent-seeking' and 'cronyism'. Such disbursement of privatization opportunities also strengthened the leadership's means for patronage, in turn encouraging competition for party and government political office and upward mobility. The selective nature of the 'bail-out' processes and procedures following the 1997–8 currency, financial and economic crises have strengthened, rather than undermined, these tendencies.

While there is little doubt that specific socio-economic targets of the NEP have been largely achieved, it is not clear that such achievement has led to national unity, understood in terms of improved inter-ethnic relations. Associating improved inter-ethnic relations almost exclusively with reduced inter-ethnic disparities among the respective business communities and middle classes has in fact generated greater ethnic resentment and suspicion on both sides. Ethnic affirmative action policies as implemented and enforced in Malaysia have associated the interests of entire ethnic groups with their respective elites, thus generalizing resentments associated with inter-ethnic, intra-class competition. Thus, it is unlikely that the ethnic affirmative action means will achieve the end of improved inter-ethnic relations. An alternative approach needs to be found to create more lasting conditions for improved inter-ethnic relations.

Quite predictably, it has been in the area of wealth ownership that there seems to have been the greatest false modesty all round. The main protagonists – the Malays and the Chinese – are both very insistent that the official figures exaggerate their respective shares of economic wealth. While there are grains of truth in such claims, the arguments are essentially self-serving. They are used to legitimize and support claims for greater shares, and for government intervention or withdrawal in this regard as the case may be. But what is most telling, perhaps, is that increased wealth ownership for any particular ethnic group actually involves only a very small minority, who are nevertheless ever ready to proclaim that they embody the interests of the particular ethnic group with which they are identified.

The relations between wealth distribution and other inter-ethnic economic disparities, such as income distribution, may be quite spurious. It is quite possible that there would be greater interest in uplifting incomes, rather than redistributing wealth. It is quite likely that there will be no further upward revision of the NEP's wealth restructuring targets above 30 per cent despite continued Malay calls for wealth redistribution to reflect ethnic demographic proportions. As post-1990 (National Development Policy and *Second Outline Perspective Plan, 1991–2000*) and post-2000 (National Vision Policy and *Third Outline Perspective Plan, 2001–2010*) policies suggest, it is likely that the 30 per cent target, which has developed such great symbolic significance and is most closely identified with the NEP in the public imagination, will be indefinitely retained for achievement at some point in the future. Depending on how one chooses to measure corporate wealth distribution, it can be shown that the 30 per cent target has already been achieved or is close to being achieved.

However, adopting such means to assuage Bumiputera demands is likely to be politically risky. Furthermore, under the NEP, many who now control UMNO and the other BN parties at various levels actually enjoy rentier incomes, largely attributable to the NEP and the climate it has fostered. These people are unlikely to give up such opportunities – perceived to have been provided by the NEP – without a fight. Hence, any government based on such patronage and support is unlikely to be capable of riding roughshod over such interests despite the better judgement of those with greater appreciation of the mixed legacy of the NEP.

The Mahathir government has already passed two opportunities (1991, 2001) to break with past policies in the interest of greater economic efficiency, more rapid growth and fairer distribution. It seems unlikely that a successor UMNO/BN government will have the autonomy or will to make such a bold break. And while the new opposition coalition must necessarily address the social, political and policy legacy around the NEP, it is more likely to take bold new initiatives for a more just and dynamic new Malaysian society.

The Malaysian government has been able to choose whether or not to announce that the NEP objectives, or more precisely the OPP targets, had been achieved. By doing so, the government could have made a clean break with the NEP in 1991 and embarked on different new policies. Instead, the government chose to continue the basic thrusts of the NEP with some changes, bearing Mahathir policy priorities, including greater emphasis on growth, industrialization and the emergence of Bumiputera Commercial and Industrial Community (BCIC) plus a new name. This compromise formula sought to insert and assert Mahathir's priorities without overly threatening his UMNO following who are still yet to be weaned off the NEP. This process has been continued in 2001 with the announcement of a new National Vision Policy to coincide with the *Third Outline Perspective Plan* period (2001–10), an obvious reference to Mahathir's Vision 2020, first enunciated in February 1991.

Whether or not the new government policy represents any significant departure from the policy in the 1990s is difficult to gauge, but seems unlikely. In view of policy trends under Mahathir, which have mainly benefited the private sector, including foreign investors, there is little evidence of any significant advances in social policy to enhance the welfare of the majority. Unlike the first decade of the NEP in the 1970s, when social policy – albeit primarily ethnic-oriented – became important, the last two decades have witnessed redistribution effects increasingly captured by politically connected Malay business and middle-class interests while private sector promotion has primarily benefited politically well-connected rentier or crony interests.

The 1997 currency crisis and the unprecedented severe contraction of 1998 owing to the very open nature of the Malaysian economy drew attention to the 'cronyistic' practices that have become an important feature of Malaysia's business landscape. Although the focus on cronyism as the cause of the 1997–8 currency and financial crises was somewhat misplaced and served the proponents of financial liberalization and capital account openness, it is now recognized as a major problem distorting and retarding the development of Malaysian modernization, industrialization as well as economic dynamism and competitiveness. After a strong recovery in 1999 and 2000, the Southeast Asian regional economic slowdown in 2001 has underscored the weakness of Malaysia's domestic engines of growth and the mixed consequences of economic openness and dependence. The prospects for Malaysia's domestic engines of growth are increasingly recognized as weak, not least because of the economy's openness and strong outward orientation as well as its historical reliance on foreign direct investment for propelling its most dynamic industries.

One consequence of foreign domination of Malaysian manufacturing has been to encourage Malaysian investors to gravitate to other rentier activities, especially finance and property. As far as most Malaysian primary commodities are concerned, the major problems on the supply-side have been rising labour costs and the exhaustion of timber and land resources. Hence, for continued economic expansion, Malaysia desperately needs new investments, technology and market access, especially for manufacturers. FDI from abroad is supposed to sustain capital inflows, provided earlier by foreign borrowings in the early 1980s and by portfolio inflows before the 1997 crisis. But with the availability of China and other competitive investment locations, Malaysia appears less attractive to prospective investors.

For ethnic-political as well as economic reasons, the Malaysian government favoured foreign investment, rather than (predominantly Chinese) domestic investment in the late 1980s. This strategy further enhanced foreign capital's dominance of Malaysian industry. However, in view of the post-1997 perception of lack of Malaysian policy consistency, it is unlikely that the massive foreign investments desired will be forthcoming, at least in the amounts desired in the near future. The government may then be tempted either to resort to foreign borrowings once again, or to offer even more attractive terms to encourage renewed foreign investments. It will be difficult to open the oil (and gas) tap much more, or cut down much more of the already seriously diminished forest, as happened in 1987. Needless to say, these options do not really offer sustainable, long-term growth and structural change for the Malaysian economy.

The debate over future Malaysian economic policy has recently surfaced again, after the economic and political crises of 1997–8, causing considerable concern in various quarters. Decisions about future economic policies are probably not going to be decided by the interests or needs of the public, but are more likely to reflect the interests and desires of those in power and others of influence, including foreign economic advisors, who usually represent the interests of transnational corporations and international economic agencies.

While there is little doubt that the Mahathir regime's economic policy rhetoric has been decidedly nationalistic since 1998 and monetary policy has been somewhat independent (although the national currency, the ringgit, has been problematically pegged to the US dollar since September 1998, there is little evidence of consistently sustained nationalistic economic policies). On the contrary, there have been a series of pragmatic policy reversals encouraged by the deteriorating situation since the strong recovery of 1999–2000. In view of economic policy shifts since the mid-1980s and late 1990s, and recent government priorities, future economic policy will probably continue to emphasize rapid growth, especially industrialization and greater reliance on the market.

Notes

1. For example, the poverty reduction between 1984 and 1987 – reported in the *Mid-Term Review of the Fifth Malaysia Plan, 1986–1990*, and based on the presumably consistent first and second Household Income Surveys – raised more troubling questions. For instance, while the number of poor rubber smallholding households was reported to have risen from 68,500 in 1984 to 83,100 in 1987, poverty incidence among them was said to have fallen from 42.7 per cent to 40.0 per cent! This decline would require the total number of rubber smallholding households to have fallen by 30 per cent – from 160,400 to 207,800 – over the same three-year period, a development unsupported by other evidence. And while the number of poor rubber smallholders is reported to have increased, poverty incidence among estate workers was inexplicably supposed to have dropped by 29 per cent – from 16,400 to 11,700 – over the same period. Meanwhile, the number of poor rice farm households was reported to have dropped by 23 per cent – from 70,500 to 54,400 – despite the reduction of government (e.g. fertilizer) subsidies and the officially fixed rice price from 1980 to 1990.

   Similarly, the disclosure of the official poverty line in mid-1989 suggests that at least some of the poverty reduction, especially between 1976 and 1984, may have been due to the reduction of the per capita poverty line income from RM33.00 in 1970 to RM30.30 in 1987 in 1970 prices, or from RM74.15 in 1970 to RM68.09 in 1987 in 1987 prices. There is also no way to independently verify the comparability of the data, e.g. in terms of methods of measurement, since they are not publicly available. Also, the different nature of the three kinds of survey involved means that they are not strictly comparable from a statistical point of view.

2. For instance, a household may well enjoy government-subsidized services valued above or below the value assumed in estimating the poverty line income (PLI). But if the full value of the services it enjoys pushes the household above the poverty line, whereas taking into consideration only the minimum quantum for the PLI would keep it below the poverty line, then clearly, the household is not receiving certain other basic needs despite being considered to be above the poverty line.

3. The *Mid-Term Review of the Fifth Malaysia Plan, 1986–1990* (p. 47) noted that if a per capita measure is used instead of a household measure, the official poverty rate in 1987 would have been 12.4 per cent, instead of 17.3 per cent, in Peninsular Malaysia.

4. The different PLIs first published in the *Mid-Term Review of the Fifth Malaysia Plan, 1986–1990* for Peninsular Malaysia, Sabah and Sarawak emphasize the considerable variation in living costs within a small country like Malaysia. For 1987, the PLIs were estimated at 'about RM350 per month for a household of 5.14 persons in Peninsular Malaysia, RM429 per month for a household of 5.24 in Sarawak, and RM533 per month for a household of 5.36 in

Sabah'. Hence, the per capita PLI was 19.8 per cent higher in Sarawak and 45.5 per cent higher in Sabah than in Peninsular Malaysia. Yet, there have not been separate PLIs for urban and rural areas, implying that the true extent of urban poverty may well be underestimated compared to rural poverty, where the urban cost of living is significantly higher, especially in the Kelang Valley and Johor Baru areas. The PLI for 1999 was RM510 per month for Peninsular Malaysia for an average household size of 4.6, RM685 per month for Sabah for an average household size of 4.9, and RM584 per month for Sarawak for an average household size of 4.8. (Malaysia, 2001b).

5. This happened despite some official discouragement of Chinese investments and capital flight attributable to the Industrial Coordination Act (ICA), higher interest rates abroad as well as emigration and investments overseas ('exit') due to Chinese frustrations in Malaysia. The resilience of Chinese capital should not be underestimated, however.

The decline in ethnic Chinese political influence after the 1960s has resulted in various responses and initiatives, varying with the specific interests concerned. From 1985, some of the more politically inspired initiatives were exposed as business scams dependent on political patronage or protection, exploited by politicians and businessmen for their own selfish ends. These exposures have further undermined the already seriously eroded position of the Malaysian Chinese Association (MCA), the second most important party in the ruling coalition. Despite its sizeable share of the economy, Chinese capital has limited control over the financial (banking, etc.) sector and the 'commanding heights' of the traditional capitalist sectors (international trade, primary production), which have mainly been taken over from foreign (especially British) capital by the state, ostensibly for the Malays.

6. In the mid-1980s, Mahathir announced to foreign investors and the Malaysian Chinese public (through the Chinese press) that NEP targets, particularly the 30 per cent objective, had been suspended in view of the economic recession in the mid-1980s.

7. Federal and state government share ownership other than Bumiputera trust agencies have not appeared in the official tables on ownership of share capital in limited companies since 1969.

References

Anand, S. (1983) *Inequality and Poverty in Malaysia: Measurement and Decomposition*, New York: Oxford University Press.

Asher, M. and Jomo, K. S. (1987) 'Recent Malaysian Tax Policy Initiatives', in Jomo, K. S. et al. (eds.) *Crisis and Response in the Malaysian Economy*, Kuala Lumpur: Malaysian Economic Association: 116–135.

Gomez, E. T. and Jomo, K. S. (1999) *Malaysia's Political Economy*, revised edition, Cambridge: Cambridge University Press.

Hashim, S. M. (1997) *Income Inequality and Poverty in Malaysia*, Boulder: Rowman.

Ikemoto, Y. (1985) 'Income Distribution in Malaysia, 1957–1980', *The Developing Economies*, 23 (4), December.

Ishak Shari (2000) 'Economic Growth and Income Inequality in Malaysia, 1971–95', *Journal of the Asia Pacific Economy*, 5(1 & 2): 112–24.

Ishak, S. and Ragayah, M. Z. (1990) 'The Patterns and Trends of Income Distribution in Malaysia, 1970–1987', *The Singapore Economic Review*, 35(1): 102–23.

Ishak, S. and Ragayah, M. Z. (1995) 'Economic Growth and Equity in Malaysia: Performance and Prospects. Paper presented at the Fifth Tun Abdul Razak Conference, Ohio University, Athens, Ohio, 12–13 April.

Jomo, K. S. (1986) *A Question of Class: Capital, the State and Uneven Development in Malaya*, Singapore: Oxford University Press.

Jomo, K. S. (1990) *Growth and Structural Change in the Malaysian Economy*, London: Macmillan and New York: St. Martin's Press.

Jomo, K. S. (1999) 'Globalization and Human Development in East Asia', in UNDP, *Globalization with A Human Face: Human Development Report 1999, Background Papers*, Vol. 2, Human Development Report Office, New York: United Nations Development Programme: 81–123.

Jomo, K. S. and Ishak, S. (1986) *Development Policies and Income Inequality in Peninsular Malaysia*, Kuala Lumpur: Institute for Advanced Studies, University of Malaya.

Jomo, K. S. with Osman-Rani, H. (1985) 'Wage Trends in Peninsular Malaysian Manufacturing, 1963–73', *Kajian Ekonomi Malaysia*, 21(1), June: 18–38.

Kharas, H. and Surjit, B. (1991) Growth and Equity in Malaysia: Policies and Consequences. Paper presented at he Eleventh Malaysian Economic Convention, 'The Sixth Malaysia Plan: The Way Forward to a Developed Nation', Kuala Lumpur, 24–26 September.

Malaysia (1971) *Second Malaysia Plan, 1971–1975*. Kuala Lumpur: Government Printers.

Malaysia (1973) *Mid-Term Review of the Second Malaysia Plan, 1971–1975*. Kuala Lumpur: Government Printers.

Malaysia (1976) *Third Malaysia Plan, 1976–1980*. Kuala Lumpur: Government Printers.

Malaysia (1979) *Mid-Term Review of the Third Malaysia Plan, 1976–1980*. Kuala Lumpur: Government Printers.

Malaysia (1981) *Fourth Malaysia Plan, 1981–1985*, Kuala Lumpur: Government Printers.

Malaysia (1984) *Mid-Term Review of the Fourth Malaysia Plan, 1981–1985*, Kuala Lumpur: Government Printers.

Malaysia (1986) *Fifth Malaysia Plan, 1986–1990*, Kuala Lumpur: Government Printers.

Malaysia (1989) *Mid-Term Review of the Fifth Malaysia Plan, 1986–1990*, Kuala Lumpur: Government Printers.

Malaysia (1991a) *Second Outline Perspective Plan, 1991–2000*, Kuala Lumpur: Government Printers.

Malaysia (1991b) *Sixth Malaysia Plan, 1991–1995*, Kuala Lumpur: Government Printers.

Malaysia (1994) *Mid-Term Review of the Sixth Malaysia Plan, 1991–1995*, Kuala Lumpur: Government Printers.

Malaysia (1996) *Seventh Malaysia Plan, 1996–2000*, Kuala Lumpur: Government Printers.

Malaysia (1999) *Mid-Term Review of the Seventh Malaysia Plan, 1996–2000*, Kuala Lumpur: Government Printers.

Malaysia (2001a) *Third Outline Perspective Plan, 2001–2010*, Kuala Lumpur: Government Printers.

Malaysia (2001b) *Eighth Malaysia Plan, 2001–2005*, Kuala Lumpur: Government Printers.

McGee, T. G. (ed.) (1986) *Industrialization and Labour Force Processes: A Case Study of Peninsular Malaysia*, Canberra: Research School for Pacific and Asian Studies, Australian National University.

Meerman, J. (1983) *Public Expenditure in Malaysia*, New York: Oxford University Press.

Mehmet, Ozay (1986) *Development in Malaysia*, London: Croom Helm.

Rasiah, Rajah, Ishak, S. and Jomo, K. S. (1996) 'Globalization and Liberalization in East and South East Asia: Implications for Growth, Inequality and Poverty'. In UNCTAD, *Globalization and Liberalization: Effects of International Economic Relations on Poverty*, New York and Geneva: UNCTAD, pp. 181–200.

8
Managing Ethnic Relations in Post-Crisis Malaysia and Indonesia: Lessons from the New Economic Policy?

Khoo Boo Teik

In Indonesia the financial crisis of July 1997 sparked a precipitious economic collapse which catalysed the *Reformasi* that ended Suharto's three-decade 'New Order' regime. The economic implosion and political turbulence brought in their wake several outbreaks of ethnic violence. These were major incidents perpetrated against the Chinese population in Jakarta and some parts of rural Java, breaking out between Christian and Muslim communities in Maluku, and mounted by Dayaks against Madurese in Kalimantan. Being telescoped into a short period of turmoil and then virtually left to fester, the violence suggested that Indonesia's ethnic relations were fast collapsing into chaos.

Instances of ethnic animosity were definitely not unknown during the New Order period. The events of 1965–6 that toppled the Sukarno regime included attacks on Chinese Indonesians as part of the terrible 'anti-communist' massacres that ushered in the New Order. During the 1970s and 1980s, there had been sporadic bursts of anti-Chinese riots often attributed to *pribumi* (indigenous) resentment of ethnic Chinese domination of the economy. In 1997 in eastern Java, there was a rash of killing of *kiai* (Muslim teachers) and *dukun* (practitioners of 'magic') – the so-called *ninjas* suspected of being sorcerers (Kristof and Denn, 2000: 3–24). In Kalimantan, just months before the financial crisis, Dayak violence against the Madurese had begun, and then it resurfaced after Suharto's regime fell.

Yet Indonesia's post-crisis outbreaks of ethnic violence surpassed previous ones in several ways. The scale of violence was much higher (with the exception of the 1965–6 massacres or the killings following the invasion of East Timor) and the incidents covered different geographical locations. Between May and June 1998, about 2,244 people died in the violence that raged in several cities, part of which was directed at ethnic Chinese (Heryanto, 1999: 320–1). Thousands of people have been killed in Maluku and in Kalimantan.[1] The character of some of the violence was shocking – the systematic rape of Chinese women (Sandyawan, 1998; Heryanto, 1999), mutiliations of the *ninjas*, ritualistic decapitations of Madurese men, women and children (Chang, 2001), and unrestrained destruction of churches and mosques (Tedjasukmana, 2000). Complex in their causes, flashpoints and antagonists, the ethnic conflicts continued to spread and flare, from Maluku's capital, Ambon, to its other islands, and from West to Central Kalimantan. In Maluku, seemingly trivial incidents sparked large-scale ethnic confrontations, which escalated into interreligious warfare, as the resentments of 'indigenous' Christians towards the preferential treatment of 'settler' Muslims were heightened by their religious differences. In Kalimantan, similarly small accidents caused a mass slaughter as the economic resentments of 'indigenous' Dayaks were intensified by their cultural suspicions of 'transmigrant' Madurese. The results in both these cases were *pribumi* vs *primbumi* conflicts,[2] which signalled that Indonesia's economically related ethnic plights were not confined to *pribumi* responses to non-*pribumi* Chinese economic domination.

The security ramifications of the ethnic violence have become quite severe. They are so whether evaluated according to the complicity of segments of the security forces in these incidents, or the partisanship of police personnel and the armed forces, or the intervention of militias. Sections of the military were suspected of planning and executing the attacks upon the Chinese and Chinese women in particular in Jakarta in May 1998 (McBeth, 1998: 27, Heryanto, 1999: 317). The violence in Maluku in 1999–2000 found police personnel aligned with the Christian community while the armed forces sided with the Muslim community (Symonds, 2000). The religious dimensions of the Maluku violence were aggravated by the intervention of the Laskar Jihad militia (Fealy, 2001). Before Suharto's fall, his centralized regime was known to practise ethnic divide-and-rule policies even as it 'resolved' interethnic conflicts by resorting to military suppression. Since then, the persistent instability of the post-Suharto regimes has left them with few initiatives to offer as solutions to the post-1997 ethnic conflicts. Thus the incidents of ethnic violence, considered together with the ongoing ethnonationalist battles in Aceh and Papua, have been regarded as signs that the Indonesian state may itself disintegrate. With the continuing economic hardship and turbulence at the apex of the present political leadership in Indonesia, some observers have begun to compare the post-crisis situation in Indonesia with the former Soviet Union and Yugoslavia before these two states broke up with accompanying ethnic violence (Booth, 1999; Uhlin, 1999).

The condition of ethnic relations in Indonesia's neighbour, Malaysia, presents a sharp contrast. Since July 1997, although it was also badly affected by the financial crisis, Malaysia has experienced only two minor incidents of ethnic confrontation. Both, happening in Kampung Rawa, Penang (April 1998) and Kampung Medan, Kuala Lumpur (March 2001), involved Malay–Indian conflict, with the Penang incident taking on some hues of a Muslim–Hindu confrontation. However, each incident was largely localized, its casualties were limited and the situation was quickly brought under control. Malay–Chinese tension, which has long overshadowed Malaysia's post-independence politics, and which remains potentially the country's most destabilizing form of ethnic conflict, was significantly absent, barring low-level controversies over familiar issues that at no point threatened to spiral out of control.

Political contention in post-crisis Malaysia has thus been generally free of ethnic tension, which is perhaps surprising when it is recalled that an economic recession in 1985–6 contributed to heightening Malay–Chinese tensions dangerously in 1987. It is perhaps remarkable that after July 1997, and especially after the sacking of former deputy prime minister Anwar Ibrahim in September 1998, Malaysia has witnessed the emergence of a novel politics of dissent (also popularly called *reformasi* after the Indonesian movement) that has consciously attempted to put forth demands for democracy, institutional reform and social justice, instead of pursuing ethnic politics for which most Malaysian political parties are known. Indeed, *reformasi* in Malaysia has sprung up around Barisan Alternatif (Alternative Front, as distinguished from the ruling coalition, the Barisan Nasional or National Front), a coalition of opposition parties and social groupings known for their diverse ethnic partnerships, religious affiliations and ideological commitments (Khoo, 2000). Given the continuing flux in Malaysian politics, it is uncertain whether or how successfully Barisan Alternatif will transform the ethnic character of Malaysian politics, but already this opposition coalition has conducted some relatively bold experiments in interethnic cooperation.

In short, it is ironic that Indonesia, which was not usually taken to exemplify a society with intractable ethnic problems, should have suffered such massive outbreaks of ethnic violence, whereas Malaysia, which has been typically portrayed as 'a case study of a deeply divided multiethnic society', maintained stable, not to say improving, ethnic relations. This stark contrast, among other things, has led some politicians, analysts and others, in Indonesia and Malaysia, maybe even elsewhere, to argue that Malaysia had been able to avoid interethnic recriminations because of the socially and politically beneficent effects of its New Economic Policy (NEP), the massive affirmative action programme it had implemented since 1970. Extrapolating from that, 'many Indonesians are urging that the solution . . . requires the adoption of something like Malaysia's New Economic Policy' (Mackie, 1999: 195).

Whatever its prospects for practical success, the idea of NEP's replicability as public policy is intriguing, and surely so for regimes anxious to find policy solutions to ethnic tensions and pressures. But a proper evaluation of NEP's record in Malaysia, or its potential as a model for adaptation elsewhere, must refrain from abstracting NEP out of the historical context in which NEP was conceived, implemented, modified and even once suspended over three decades. There is good reason for this caution: NEP, at its core, was a statement of goals and objectives – namely those of 'eradicating poverty irrespective of race' and 'restructuring to abolish the identification of race with economic function' in order to achieve 'national unity'. After the 13 May 1969 ethnic violence in Kuala Lumpur, some such visionary statement would have had to be invented had the Tun Abdul Razak-led National Operations Council not in fact promulgated NEP. But the specific measures and programmes of affirmative action which were adopted in NEP's name were frequently matters of political contention, state intervention and bureaucratic invention. They were scarcely the stuff of a 'do-it-yourself' kit for mending ethnic disrepair. Besides, although ethnicity ruled its rhetoric, NEP was, ultimately, a massive social engineering project undertaken to redress 'ethnic economic imbalances' but, in doing so, it recomposed Malay society and Malaysia's class structure sometimes with unintended consequences.

As this chapter shows, the NEP project demanded far-reaching re-definitions of nationhood; alterations in the balance of economic and political power; construction of state capacities for economic interventionism; changes in modes of governance and regulation; and the promotion of an ideology of developmentalism – and all these coming together under specific global and domestic conditions. On the basis of this analysis of key changes to Malaysian political economy since 1970, and their impact on ethnic relations, the chapter concludes by considering whether some lessons from NEP might be relevant to Indonesia's future management of ethnic relations.

Ethnic division of labour

Official classification divides the Malaysian population between the Bumiputera, or indigenous, people and non-Bumiputera, or non-indigenous people. By this classification, the Bumiputera consist largely of the Malays and the aboriginal communities of Peninsular Malaysia, and the various 'natives' of Sabah and Sarawak. The Sabah and Sarawak Bumiputera include numerous groups, such as the Kadazan, Murut and Bajau of Sabah, and the Iban, Melanau, Bidayu, Kayan, Kenyah, Kelabit, Berawan and Penan of Sarawak. The non-Bumiputera category chiefly refers to the Chinese and Indians whose presence in Malaysia became significant with the waves of immigration encouraged or tolerated by the British colonial administration during the nineteenth and early twentieth centuries. In recent years, there has been an official tendency to differentiate the population along religious lines as well, the most important distinction being that made between Muslims, who are pre-dominantly Malays, and non-Muslims. There are sizeable numbers of indigenous non-Malay Muslims in Sabah and Sarawak, as well as Indian Muslims in Peninsular Malaysia, and a small proportion of Muslim converts of other ethnic backgrounds. Other Malaysians are classified or regard themselves as non-Muslims. Although these major ethnic and religious differentiations do not exhaust Malaysia's cultural complexity, they reflect the reality of its plural society, particularly a pronounced pre-NEP ethnic division of labour that has been the source of much political contention.

On the eve of Merdeka (independence) in 1957, Malaysia's political economy, shaped by colonial capitalism, had created certain patterns of uneven development, economic disparities and social divisions. The locus of advanced economic activity lay in foreign-owned plantations, mines and agency houses which produced and exported primary commodities (rubber and tin being the most important) to the rest of the world.[3] Domiciled Chinese capital maintained a sufficiently strong presence in *comprador* activities, banking, small-scale manufacturing, retailing and services so that the 'ubiquitous activity of the Chinese middleman' lent weight to the 'popular misconception that commerce is controlled by the Chinese' (Puthucheary, 1960: xv). Political control and the administration of the state apparatus had been mostly turned over to Malay aristocrats who had been trained for civil service by the colonial state. Hence the social origins of the ruling elite were those of the expatriate representatives of foreign capital, indigenous Malay aristocrats and domiciled Chinese capitalists and traders.

The economic disparities and social divisions were complicated by an ethnic division of labour not uncommon to the social organization of labour in other former colonies, such as Burma, Fiji and the countries of East Africa. Colonial design (Lim Teck Ghee, 1984) as well as the peasantry's 'refusal to supply plantation labour' (Alatas, 1977: 80) left the Malay peasantry chiefly engaged in food production. Migrant Chinese and Indian labour mainly worked in the tin mines, and rubber estates and public works projects, respectively. Thus the Malay peasantry escaped the harsh conditions of colonial capitalism, but the rural Malay community was thereby locked into an immiserating close-to-subsistence sector. Colonial capitalism took a heavy toll on migrant labour, but sections of Chinese and Indian migrants took advantage of an expanding urban sector to gain upward mobility through commerce, education and the professions.

The tripartite division of power at the elite level and the ethnic division of labour found a peculiar expression in the basic 'formula' of the Alliance, Malaysia's first ruling coalition, which comprised the United Malays National Organization (UMNO), Malayan Chinese Association (MCA) and Malayan Indian Congress (MIC). The Alliance protected foreign economic interests (which were not nationalized, as happened, say, in Indonesia under Sukarno), preserved the position of domiciled Chinese capital, and largely ceded the control of the state apparatus to the Malay aristocrats who led UMNO. Politically, a federal constitution reserved a 'special position' for the Malay community in recognition of its indigenous status but guaranteed the non-Malays a newfound citizenship and accompanying rights. Hence the Alliance's 'formula' became known as a compromise that left 'politics for the Malays' and 'economics for the Chinese'. The Alliance's economic management was conservative. The thrust of economic development under the Alliance was directed at improving urban infrastructure, implementing limited rural development schemes and providing small-scale assistance to incipient Malay business. Few things more clearly showed the regime's commitment to a 'free market' and its reluctance to tackle the ethnic division of labour than the regime's reluctance to intervene on behalf of sections of UMNO's Malay base. Despite a growing Malay frustration with the lack of progress in redressing their 'relative economic backwardness', the regime's orientation in this area was supportive rather than aggressive (Jomo, 1986: 253–4).

Left to itself the market could not resolve problems of rising unemployment, declining incomes and widening inequalities. By the late 1960s, the Alliance was hard pressed to meet social expectations coming from different quarters. The expectations were *economic* because *laissez faire* capitalism and its ethnic division of labour could no longer match the social pressures arrayed against it. A marginalized Malay peasantry sought release from rural poverty, most dramatically by seizing uncultivated state land. A combination of Malay bureaucrats, intelligentsia and middle class wanted to end their 'relative backwardness' vis-à-vis their Chinese counterparts and Chinese capital in particular (Mahathir, 1970). The non-Malay middle and working classes refused to accept that their opportunities for employment, education and upward mobility could be prejudiced by the constitutional safeguards of certain 'Malay special rights'. The expectations were *cultural* in that the fissures of Malaysia's multiethnic society presented serious problems in the areas of language, culture and citizenship. These were susceptible to ethnic sentiments during the formative years of a Malaysian nationhood which was still haunted by the separate memories and complex demands of pre-war and post-war Malay, Chinese and Indian nationalism. Finally, the expectations were *political* as the popular grievances were expressed via political parties and electoral competition. In short, the ethnic politics of the 1960s pitted the Alliance's *laissez faire* capitalism and 'Merdeka compromise' against a rising *democratization of expectations* – that is, mass but frequently conflicting expectations of what decolonization and independence should mean.

At the May 1969 general election, the coincidence of mass expectations crystallized into an electoral revolt against the Alliance. An informal pact helped diverse opposition parties – the Pan Malaysian Islamic Party (PMIP, now Parti Islam, or PAS), Democratic Action Party (DAP) and the Gerakan Rakyat Malaysia (Gerakan, or Malaysian People's Movement) – erode the Alliance's hold on power. On 13 May, Kuala Lumpur was engulfed in ethnic violence.

NEP: Politics and social transformation

With the violence the Alliance's elitist framework, the political economy that underpinned it, and the cultural compromises that were its supposed success, collapsed.[4] The National Operations Council (NOC), headed by Deputy Prime Minister Tun Abdul Razak, which ruled under a state of emergency from 1969 to 1971, had no more use for *laissez faire* capitalism. Razak's regime promulgated the New Economic Policy (NEP), the premises of which were that widespread poverty, the ethnic division of labour and Malay resentment of interethnic 'economic imbalances' lay at the heart of the May 1969 violence. NEP's two major objectives were 'poverty eradication irrespective of race', and 'restructuring to abolish the identification of race with economic function'. To 'eradicate poverty irrespective of race', the state's 'Outline Perspective Plan 1971–90' targeted a decline in the incidence of poverty, from 49 per cent of all households in 1970 to 16 per cent in 1990. To accomplish 'restructuring to abolish the identification of race with economic function', the state planned to raise the *bumiputera* (indigenous, but predominantly Malay) share of corporate equity from 2.5 per cent in 1970 to 30 per cent in 1990.

During NEP's first decade of implementation, the pursuit of its objectives entailed several major socio-political departures from the Alliance period. BN (effectively UMNO) redefined the parameters of Malaysian nationhood so as to place the dominant position of the Malay community vis-à-vis other ethnic communities beyond contention. BN imposed this redefinition by entrenching the Malay language as the national language and the medium of instruction in state schools, reorganizing the educational system to reflect NEP's priority of producing greater numbers of Malay graduates, and proclaiming a Malay and Islamic culture as the national culture. With NEP's affirmative action imperatives, the state systematically used ethnic quotas and targets to regulate access to state assistance, business opportunities, tertiary education and civil service recruitment – primarily in favour of the Malay community. In this regard, no one doubted that NEP was meant to meet Malay expectations much more than non-Malay expectations, or that meeting the former frequently meant curbing the latter. Mahathir Mohamad, NEP's most articulate ideologue, could bluntly say: 'The only thing to do is to admit that in giving the Malays their place in the sun, there must be denial for some non-Malays. Some non-Malays will have to be sacrificed in order to bring the Malays up.'[5] NEP's architects more tactfully said that NEP's projected high growth would achieve 'restructuring' without provoking a sense of deprivation among the non-Malays.

This reassurance often meant little at the level of political parties where ideological contestation and electoral competition retained much of their pre-1970 character of ethnic disagreement. For many Chinese, NEP meant a shift to 'more politics for the Malays' and 'NEP economics', which doubly disadvantaged non-Malays. At the elite level, BN (which was the old Alliance enlarged by the cooptation of several opposition parties) practised an institutionalized politics of ethnic relations and power-sharing, but demonstrably under UMNO's dominance. Before 1969, MCA leaders held the Ministries of Finance and Trade, and exert considerable 'Chinese influence' over economic planning and policy-making. By the mid-1970s, however, UMNO leaders had monopolized policy-making. At a quite different level, official attitudes all but identified poverty with rural Malay poverty so that NEP's 'poverty eradication' programmes rarely reached the non-Malay poor, such as the so-called 'Chinese New Villagers' or the urban poor. Yet several factors moderated non-Malay expressions of their 'sense of deprivation'. One factor was the resilience of the Chinese community. Their business operations had to contend with stricter bureaucratic regulation but were not seriously hindered. Their community and social infrastructure – schools, associations and religious and other institutions – continued to function and provide expressions of their identity and culture. A second factor was the recognition that NEP could not be dislodged as a policy framework. Accordingly, the Chinese community's main tactical response to NEP was to accept its *objectives* while trying to moderate its *implementation*. Hence ethnic politics under NEP was consistently conducted around targets, quotas and percentages. The third factor, discussed at greater length below, was the high economic growth under NEP which generated new opportunities for the business and professional and middle classes as a whole.[6]

NEP's ethnic dimensions were explicit, but its underlying class content was not less significant: 'restructuring' rapidly transformed Malay society and recomposed the Malaysian class structure. In both these processes lay the state-engineered emergence of a combination of a Malay capitalist class and Malay middle and professional classes, later called the Bumiputera Commercial and Industrial Community. But the Malay peasantry was likewise transformed. NEP offered no land reform, but the Federal Land Development Authority implemented large-scale land settlement schemes to absorb landless peasants with the promise of eventual landownership (Halim, 1992). Young rural Malays (a large proportion of whom were women) were inducted into the manufacturing sector. Yet others were sent for training at all levels, absorbed into the civil service, or helped with opportunities for business. They all contributed to swelling rural-to-urban migration which NEP's advocates regarded with equanimity. But an unintended consequence of NEP's rapid transformation of Malay society was the resurgence of Islam as an ideological rallying point for dissident Malays. Prominent participants in that resurgence were young Malays, students and professionals. They were the targeted beneficiaries of NEP's educational, commercial, urbanization and industrial programmes. But they were simultaneously subjected to a wide range of social, economic, spatial and psychological dislocations, and moved by a composite of personal, ethnic and class impulses to turn to Islam as the fount of dissenting alternatives to NEP policies, practices and priorities. In an unexpected turn for ethnic relations, this Islamic resurgence eventually explored a discourse of Malaysian politics that claimed a 'non-chauvinistic' engagement with non-Malay and non-Muslim sensitivities on ethnic, religious and other issues.

State economic intervention

NEP's social engineering was managed by a decidedly interventionist state that played three key roles. As a *provider* of opportunities for Malays, the state enlarged the existing corps of Malay entrepreneurs, graduates and professionals. The state gave Malay entrepreneurs financial assistance, credit facilities, contracts, preferential share allocations, subsidies and training. It established new public universities and all-Malay residential schools and colleges at home, and sent tens of thousands of Malays, young students and mid-career officers to universities abroad. This social engineering produced a full range of Malay entrepreneurs and capitalists (Searle, 1999: 81–95), a sizeable Malay middle class (Abdul Rahman, 1995), and a considerable '*bumiputera* participation rate' in the professions (Jomo, 1990: 82–3, Table 4.2; Malaysia 1999: 85, Table 3-7).

The state also became a determined *regulator* of business, both local and foreign, although the regulation of the former was politically more contentious. The state strengthened its regulatory powers and enforced compliance with NEP's restructuring requirements by using legislative means (Industrial Coordination Act [ICA] 1975) and bureaucratic procedures (set by the Foreign Investment Committee). NEP's restructuring requirements set a quota of at least 30 per cent bumiputera equity participation and employment in companies covered by ICA.[7] In 'expanding government power over firms', ICA gave the Minister of Trade and Industry wide discretionary power over licensing, ownership structure, ethnic employment targets, product distribution quotas, local content and product pricing (Jesudason, 1989: 135–8).[8]

Finally, the state emerged as a major *investor* in many sectors of the economy. The state expanded public sector ownership of corporate equity by acquiring assets on behalf of the Malays. Public enterprises proliferated in number from 22 in 1960 to 109 in 1970, 656 in 1980 and 1,014 in 1985. State agencies, banks and funds sought, bought and otherwise held equity 'in trust' for bumiputeras. Some of the best known of these state agencies were Bank Bumiputera, Urban Development

Authority (UDA), Perbadanan Nasional (Pernas, or National Corporation), Permodalan Nasional Berhad (PNB, or National Equity Corporation), Amanah Saham Nasional (ASB, or National Unit Trust Scheme)
and the state economic development corporations (SEDCs) (Searle,
1999: 61–6; Gomez and Jomo, 1997: 29–39).

NEP's first decade was the heyday of state bureaucrats and technocrats
who played the three roles of provider, regulator and investor with
single-minded purpose, technical planning and enormous levels of
resources. Fortuitous circumstances helped as well. The bureaucrats and
technocrats who pursued NEP's 'poverty eradication' and 'restructuring'
were helped in the 1970s by an international commodities boom and
the discovery of offshore petroleum, both of which boosted state
revenues. On the strength of these sharply increased revenues, the state
was able to finance its intervention in the economy without imposing
undue stress upon the national budget or the country's balance of payments. For example, public enterprises under the stewardship of Tengku
Razaleigh Hamzah (Minister of Finance in the mid-1980s) readily
employed state resources to buy into, buy out or otherwise start companies that were pivotal to securing Malay control of the 'commanding
heights' of the economy.

The boost to NEP came from yet another source. One of the state's
domestic priorities, that is, mass employment, which ISI could not
generate, coincided with an external development, namely the search
by foreign multinational corporations (MNCs) for politically stable
offshore production sites and cheap labour. Thus began Malaysia's shift
to an export-oriented industrialization (EOI) programme by offering
the comparative advantages of lower wages, the prohibition of unionization among a new industrial labour force, the provision of sound physical and social infrastructure, and the utilization of fiscal, tax and other
incentives to attract foreign direct investment. This shift to EOI
attracted manufacturing MNCs from the West and East Asia to new
export processing zones, and transformed a previously commodity
export-based economy into an industrialized economy.

Economic nationalism

In other respects, the state's economic intervention altered the balance
of power among the state, foreign capital and domestic capital. The fundamental change was revealed by the state's economic nationalist attitude towards foreign and Chinese capital. NEP targeted a 30 per cent
Malay share of corporate equity by 1990, but allowed for a rise in non-

Malay ownership from about 34.3 per cent in 1970 (with the politically more contentious Chinese share accounting for 22.8 per cent in 1969) (Malaysia, 1971: 40, Table 3.1) to 40 per cent in 1990 (Malaysia, 1976: 86, Table 4-16). Thus, Malay and non-Malay shares would increase at the expense of foreign ownership, which was targeted to decline from 63.3 per cent in 1970 to 30 per cent in 1990 (Malaysia, 1976: 86, Table 4-16). The state began to acquire foreign companies or foreign equity. State enterprises, led by Pernas and Permodalan Nasional Berhad (PNB), bought over foreign companies – such as London Tin, Chartered Consolidated, Sime Darby and Guthrie – that had long dominated the mines, plantations and trading houses. Faced with state acquisitions or restructuring, certain foreign companies chose to relinquish ownership or control of their Malaysian subsidiaries (Searle, 1999: 72–4).[9] Yet foreign capital could be mollified. The old foreign capital of the plantation houses, mines, banks and trading houses was never threatened with outright nationalization. 'Malaysianizing' the ownership of established companies by restructuring was accomplished by market transactions. NEP's 'backdoor nationalization', as foreign critics characterized the state acquisitions, entailed 'relatively gentle . . . encroachments on the terrain of foreign capital' (Jomo, 1986: 281, fn. 68). Meanwhile the new foreign capital of the MNCs was highly favoured. The MNCs were not subjected to NEP's 'wealth restructuring' requirements, but they met NEP's 'employment restructuring' goal by proletarianizing large numbers of young rural Malays within the modern sectors of the economy.

For Chinese capital the danger was that the state's economic nationalism was inclined towards 'Malay nationalism' which the Chinese business community and political parties were too weak to resist. Chinese capital could not match the state's penetration of key economic sectors. In banking, for example, where Chinese capital had expanded in pre-NEP years, the state enlarged its assets and restructured both foreign-owned and Chinese-owned banks. By 1990, the state had owned the three biggest banks, Malayan Banking Berhad, Bank Bumiputera Berhad and United Malayan Banking Corporation (Searle, 1999: 75, Table 3.2). Nor could Chinese capital escape stricter regulation as was demonstrated by the failure of MCA and the Associated Chinese Chambers of Commerce and Industry of Malaysia, despite repeated attempts, to have the ICA repealed (Jesudason, 1989: 134–42). Chinese capital never enjoyed the MNCs' privileged treatment. Portions of Chinese 'old wealth', typically family businesses controlled by individual tycoons, were unable or unwilling to adjust to NEP. These 'pursued easy and safe areas of expansion, investing heavily in property development and finance, and avoiding sectors like manufacturing, which entailed larger risks and longer periods to recuperate investment outlays' (Jesudason, 1989: 163).

Other Chinese businesses, however, discovered opportunities that were, arguably, attributable to NEP. During NEP's first decade real GDP growth averaged 7.6 per cent per year (or 7.3 per cent over the Second Malaysia Plan period of 1971–5 and 8.6 per cent in the Third Malaysia Plan period of 1976–80). Under such conditions, business generally prospered and the (predominantly Chinese) non-Malay share of corporate equity rose between 1970 and 1985. Some, typically big, Chinese businesses adapted to the NEP-altered balance of power at elite levels. Offering varying combinations of capital, networks and expertise, they courted, were courted by or otherwise built commercial relationships with aspiring Malay capitalists or influential Malays situated in the aristocracy, bureaucracy, military and the dominant Malay political party (Heng, 1992: 132–4; Sieh, 1992: 110–11). Soon a distinctive NEP creation – the 'bumiputera–non-bumiputera joint venture' – emerged as a corporate platform from which adaptable Chinese capital, both 'old wealth' and 'new money', partook in the state-led demand and public enterprise investment boosted by high commodity and oil revenues.

Emerging intra-Malay conflicts

Away from ethnic considerations, the state sponsorship of Malay capital was dependent upon three critical factors. UMNO, as the dominant party in government, supplied the political power to push through NEP's social engineering. The Malay-dominated bureaucracy provided the capacity for implementing NEP programmes. The performance of an incipient class of Malay capitalists had to vindicate the state assistance and nurture they received. Influential coalitions soon emerged from among the ranks of party, bureaucracy and class, only to become new sources of intra-Malay conflict, which could not be posed in interethnic terms.

In the mid-1970s, one flashpoint emerged between the party and the bureaucracy. Razak's regime had rapidly enlarged its corps of bureaucrats and technocrats as Razak insisted that development required more 'administration' than 'politics'. A whole generation of Malay administrators, technocrats and professionals was trained at state expense and equipped with the resources to take charge of economic development under NEP. But the transition to an NEP state required a power shift, too, from UMNO's 'old guard' to younger UMNO politicians who were being groomed by Razak. And just as NEP repudiated the Alliance's *laissez faire*, so the rise of Razak's 'young Turks' marginalized UMNO's 'old-style politicians', who supposedly lacked 'the vision and technocratic skills to carry through the restructuring of society' (Crouch, 1980: 17, 32–3).

Another source of conflict lay in the bureaucracy as it expanded in terms of funding, resources and personnel. Bureaucratic involvement in economic activities grew such that by 1983 public enterprises had controlled an estimated 45 per cent of 'modern agriculture', 50 per cent of mining and between 70 and 80 per cent of banking (Parti Gerakan, 1984: 187, Table 2). But the performance of public enterprises was itself a major problem. Many public enterprises could not meet market criteria of efficiency and profitablity (Rugayah, 1995: 75–8; Gomez and Jomo 1997: 76–7). Many officers regarded their public enterprises as 'social enterprises', whose 'restructuring' goal was not readily measured in pecuniary values. The state tended to overlook the public enterprises' deficits, debts and losses as the price of providing the Malays with experience, employment and skills. But the scale of deficits and losses was daunting. Total public sector deficit rose from RM400 million in 1970 to RM15.2 billion in 1982. State governments, statutory bodies and public enterprises owed the federal government RM8.743 billion in 1982 (Mehmet, 1986: 133–4) while 'approximately 40–45 per cent of all SOEs [state-owned enterprises] have been unprofitable throughout the 1980s', of which 'almost half (or 25 per cent of all SOEs) had negative shareholder funds' (Adam and Cavendish, 1995a: 25). A politically more contentious issue was the transfer of public enterprise assets. In principle, public enterprises run by political appointees and state managers held those assets 'in trust' for the Malays. But the more commercially oriented trust agencies, like PNB, were empowered to acquire profitable companies. Even so powerful a public corporation as Pernas was required to transfer eleven of its most profitable companies to PNB in 1981. Commercial imperatives became more urgent after PNB established Amanah Saham Nasional (ASN, or the National Unit Trust Scheme). ASN bought PNB's assets at cost, while individual Malays bought units of ASN shares. The companies remained 'within the community' while individual shareholders received returns on their investment. ASN was a novel solution to the problem of asset transfer. Yet some managers of public enterprises were burdened by a 'disincentive to profit-making' for fear of PNB's taking over their enterprises (World Bank, cited in Gomez and Jomo, 1997: 77).

Public enterprises also faced pressures from Malay entrepreneurs who wanted the assets to be directly transferred to them, or complained of 'unfair state competition'. Not a few state managers chose to become entrepreneurs, sometimes by acquiring the very enterprises they managed. Contention over the transfer of public assets grew acute as UMNO entered business, and its managers used the party's dominance to compete for state projects, contracts and assets. Within a few years of starting Fleet Holdings (for the purpose of generating party funds), UMNO had built up an economic empire that penetrated most economic sectors (Gomez, 1990; Searle, 1999: 103–26). Subsequently notable UMNO 'nominees, trustees or proxies' – people to whom the party assets were entrusted – became big capitalists in their own right (Searle, 1999: 135–53).

In summary, as resources were controlled by bureaucrats and technocrats, as UMNO entered business on a large scale, and as individual Malay capitalists emerged, new coalitions between groups located within the Malay party, bureaucracy and capitalist class arose, which contended for power, access to resources and opportunities for accumulation. Over time, their agendas could less and less be amicably subsumed under NEP: all based their claims on 'restructuring', but each pursued its disparate interests.

Mahathir: reinterpreting NEP

By the time Mahathir Mohamad became Malaysia's fourth prime minister in July 1981, many flashpoints of intra-Malay competition had emerged, which would continually test the integrity of the party–bureaucracy–class axis so critical to NEP's realization. And they generated conflicts that could not be readily posed in the familiar interethnic mould. Mahathir himself would not and could not *replace* NEP's objective of restructuring but he meant to *displace* NEP as the overriding concern of Malaysian society. Mahathir is famous for formulating the 'Malay dilemma', which was usually understood to mean the correction of 'Malay relative backwardness' vis-à-vis the non-Malays. But the crux of Mahathir's 'Malay dilemma' was that the 'relative backwardness' of the Malay community, if uncorrected, would be the millstone that prevented the nation from catching up with the advanced nations of the world. It would be more accurate to characterize Mahathir as *a nationalist with capitalist aspirations*, or *a capitalist with nationalist aspirations* – and one who came to power just as the so-called 'East Asian miracle' unfolded. Consequently, Mahathir opted to steer Malaysia towards modernization, industrialization, privatization and bureaucratic reform with significant implications for ethinic relations.

For a start, Mahathir extended and planned even to accelerate NEP's high-growth developmentalism, which would consolidate NEP's basic aims while lessening the likelihood of ethnic acrimony. One of his ways of doing so was to re-establish an alliance between state and domestic capital via his 'privatization' and 'Malaysia Incorporated' policies. Here the relative success of NEP's 'restructuring' ensured a critical difference between Malaysia Inc. and the state–capital ties under the Alliance: the state now promoted a goal of Malaysian economic nationalism within which a leading role was reserved for the Bumiputera Commercial and Industrial Community (Khoo, 1995: 333–8). In that sense, the domestic goal of 'restructuring' concerned Mahathir much less than providing directions for a state-sponsored drive towards heavy industrialization and industrial deepening, following the East Asian model of late industrialization associated with the economic successes of Japan and the 'East Asian tigers'. Consequently, the Mahathir regime offered a restatement of national aspirations as a quest for NICdom (newly industrialized countries) in the mid-1980s, and, after 1990, as a march towards developed country status, which would stop Malaysian society from 'looking inwards with prejudice but rather outwards with pride' (Das, 1982).

The first decade of Mahathir's premiership did not see a trend of diminishing interethnic conflicts. The reverse was true, although his regime did not institute any particular NEP-type policy to heighten ethnic tensions. But the 1985–6 recession strained the management of ethnic relations. On the one hand, the end of high growth intensified the (Chinese) sense of deprivation – in economic and cultural matters – that NEP was supposed to pre-empt. On the other hand, the Malay party–bureaucracy–class axis was split over how NEP's 'restructuring' objective would be affected by the recession. An anti-Mahathir camp wanted to pursue 'restructuring' and 'wealth redistribution' (along ethnic lines), if necessary with more vigour. Mahathir and his allies decided to 'hold the NEP in abeyance', that is, to suspend NEP's 'restructuring' requirements to pursue 'growth' rather than 'redistribution'. This intra-Malay conflict deeply split the Malay community and, in the face of a rising, urban non-Malay opposition, brought Malay–Chinese tensions to a dangerous level in 1987. The tensions were immediately dampened by police repression in October 1987.

What truly defused the tensions was the return to high economic growth. Once more internal policies coincided with external conditions. 'Holding NEP in abeyance', the state offered foreign direct investment more liberal equity requirements, easier start-up conditions, substantial ringgit (Malay currency) depreciation and lower labour costs. This

investment regime attracted investment inflows principally from Tai-
wanese, Japanese and Singaporean manufacturers, prompted to relocate
some of their activities because of rising production costs, tightening
labour markets and stricter environmental restrictions at home.
Just between 1988 and 1990, NEP's concluding year, the average growth
rate exceeded 9 per cent. Indeed, official statistics showed that the
targets for 'poverty eradication' and 'restructuring' had been substantially met. Between 1970 and 1990, the incidence of poverty had
declined from 49 per cent (of all households) to 17 per cent. Over the
same period, despite controversy over the exact extent of 'restructuring', the bumiputera share of corporate equity had risen from 2.4 per
cent in 1970 to at least (and probably considerably more than) 20 per
cent. And bumiputera professionals, who formed less than 5 per cent
of major professional categories in 1970, constituted over 29 per cent
in 1990.

By its own standards, NEP had been a success. But what really set aside
the ethnic politics of NEP was the wave of prosperity of the early to
mid-1990s. With it came rises in income and living standards for most
sections of Malaysian society (with the exception of the new underclass
of unskilled and semi-skilled, legal and illegal migrant labour). Then,
from a position of strength, Mahathir redefined Malaysian nationhood
yet again. He confidently claimed that the 'Malay dilemma' had ended.
In place of NEP, Mahathir offered *Wawasan 2020* (Vision 2020), which
expressed a vision of a *Bangsa Malaysia* (Malaysian nation) attaining the
status of a developed country by the year 2020. Vision 2020 was proclaimed in 1991, and soon became hugely popular. Never had Mahathir
or any of the previous ruling regimes obtained more multiethnic
support than in the 1995 general election. By then, the overt manipu-
lation of ethnic sentiments and grievances had become less habitual
among politicians of both the ruling coalition and the opposition
parties. To the extent that ethnic differences and cultural grievances in
Malaysia had always had an economic 'essence' to them, the Mahathir
regime in the 1990s seemed to have supplied economic solutions to cultural problems. The privatization of tertiary education, corporatization
of public universities and Mahathir's insistence on reviving the use of
English on pragmatic grounds combined to defuse interethnic squab-
bles over issues of language, tertiary educational quotas for students of
different communities and the Chinese independent schools. No non-
Malay then would dispute the status of Bahasa Malaysia. Only some
Malay 'linguistic nationalists' questioned Mahathir's renewed promotion of the English language, while increasing numbers of non-Chinese

(mostly Malay) children began to attend Chinese schools without a hint of controversy.[10]

Lessons from NEP

For most Malaysians in the 1990s, interethnic tolerance took on new meaning and greater value when contrasted with ethnic warfare in the Balkans and the former Soviet bloc. It was common for Malaysians to hear hopeful and not just propagandistic talk of the unifying national goals of *Wawasan 2020* and *Bangsa Malaysia*. Then, Malaysians, according to one strand of BN ideology, had become one family. Nationhood, the elusive state that defined the Alliance elites, and national unity, which was NEP's distant goal, seemed attainable. It will never do for Malaysians to be complacent about ethnic relations and potential tensions. Yet one can now better understand how it was that things appeared to be quiet on Malaysia's ethnic front on the eve of the July 1997 crisis, and why, despite other kinds of political conflicts, no major ethnic conflicts surfaced in the aftermath of the crisis.

What then are the 'lessons from NEP' that one can draw for the management of ethnic relations? They include the following:

1. NEP's socio-economic reforms required a high degree of state intervention. The post-1969 regimes continually sought to 'govern the market', even when Mahathir's 'privatization' offered an important nod in the direction of a domestic capital that had become much more multiethnic. Despite opposition and some problems which have lingered to this day, it was the state's assumption of the roles of provider, regulator and investor that made possible the initial burst of NEP implementation.

2. NEP recognized that the ethnic division of labour which divided the society along intersecting ethnic and class lines had to be tackled on both counts. NEP expressly prescribed ethnic solutions to ethnic problems but its underlying class content was not less important. 'Restructuring' to sponsor the rise of Malay capitalist, professional and middle classes was often presented as NEP's explicitly ethnic dimension. In reality, it was more than that. And, in the absence of land reform, the Felda land resettlement schemes and the mass industrial employment spearheaded by the MNCs rounded off a deep transformation of Malay society and the Malaysian class structure.

3. The post-1969 regimes redefined the parameters of nationhood and nationality but without abandoning some of the basic tenets of

interethnic relations that were inherited from the Alliance period. Razak's regime established Malay dominance vis-à-vis the non-Malays. The subsequent formulation of a Malay-Muslim national culture consigned expressions of non-Malay identities and cultures to 'begin neglect' but not an outright hostility that threatened the basic economic and social infrastructure of the non-Malay communities.

4. Economic nationalism played a big role in NEP but came in different guises and was practised to different degrees. NEP reduced an older form of foreign ownership of the national economy for the benefit of domestic capital, but favoured EOI-based manufacturing foreign direct investment (FDI). At the level of corporate wealth, restructuring embodied strands of Malay economic nationalism vis-à-vis non-Malay capital, but small and medium Chinese businesses were not subjected to restructuring. Mahathir's 'Malaysia Inc.' stance reinterpreted NEP to express a vision of a multiethnic 'national capital' capable of leading a unified nation.

5. NEP's transformation of Malay society generated new 'intraethnic' tensions and conflicts. 'Restructuring' at corporate levels created new coalitions of economic and political power whose agendas could not be subsumed amicably under NEP. At the mass level, the subjection of the Malay masses to rapid change and dislocation brought out forms of Malay-Muslim disaffection with the 'Malay state'.

6. BN, like the Alliance before it, institutionalized power-sharing among the ethnic communities. Even after the balance of power was tipped in UMNO's favour, UMNO's non-Malay partners in BN remained not only symbolic but also real, if limited, representatives of 'their' communities. Power-sharing was practicable because the core of Malaysia's ethnic divisiveness was mostly limited to Malay–Chinese differences, rather than much more complicated sets of ethnic conflicts.

7. Successive regimes were committed to NEP's premise of promoting high economic growth to facilitate redistribution without placing undue stress upon ethnic relations. At a critical juncture during the recession of the mid-1980s, Mahathir's regime chose to suspend restructuring in favour of growth and employment generation while keeping the option of returning to restructuring under more conducive conditions.

8. Changing conditions or fortuitous circumstances variously affected NEP's performance. Some conditions were favourable, such as the oil price increases and commodities boom of the 1970s, which gave an impetus to restructuring. Other conditions were unfavourable, such

as when oil and commodity prices crashed in the 1980s, forcing a suspension of restructuring. Other circumstances were fortuitous – the changes in the global industrial and financial system, which brought the first wave of manufacturing FDI in the 1970s, and the second wave in the late 1980s. One key factor was the ability of the state to manage the destabilizing effects of economic crises and to modify policies to respond to, or take advantage of, changing conditions.

9. NEP could as much heighten as diminish ethnic differences to the extent that issues of ethnic identity and problems of cultural grievances in Malaysia had always had an economic 'essence' to them. In the event, the substantive attainment of NEP's socio-economic goals diminished the likelihood of intense ethnic economic rivalry, while the Mahathir regime's economic solutions to cultural problems in the 1990s encouraged a deeper sense of national purpose and identity.

Conclusion: prospects for Indonesia

Looking at Indonesia today through NEP lenses, as it were, one will see more 'contrasts and obstacles' than 'similarities and opportunities' for the management of ethnic relations in the immediate future.

Indonesian society today has less room for manoeuvre than Malaysia under NEP. Malaysia was never the exemplar of the East Asian model of development, but the state could take advantage of prevailing global circumstances to intervene heavily in the economy, impose a reformist agenda on foreign and local capital, utilize the emerging 'new international division of labour' to break the ethnic division of labour, nurture state-owned enterprises, and so on. This opportunity, lost to Indonesia under the New Order regime, is not likely to be regained by the state in post-crisis Indonesia. The current phase of globalization is dominated by mobile multinational corporations and even more mobile finance capital. The state in post-crisis Indonesia can scarcely hope to operate with the degree of state intervention or the kinds of economic nationalism that propelled NEP without provoking a massive capital strike, both foreign and domestic. Here, if post-crisis Malaysia has been able to maintain a semi-autarkic stance vis-à-vis the international money market since September 1998 without adverse effects for ethnic relations, it is partly because the political economy of NEP began before the advent of neoliberal demands to 'roll back the frontiers of the state'. Over a period, the state in Malaysia was able to build the institutional capacity needed to support state-led growth. And despite inefficiencies and excesses justified by 'restructuring', state revenues were invested in public projects that were committed to 'poverty eradication'. In contrast, the Indonesian bureaucracy 'suffered from a surplus of departments filled with underpaid and underemployed staff, charged with carrying out overlapping and uncoordinated regulations' (Vickers, 2001: 77). To take a notable example, Malaysia's national petroleum company, Petronas, has long been one of the best managed state enterprises. Petronas served as the state's cash cow, milked to fund development in good times and to bail out the state in times of financial crunch. In contrast, Indonesia's Pertamina had been captured by private interests before, even bankrupted, and needed to be saved by the state. Between Petronas and Pertamina lies the gulf between a developmentalist state having bureaucratic and technocratic capabilities, and a largely predatory state. It is difficult not to recall the characterization of post-crisis Indonesia as one of 'those places where capitalism has been and gone, leaving behind scarred landscapes and ruined social edifices' (Anderson, 1998: 299).

One can, of course, draw parallels between the politically sensitive Malay–Chinese divide in pre-NEP Malaysia and the uneasy relations between *pribumi* Indonesians and the non-*pribumi* ethnic Chinese. Indonesia's situation has not been improved by meaningful corrections of '*pribumi* relative backwardness', leaving aside the emergence of powerful *pribumi* economic interests. Calls for NEP-type restructuring had been issued in Indonesia before. Some were made on ethnic grounds by vested and powerful *pribumi* interests seeking to expand their economic empires, some on class grounds by 'radical critics of the New Order' moved by 'populist concerns for a more equitable distribution of wealth' (Robison and Hadiz, 1993: 26). In circumstances of prolonged economic hardship, any Indonesian initiative that targets Chinese ownership for 'restructuring' will contain 'dangerously disruptive potential' (Robison and Hadiz, 1993: 26) no matter how it is justified. Mackie recently considered it 'highly unlikely that an NEP would be anything short of disastrous' since 'confiscatory measures against the Chinese would be unavoidable' and the absence of 'a highly competent and uncorrupt bureaucracy' would mean that neither 'redistribution of property nor even an NEP-style one could be carried out cleanly or without immense disruption' (Mackie, 1999: 196). But given that desperate economic resentment still lies at the heart of anti-Chinese sentiment in Indonesia, is there any practicable alternative to adopting some variant of NEP's restructuring objective? There may not be. One basic lesson from Malaysia's NEP is that where class divisions closely overlap ethnic differences, economic disparities and cultural grievances will exacerbate each other. There may not be a practicable alternative to having 'class *and* ethnic' solutions'. But if 'restructuring' is applied to moderate 'ethnic Chinese economic domination', any future management of *pribumi–non-pribumi* relations must learn from another basic NEP lesson, that is, 'restructuring' cannot work efficiently without growth, or equitably without recognizing the need to preempt a 'sense of deprivation'.

This last point is especially critical since Indonesia's ethnic relations are vastly complicated by certain *pribumi–pribumi* relations. Relations between 'indigenous Christians' and 'Muslim settlers' in Maluku and between 'native Dayaks' and 'migrant Madurese' in Kalimantan combine a heightened sense of economic deprivation with cultural or religious suspicions. To those problems might be added regionalist resentments of previous marginalization by the highly centralized New Order regime.[11] It is no easy task to address adequately these mixes of economic, cultural and regionalist grievances. Some degree of decentralizing political authority is necessary despite concern that decentralized control over resources will become the regional elites' vehicle for self-aggrandizement. Some degree of regional autonomy is probably necessary to avoid an intensification of interethnic violence that could result in the ethnonationalism seen in Acheh or Papua.[12] At least in principle, the precondition for a solution to these difficult *pribumi–pribumi* relations has to be a more equitable distribution of economic opportunities and resources, between the centre and the regions, and within the regions themselves – some form of federalism, in a word. As Legge (2001: 25) has rightly observed, whereas 'in the 1950s federalism was a dirty word in the backlash against the Dutch efforts to retain influence by creating a United States of Indonesia', today 'one may wonder whether a federal type of solution might not be the only way of satisfying some regional demands'.

Problems of ethnic relations are rarely problems in and of themselves. They are embedded within political economy, society and culture. The real question may not be whether post-crisis Indonesia needs an NEP to solve its ethnic problems which are more varied, more complex and operate on a larger scale than Malaysia's before NEP. The real question is what *Reformasi* ultimately means for the majority of Indonesians, two-thirds of whom (or nearly 80 million people, just short of eight times the *total* Malaysian population in 1970) were reported to live below the poverty line in 1999 (ILO 1999).[13] For them any economic 'restructuring' must mean significant 'poverty eradication' above all else. To accomplish that requires a massive social transformation that is far more the stuff of ongoing political struggles than any particular exercises in public policy. In this, post-crisis Indonesia has, arguably, one bright spot. The 1997 crisis brought popular resistance to *'korupsi, kolusi dan nepotisme'* – the practices of 'cronyism, collusion and nepotism'. As a corollary, the economic and social reforms needed to correct the concentration of wealth in the hands of powerful, but not exclusively ethnic Chinese, coalitions need not be anti-Chinese in social impulses and popular understanding. If *Reformasi* brings a significant transformation of Indonesian political economy and society that gives substantive meaning to competing notions of democracy and social justice – including an equitable distribution of wealth along ethnic, class and regionalist lines – then other conditions of decent ethnic relations – cultural freedom, religious tolerance and regional autonomy – would be attainable. If *Reformasi* fails to do so, then the prospects for ethnic relations would be just as dismal as for other social issues.

Acknowledgements

I would like to thank Ariel Heryanto, Francis Loh Kok Wah, Vedi Hadiz, James Jesudason and Khoo Khay Jin for helping me with materials and comments, and Ho Phaik Li and Wu Yoke Li for their assistance. Funding from Sida, Sweden, in conjunction with the 'Discourses and Practices of Democracy in Southeast Asia' project, led by the Goteborg Centre for Asian Studies, which supported the preparation of this chapter is gratefully acknowledged.

Notes

1. Estimates of the number of people killed in Maluku from January 1999 to June 2000 ranged from 4,000 (Tedjasukmana, 2001: 28), to 8,000 (Liu, 2001: 26) to 10,000 (Chew, 2000: 51). The violence in Kalimantan broke out in December 1996–January 1997 (Human Rights Watch Asia, 1997), March 1999 (McBeth and Cohen, 1999; Tesoro and McCawley, 1999), and in March 2001 (Elegant, 2001).
2. See Anggraeni (2001) for Herb Feith's comments on a history of conflicts between 'indigenous communities' and 'immigrant minorities' in Maluku and Kalimantan.
3. A pioneering study of 'ownership and control in the Malayan economy' in the 1950s found that European-owned companies controlled 84 per cent of large rubber estates (of over 500 acres each), 60 per cent of tin output, 65–75 per cent of exports, and 60 per cent of imports (Puthucheary, 1960: xv, 26–7, 85–6).
4. Mahathir (1970: 15) wrote: 'The Government started off on the wrong premise. . . . It believed that the Chinese were only interested in business and acquisition of wealth, and that the Malays wished only to become Government servants. These ridiculous assumptions led to policies which undermined whatever superficial understanding there was between Malays and non-Malays'.

5. A 1971 statement by Mahathir, cited in Yap (1976).
6. Many Chinese who truly refused to accept NEP emigrated.
7. Originally, ICA provisions applied to any manufacturing firm having at least RM100,000 in shareholder capital and employing a minimum of 25 workers.
8. Even at the level of state and local government, (non-Malay) businesses came under stringent bureaucratic regulation. In a non-manufacturing area such as real estate development, for example, many authorities – including land offices, town and country planning departments, municipal councils, and state economic development corporations – imposed 'NEP requirements' on seemingly technical matters as land-use conversion or planning guidelines.
9. One exception to the success of the state's acquisitive trend was the foreign oil companies' refusal to share management control with Petronas (Petroliam Nasional, or National Oil Corporation), as stipulated by the Petroleum Development Act 1974 (Searle, 1999: 69–70). In response to the Petroleum Development Act, 'which smells of nationalization, and . . . cannot be acceptable to any foreign interests. . . . foreign investment in Malaysia has come to a standstill' (Grace, 1976, cited in Jomo, 1986: 281, fn. 69). There was an investment strike which ended only after the state had renegotiated with the oil companies and dropped the management conditions.
10. The current estimate is 65,000 non-Chinese students, or about 10 per cent of the student population in Chinese schools.
11. Commenting on the 'debate surrounding regional political autonomy and the demand to reformulate the existing national-state formation', Tirtosudarmo (2000: 28) remarked that 'the emergence of various ethnic based organizations, demanding for a recognition of their indigenous rights, is likely to be interconnected with the demand for more autonomy and independence [for] the regions.'
12. '[I]f Jakarta wants to find a fundamental solution to the Dayak rebellion in Central Kalimantan, and prevent it from spreading to the other Kalimantan provinces, and turn it into an island-wide movement for Dayak self-determination, Megawati and her military supporters had better fly over and start talking to the Dayak leaders, rather than simply using the Wild West style of "sending in the cavalry"' (Aditjondro, 2001). Aditjondro wrote this in May 2001, two months before Megawati Sukarnoputri replaced Abdurrahman Wahid as president of Indonesia.
13. ILO (1998) had this dire report on the poverty situation in post-crisis Indonesia:

> Due to stagnant wages and incomes in nominal terms, on one hand, and high inflation on the other, around 75 million people, or 37% of the population, will fall below the poverty line by mid-1998. The corresponding figures by the end of 1998 will be around 100 million people, or 48% of the population. This is a three to four-fold increase from the officially estimated 11% poverty incidence in 1996, and comparable to levels prevailing in the mid-1970s. In the absence of improvements in household income, further price rises in 1999 will push some 140 million people, or 66% of the population, below the official poverty line, at poverty levels not seen since the 1960s.

The incidence of poverty in rural areas, at 53%, will be higher than that in urban areas, at 39%, by end of 1998. Also, over 70% of poor people will live in rural areas. Based on alternative, internationally comparable, poverty lines of US$1.0 and US$0.80 in urban and rural areas, 57% of the population still lived below the poverty line even before the crisis in 1996, or more than five times the official estimates of CBS. The latter's estimates were based on a poverty line of US$0.45 per capita per day in 1996. These alternative estimates call into question the government's main approach of focussing on pockets of poverty in so-called least developed villages. Clearly, when poverty is as widespread as indicated by internationally comparable poverty lines, poverty alleviation efforts should be directed at the majority of the population.

References

Abdul R. E. (1995) 'Malaysian Middle Classes: Some Preliminary Observations', *Jurnal Antropologi dan Sosiologi*, 22: 31–54.

Adam, C. and Cavendish, W. (1995a) 'Background'. In Jomo K. S. (ed.), *Privatizing Malaysia: Rents, Rhetoric, Realities*, Boulder, Colorado, Westview Press, pp. 11–41.

Adam, C. and Cavendish, W. (1995b) 'Early Privatizations'. In Jomo K. S. (ed.) *Privatizing Malaysia: Rents, Rhetoric, Realities*, Boulder, Colorado, Westview Press, pp. 98–137.

Aditjondro, George J. (2000) 'The Political Economy of Violence in Maluku, Indonesia', reprinted in *Aliran Monthly*, 20 (2): 25–7.

Aditjondro, George J. (2001) 'Avoiding the Mistakes of Ambon', *The Jakarta Post.com*, 22 May.

Alatas, S. H. (1977) *The Myth of the Lazy Native*, London: Frank Cass.

Anderson, B. (1998) *Spectres of Comparison: Nationalism, Southeast Asia and the World*, London: Verso.

Anggraeni, D. (2001) 'Images of Injustice in the History of Kalimantan', *Jakarta Post*, 15 March (http://www.thejakartapost.com/detailededitorial).

Booth, A. (1999) 'Will Indonesia Break Up?', *Inside Indonesia*, No. 59, July–September: 5–6.

Chang, A. (2001) 'Bloodbath in Indonesia', *ABCNews.com*, 27 February.

Chew, A. (2000) 'Fight for Maluku', *Asiaweek*, 27 October: 50–4.

Coppel, C. (1983) *Indonesian Chinese in Crisis*, Kuala Lumpur, Oxford: Oxford University Press.

Crouch, H. (1980) 'The UMNO Crisis: 1975–1977'. In H. Crouch, L. K. Hing and M. Ong (eds.) *Malaysian Politics and the 1978 Election*, Kuala Lumpur: Oxford University Press, pp. 11–36.

Das, K. (1982) 'Mahathir's "Restoration"', *Far Eastern Economic Review*, 11 June: 38

Elegant, S. (2001) 'The Darkest Season', *Time*, 12 March: 14–20.

Fealy, Greg (2001) 'Inside the Laskar Jihad', *Inside Indonesia*, No. 65, January–March: 28–9.

Gomez, T. E. (1990) *UMNO's Corporate Investments*, Kuala Lumpur: Forum.

Gomez, T. E. and Jomo K. S. (1997) *Malaysia's Political Economy: Politics, Patronage and Profits*, Cambridge: Cambridge University Press.

Hadiz, V. R. (1999) 'Contesting Political Change After Suharto'. In A. Budiman, B. Hatley and D. Kingsbury (eds.) *Reformasi: Crisis and Change in Indonesia*, Clayton, Victoria: Monash Asia Institute, Monash University, pp. 105–26.

Halim Salleh (1992) 'Peasants, Proletarianisation and the State: FELDA Settlers in Pahang'. In Joel S. Kahn and Francis Loh Kok Wah (eds.) *Fragmented Vision: Culture and Politics in Contemporary Malaysia*, Sydney: Allen & Unwin, pp. 107–32.

Heng Pek Koon (1992) 'The Chinese Business Elite of Malaysia'. In R. McVey (ed.) *Southeast Asian Capitalists*, Ithaca, NY: Cornell University Southeast Asia Program, pp. 127–44.

Heryanto, A. (1998) 'Ethnic Identities and Erasure: Chinese Indonesians in Public Culture'. In J. S. Kahn (ed.) *Southeast Asian Identities: Culture and the Politics of Representation in Indonesia, Malaysia, Singapore and Thailand*, Singapore: ISEAS, pp. 95–114.

Heryanto, A. (1999) 'Rape, Race and Reporting'. In A. Budiman, B. Hatley and D. Kingsbury (eds.) *Reformasi: Crisis and Change in Indonesia*, Clayton, Victoria: Monash Asia Institute, Monash University, pp. 299–334.

Human Rights Watch Asia (1997) 'The Horror in Kalimantan', *Inside Indonesia*, No. 51, July–September: 9–12.

Jesudason, James V. (1989) *Ethnicity and the Economy: The State, Chinese Business, and Multinationals in Malaysia*, Singapore: Oxford University Press.

Jomo K. S. (1986) *A Question of Class: Capital, the State, and Uneven Development in Malaya*, Singapore: Oxford University Press.

Jomo K. S. (1990) *Growth and Structural Change in the Malaysian Economy*, London: Macmillan.

Khoo Boo Teik (1995) *Paradoxes of Mahathirism: An Intellectual Biography of Mahathir Mohamad*, Kuala Lumpur: Oxford University Press.

Khoo Boo Teik (2000) 'Unfinished Crises: Malaysian Politics in 1999'. In *Southeast Asian Affairs 2000*, Singapore: Institute of Southeast Asian Studies, pp. 166–83.

Kristof, N. and Denn, S. W. (2000) *Thunder From the East: Portrait of a Rising Asia*, London: Nicholas Brearley Publishing.

Legge, J. (2001) 'The Contingent and the Unforseen'. In G. Lloyd and S. Smith (eds.) *Indonesia Today: The Challenges of History*, Singapore: ISEAS, pp. 14–26.

Lim Teck Ghee (1984) 'British Colonial Administration and the "Ethnic Division of Labour" in Malaya', *Kajian Malaysia*, 2, 2 (December): 28–66.

Liu, M. (2001) 'Terror Islands', *Newsweek*, Feburary 12: 26–8.

ILO (International Labour Organization) (1998) *Employment Challenger of the Indonesian Economic Crisis: Executive Summary*, ILO Jakarta Office, United Nations Development Program (http://www.ilo.org/public/english/region/asro/jakarta/summary.htm).

Mackie, Jamie (1999) 'Tackling the "Chinese Problem"'. In Geoff Forester (ed.), *Post-Soharto Indonesia: Renewal or Chaos?*, Singapore: ISEAS, pp. 187–97.

Mahathir Mohamad (1970) *The Malay Dilemma*, Singapore: Donald Moore.

Mahathir Mohamad (1991) 'Malaysia: The Way Forward', *New Straits Times*, 2 March.

Malaysia (1999) *Kajian Separuh Penggal Rancangan Malaysia Ketujuh 1996–2000* (Mid-term Review of the Seventh Malaysia Plan 1996–2000), Kuala Lumpur.

Malaysia (1971) *Second Malaysia Plan 1971–1975*, Kuala Lumpur.

Malaysia (1976) *Third Malaysia Plan 1976–1980*, Kuala Lumpur.

McBeth, J. (1998) 'Shadow Play', *Far Eastern Economic Review*, 23 July: 23–7.

McBeth, J. and Cohen, M. (1999) 'Dayak Destruction', *Far Eastern Economic Review*, April 1: 20.

Mehmet, O. (1986) *Development in Malaysia: Poverty, Wealth and Trusteeship*, London: Croom Helm.

Parti Gerakan Rakyat Malaysia (1984) *The National Economic Policy – 1990 and Beyond*, Kuala Lumpur.

Puthucheary, James (1960) *Ownership and Control in the Malayan Economy*, Singapore: Eastern Universities Press.

Robison, R. and Hadiz, V. (1993) 'Privatization or the Reorganization of Dirigism? Indonesian Economic Policy in the 1990s', *Canadian Journal of Development Studies*, Special Issue: 13–32.

Rugayah Mohamed (1995) 'Public Enterprises'. In Jomo K. S. (ed.) *Privatizing Malaysia: Rents, Rhetoric, Realities*, Boulder, Colorado: Westview Press, pp. 63–80.

Sandyawan Sumardi (1998) 'Rape is Rape', *Inside Indonesia*, No. 56, October–December, pp. 19–20.

Schwarz, A. (1999) *A Nation in Waiting: Indonesia's Search for Stability*, St Leonards, NSW: Allen & Unwin.

Searle, P. (1999) *The Riddle of Malaysian Capitalism: Rent-seekers or Real Capitalists?*, St. Leonards, New South Wales: Allen and Unwin.

Sieh Lee Mei Ling (1992) 'The Transformation of Malaysian Business Groups', in R. McVey (ed.) *Southeast Asian Capitalists*, Ithaca, NY: Cornell University Southeast Asia Program, pp. 103–26.

Suryadinata, L. (ed.) (1997) *Political Thinking of the Indonesian Chinese 1900–1995*, 2nd edition, Singapore: National University of Singapore Press.

Symonds, P. (2000) 'Fighting in the Malukus Heightens Tensions across Indonesia and within the Wahid Cabinet', *World Socialist Web Site*, 10 January.

Tedjasukmana, J. (2000) 'The Mysterious Roots of Mayhem', *Time*, 24 January: 21.

Tedjasukmana, J. (2001) 'Looking for a Miracle', *Time*, 5 February: 28.

Tesoro, J. M. and McCawley, T. (1999) 'Murder and Mayhem', *Asiaweek*, 30 April: 28–31.

Tirtosudarmo, R. (2000) 'Demographic Engineering, Uneven Development, and the Emerging Ethnic Politics in Indonesia', Working paper presented at the workshop on *Discourses and Practices of Democracy in Southeast Asia*, Institute of Malaysian and International Studies (IKMAS), Bangi, Malaysia, 10–13 April.

Uhlin, Anders (1999) 'The Russian Road', *Inside Indonesia*, No. 59, July–September: 7–8.

Uhlin, A. (1997) *Indonesia and the 'Third Wave of Democratisation'*, New York: St Martin's Press.

Vickers, A. (2001) 'The New Order: Keeping Up Appearances', in G. Lloyd and S. Smith (eds) *Indonesia Today: The Challenges of History*, Singapore: ISEAS, pp. 72–84.

Yap, S. (1976) 'The Prodigal Who Made His Way Up', *New Nation*, 9 March.

Young, K. (1999) 'Post-Suharto: A Change of Regime'. In A. Budiman, B. Hatley and D. Kingsbury (eds) *Reformasi: Crisis and Change in Indonesia*, Clayton, Victoria: Monash Asia Institute, Monash University, pp. 69–104.

9

The Politics of Land Distribution and Race Relations in Southern Africa

Sam Moyo

Introduction

This chapter discusses the politics of land distribution and race relations is Southern Africa, with a particular focus on the experiences of the former settler colonial states of Zimbabwe, South Africa and Namibia. It examines how inequitable land relations have contributed to intensified race-based conflicts in the southern African region and shaped specific demands for land redistribution and land reform policies. The chapter relies on detailed case study evidence from Zimbabwe, as well as South Africa and Namibia, and implicitly assesses their implications for the entire southern Africa.

Recent land reform debates in southern Africa, predicated on the Zimbabwe land conflict, have rekindled discourses on unequal race relations within the region. Land policy formation is increasingly shaped by racial patterns, land and natural resource ownership and social justice arising from historic grievances. The indigenous black population continues to be marginalized in national and global politics and economic benefits that are derived from land and natural resources. Although liberation struggles represented real attempts to address racial land inequalities, the black majority in most southern Africa countries remain landless and excluded from development, although they have formal political and economic sovereignty. Strategies to reclaim land and natural resources has refocused the need to address the race question in the sub-region and re-examine sovereignty, independence, development aid and reparations as these relate to the land question.

Colonial land policies institutionalized racial inequity in land in southern Africa. Recent attempts to confront the consequences of historical land expropriation, as well as to redress contemporary land-based inequities and discriminatory legislation and institutions, have generated renewed racial conflict in the sub-region. Land-related conflicts today increasingly arise from initiatives to forcibly repossess rights to land and embedded natural resources. The greatest threat to security in southern Africa lies in unequal land ownership patterns in countries where poor people's livelihood depends on farming. Formal employment is unable to absorb the numerous unemployed, land-short, land-less and homeless (Tevera and Moyo, 2000). Land conflicts along racial lines in Zimbabwe suggest that reconciliation without justice and social integration of whites is fragile.

The legacy of racially unequal land control confronts mainly the former settler colonies of Zimbabwe, Namibia and South Africa as well as the other countries such as Malawi, Swaziland and Botswana, which experienced low-intensity settlerism. Independence agreements in these states sought to protect white capital, including large-scale white commercial farmers' control of prime lands. The independence constitutions guaranteed the protection of private property by sanctifying willing seller–willing buyer approaches to the disposal of freehold land for its redistribution.

A major problem in addressing the land conflict is the racially based ideological distortion that shrouds social, political and economic debates on land in southern Africa. The key land reform myths of interest here are:

- that the land rights held by white minorities over the land they expropriated historically are not only legally valid but also socially and politically legitimate;
- the freehold landholding system, which in the case of Zimbabwe, Namibia and South Africa is white-dominated, and private land markets are efficient and superior to customary (so-called 'communal') tenure, thus justifying their preservation in the hands of minority white landowners. The latter are considered a constraint to productivity and commercial farming;
- that the postcolonial land reform policies are irrational and undermine food security and confidence in the economy because they place the short-term political problem of redressing historical and racial imbalances ahead of economic stability;
- that smallholders misuse their land ecologically, while whites efficiently utilize their land in terms of the scale of area used and yields per unit of land; and

- that white farmers are generically superior technologically and are efficient producers, while blacks farmers are subsistence farmers who contribute little to the economy.

These myths reflect an ahistoric understanding of the origins and development of white-controlled large-scale farm sector, ignorance of the important role black smallholder farming has played in the region, and the deep-rooted racism used to justify inaction on land reform.

Conceptual issues

A historical and political economy framework is necessary to understand the evolution of racial inequalities, conflicts and struggles over land and polices to address these. Such analyses need to be contextualized within the rubric of popular demands for social justice and equity rather than subsumed by neoliberal notions of governance and rule of law, which propose trickle-down and welfarist poverty reduction approaches to a problem that requires major structural change.

Institutionalized racism and economic control through land monopolies

Settler colonialism and land expropriation are at the root of the land and race problem. Conflict today results from past violence over access to land and natural resources during pre-colonial conquest that continued during the colonial period. During the colonial period there was polarization along racial lines due to ill-treatment of blacks by whites on farms, mines and towns. Whilst the primary motive was land expropriation, proletarianization was instituted as a means of making blacks a cheap labour force on farms and mines (Arrighi, 1967). In order to develop a manufacturing base for white consumption, the white settler regime had to expropriate land as the key means of production, followed by exploitation of cheap black labour (see above). Greater national control by whites in colonial legislatures found expression in an institutional framework strongly biased in favour of the interests of monopoly control over land by whites (Umhlaba, 1989). By owning the best and most of the land, whites gained control over black farmers in the hinterlands by forcing them to work for them on their terms.

White farmers have always been able to rely on the police, the judiciary, the white parliament and white technical experts to protect their absolute control over land. White farmers in turn often acted as though they had absolute power and control over the lives of the black farmworkers and other people who lived on their land. 'Assault and murder are commonplace and very few of the whites were prosecuted even when charges were laid' (see above). In the guise of protecting landed property, the colonial state created administrative systems for the white settlers and excluded the indigenous blacks.[1] For instance, 'all institutions in the Transvaal platteland are fundamentally racist: shops, the police, the post offices and the courts. This can be related to the way in which race is functional to the balance of power in the areas' (Umhlaba, 1989).

Beyond race, there are other land conflicts precipitated by ethnicity with numerous minority groups being denied access to land. In Botswana, the so-called 'bushmen' land was expropriated by large mining concerns due to diamond mining, with piecemeal compensation to the *tribes*. In Zimbabwe, whilst the ethnic dimension is currently clouded, there are tendencies to question the land rights of minorities and long-standing migrants. The Herero in Namibia, and the Maasai in Tanzania, have suffered the same fate as land expropriated from the white landowners was said to have been transferred to the majority ethnic groups (Shivji, 1998). As a result, the original claimants have suffered from a lack of land rights.

The root of destruction of black cultures can be traced to missionaries (Rhodes, Moffat, Livingstone), which promoted the so-called 'civilization' of the African as 'pagans', while black traditional leaders were evicted from places of their traditional rituals as the white missionaries took over the control of land. White land administrators formed an alliance with such missionaries in sanctifying the conquest of land. The mission educational system, for instance, segregated blacks from whites and condoned white supremacist ideologies. Longstanding ethnic diversity was recast into deep hostilities and segregation by the white missionary administrators and landowners. Subjugation of traditional leader (chiefs, spirit mediums) and promotion of Christianity led to divide-and-rule tactics in controlling land and minerals, such as diamonds and gold.

The white commercial farm economy

It has become an almost indelible southern Africa perspective that commercial farming is large-scale and done by white landowners, while subsistence farming is practised by the black peasantry. Although in a few instances there are piecemeal efforts to 'buy out' black elites into large-scale farming through affirmative action programmes, large-scale commercial farming remains dominated by whites in terms of land ownership, value of production and the 'social status' associated with it.

Competition for land from black elites tends to have been contained through restrictions on land sales in the communal areas and, on racial grounds, on freehold zones during the colonial and postcolonial period. Thus a few rural elites have been able to use land as a basis for attracting credit, while whites dominate agricultural financial loans. Moreover, blacks could not by law consolidate their communal area land for commercial production, as this was seen to lead to stiff competition against white farmers (Arrighi, 1973). The protection of the white farming economy was also found within export agriculture, through marketing policy and infrastructure, and production. Increasingly, domestic food markets and labour-intensive commodities for export markets, such as cotton, are dominated by black smallholders. However, due to the location of communal areas far away from main lines of transport, their returns are relatively marginal.

State subsidies have historically been used to support white farmers because they are considered key in exports, while the food security concept was used to augment subsidies to the large-scale commercial farming sector.[2] Colonial and postcolonial regimes have supported research stations located in white farming areas, and focused the development of infrastructure (public dams, roads, communications and power) among white farmers to the exclusion of blacks. This widened the differential productivity of white agriculture compared to the black peasantry.

To date, the racially blind land policy in southern Africa does not accept international mainstream agricultural economics debates, which argue that smaller sized farms tend to use their land more productively, in terms of higher unit yields and use of labour. The trend, based on self-exploitation of domestic labour in peasant households, particularly of female and child labour, which has led to impressive small farmer performances in Malawi and Zimbabwe, has not adequately changed beliefs in black smallholder efficiency (Weiner et al., 1985; Moyo, 1987). The belief in the greater efficiency of large farms has also been a key constraint to progressive land policy in non-settler states before and after independence. Various governments, including Malawi, Swaziland and Botswana, developed their agricultural and land policies from the late 1960s on the basis of promoting large estates because of the need for economies of scale and the presumed superiority of large farms.

In the 1980s, land policies in Southern Africa promoted individual indigenous capitalist farmers, drawn from senior politicians and civil servants, retirees and other formerly non-agrarian indigenous business people.[3] Once again macro-economic and agricultural policy regimes ensured that various resources such as credit, foreign currency and infrastructure were mainly allocated to both white and indigenous large capitalist farmers. The effects of such preferential resource allocations were wrongly taken to imply that large-scale farming was more effective than smallholder farming in Southern Africa.[4] This had the effect of legitimizing the expansion of large-scale landholdings and discouraging land reform in those countries where growing land ownership imbalances were exacerbating land shortages, land degradation and rural poverty.

Environmentalism and white control of tourism

Again, southern African environmental discourses tend to regard land husbandry by blacks as intrinsically poor, implying that the environment will collapse if land is redistributed. The perception is that it is only whites who value and nurture the environment, while agronomic practices of blacks, such as intercropping, are thought to destroy the soil. Thus the 'conventional' settler-introduced system of agriculture with crops in straight lines, using advanced technology and chemicals, which again the blacks are thought to be incapable of using, are considered superior systems. Recent research has, of course, disproved these notions.

Yet, indigenous technical knowledge promoted by liberal environmental NGOs seems to suffer from its lack of real agronomic alternatives that can take blacks in communal areas beyond current community-based natural resources projects that do not improve the standards of living of the majority. The common middle-class perception is that the poor degrade land and that the white large-scale commercial sector uses land efficiently. This ideology underlies the excessive focus of NGO schemes on 'protecting' land and 'educating' the peasantry on sustainable land use, rather than their advocacy for land redistribution.

Generally, NGOs have been and remain a reactionary force on land reform rather than an agenda-setting movement. NGOs can be conceived as a new mechanism for promoting the so-called 'indirect rule system' wherein they increasingly substitute the local state and traditional authority in organizing communities in the co-management of state and donor-initiated development projects. This tendency begs further questions in the debate on the nature and weakness of NGOs to champion the rights of indigenous people to their land and better standards of living (Mamdani, 1996).

NGOs are at the root of the further alienation of natural resources and monopolistic control of tourism by white minority companies in alliance with regional and multinational corporations (Moyo, 2000). In countries such as Mozambique, Namibia and South Africa, white individuals, companies and regional mega-tourism ventures have expropriated land at the coastal zones. In the past, racial discrimination meant that blacks could not access holiday resorts. Yet more importantly, the cost of coastal prime lands for tourism development was made artificially high to deny access to blacks. Fighting for access to beaches and fishing rights on oceans was central to the liberation struggles in those countries that are not landlocked.

The project of subjugating blacks is underpinned by the discourses on environmental aestheticism (eco-culture, eco-tourism), which now claim to preserve primordial black cultures as part of the image of the African wilderness. Thus, eco-tourism allocates monies to trickle into the landless black communities, while the bulk of benefits of land control rests with external financiers and safari operators. Furthermore, through the so-called transboundary peace parks involving two or more countries, global capital has found an avenue for land expropriation in the context of foreign direct investment. In Namibia, Zimbabwe and South Africa many of the black, white and foreign elites tend to allocate to themselves large tracts of land for commercial farming or tourism and in addition lobby the state for favourable tourism polices (see above). The marginalization of the majority of the people tends to create political conflicts with those minority groups who seek to control such benefits. The political and economic consequences of these problems in the region are broadly the same: poverty, enforced high population density in customary lands, land degradation, lack of resources to invest in adequate land management and political uncertainty.

Postcolonial forces of the land problem and its global dimensions

The current wave of neoliberal interpretations of the land question, which emphasizes liberal political and market rights of existing landowners rather than social justice, popular social rights and the redistribution of resources, are fundamental to the structural adjustment prescriptions facing most African countries. These economic and political reforms in southern Africa promote the interests of white business, black middle classes and global capital rather than the survival and economic needs of the rural poor and working class. The present focus on democratization and the rule of law in the land reform discourse does not only protect the minority land rights over those of the indigenous people;

Table 9.1 Polarized Values on Land Reform and Democratization

Land Redistribution		Democratization
Equity	vs.	Democracy
Social Rights	vs.	Liberal Political Rights
Need/Poverty and Reparations	vs.	Efficiency
Historical Social Justice	vs.	Contemporary Governance Problem
Majority/Indigenization Property Rights	vs.	White Minority Property Rights
Reinvention of Law (Legal property rights regime, Popular interest)	vs.	Received Rule of Law
Customary Law or Indigenous/ historic and Legitimate	vs.	Existing Universalized System of Law and Property Rights

it also polarises society along artificially defined value differences (Table 9.1).

There is a perception that national and global coalitions of industrial and agricultural capital aim to protect the property rights and benefits of a few white minorities, while paying lip service to land reform and poverty reduction. Increasingly, global conventions such as WTO, UNCED and Kyoto, place countries in the South under pressure to strike a balance between so-called sustainable development and land reform. The middle-class-led NGOs, following neoliberal development agendas, emphasize the 'community-based natural resources management' (CBNRM) discourses rather than land reforms that challenge resource ownership patterns as a basis for addressing the environmental problems.

Negotiated and market-assisted land reforms are now being promoted by global institutions such as the World Bank (Binswanger and Deininger, 1993; Binswanger, 1996; Deininger, 1998) as a way of conflict resolution through provision of funding, although for the last two decades their emphasis has been on market-based reform. However, market-assisted land reforms tend to protect and empower white landowners who have greater leverage in land transactions, leading to the transfer of unsuitable land for popular resettlement requirements (Moyo, 2001). Yet, the same global institutions also call for export incentives and the protection of private investment through national laws and global conventions such as WTO that do not favour the small-holders, who are mainly black. The most destructive of these contradictory global market-based policies is the European Union's Common Agricultural Policies, whose subsidies have increased smallholder poverty, while not supporting land reform.

Land holding patterns in the region

Background to land holding patterns

The existing structure and patterns of race relations, which underlie land inequalities in southern Africa, are based on a relatively unique distribution of demographic features, including population, wealth, income and employment patterns, which define economic control and management. Even political party and civil society participation and social relations are heavily polarized racially in these societies. This racial framework defines the social basis for land demand and the struggles that shape policy-making.

Whites, as individuals, and multinational companies have been predominant in the control of the economy, including agriculture, manufacturing industry, tourism and commerce.[5] In South Africa, the land problem is complex mostly because of its deep-seated manifestations in both massive urban slums and marginal rural areas under extreme population pressure. The long political struggle against apartheid and land expropriation over many centuries has been resisted by a numerically large and organized white minority population.[6] The rest of the southern African countries have low white populations and fewer white farmers, yet they control a large part of the land and the few industries.

Income distribution patterns in the region show that whites have high incomes, in a sea of massive rural and urban poverty in black communities. Most blacks have no access to a sustainable income base outside agriculture and the high unemployment levels exacerbate the demand for land. In the former white settler colonies, land ownership patterns in urban areas physically segregated blacks and whites residences, and whites developed their own social enclaves of separate schools, hospitals, country clubs, and so forth. This segregation tends to underlie some of the black-on-white violent conflicts on the farms in South Africa and Zimbabwe, although violent criminal activities have capitalized on contested land and economic conditions. The root of much racial animosity in the region is the fact that whites are considered to have 'conquered' the indigenous groups, leading to the dislocation of the latter and creation of a pseudo-feudal system.

Land expropriation was rampant in southern Africa. It is only Botswana that had no white settlers by 1958. On the other hand Angola,

Table 9.2 Settler Alienation of Land in Southern Africa

Country	% Land Alienated by Settlers		White Settler % of population	
	1958	2000	1960	2000
Angola	6.0	5.4	1.0	0.2
Botswana	0.0	5.0	0.3	0.5
Lesotho	5.0	5.0	0.3	0.8
Malawi	43.0	4.3	8.0	0.4
Namibia	43.0	44.0	19.4	11.1
South Africa	89.0	83.0	2.8	13.7
Swaziland	49.0	40.0	0.2	–
Zambia	3.0	3.1	3.0	0.1
Zimbabwe	49.0	41.0	7.1	0.8

Sources: Hendricks (1995). Department of Land Affairs, South Africa, Land reform experiences in South Africa and the options for future, SADC land conference paper CIA, World Fact book, 2001 Atlapedia.com (website last updated 2001). DR Congo statistics, Land Tenure Centre, Country Profiles of Land Tenure in Southern Africa, Namibia.

Lesotho and Zambia had lower percentages of land alienation (Table 9.3). In terms of settler population, Namibia seems to have had a significant white settler population (19 per cent), mainly composed of the Afrikaners, Germans and Austrians in 1960. The greatest white settler land alienation occurred in South Africa with 89 per cent with the Dutch and English jostling for the control of land since the eighteenth century.

In the 1960s, Botswana, Lesotho, Swaziland and Angola had a smaller white settler population. Significantly, during the war of conquest, traditional leaders in Botswana sought protectorate status from the United Kingdom. Namibia had the unfortunate experience of being declared a South African protectorate under the League of Nations, after having been a colony of Germany. This administrative arrangement denied independence to the indigenous people and sanctioned the racist laws that protected the interest of white farmers in the form of freehold title to land.

The white population tends to be grossly over-represented in land ownership in terms of population structure. South Africa, Namibia and Zimbabwe have the largest number of whites and white farmer population compared to the other countries. In Zimbabwe the 100,000 whites command a significant influence in the economy through the control of land, industry, commerce and manufacturing.

Table 9.3 Land and Population in Southern Africa

Country	land Area (000 ha)	Potential Agricultural Area (000 ha)	Population Density (persons/000 ha)	Total Population	Whites (%)
Angola	124,670.0	31,167.5	81	10,145,267	1
Botswana	60,037.0	28,217.39	26	1,576,470	4 (est.) (White and Kgalagadi = 7 per cent)
DR Congo	234,541.0	23,454.1	222	51,964,999	9
Lesotho	3,035.5	2,337.34	706	2,143,141	0.3
Malawi	9,400.0	6,400.0	1,104	10,385,849	0.06
Mauritius	186.0	102.3	6,341	1,179,368	Indo-, Sino- and Franco-Mauritian
Mozambique	79,938.0	41,056.89	201	17,700,000	0.06 European, 0.08 Indians
Namibia	82,541.8	38,794.65	21	1,771,327	6
South Africa	121,991.2	95,153.14	356	43,421,021	13.6 where, 2.6 Indian
Swaziland	1,736.3	1,267.5	624	1,083,289	3
Seychelles	45.5	6.83	1,743	79,326	Seychellois (mix of African, European, Asians)
Tanzania	94,508.7	48,710.0	374	35,306,126	1
Zambia	75,261.4	35,372.86	127	9,582,418	1.1
Zimbabwe	39,058.0	32,027.56	290	11,342,521	0.8
Totals	1,777,449.9	384,068.06		196,681,122	

Sources: CIA, The World Factbook, 2001 – Country land areas, potential agricultural land (except Malawi and Tanzania), White % (except for Malawi) US Bureau of the Census, International Data Base 2001; Ministry of Lands and Human Settlements Development, Tanzania, National Land Policy, 1995 Potential Agric Land Bloodbook.Com. (website last updated 1 October 2001), Race and Ethnicity Analysis – White % for Malawi hectares of the commercial farmland belong to black farmers. By contrast, communal lands comprise 138,000 households with an area of 33.5 million hectares, which is only 41 per cent of the land available.

Present regional land holding patterns

Countries such as South Africa, Namibia and Zimbabwe are confronted with unequal land holdings with titled land in the hands of a few white commercial farmers. The skewed land holding is excessive in South Africa, where 60,000 white South African farmers who make up only 5 per cent of the white population, own almost 87 per cent (85.5 million) of the land. Only 20,000 white commercial farmers produce 80 per cent of the gross agricultural product. A further 40,000, including some 2,000 black farmers, produce 15 per cent, while 500,000 families living in the former homelands produce an estimated 5 per cent. At least 12 million blacks inhabit 17.1 million hectares of land and no more than 15 per cent (or 2.6 million hectares) of this land is potentially arable (Wildschut and Hulbert, 1998). Thus whites own six times more land in terms of the quantity of land available and its quality.

However, Namibia has the highest number of white settlers, with 19 per cent of the total population. Commercial land under freehold comprises 6,300 farms measuring about 36.2 million hectares belongs to 4,128 mostly white male farmers of either German, Austrian or South African origin as well as companies closely linked to the former colonial masters. The freehold land covers 44 per cent of available land and 70 per cent of the most productive agricultural land covering 362,000 square kilometres. Only 2.2 million hectares of the commercial farmland belong to black farmers. By contrast, communal lands comprise 138,000 households with an area of 33.5 million hectares, which is only 41 per cent of the available land. Swaziland and Lesotho have high population densities around largely mountainous areas and scarce arable land. Customary land tenure is predominant, while these countries struggle for equitable land ownership in the context of traditional leaders' control over land allocation (Mashinini, 2000). Increased privatization of state lands as part of the foreign investment drive has pushed the majority of the people on the worst lands.

In Mozambique, although all land is constitutionally state land, privatization of land started in 1984 as part of the implementation of the structural adjustment programmes. This has created grounds for racial animosity as foreigners and white South Africans tend to dominate this investment. Confrontation over land in Zimbabwe has seen the emigration of white Zimbabweans to Mozambique.[7] Mozambican officials have called for greater social integration of incoming white farmers to avoid creation of 'white islands' of development. Prospective farmers negotiate for access to land with the state and local communities to pre-

Table 9.4   Land Tenure in Southern Africa (Approximate % of National Territory)

Country	Freehold/ Leasehold	Communal/Tribal/ Customary	Conservation/Minerals/ Water/Catchments/ Reserves and Other State Land
Angola	6 (est)	51 (est)	43.0
Botswana	6.0	71.0	23.0
DR Congo	8.9 (est)	28 (est)	63.1
Lesotho	22.0	77.2	0.8
Malawi	27.4	65.0	7.57
Mauritius	77.4	9.8	12.8
Mozambique	22.5	32.4	45.1
Namibia	36.3	41.0	22.7
Seychelles	22.0	69.0	9.0
South Africa	44.3	53.0	2.67
Swaziland	43.2	49.8	7.0
Tanzania	6.6	47.4	46.0
Zambia	6.0	58.0	36.0
Zimbabwe	41.0	43.0	16.0

Sources: Botswana Country Paper, Land Questions and Land Tenure, presented at the SADC regional land conference in Namibia, 2001; Malawi Population and Housing Census, 1998; Tanzania National Land Policy (1995), and Country Paper presented at the SADC regional conference in Namibia 2001; Land Question and Land Reform in Zimbabwe, 1980–Present, World Bank, AFTES Working Paper No. 19, 1996, Economist Intelligence Unit, Country profiles, 2001 – figures for Seychelles, Rihoy E. and Jones B., A Stakeholder Guide to Community-Based Natural Resources Management and Tenure in Southern Africa, 1999; Current statistical figures could not be found for Angola and DR Congo for areas of land under leases and customary tenure, estimates are projections form 1993 figures.

empt future land conflicts. Half of Mozambique's 40 million hectares of arable land is uncultivated, and is viewed as the largest pool of available land in southern Africa.

In Zimbabwe most of the freehold lands are in the hands of whites and are located in the most fertile parts of the country, with the most favourable climatic conditions and water resources.[8] Approximately 4,500 white commercial farmers (0.03 per cent of the population) control 31 per cent of the country's land under freehold tenure or about 42 per cent of the agricultural land. On the other hand 1.2 million black families in Zimbabwe subsist on 41 per cent of the country's area of 390,076 square kilometres.

Contested settler notions of land size

In the former settler colonies per capita arable land ownership has been declining due to an increase in population in the communal areas. The little gains made by piecemeal land resettlement have been severely eroded due to population increase. However, the greatest security threat remains: that a few white farmers own most of the best arable land, and that their farms are oversized, while poverty amongst the majority has been increasing. While poor black smallholders and the landless call for increased land redistribution, rural elites call for access to larger plots on the commercial farms. Zimbabwean bureaucrats have recently prescribed land size ceilings in all the natural regions based on rather outdated notions of what farm sizes are required for 'viable' commercial farming.

Farm sizes in the region reflect the trends in land ownership. In Namibia the average white LSCF farm sizes is 5,700 hectares. In Zimbabwe the average is 2,500 with variation from NR II to V. In the communal areas the average farm size is around 2 hectares and in resettlement areas it is 5 hectares. In South Africa 28.5 per cent of the farms are larger than 1,000 hectares (Wildschut and Hulbert, 1998). The resettlement programmes in the region are proceeding on the basis of small-sized farms for blacks averaging less than 10 hectares of arable land in areas such as NR II in Zimbabwe. Land reform based on controlling farm sizes through ceilings has not been pursued in most of the countries.

This leaves a few landowners holding outrageously large tracts of land. Using the cut-off point of over 10,000 hectares owned either through company or individual title and as single or multiple farms, about 66 landowners (with 158 farms) occupy over two million hectares of Zimbabwe's land. Most of these farms are multiple-owned company farms. Eight individuals, for instance, together owned 13 farms occupying 158,531 hectares, of which 29 per cent of the area was owned as multiple farms. Multiple farm ownership is thus a decided feature of Zimbabwe's landed gentry, whether these are company or individually owned.

The criterion used to determine viable farm sizes is based on a legacy of white settler notions of the 'small scale' being subsistence-oriented and the 'commercial' being large-scale white farms. Although the categorization is posited as a function of different resource levels, there is still a clear class or racial (social) element to it. Large land sizes are said to be necessary for mechanized agriculture, such as the use of combine harvesters, which blacks are said to be unable to acquire. The large land sizes are said to provide leverage for multiple land uses on a single farm, including leaving some of the land fallow for some time.

In order to conceal land under-utilization and speculative uses of land, white commercial farmers and multinational companies have tended to put their land under wildlife ranching. None the less invest-

Table 9.5   Per Capita Arable Land in the SADC Region

Country	Per Capita Arable Land Area (Hectares)				
	1965	1980	1987	1990	2000
Angola	0.53	0.41	0.34	0.31	0.25
Botswana	0.73	0.44	0.35	0.33	0.22
D.R. of Congo	0.36	0.25	0.20	0.18	0.14
Lesotho	0.37	0.22	0.20	0.18	0.16
Malawi	0.28	0.20	0.20	0.18	0.18
Mauritius	0.12	0.10	0.10	0.09	0.08
Mozambique	0.30	0.24	0.21	0.20	0.17
Namibia	0.92	0.64	0.53	0.49	0.47
Seychelles	0.02	0.02	0.01	0.01	0.01
South Africa	0.62	0.45	0.38	0.38	0.28
Swaziland	0.38	0.33	0.23	0.23	0.18
Tanzania	0.17	0.12	0.12	0.12	0.12
Zambia	1.34	0.89	0.73	0.67	0.55
Zimbabwe	0.46	0.35	0.30	0.28	0.24
Sub-Saharan Africa	0.47	0.33	0.28	0.26	0.24

Sources: World Bank, Human Development Indicators, 2001 – for 1965–90 CIA's World Factbook, (country arable land areas), 2001 and US Bureau of the Census (population figures), 2001 for computing year 2000 column.

ing in game ranching, tourism in the form of conservancies, requires expropriation of large-sized land which in some countries they achieve through land consolidation. Various shareholding structures that remain in the clique of white farmers are exclusionary to the blacks contesting such arrangements through land occupations. The tourism sector has excluded blacks, given that it is regarded as too technical for black smallholders, in terms of marketing its products, whom it is argued should concentrate on less technical crops such as maize and sunflower rather than horticulture (World Bank, 1991; 1995: vol. 2).

This racist notion is buttressed by the belief that blacks yearn for home consumption and residence and do not require land for commercial uses. However, the output performance of smallholders including resettled black farmers and those who have invested in peri-urban areas demonstrates that with adequate access to land blacks can contribute substantially to domestic and export markets. Unfortunately, white farmers and some donor circles continue to pursue the misplaced notion that when blacks obtain large-sized land through state support it is only a reflection of unproductive cronyism. However, since whites obtained large-sized land through the same procedures, which were aimed at commercializing farming, such notions are unfounded.

Politics and demand for land redistribution

The demand for land redistribution in terms of both redressing histori-cal and racially grounded inequities and of the growing need by both the black poor (rural and urban) and black elites has been a consistent feature of southern African politics and policy-making. Recently most of these countries have been formulating land policies in response to both public pressure for redistribution and official perspectives that insist on the crucial role of tenure reform in development. Most official analyses of the land question have, however, tended to underestimate the nature and scale of demand for land redistribution, and to ignore the racial tensions that have persisted as a result of the unfinished land reform agenda.

The demand for land reform takes various forms and arises from various sources. These include formal and informal demands, legal and underground or illegal forms of demand for land redistribution, and demands which may be based upon the restitution of historic rights or contemporary demands based upon different needs. The different socio-political organizations, which mediate such demands, include the civil society organizations, farmers unions, political parties, War Veterans Associations, business representative organizations, community-based organizations and traditional structures. Such structures are central in the evolution of the demand for land redistribution. The social content of these structures, however, is decidedly racially polarized in southern Africa, while the class composition of the 'visible' policy actors has been elitist.

Since the decolonization of Zimbabwe, South Africa and Namibia from the 1980s, the debate on land reform was mainly focused on market instruments of land transfer, although these failed to redress the legacy of racially inequitable land ownership. Despite broad consensus among governments, the landless, landowners and the international community on the need for land reform in the sub-region, the land reform debate has remained shallow. The main reason for this is that the predominantly urban-led civil society has not formally embraced the land reform agenda due to the enduring, class-based orientation of its leadership, especially in the NGO movement. This has relegated rural social movements on land reform to informal politics while giving prominence to more organized, middle-class civic groups and policy organizations that typically advocate market-based methods of land reform and liberal rights issues.

The onset of structural adjustment, as well as multiparty 'democratization', reinforced the liberal dimension of the land debate, which 'opposition' movements have adopted. In the process of transition to a liberal economy, however informal rural politics, and land occupations in particular, have remained the primary source of advocacy for radical land reform and indeed have succeeded in maintaining land reform on the agenda. Over time, the salient land demands of the black middle classes and elites within civil society organizations and both the ruling and opposition parties, were made within a liberal electoral and human rights framework, which avoided the fundamental issues of economic restructuring and redistribution of resources.

In debates around land reform the race issue emerges because the land to be acquired is expected to come from land largely owned by whites and the beneficiaries are black. The reality is that the state has had to respond to agitation by black social movements, traditional leaders, rural community leaders and black affirmative action pressure groups to facilitate land reform as a basis of healing the wounds of past grievances. Attempts to address the land question tend to be construed as overt racism on the part of those demanding land from the state, although land shortages and needs are real.

Southern Africa in general has not, historically, had an organized civil society that has made radical demands for land reform or land redistribution. Under colonial rule, the land cause was led by the liberation movements, and in the 1970s, was pursued by means of armed struggle (Chitiyo, 2000). In the post-colonial period, the civil society groupings that have existed have been predominantly middle class and with strong international aid linkages that have militated against radical land reform, while formal grassroots organizations have tended to be appendages of middle-class driven intermediary civil society organizations (Moyo, 1994). The rural operations of civil society within a neoliberal framework has been characterized by demands for funds for small 'development' projects aimed at a few selected beneficiaries (Moyo et al., 2000). This state of affairs has left a political and social vacuum in the leadership of the land reform agenda.

The indigenization lobby seems to have transformed the meaning of land reform and the 'return of lost lands' by appealing for the de-racialization or 'blackening' of the ownership base of commercial farmland. Some of its proposals appear to be a racial substitution formula for capitalist farming. The emerging indigenous capital, large white farmer organizations, black technocrats and many NGOs have however tended to support the shift of eligibility criteria for access to land from the 'landlessness' and 'insecure' to the 'capable', 'productive' and 'efficient', within the terms of the neoliberal global development paradigm (Ashworth, 1990; World Bank, 1995). This changing terms of the land reform debate was buttressed by optimistic expectations of foreign investment that were expected to submerge land reform through other socioeconomic developments, including employment creation. In this context, land reform came to be perceived as almost unnecessary.

The re-emergence of land reform on the developing world agenda (Brazil, Colombia, etc.) in the mid-1990s and the relaunching of the resettlement programme in Zimbabwe mark the current phase of a dialectic relationship between peasants, government and global institutions. After the failure of structural adjustment to live up to its rural development promises, the land question has resurfaced as a legitimate item on the poverty reduction agenda of the World Bank while, at the national level, the same failure has brought demands on the ruling party to resuscitate its liberation promise.

Given Zimbabwe's colonial legacy, the long-standing conflicts over the land question translate into intense electoral political competition, which in turn is marked by polarization between land reform radicalism and conservative land transfer strategies. Indeed, the land question could not be dislodged from the electoral debate. Opposition parties in Zimbabwe, South Africa and Namibia have sought to depoliticize the land issue on technical grounds for the same reasons advanced by the external-funding institutions. The ruling party argued that the opposition intended to reverse land reform, and were sellouts to the former colonial masters, given their alleged receipt of financial assistance from white farmers and businesses, and from civil society organizations linked to donor funding.

In the face of strong post-liberation war movements demanding access to land, the white farmers appear to have sought political solace through the opposition movements. The strongest white participation in politics defending their so-called land rights is found in South Africa, Namibia and Zimbabwe in line with the numerous whites in these countries and the apartheid structures still existing. However, in Zimbabwe an economic decline in the 1990s coinciding with threats of compulsory land acquisition opened the scope for white farmers for the first time to take an open political path to protect their interests.

In Zimbabwe, white farmer participation in politics to protect their land rights took the form of the support against the *yes* vote in the constitutional referendum in 2000. The government alleged that the farmers were responsible for financially supporting opposition political parties. Nevertheless, the Zimbabwe opposition movements have had narrow political interests. While they have pursued valid demands for democratization, within a liberal electoral and human rights framework, they have limited social democratic demands, especially regarding the redistribution of land resources or economic restructuring. In many cases the opposition movements have presented land reform as a non-political issue to be determined by economic considerations only.

However, the pressure for land reform must, as usual and of necessity, given Zimbabwe's history, build up around elections, making it trite to say that the issue of land reform is being politicized. Rather, the point is that various political parties need to develop a vantage point on land reform so that their social delivery agenda remain relevant to popular demands. Given the potential for land conflicts in South Africa and Namibia, there has been some tussling over the manner in which the Zimbabwe land problem should be handled in their respective parliaments. While the black legislators from the liberation movement backgrounds in Zimbabwe tend to expect such conflicts to spread into South Africa and Namibia, if land reform is not pursued, their white counterparts from liberal political parties have tended to put pressure on their governments to condemn land occupations and to ensure that the Zimbabwe situation would not happen in their countries.

Land redistribution policies and balancing racial land inequality

Little progress has been achieved in southern African land reform policies, especially in redressing racial land inequalities, colonially based discriminatory land use regulations and land tenure systems. A generic set of land problems, which requires policy attention (Table 9.6), remains unaddressed in southern Africa.

Racially biased ownership of land tends to accompany discriminatory land use polices and practises, and land tenure laws. The redistribution of land could shift the underlying causes and effects of such biases. For instance, inefficient land use among large farmers, over-utilization of overcrowded areas and the insecurity of tenure among the landless and land-short could be changed by expanding the numbers of those benefiting from land redistribution. Instead, southern African land reform policies have focused on reforming the *in situ* regulation of land use and environmental management practices among smallholders, and

Table 9.6 Land Policy Problems and Issues

Issue	Problems
Land Distribution	• Inequitable and unjust distribution of land • Limited rights/access for majority • Costly and cumbersome transfers of land
Land Utilization	• Discriminatory regulations against customary tenures • Speculative underutilization of freeholds • Unsustainable use in overcrowded areas • Coercive regulations in some tenures
Land Tenure	• Insecurity of some tenures • Discriminatory protection system • Over-centralized regulations
Land Administration	• Coercive and centralized approach • Dispersed institutions • Poor representation of majority • Weak transparency
Land Adjudication	• Biased towards market and state sectors • No restitution/victims compensation • Merged powers of local courts/authorities • Inaccessible courts/mediation

Sources: Shivji et al. (1998).

attempts to reform customary tenures towards freedhold land tenure and developing a land market among the black communities.

The little land redistribution that has been attempted in the sub-region has been constrained by unrealistic legal and constitutional frameworks, which led to costly and slow processes of land acquisition and transfer of land rights to various beneficiaries. Land redistribution policies have been unduly influenced by market-oriented preconditions, which eventually militate against the poorest and landless people's land needs. The land redistribution experiences in the region have been based upon four broadly related approaches.

State-centred but market-based approach

The most dominant approach used, mainly in Zimbabwe and Namibia before the introduction of compulsory land acquisition approaches in the former, can be referred to as a 'state-centred but market-based' approach. Land was purchased by the state for redistribution following willing seller–willing buyer procedures. The private sector led land identification and supply through the market, and central government was a reactive buyer choosing land on offer. Governments provided land to beneficiaries selected mainly by land authorities under the direct supervision of central government. The land restitution approach followed in South Africa is essentially a state initiative in which government pays mostly market prices for land claims of individuals and communities in a limited land rights and time-bound framework.

State compulsory acquisition of land at market prices

In the last decade land redistribution, using compulsory methods of land acquisition by the state, which pays market prices for the land and its developments or for developments only, has been pursued in Zimbabwe and is being debated in other countries. In this approach the government also controls the resettlement process, although settler selection is more locally controlled. In Zimbabwe up to 3,000 farms were gazetted for acquisition between 1992 and 2001. However, cumbersome litigation has been a key constraint. In South Africa, a few cases of compulsory acquisition have recently evolved out of its land restitution programme, given the resistance of landowners to part cheaply with their land. Even where the aim is a limited redress of the injustices of forced removals of blacks by white settlers and the historical denial of access to land to the majority of the South African population, compulsory land acquisitions have received little public support by civil society organizations (Department of Land Affairs 1996: 15; Commission on Restitution of Land Rights 1997: 23; National Land Committee 1997: 31).

Market-led land redistribution assisted by the state

A third approach to land redistribution that has been attempted in South Africa, and which was discussed at Zimbabwe's Land Donors' Conference of 1998 in the context of testing 'alternative' approaches, is the so-called market-assisted land reform approach. In the 1990s, multilateral institutions responded to widespread radical land seizures in Brazil, by promoting the market-assisted land reform approach on grounds of its being more cost-effective, transparent, fair and speedier. The entire land reform process has to be led by the private sector, communities and NGOs within a market framework. This framework of land acquisition seems to favour the large landowners' compensation requirements. However, most black communities resist paying for land they feel has been stolen. This approach has been implemented rather slowly in South Africa and has yet to be implemented in Zimbabwe and Namibia. Only a few NGOs and farmers believe in the efficacy of this approach.

This approach tends to be populist in that it expects land reform to be community-driven but legally grounded. Communities are expected to develop local land reform plans, identifying the demand for and potential supplies and pricing of land, and negotiate land transfers that are fair to both landowners and the impoverished and marginalized rural populations. Given that social movements and NGOs in southern Africa have yet to drive radical land reform, this approach masks the dominance of conservative technocrat consultants and NGOs, as evidence from the South African experience has begun to show.

Community land occupation and state-facilitated approach

Finally, there is the community-led land occupation strategy, whether state facilitated or formalized. This approach as a formal strategy to land redistribution has not been implemented on a grand scale in most of the countries. In Zimbabwe it was implemented during the first four years after independence. Land identification was led by communities through 'squatting' and government purchased the land at market prices in what was officially coined the 'Accelerated Resettlement Programme'. Local 'squatter' communities selected themselves as beneficiaries by occupying mainly abandoned and under-utilised lands, most of which were in the liberation war frontier zones. Subsequently, the government used forced evictions to restrain this approach until land occupations re-emerged during 1998 on farm that government had identified for compulsory acquisition. More recently this form of land occupation, albeit led centrally by the war veterans association, has dominated land reform policy, leading to the current fast-track programme. In South Africa numerous peri-urban 'informal settlements' that began in the late 1980s are a product of this approach.

These various approaches to land redistribution increasingly tend to be used in combination, although the market-based approach remains dominant. Recent donor support to governments' land reform programmes tends to favour the untested market approach to avoid efforts at compulsory acquisition on a large scale. Until recently, these land redistribution programmes have aimed to rehabilitate and politically stabilize countries torn apart by armed struggles through the following generic objectives:

- decongestion of overpopulated areas;
- increasing the base of productive agriculture;
- rehabilitation of people displaced by war;
- resettlement of squatters, the destitute, the landless;

- promotion of equitable distribution of agricultural land;
- deracialising commercial agriculture.

Increasingly, land reform programme objectives are being stylized towards addressing poverty reduction in keeping with the new development grounded in poverty reduction strategy processes.

Since 1998, the internationalization of Zimbabwe's land problem through the donors conference and other initiatives has placed greater pressures on the sub-region's land reforms to focus on addressing poverty reduction. Given that this approach is not grounded in redressing historical grievances or restituting land rights *per se*, it underplays the importance of balancing the racial composition of farming and confronting racial imbalances in land control.

Most of the southern African countries facing demands for land reform may require strong state intervention of the land markets, given inherited uneven racial distribution of social capital and control of markets. The adoption of the policy of reconciliation, which began in Zimbabwe and spread to the governments of South Africa and Namibia, has meant that many governments in the region treated radical land reform as racially sensitive and unnecessary. This perspective has changed as threats of massive land repossession suggest the need for extensive and speedier approaches to land reform.

The scale and social composition of those benefiting from land redistribution has been narrow given the limited transfers witnessed so far. Since independence from South Africa in 1990, only about 35,000 black Namibians have been resettled on white commercial farmland.[9] In South Africa as of 2001, 1,203 claims had been settled, representing some 162,000 beneficiaries (Department of Land Affairs, Restitution statistics). The land restitution programme deals with justice in a material, tangible sense through acknowledging the injustice of the past and addressing these through concrete action.

By 1998, in Zimbabwe 3.6 million hectares mainly large-scale, white-owned land had been redistributed to 70,000 families. The government states that to date 3.5 million hectares and 118,000 families have been settled under the fast-track programme, although much of the land is being contested by owners and some land is under illegal occupation (*Daily News*, 2001) Most of the resettlement took place during the first five years of independence, while the rural black population continued to increase without a concomitant increase in land holdings to reflect these demographic changes. Furthermore, government policy is to provide infrastructure and resource back-up to the resettled families.

Recently, the lack of resources in the context of massive land transfer programmes means that the state has had to resettle people on the basis of minimal support.

Deracializing commercial farming has been gaining importance in current land redistribution programmes at the expense of the landless. In Zimbabwe, the Land Reform Policy of 1990 emphasized support for promoting emergent black large-scale farmers in what appeared less as a resettlement than a land reallocation programme intending to redress racial imbalances. South African and Namibian policies also sought to empower black commercial farmers as an integral aspect of land reform. In this context, special groups such as war veterans have received particular attention. In Zimbabwe, for instance, the government reserved a 20 per cent quota of resettlement land for war veterans in 1995, while master farmers and agricultural graduates were to benefit from the land allocations of medium to large-scale farms under the newly established Tenant Farmer Scheme.

Different forms of deracialization have emerged in the form of affirmative action and indigenization in Zimbabwe and South Africa respectively, given their stated objectives of creating a black agrarian bourgeoisie. The land currently controlled by the state is being used to facilitate blacks' access to land if they have the resources to invest in agriculture.[10] In Zimbabwe about 400 blacks have gained 420,000 hectares through this route. Another 1,000 blacks have used their own resources to acquire about 760,000 hectares on the open market. However, it is argued that prime land still remains in the hands of the white farmers, who are not prepared to dispose it (Moyo, 1995).

Land reform policies of occupations in southern Africa seem to evolve through the interaction of market and compulsory approaches to land acquisition for redistribution to both the landless and an emerging black agrarian bourgeoisie. Official land reform policies seem to respond to increasing land demands and land occupation pressures. The Zimbabwe government for example, co-opted land occupations, using the ruling party and the War Veterans Association, into a formalized land acquisition strategy, in response to the changing political and economic context and pressures of the times. A persistent feature of the land reform experience is that racial imbalance and historic grievances over land expropriation are the binding force underlying social mobilization for land reform, which the black middle classes lead or co-opt. This in turn reflects the slow pace of land redistribution and the legacy of white monopolistic control of land and the agrarian-related sectors.

Conclusion

Independence and reconciliation policies in Zimbabwe and Namibia and the demise of apartheid in South Africa persuaded many to believe that racial conflicts would disappear. Regional integration and the 'peace dividend' were expected to lead to economic growth throughout the region, and obviate the need for major structural changes. There are important lessons to be learnt from political independence settlements of the sub-region that did not address the core racial problem of inequitable land and natural resources ownership, as well as the downstream economic opportunities ensuing from such control.

This chapter has argued that land redistribution through redressing historical problems and social justice are crucial ingredients of reconciliation and development in the sub-region because of the broadly based demand for such reforms. Since political independence settlements did not consider compensating victims of past losses of land, human resources, livestock, wildlife resources and home, land redistribution can be seen as some form of reparations. It is within this context that countries such as Zimbabwe view the former colonial masters as having an obligation to pay for the land that was expropriated during the colonial period. The failure to mobilize finance for land reform by the international community, for various reasons, has tended to fuel indigenous people's perceptions that the white landowners are being protected by the donor community because white landowners are their 'kith and kin'. In this way, the land question in southern Africa is increasingly viewed as an internationalized form of racist privileging of white minorities in the face of their historical victims' demand for redistribution.

A related vexing question is the extent to which land can be treated as a development project managed through normal donor funding procedures. Many donor countries have supported land reform as an economic development project, while neglecting the enduring political and social justice issues that underlie it. This perspective contradicts demands that former colonial masters should be responsible for paying for land transfers, which individual white farmers are expected to facilitate. Instead, landowners have found it more expedient to focus on market principles of compensation for their land transfers.

Race relations in Southern Africa can be improved through land reform policies, if the historical and social justice and contemporary problems of equity, poverty reduction and broader economic growth are acknowledged and redressed directly rather than subsumed by development parameters and aid preconditions. Attempts to reduce complex racial and political conflicts into simplistic components of economic reforms, premised upon distorted and inadequately developed market processes and narrowly founded approaches to good governance and the 'rule of law', can serve only to polarize further socially charged southern African societies. Social justice based upon more equitable race relations and land distribution is integral to longer-term political reform and economic development. Interestingly, the land occupations experience of Zimbabwe and threats of the same in South Africa and Namibia have at least forced policy-makers and various publics to confront past and present race grievances and force dialogue between whites and blacks over race relations in general and land reform in particular. Resolving racial land conflicts requires new notions of reconciliation, which entail exposing the wider historic truths of past and present race relations, and the redistribution of resources such as land.

Notes

1. The term indigenous people generally refers to black Africans born in countries of southern Africa. It is not associated with the generic use of the term such as aborigines or Khoisan. In Zimbabwe, whites born in Zimbabwe tend to be excluded from this category as they are regarded as descendants of illegal settlers who gained land through conquest.
2. The large-scale farmers, who have large pieces of land, are regarded as critical for food security. It is for this reason that a lot of subsidies go into large-scale commercial farming to the exclusion of smallholders, who depend on food subsidies because the land they have cannot sustain commercial production.
3. Indigenous elite farmers tend to seek large farms, which promotes temporary alliances emerging between them and large-scale white farmers thereby further derailing state efforts to acquire and redistribute land.
4. In Mozambique massive land reoccupation after the civil war managed through customary systems occurred without outside help. Despite the lack of basic social services and other infrastructure, including the widespread presence of land mines the peasants contributed massively to the 18 per cent rise in GDP through agricultural production in three years after the end of the civil war.
5. The predominant labour force in industry and manufacturing sector are blacks, with whites dominating in the managerial positions and proprietorship of companies. Even though the number of commercial farmers in the large-scale commercial farming area is very low, they do employ a large percentage of the black labour force. Many studies have shown that countries such as South Africa and Zimbabwe have a 'foreign' legion of black farm labour whose condition of living is pathetic.

6. South Africa, Namibia and Zimbabwe have a 'well-organized' farming community led by unions in conformity with their long presence in the farming sector.
7. Mozambique expects 100 white Zimbabwean commercial farmers, while ten have been allocated 4,000 hectares in Manica province. A group of 63 white Zimbabweans had requested 400,000 hectares, but the government of Mozambique has put a ceiling of 1,000 hectares per individual application (*Daily News*, 20 July 2001).
8. Water resources (dams, etc.) are found mainly in white-owned highvelds. A land reform programme that redistributes prime land will also broaden access to water for irrigation.
9. Some 243,000 are still waiting for land. In order to resettle them the government needs N$900 million (US$112 million) to buy 9.5 million hectares (*Financial Gazette*, 5 July 2001).
10. It has been noted that blacks who have gone into the open market to acquire land using their own resources have tended to perform badly due to high debts and incapacity to capitalize as all the resources are put into the acquisition of land.

References

Arrighi, G. (1967) *The Political Economy of Rhodesia*. Publications of the Institute of Social Studies, Series Major, Vol. XVI, 1st edition.

Arrighi, G and Saul, T. (1973) *Essays on the Political Economy of Africa*, New York: New York Monthly Press Review.

Ashworth, A. A. (1990) Agricultural Technology and the Communal Farm Sector. Background paper to the World Bank, Zimbabwe Agricultural Sector Memorandum, The World Bank, Harare.

Binswanger, H. (1996) 'The Political Implications of Alternative Models of Land Reform and Compensation'. In K. Van Zyl and H. Binswanger, *Agricultural Land Reform in South Africa*, Cape Town: Oxford University Press.

Binswanger, H. and Deininger, K. (1993) 'South African Land Policy: The Legacy of History and Current Options', *World Development*, 21(9), September: 1451–75.

Chitiyo, T. (2000) *Land Violence and Compensation: Reconceptualising Zimbabwe's Land and War Veterans Debate*, Track Two, Vol. 9, No. 1.

CIA World Factbook (2001) Country land areas, potential agric. land (except Malawi and Tanzania), White % (except for Malawi). Washington: US Bureau of the Census.

CIA World Factbook (2001) SADC land conference paper. Atlapedia.com (website last updated 2001) DR Congo statistics, Land Tenure Centre, Country Profiles of Land Tenure in Southern Africa, 199 Namibia.

CIA World Factbook (2001) Country Arable Land Areas.

Commission on Restitution of Land Rights, Annual Report 'Problems and Obstacles Faced in the Field' (Republic of South Africa, 1997), p. 23.

Deininger, K. (1998) *Making Negotiated Land Reform Work: Initial Experience from Colombia, Brazil and South Africa*, World Bank Working Paper No. 2451, Washington, DC.

Department of Land Affairs (1996) South Africa. Land Reform Experiences in South Africa and the Options for Future. SADC land conference paper, p. 15.

Economist Intelligence Unit (2001) Country profiles – figures for Seychelles.

Government of Botswana (2001) Botswana Country paper: Land Questions and Land Tenure. Presented at the SADC regional land conference in Namibia.

Government of Malawi (1998) Population and Housing Census.

Government of Tanzania (1995) National Land Policy. Ministry of Lands and Human Settlements Development – Potential Agric Land Bloodbook.Com. (website last updated on 01 October 2001).

Government of Tanzania (2001) 'Tanzania Country Paper in Land Policy'. Paper presented at the SADC regional conference in Namibia.

Government of Tanzania (2001) International Data Base. Ministry of Lands and Human Settlements Development, Tanzania.

Hendricks, F. (1995) *Questioning the Land Question, Agrarian Transition, Land Tenure, Rural Development in the Former Settler Colonies of Southern Africa*, Cape Town, South Africa.

Mamdani, M. (1996) *'Citizens and Subjects: Contemporary Africa and the Legacy of Late Colonialism'*, Princeton NJ: Princetown University Press.

Mashinini, V. (2000) The Land Problem in Lesotho: Focus on Contestation and Conflicts. Paper Presented at the SARIPS/Sapes Trust Annual Colloquium, Harare, 24–27/September.

Moyo, S. (1987) 'The Land Question in Zimbabwe', in Mandaza (ed.), *Zimbabwe: The Political Economy of Transition*, Codesria, Dakar.

Moyo, S. (1994) 'Conceptualising Land Tenure in Southern Africa: The Case of Zimbabwe', SAPEM, Vol. 7, No. 8, May.

Moyo, S. (1995) *The Land Question in Zimbabwe*, Harare: Sapes Books.

Moyo, S. (2000) *Land Reform under Structural Adjustment in Zimbabwe*, Uppsala: Nordic Africa Institute.

Moyo, S. (2001) The Interaction of Market and Compulsory Land Acquisition Processes with Social Action in Zimbabwe's Land Reform, mimeo.

Moyo, S., Raftopolous, B and Makumbe, J. M. (2000) *NGOs and Development in Zimbabwe*, Harare: SAPES Books.

National Land Committee (1997) Affiliate Report, Surplus People Project, Published in South Africa, p. 31.

Rihoy, E., Jones, B., Anstey, S. and Raflos, M.(1999) Tenure in Transition: A Stakeholder Guide to Community-Based Natural Resources Management and Tenure in Southern Africa, SADC Natural Resources Management Project/USAID/ART.

Rukuni, M. and Eicher, C. K. (eds.) (1994) *Zimbabwe's Agricultural Revolution*, Harare: University of Zimbabwe Publications.

Shivji, I. (1998) Not Yet Democracy: Reforming Land Tenure in Tanzania, IIED/HAKIARDHI/Faculty of Law, University of Dar es Salaam.

Shivji, I., Moyo, S., Ncube, W. and Gunby, D. (1998) Draft National Land Policy for the Government of Zimbabwe. Discussion Paper. Harare: FAO and Ministry of Lands and Agriculture.

Tanzania National Land Policy, 1995.

Tevera, D. and Moyo, S. (2000) *Environmental Security in Southern Africa*, Harare: Sapes Books.

Umhlaba (1989) *Rural Land Struggles in the Transavaal in the 1980s*, Johannesburg: A Trac/Black Sash Publication, p. 15.

Weiner, D., Moyo, S., Manslow, B. and Okeefe, P. (1985) 'Land Use and Agricultural Productivity in Zimbabwe', *Journal of Modern African Studies*, Vol. 23, No. 2.

Wildschut, A. and Hulbert, S. (1998) A Seed Not Sown: Prospects for Agrarian Reform in South Africa, German Agro Action, and the National Land Committee, mimeo.

World Bank (1991) Zimbabwe: Agricultural Sector Memorandum: Vols I and II, Washington DC.

World Bank (1995) Zimbabwe Agricultural Sector Memorandum, Washington DC.

World Bank (1995) *Zimbabwe Achieving Shared Growth: Country Economic Memorandum*, Vol. 2. Washington: World Bank.

World Bank (1996) *Land Question and Land Reform in Zimbabwe*, 1980–Present, World Bank, AFTES Working Paper No. 19.

World Bank (2001) Human Development Indicators, 1965–1990.

10

Intersections of Race, Gender and Social Policy in Aotearoa/New Zealand: *Waihi I te toipoto, kaua I te toiroa*[1]

Tracey McIntosh

Introduction

Identity, both personal and collective, is formed in the material reality in which we live. Our gendered identities determine to a large degree the way that we see ourselves and are seen. Similarly, our class location is important to these same perceptions. Ethnicity is another layer, and some ethnic identities produce a far greater and more pronounced reaction than others. The Maori experience of colonization and the contemporary reality of marginalization and deprivation in everyday life mean that ethnic identity in Aotearoa/New Zealand is a site of struggle and resistance.[2] There is no single Maori experience. We do not all suffer the same burdens or enjoy the same privileges. Though there is a strong sense of our connectedness, of our belonging to each other by descent, by land and by sharing a common history, our experience of being Maori is inflected in myriad ways. If we understand social policy to be those 'actions which affect the well-being of members of society through shaping the distribution of and access to goods and resources in that society' and note that by this process 'some groups and individuals will be advantaged and others disadvantaged' (Cheyne et al., 1999: 2–3), we understand how social policy influences and moulds these experiences.

To say that I am a Maori woman, which I do, is not to make a claim that is free from ambiguity. Maori as an ethnic classification is understood in a variety of ways by a variety of actors. Self-perception is an important aspect of identity politics but it may not be the primary one; the perceptions of others may have far greater implications on 'who' you are.

Ambiguity and identity

I have been asked many times why I self-identify as Maori, the under-lying thrust of the inquiry being less an inquiry of interest and more a challenge;[3] that is, a questioning of the authenticity of my claim. My authenticity is questioned due to the simplest of things: colour. Being of fair complexion means that for many my persistence in identifying myself as Maori is seen by some (non-Maori) as a form of romantic stub-bornness, while for others it is seen as merely perverse. The issue of 'passing' – that is, of being a 'person of colour' but identifying with the dominant ethnic group – has generated scholarly and popular works in the United States. Two publications (Ginsberg, 1996; Sollons, 1997) look closely at the constructive features and fictive narratives of identity making, particularly with regard to ethnic hybridity and the ability to pass as white. Given the far greater level of intermarriage in Aotearoa/New Zealand and a less heightened and hysterical regard to race,[4] the issue of 'passing' has not been as pertinent to our ethnic dis-course. However, it does not go unquestioned. The question pertaining to my ethnicity could as easily be 'Why say you are Maori if you don't have to?' (McIntosh, 2001: 142).

This form of questioning contains an interesting policy dimension. As a young person I was asked, within the context of assimilation, if I could pass as Pakeha,[5] why persist in being seen as Maori if this serves only to act as an obstacle to my becoming a 'full, contributing member of New Zealand society'. A call for all to be 'New Zealanders' was a call for Maori to embrace Pakeha values and societal structures while carving out a space of inclusion for (non-threatening) aspects of Maori culture. To sing Pokarekare Ana,[6] even if you do not know what the words mean, was seen, particularly by Pakeha, as signifying the unity and particu-larity of our joint cultures. It was portrayed as a token of the way 'we' embrace each other's culture. In reality, it signified no more than tokenism. The question posed in this context reflected a belief that New Zealand had the best race relations in the world. As Walker has noted, 'the ideology of one people functioned to hide the relationship of Pakeha dominance and Maori subjection' (Walker, 1990: 186). Later, when I was asked the same question, it was laced with suspicion and cynicism. Framed within a heightened awareness of historical griev-ances and Maori claims, my self-definition as Maori was thought by some to be about accessing resources and privileges reserved for Maori. Calls for us to be one people now come from those who believe that Maori have preferential treatment at the expense of non-Maori. For many Pakeha any initiative that seeks to redress Maori disadvantage is seen to be at the great cost of 'ordinary' (read non-Maori) New Zealanders. This has meant that most state social policy has steered away from using 'affirmative action' rhetoric, instead speaking of targeting Maori 'problems' rather than redressing systemic disadvantage. The stigmatizing of the Maori condition leads to further individual and collective degradation. The different ways my Maoriness has been perceived over time mirrors current political and policy debates. The way I understand myself as Maori may have little in common with ways that non-Maori understand me.

This raises a number of issues, particularly in regard to notions of homogeneous ethnic identity. While not disputing the idea that to be Maori means that one would recognize or acknowledge the significance of certain things (for example, *whakapapa, iwi/hapu* affiliations, *te reo, kawa, tikanga*)[7] it does not mean that to identify as Maori means that one is absorbed into an undifferentiated ethnic mass. My identity as Maori is inextricably caught up with my working-class background and the fact that I am a woman. Different aspects of my identity provide the shades and contours in creating the multiple realities which are the self. The Maori whom I grew up with, who lived in the same street, shared similar struggles; struggles as likely to be connected to the inequalities inherent in a capitalistic system as to struggles directly connected with being Maori. Nearly all the Maori men in the street (and my Pakeha father) worked at one of the three abattoirs ('freezing works') in the Otahuhu-Penrose area of south Auckland. This too is a part of *my* experience of being Maori. While other 'common' Maori experiences may have been outside my sphere of knowledge, the ones I had are a part of my authentic experience of being Maori. To be Maori is to be part of a collective but heterogeneous identity, one that is enduring but ever in a state of flux.

Maori identity

The history of Maori struggle and its implications in the formation of Maori identity is well documented (Walker, 1990; Greenland, 1991; Poata-Smith, 1996). Greenland (1991) explores the way that Maori identity has developed over the last 30 years or so. In this way we can map how, over different periods, and due to specific political and economic conditions often underscored by changes in policy direction, identity has been more closely linked to certain aspects than others. Shifts of emphasis do not go uncontested by Maori. Coates and McHugh's (1998) collection canvasses the wide number of views held in the way that Maori identity is understood. In the light of moves towards compensation and new policy directions from government for Maori, the issue of Maori identity becomes even more salient. For example, urban Maori who have become disenfranchised or disaffiliated from traditional tribal ties seek new ways of constituting a Maori collective identity that emphasizes ethnicity and class interests over tribal allegiances. Apirana Mahuika acknowledges that Maori differ on this issue and sees that discussion as healthy and to be expected. While he believes there are legitimate claims to tying identity to ethnicity over tribal ties in a few selective cases, he argues that ethnicity 'cannot usurp the mana[8] and role of whakapapa as the determinant of who one is affiliated to, and who are one's kind based on descent and blood' (1998: 218). In the same collection, Mason Durie, Roger Maaka, Joe Williams and others offer commentaries that illustrate the richness and diversity of issues pertaining to what is at the heart of Maori identity.

Mana wahine[9]

Linda Tuhiwai Smith looks at the way Maori women are reasserting their specific identities. Europeans of the nineteenth century depicted, objectified and represented Maori and other indigenous women in ways that have 'left a legacy of marginalization within indigenous society as much as within the colonizing society' (Smith, 1999: 46). Many modern Maori organizations that are perceived as traditional indigenous structures are colonial constructs put in place for purposes of colonial rule and administration. These organizations have often privileged certain groups or families over others, in many cases making positions of power and decision-making an exclusively male domain. In an attempt to reclaim and acknowledge Mana wahine Maori a group of prominent Maori women have made a claim to the Waitangi Tribunal which hears petitions by Maori relating to the contraventions of the Treaty of Waitangi.[10]

Before this Tribunal, the Maori women taking the claim are having to establish and argue, using historical texts, research and oral testimonies, that the Crown has ignored the *rangatiratanga* (chiefly or sovereign) status, of Maori women. To argue this, the claimants are compelled to prove that Maori women were as much *rangatira* (chiefs) as Maori men. At a very simple level the 'problem' is one of translation. *Rangitiratanga* has generally been interpreted in English as meaning chieftainship and sovereignty, which in colonialism was a 'male thing' (Smith, 1999: 46).

As the Maori lawyer Annette Sykes argues, the implications of believing that Maori power regimes replicated nineteenth-century European ones has led to a loss of status for Maori women in their own communities, effectively devaluing them and their roles and denying them their rightful voice in helping determine their communities' futures.

> The essence of the claim is to bring to the forefront of the current Treaty jurisprudence, the need to look at notions of govenance in Aotearoa and the exclusionary practices that exist, which inhibit and prevent participation by Maori women in tribal models for self-determination, that have been erected under New Zealand legislation, and the erosion that this itself has had on Te Mana Wahine in Te Ao Maori [the mana of women in the Maori world]. (Sykes, cited in Smith, 1999: 156)

Reclaiming, reasserting and, in some cases, reconfiguring Maori identities and Maori relationships has become a crucial part of Maori personal and collective politics.

Radical identities

My previous discussion on personal ethnic identity formation was an attempt to portray identity as a 'process rather than a result' (McHugh, 1998: 149). Since the 1970s, the most common face of Maori presented to the non-Maori audience has been the 'radical' one. For the most part it was a very specific face – young, urban and angry – and it was not only Pakeha that withdrew from it. Many Maori elders were disturbed by the way these young people chose to air their grievances. But as the assault continued unabated there was a need to try to determine the type of people the 'radicals' were and to ascertain the nature and legitimacy of the grievances they had. Greenland notes that radicals were typically criticized as 'false Maori who adopted Pakeha techniques to protest Maori take [causes]' (1991: 91). This drew on the stereotype of the radical as being a disaffiliated, disrespectful, shiftless individual who had ceased to listen to the counsel of those who knew better and was unable to take responsibility for his/her own obvious shortfalls. However, Maori protest did not exist within a vacuum but should be seen within a global context of protest movements. Civil rights movements, Black Power, women's liberation, student political activism, the Vietnam War, the rise of the New Left and the influence of Marxism and feminism all created a greater awareness of conditions of oppression, conflict and the desire for redress. The level of discontent, the dire picture that was painted of the living conditions of Maori and their demands for revolutionary change were disconcerting to many. The 'best race relations in the world' myth was shattered as young Maori men and women exposed the level of oppression and deprivation that existed in Maori life. An international focus on inequities, coupled with the consequences of urbanization that led Maori and Pakeha to face each other in everyday life, sometimes for the first time, meant that Maori began strongly articulating their struggle for self-determination in public fora.[11] This articulation has been continued in a range of voices.

Location

As *tangata whenua* (people of the land, indigenous people), Maori find their social location in New Zealand society to be a highly contested one. The struggle to achieve *tino rangitiratanga* (self-determination, sovereignty) is seen as primary to most Maori but its achievement and interpretation are both areas of some dispute. Social policy in New Zealand of the last thirty years has been informed by these debates and the meeting of Treaty of Waitangi obligations has become a central objective of policy outcomes.[12] Though the present government has clearly articulated its intention to uphold the Treaty of Waitangi and to 'close the gaps' between Maori and non-Maori achievement in education, labour force involvement, housing and health, this has been met with a certain cynicism by many Maori and strident opposition from other sectors of New Zealand society. Many Maori doubt that there is sufficient political consciousness and will to address the causes for the ongoing social and economic disparities, while some non-Maori strongly resent policies and programmes that they perceive as privileging Maori over 'ordinary' New Zealanders. Criticism of the Treaty itself is broad. It ranges from the belief that the Treaty is used as a cloak for 'dubious Maori activities, from violent protests and civil disobedience on the one hand, to illegal plunder of customary resources on the other' (Fleras and Spoonley, 1999: 16). For others, Treaty entitlements are compared to apartheid strategies where privileges are given out on the basis of 'race' (ibid.). For still others, there is a sense that the Treaty is being used to fool successive governments into making 'extravagant payments in perpetuity to Maori' because of ill-founded sentiments of guilt based on actions in the past (ibid.). Against this backdrop we find that all things Maori are political.

Social gaps

That major cleavages exist between Maori and non-Maori is clear. Extensive research on the Maori condition shows that Maori suffer disadvantage from birth. The Maori infant is more likely to die than the non-Maori infant. The Maori child is less likely to participate in early childhood education. Though significant data on performance at primary school level are scarce, we know that young Maori are leaving secondary school with much lower levels of qualifications than non-Maori. Maori are much more likely to be suspended and expelled from school, which increases the likelihood that they will have fewer educational achievements and be more significantly involved in youth offending.[13] Maori unemployment rates are considerably higher than for non-Maori and Maori income is considerably lower.[14] Maori are more likely to require government assistance or be totally dependent on a government benefit.[15] Many Maori live in inadequate housing and suffer a poorer mental and physical health status than non-Maori (Te Puni Kokiri, 2000a: 6–7).

Disadvantage and difference are marked in Maori participation in the criminal justice system. Maori are over-represented as victims and as offenders. In 1998, the Maori population represented 13 per cent of the population aged 14 and over, yet Maori comprised 40 per cent of all apprehensions (that is, arrests, cautions, diversions), 41 per cent of all prosecuted cases and 44 per cent of all people convicted of an offence (Te Puni Kokiri, 2000a: 34). The face of the criminal is increasingly perceived as Maori. This is alarmingly reinforced by the fact that almost half the prison population is made up of Maori (ibid.). Since 1991 the disparities faced by Maori and non-Maori in the criminal justice system have widened. In 1998, 'Maori were 3.3 times more likely to be apprehended, 3.6 times more likely to be prosecuted and 4.1 times more likely to be convicted of an offence compared to non-Maori' (ibid.). Maori are almost four times more likely to be apprehended for violent crime than non-Maori, which is of particular concern because of the critical and continuing effect it has on its victims and because violent offences are afforded a high profile in the media further presenting Maori as criminal. For too many people, unemployment, illness, psychiatric conditions, poverty and prison life is what being Maori means. Though the position and legitimacy of Maori culture within New Zealand society has been greatly enhanced since the 1970s, with greater respect afforded to our *tikanga* (culture) and *te reo* (language), the Maori renaissance has been far less successful in addressing the many other social inequities that Maori face in their daily lives. There is a danger of speaking of a culture as a whole way of life outside its own political economic history (Webster, 1998). While culture is obviously vitally important to physical and spiritual well-being, for this to be fully achieved we need to ensure that day-to-day struggles and the solutions to them are met with the same determination that we give cultural considerations. There is the need not only to fight for the preservation and vitality of culture, but also to assure equity with regard to economic and political standing and the accessing of resources, power and knowledge.

Intersections of gender

Race,[16] gender, sexuality and class interlock: each of these factors impacts on the way the other is experienced. Maori attempts to address issues of their own oppression have been multifarious. There is a tendency to privilege cultural discourses that stress the differences between Maori and Pakeha cultural values and to ignore the way that oppressive relationships are inflected by gender and class. Some commentators have noted the need to explore how attempts to tackle forms of racial discrimination may benefit different sectors of Maori more than others and in some cases continue to perpetuate forms of gender oppression. Maori women are at the forefront of the struggle to improve the social position of their communities, yet they continue to bear the greatest burden of social, political and economic oppression. Maori women continue to examine their position critically as Maori and as women in New Zealand society. This has led them, amongst other things, to challenge Pakeha feminists and question their own allegiances. This challenge is passionately articulated by Donna Awatere (1984).[17] Written as a series of articles for the New Zealand feminist magazine *Broadsheet*, it is a blistering attack on racism, sexism and capitalism. In it she is sharply critical of the feminist movement, the trade unions and the left, positing that their inability to align with the Maori sovereignty cause is because, in the end, 'all white people are captives of their own culture' (Awatere, 1984: 9).

Her section on the feminist movement first looks at what Maori women have achieved. She argues that the Maori Women's Welfare League[18] is the strongest indigenous women's movement in the world. She notes how in its formation Maori women had to 'step outside traditional Maoridom leadership's paths to provide leadership for ourselves and for Maoridom as a whole' (1984: 41). Mira Szaszy, a founding member of the League and a past president, also speaks of the necessity 'to set up a structure which was not dominated by men, i.e. on non-Maori lines' (in Hoskins, 2000: 43). Maori women, through their efforts to bring more balance to leadership roles, sometimes sought alliances with Pakeha women. However, Awatere asserts that Pakeha women cannot understand the need for Maori to see Maori issues as primary. Maori allegiance first and foremost is to other Maori rather than to other women. Pakeha women, she argued:

> vent their anti-Maori xenophobia on Maori men. In the early 70s white women's paranoia about Maori men 'rapists' and 'gang members' matched equally that of white men.
>
> White women sought to set Maori women against Maori men. Some white women are still into this. The first loyalty of white women is always to the White Culture and the White Way. This is true as much for those who define themselves as feminists as for any other white women. This loyalty is seen in their rejection of the sovereignty of Maori people and in their acceptance of the imposition of British culture on the Maori. This is to be expected as the oppressor avoids confronting the role they play in oppressing others. (1984: 42)

She claims that Pakeha feminists use their race power, privilege and status to ensure that their way of understanding feminism supersedes the way that Maori women understand it. White feminists assume that issues that they see as vitally important to their interests (debates around abortion, equal pay, sexuality, etc.) are universal women's issues. Awatere notes how oppression is rarely a discrete entity. A focus solely on patriarchy may render invisible other virulent forms of domination.

> The oppression of women *does not* exist in a vacuum: economic and racial privileges cannot be separated from sexual power. Try telling a black Azania woman today that she should unite with white women to overthrow the patriarchy, and the stupidity of treating sex oppression on its own can be seen. (ibid.)

Awatere seeks to redefine feminist issues from a Maori perspective. She argues that for Maori women the primary issue is one of sovereignty. She sees this as the ability to determine one's own destiny from the basis of the land and resources:

> For Maori women, all our concerns as women center around the fact that we and our people have no say in the shaping of our own destiny

as a people. That the rules in this country were made by immigrant races and nations, and were *not* made for the Maori by the Maori. We are *forced* to live apart from the resources of the land and apart from the cultural and spiritual values which made us what we are.

The Maori language is a feminist issue, the land is a feminist issue, separate development is a feminist issue, the venomous hatred of the Maori by the Pakeha is a feminist issue. (1984: 43–4)

Awatere recognizes that Maori women and Pakeha women have a common oppression. It is an oppression that 'requires a political, economic, social and philosophical upheaval to achieve its goal of eliminating all forms of iniquity based on race, sex and class' (1984: 44). Yet, she argues, the truly revolutionary action that must be taken will not be considered by white women, as this would undermine their race and class privileges. Michael Reilly argues that Awatere's work forces us to be aware that worthy causes may serve the interests and needs of advocates differentially. For Awatere it was clear that Maori sovereignty must remain the central focus for Maori:

> What does she say to history? Maori sovereignty must always be the guiding criterion: study of Maori must serve Maori ends, articulate the Maori struggle, relate a history too conveniently laundered by historians in the service of Pakeha society. (Reilly, 1996: 85)

Inside inequality

There have been a number of Maori women (Te Awekotuku, 1991; Irwin, 1992; McArdell, 1992; Szaszy, 1993; Evans, 1994; Johnson and Pihama, 1994; Hoskins, 2000) and non-Maori women (Jones and Guy, 1992; Simpkin, 1994; Larner, 1996), who have further explored the relationships between Maori and non-Maori feminists. Along with these women, others have looked at gender tensions *within* Maori society. Linda Tuhiwai Smith asserts that since our first contacts with Europeans our identities, cultural life and political arrangements have irrevocably changed. She believes that all Maori social structures have been 'colonized, distorted and rearranged' and that colonization coupled with the imposition of Western hegemony has meant the construction of new forms of social relationships within Maori culture and between Maori and Pakeha (in Hoskins, 2000: 35).

Johnson and Pihama assert that 'Maori are constructed in opposition to Pakeha, a constructed duality which predominantly locates Maori in

deviant and inferior locations' and that this is to be expected in relationships associated with dominance and subordination (1994: 88).
They also note that since colonial times Maori women have been treated
differently from Maori men because colonialists saw women primarily
as male possessions. Maori women's and girls' place in society was
devalued during this time as they were seen as playing no role in determining the direction of Maori society; 'Pakeha men dealt with Maori
men. The roles proffered for Maori women were mainly those of servitude, as either maidservants for Pakeha households or 'good wives and
mothers' for Maori men (1994: 89).

Early social policies acted to marginalize Maori women further on the
basis of their ethnicity and gender. Smith argues that Maori were seen
as the 'Other' of all categories:

> As women we have been defined in terms of our differences to men,
> as Maori we have been defined in regard to our differences to the col-
> onizer. As Maori women we have been defined in terms of our dif-
> ferences to Maori men, Pakeha men and Pakeha women. (in Johnson
> and Pihama, 1994: 93)

Johnson and Pihama's work on the processes of marginalization of
Maori women convincingly expresses how negative perceptions that
then feed social policy and legislation have had massive and long-term
implications. Their discussion on the educational experience of Maori
women from colonial times until recently reveals how it has locked
Maori women into a cycle of deprivation:

> For Maori, the implications of our historical experiences are such that
> we have been denied access to Te Reo me nga Tikanga, our language
> and culture. We have been denied access to the credentials and qual-
> ifications that would provide Maori women with options other than
> those of domestic and service workers. We have been denied access
> to full participation and input into the wider society. We have been
> denied access to full participation in policy formation and key deci-
> sion making for our own people. Colonial discourses have operated
> on the whole effectively to lock Maori women out of crucial posi-
> tions – positions which impact on our day to day lives and the lives
> of our peoples. (1994: 99)

The devaluation of Maori women has impacted negatively on all aspects
of Maori life. Our children, our relationships, our families and our

communities have suffered. It has occurred to the detriment of the lived reality of both Maori men and women. However, it has also allowed Maori men to extend their areas of power and dominance in respect to Maori women. Hoskins argues that Maori men within Maori society:

> have largely become the legitimated keepers, interpreters and pro-moters of what is considered authentic, traditional knowledge and tikanga and kaupapa Maori.[19] It is *they*, therefore, who are primarily articulating our past – in their own interests and political goals . . . The popular notion of traditional gender complementarity – defined as different/separate spheres in work and social relations for women and men does not, in my opinion, necessarily mean that 'material and power considerations' automatically flow to all Maori women. Indeed, patriarchally and Christian inspired missionary/colonizer-conveyed notions of gender role 'complementarity' were *not* about the sharing of decision making and power, but about separate roles with women clearly positioned as subservient to men. (2000: 39)

Distinct 'traditional' gender roles do not necessarily mean that gender inequities become less problematic. The issue of speaking rights on the *marae*[20] has ensured that gender issues in Maori society have continued to have a high profile in New Zealand. The belief that women have no speaking rights on the *marae* has often been cited as proof that Maori society is inherently sexist and oppressive of women. The collapsing of the meanings of *marae*, the debate about what constitutes 'speaking' in a Maori context, the increasing importance of Maori protocols in formal and state occasions and the invitations to non-Maori to speak on the *marae* have meant that these are issues that are hotly contested by Maori and non-Maori alike. Kathie Irwin contests that it is only due to Western notions of what constitutes speaking that there is a failure to recognize *karanga* as a form of speech.[21] Women do have power, status and voice on the *marae*, a fact that many non-Maori do not understand. *Marae* has spiritual, cultural and political significance to Maori, and we are often hurt when it is abused and misunderstood. However, it would be difficult to argue that gender power relations on the *marae* are equal. Though Irwin believes that the speaking rights issue has been used by Pakeha to belittle Maori and to justify 'both their ignorance about the Maori language and culture and their refusal to become informed' (1992: 8), she acknowledges that while certain aspects of *marae* proto-col have changed to meet contemporary needs, these changes have rarely benefited Maori women:

All cultures are dynamic and continually changing. However, it is clear that many of the 'newly traditional' Maori cultural practices that are emerging are serving the interests of Pakeha men while disempowering Maori women, in the name of "Maori cultural practices' ... It is a strange culture that legitimizes the rights of male outsiders over and above the rights of its own women. These new 'tikanga' seem to many Maori women to be practices of male bonding, not Maori culture, and they should be recognized as such. (Irwin, 1992: 16)

Ripeka Evans believes the restricted speaking rights on the *marae* are increasingly pervading other non-*marae* situations enhancing male hegemony and further oppressing and silencing the collective voice of women (in Hoskins 2000: 42). Mira Szaszy argues, 'our marae are patriarchal institutions pervaded by assumptions of male dominance' (ibid.). Hoskins observes that a feature of the 'Maori renaissance' has been that *marae* protocols are now found in many other Maori and non-Maori fora (2000: 43). Maori men, by grace of their gender, already have an advantage over Maori women and it is unlikely they will willingly relinquish it, or even share it. Current policy and Treaty settlement practices mean that certain Maori men are benefiting substantially. While the Treaty of Waitangi recognizes and promises to protect group rights (in both the Maori text and English translation), government policy towards Maori historically and presently has sought to extinguish these rights, and replace them with individual rights as these are understood in European legal and social policy terms (Cheyne et al., 1999: 168). The individuals who have benefited from this approach have been overwhelmingly male. Maori male interests are perceived as simply Maori interests. Evans observes that within many Maori institutions, organizations, trusts and the like:

The power and decision making process of these organizations is in the hands of a small oligarchic menagerie of Maori men, businessmen, politicians, bureaucrats and lawyers, or otherwise more commonly known as the boy's club ... There is no system guaranteeing a place for Maori women within our own institutions or within new organizations which have evolved to manage our assets. Any talk of structural change sends some of our Maori men into a tail-spin about 'cultural correctness' and 'making waves'. There is high powered selective amnesia about what it takes to make change. (in Hoskins, 2000: 46)

Maori women continue to want to be linked to and stand by our Maori men. We recognize that to achieve our aims and maintain our own cultural values continued solidarity is essential. We must, however, also continue to strive for equal positions of power and responsibility. Social policy, legislation and action, if they are to create greater well-being, must enhance the mechanism for power-sharing and inclusive participation rather than replicate and legitimate unequal power relations.

Intersections of race

Issues of unequal power relations and barefaced hypocrisy came to the fore in the anti-racist movements of Aotearoa/New Zealand. In the 1960s a 'close working relationship was forged between Pakeha anti-racist groups and what eventually evolved into the Maori protest movement' (Poata-Smith, 1966: 99). This relationship was originally formed around opposition to the New Zealand Rugby Football Union's decision to exclude Maori rugby players from the 1960 All Black tour of South Africa. This generated intense opposition, and the 'No Maori, no tour' protests extended to look at the ethics of any contact with South Africa and a closer examination of the apartheid system. This examination led to some predominantly Pakeha anti-racist organizations to start to question more deeply the relationship between Maori and Pakeha in New Zealand society. Halt All Racial Tours (HART), an umbrella organization of anti-racist groups formed in 1969, was a result of the interaction between Maori groups and anti-racist groups. Though not without conflict inflected by both gender and race (Awatere 1984, 1996), the relationship was an enduring one which culminated in the tremendous opposition to the 1981 Springbok Tour (Poata-Smith, 1996: 99–100). The 1981 Springbok tour forced many Pakeha to face up to the daily racism that Maori faced. They were also challenged by Maori groups to explain why they protested so ardently against apartheid in South Africa, yet were strangely silent about commenting on forms of racist oppression in their own country. The Maori Organization on Human Rights (MOOHR) publicized the racism and discrimination that Maori faced in housing, sport, employment and elsewhere. As a group which drew on class analysis to explain Maori oppression it urged both Pakeha and Maori to join the struggle against discrimination stressing that it was 'rich Pakeha to blame for racism, not all Pakeha' (in Poata-Smith, 1996: 101). While MOORH took this position to champion the rights of all 'minorities' based on class and/or ethnicity, Poata-Smith asserts that since the 1980s many Maori movements have tended to fight for the political changes of greatest benefit to those Maori who are already middle class or wealthy. In this regard, cultural nationalism and the politics of Maori identity have been the perfect social theory for the upwardly mobile Maori middle class because it presents the interests of Maori in contemporary capitalist society as essentially unitary ... This ignores the critical importance of differential access to economic and political power within and across Maori society.

Indeed, Maori are all too frequently discussed by cultural nation-alists as if forming one homogenous entity, its members possessing exactly the same experiences of oppression and exactly the same political aspirations. (Poata-Smith, 1996: 112)

An emphasis solely on cultural solidarity obscures the very real differ-ence of social class and social relations in Maori society in the same way that it obscures the inequalities between men and women.

Intersections of policy

The Royal Commission on Social Policy of 1988 acknowledges the dual heritage of New Zealand society, namely Maori and Western/Pakeha cultures. The Commission document states that the standards and foundations of Maori society were identified as the following four cornerstones:

- *Te Ao Turoa* (the environment);
- *Whanaungatanga* (bonds of kinship);
- *Taonga tuku iho* (cultural heritage);
- *Turangawaewae* (place of security).
  (in Cheyne et al., 1999: 53)

This stresses the interrelationship between physical, human, spiritual and cultural dimensions of life (ibid.) Social policy needs to be mindful of these foundations, but see them as dynamic, not static, foundations.

Maori social policy, as understood and directed by Maori with its roots in the Treaty of Waitangi, has sought to maintain and improve the well-being of Maori based on a world-view and values that emphasize col-lective identity and a unity between the spiritual and material worlds (Cheyne et al., 1999: 47). Over time, under different social conditions, Maori have employed different approaches and strategies with the state. The state itself has seen itself as benefactor, minder, enforcer, director and facilitator, sometimes playing a number of roles concurrently. In regards to Maori, the state has achieved some success in improving well-being, but social indicators are a damning indictment. The *Closing the Gaps* report acknowledges that there have been few reductions in the social and economic disparities between Maori and non-Maori in the last few years (Te Puni Kokiri, 2000a: 6). Where the status of Maori has improved, we find that equivalent improvements in the status of non-Maori have occurred so that the 'gaps' remain. Disadvantage remains entrenched. For many, social policy is understood as an abstract or bureaucratic process that occurs some distance from the lived realities of one's day-to-day existence. Yet for all people, and most particularly for those who are from deprived and devalued sectors of society, social policy can be literally a life-and-death issue. Health indicators serve as a potent reminder of Maori deprivation in Aotearoa/New Zealand and alerts us to the fact that social policy can impact at the most critical levels.

An examination of health statistics for Aotearoa/New Zealand forces us to conclude that death, like life, is unequal. Social location, to a great extent, determines the type of death we are likely to experience (McIntosh, 2001: 238). Class, gender and ethnicity play an important role in locating our probable cause of death. Over the last century the average life expectancy of New Zealanders has risen significantly. A temperate climate, low population density, lack of heavy industry and good nutrition meant that from the middle of the nineteenth century until the 1930s, New Zealand had the lowest mortality rate in the world (Statistics New Zealand, 1998). The improvement of longevity mostly occurred prior to the 1930s and was due to saving lives at younger ages. The infant mortality rate fell in association with a major reduction in infectious and respiratory diseases, which were previously the main cause of death. Recent data indicate that heart disease, cancer and cerebrovascular diseases are the three leading causes of death in New Zealand, and together account for 60 per cent of all deaths among the adult population in any year. Respiratory diseases claim another 10 per cent. Motor vehicle accidents cause another 3 per cent of all deaths in a year, with people in the 15–24 age group accounting for over 80 per cent of these fatalities (ibid.). Since 1972 there has been a gain of a little over five years in the life expectancy at birth of men and 4.5 years in women. Although the nation has benefited from better living standards, advances in medical technology and improvements in health services, the benefits have been unevenly distributed. In 1990–2, the average life expectancy of Maori males was 68 years, compared with 73 years for Maori females, while for non-Maori, life expectancies were 73.4 years for male and 79.2 years for females (ibid.). Statistics are useful in giving an overview of a social phenomenon, but there is a need to be mindful that numbers alone can obscure the lived reality of many people. What are the social consequences of Maori men living five years less than their non-Maori counterparts, or the consequences of Maori women having a rate of cervical cancer nearly six times greater than that of non-Maori women (Te Puni Kokiri, 2000a: 45), or the consequences and social implications of the Maori lung cancer death rate being over four times greater than the non-Maori rate (Te Puni Kokiri, 2000a: 44)? Is it nothing more than mere numbers? The health and life expectancy of individuals and collectives have always differed according to their position in society. The types of death we die may change, but overall 'wealthy people continue to have better health and live longer to enjoy it than poorer people' (Evans et al., 1994, in Davis and Dew, 1999).

There is strong evidence linking vulnerability to ill health to low income. Income inequalities in New Zealand diminished post-World War II until the 1970s, but increased markedly between 1987 and 1991. This growth in inequalities is particularly marked in relation to Maori and Pacific Island communities, who are acutely disadvantaged on a number of health indicators. Health issues and their analysis 'remains an important tool for policy development, resource allocation and programme implementation' (Te Puni Kokiri, 2000b: 1). The persistence of health inequalities in New Zealand suggests that these are linked to socio-economic factors and the consequences of marginalization. Recent research in New Zealand underscores international findings that social, physical, cultural and economic factors are the main determinants of health (Te Puni Kokiri, 2001b: 2). The *NZDep96 Index of Deprivation* looks at relative disadvantage for various population groups throughout New Zealand (Salmond et al., 1998). The index shows that Maori are far more likely to live in the most deprived areas than are non-Maori (56 per cent of Maori live in areas with an index of 8 or more compared to 24 per cent of non-Maori) (Te Puni Kokiri, 2001b: 2).[22] Maori men living in the most deprived areas have a seven-year difference in life expectancy compared to Maori men living in the least deprived areas. There is a similar difference for female Maori as well. However, the index also notes that there are considerable differences between Maori and Pakeha as well. Pakeha men and women living in the *most* deprived areas have longer life expectancies than Maori men and women living in the *least* deprived areas. This measure 'highlights the entrenched disparities that exist across all levels of socioeconomic status' between Maori and Pakeha (Te Puni Kokiri, 2000b: 2).

Philippa Howden-Chapman notes that the behavioural and health effects of unequal resource distribution indicate a breakdown in social and community relations (Howden-Chapman, 1999: 73). She further notes that health and well-being is more than just the absence of personal illness or injury, 'well-being involves consideration of collective well-being, sense of community and the community's pool of organized 'social capital' from which individuals can draw' (1999: 80–1). She feels that to arrive at more equal health outcomes in society there is a strong case for better distribution of economic and social resources. The statistics also support the idea of cycles of disadvantage that indicate a need to look at lifecycle but also examine historical patterns of disadvantage. Levels of deprivation and community health, research suggests, have a significant impact on the health of a population. This fits well with Maori views of health and the belief that policy that targets the individuals rather than the wider communities are likely to be of less benefit to Maori than collective initiatives (1999: 76).

Addressing power

From the late 1980s governments have turned their attention to reforming health, welfare and education services. The Ministry of Health has as one of its sets of goals to:

> improve, promote and protect Maori health status so in the future Maori will have the opportunity to enjoy at least the same level of health as non-Maori. The objectives are:
>
> - to ensure that all services funded are culturally appropriate and compatible with gains in Maori health
> - to show an understanding of and commitment to the Treaty of Waitangi.
>
> (Manatu Hauora, 2003: 3)

Though there are numerous references to the Treaty of Waitangi in many governmental goals and objectives, the New Zealand Parliament has continued to resist inserting legally binding references to specific Treaty or other Maori rights in social legislation (Cheyne et al., 1999: 154). There continues to be an enthusiasm in attempting to meet 'culturally appropriate' goals that may be met with increased sensitivity to cultural practices rather than to looking at true power-sharing which would be needed to honour Treaty of Waitangi commitments. The health statistics of Maori speak to a history of exclusion, institutional racism, material deprivation, cultural degradation and marginalization. To overcome these there is a need not only to recognize and respect cultural difference but to create structural change which produces true economic and political power-sharing. Shifts in the debates about biculturalism and *tino rangatiratanga* in New Zealand since the 1980s have been about the need for economic and political power-sharing and not merely an awareness of and respect for Maori values, language and culture. This can take many forms and requires political courage to create the mechanisms and institutions that would make 'closing the gaps' more than mere rhetoric: 'such power sharing may require autonomous political institutions and an independent economic base, or it may involve equal participation in bicultural institutions (Cheyne et al., 1999: 122). Oppression cannot be lifted solely by facing up to or even appreciating difference. It can come only with the shifting and transforming of power relations.

Notes

1. This *whakatauki* (Maori proverb) translates as 'Let us keep close together, not wide apart'. In this instance I am using it to reflect on the social fissures that exist in New Zealand society. Aotearoa is the Maori name for New Zealand.
2. New Zealand/Aotearoa has a population of 3,737,277. One in seven people (526, 281) defined themselves as being of Maori ethnicity in the 2001 National Census. There has been an increase of 21 per cent for the count of people of Maori ethnicity between 1991 and 2001 (Statistics NZ, 2001).
3. It is interesting to note that those who offer this challenge have changed over time. When I was younger it was mostly made by Pakeha New Zealanders, as I have grown older it has mostly been made by non-New Zealanders outside of New Zealand. I have never been asked by Maori, but this is not to say that they have not challenged my authenticity in other ways. The change in who asks the question over the years reflects the changing political status of things Maori.
4. This is, of course, not to argue that race and colour do not matter in Aotearoa/New Zealand. They do and they have always mattered. The history of Aotearoa/New Zealand since European settlement is one that is shaped and informed by discrimination and prejudice. Legislation has, at times, blatantly discriminated against Maori, but our experience can be compared only with difficulty to the legal processes of segregation and racism that occurred in South Africa or the United States. While these countries had segregation embedded in their systems in the legal, political and cultural senses, in Aotearoa/New Zealand we have relied far more heavily on what Ranginui

Walker has termed 'the informal social divide between Maori and Pakeha' (1996: 9).

5. The meaning of the word Pakeha is still contested and can change in a variety of contexts. However, generally it refers to descendants of immigrants from Europe who have been in Aotearoa/New Zealand for several generations.

6. A popular Maori love song.

7. *Whakapapa* refers to genealogy and descent; *iwi* refers to tribal group; *hapu* to sub-tribe or clan within an *iwi*; *te reo Maori* refers to the Maori language; *kawa* to protocols and customs; and *tikanga* to appropriate cultural practices.

8. *Mana* cannot adequately be translated, but it speaks to spiritual power and authority. It can also be more loosely referred to as status and prestige.

9. *Mana wahine Maori* is the spiritual power and authority of women. *Mana wahine* is also used to denote Maori forms of feminism.

10. The Treaty of Waitangi was signed between Maori chiefs and the British Crown in 1840. The Treaty had three provisions and two versions, one in English the other in Maori. The competing interpretations that exist within and between the two versions have 'played havoc with politics and policy' (Fleras and Spoonley, 1999: 9). The Waitangi Tribunal was established by parliament under the Treaty of Waitangi Act 1975. This Act establishes the Tribunal which is charged with hearing claims by Maori that the Crown has contravened the principles of the Treaty of Waitangi. At first this applied only to contemporary grievances. The Tribunal was able to recommend action by the Crown, but the recommendations were not binding. The Act was amended in 1985 to extend the scope of claims back to 1840 (Smith, 1999: 57). There is a vast literature on the Treaty of Waitangi. See, for example, Walker (1990, 1996); Cox (1993); Durie (1995, 1998); Kelsey (1996), Graham (1997) and Fleras and Spoonley (1999).

11. The struggle itself was not new, only the forms that it undertook. Walker (1990) provides evidence and analysis of the Maori struggle for social justice, equality and self-determination since European contact.

12. The Treaty and its importance in contemporary Maori lives is not something that can be taken for granted. Not long after it was signed it was dismissed as a 'nullity' by the colonial government. In the space of the last 30 years the Treaty has gone from a document of historical interest to a 'blueprint for a bicultural New Zealand and from a "fraud" to a framework for living together with our differences' (Fleras and Spoonley, 1999: 14).

13. In April 2001 the Suspension Reduction Initiative (SRI) was introduced by the Government with the aim of reducing the suspension rate of Maori to the non-Maori rate. Initially, 86 secondary schools were targeted and Maori suspensions were reduced from 76 per 1,000 in 2000 to 56 per 1,000 in 2001 (ministerial announcements, 7 May 2002). Working in regional school clusters with extended family and community involvement seems to have had beneficial results, though it is too early to determine if the results will be ongoing or statistically significant.

14. The official Maori unemployment rate remains high. While the non-Maori rate is presently 5.4 per cent the Maori rate is 16 per cent (NZ Statistics 2001). Maori women are particularly vulnerable to unemployment. From the 1970s until the late 1980s Maori women were more likely to participate in the labour force than non-Maori women. However, with the onset of a recession

and the implementation of economic restructuring, the participation of women has fallen while non-Maori participation in the labour force has remained fairly constant (Te Puni Kokiri, 1999: 14). Though the 1996 census showed a slight improvement, Maori women remain less likely to be employed (47 per cent compared to 54 per cent of non-Maori) (ibid.). Maori women in the labour force continue to be concentrated in low employment growth sectors. Income disparity between Maori and non-Maori is a potent indicator of the disparities that exist in New Zealand society. As income can be associated with access to adequate housing, educational attainment, health status and criminal activity it is significant to note that Maori receive lower incomes than non-Maori for almost all occupations (Te Puni Kokiri, 2000: 26). Maori women earn significantly less than Maori men. Given that Maori women are much more likely than non-Maori women to be raising children on their own, the implications of income disparity are even more alarming. In 1996, 43 per cent of Maori women with dependent children were sole parents compared with 19 per cent of non-Maori women (Te Puni Kokiri, 1999: 8).

15. In the twelve months leading up to the 2001 Census three in eight adult Maori had received a government benefit (Statistics NZ 2001: 3).

16. The term 'race' is rarely used in the Aotearoa/New Zealand context. Though colonial and historical documents speak about the 'Maori race' it is no longer in common usage. The term ethnicity is used to refer to specific and general group identity.

17. Awatere-Huatas (1996) views on Maori sovereignty and many other issues have shifted dramatically since 1984. In 1984 she was in the vanguard of Maori calls for total autonomy, now as a Minister of Parliament and ACT party member (a right-leaning party) her views on these issues have changed. However, her 1984 work remains one of the clearest articulations of young radical Maori voice of the period.

18. Founded in 1951 the MWWL was the first national Maori organization to be formed. It set out to promote 'activities that would improve the position of all Maori, particularly women and children, in the fields of health, education and welfare' (Szaszy, 1993: xvi).

19. *Kaupapa Maori* refers to Maori philosophies, values, principles, rationales and approaches.

20. Traditional Maori gathering place; the *marae atea* is the space directly in front of the meeting house where rituals of encounter take place. Irwin (1992) alerts us to the fact that the term *marae* has at least two distinct meanings. The first refers to the whole complex made up of the encounter area, meeting house, cooking areas, dining areas and ablution blocks, while the second refers to the *marae* proper, i.e. the open space in front of the ancestral meeting house where hosts and guests first meet.

21. *Karanga* is the call of welcome that is ritually performed on the *marae*. It is performed by Maori women.

22. The NZDep96 scale of deprivation ranges from 1 to 10, where I represents the least deprived areas and 10 the most deprived areas. NZDep96 combines nine variables from the 1996 census and provides a deprivation score for each meshblock (a geographical unit defined by Statistics New Zealand containing a median of 90 people).

References

Awatere, D. (1984) *Maori Sovereignty*, Auckland: Broadsheet Publications.

Awatere-Huata, D. (1996) *My Journey*, Auckland: Seaview Press.

Cheyne, C., O'Brien, M. and Belgrave, M. (1999) *Social Policy in Aotearoa New Zealand*, Auckland: Oxford University Press.

Coates, K. S. and McHugh, P.G. (1998) *Living Relationships: Kokiri Ngatahi: The Treaty of Waitangi in the New Millennium*, Wellington: Victoria University Press.

Cox, L. (1993) *Kohitanga: The Search for Maori Political Unity*, Auckland: Oxford University Press.

Davis, P. and Dew, K. (eds.) (1999) *Health and Society in Aotearoa New Zealand*, Auckland: Oxford University Press.

Du Plessis, R. et al. (eds.) (1992) *Feminist Voices*, Auckland: Oxford University Press.

Durie, M. H. (1995) 'Tino Rangatiratanga', *He Pukenga Korero*, Vol. 1: 1.

Durie, M. H. (1998) *The Long Dispute: Maori Land Rights and European Colonization in Southern New Zealand*, Christchurch: Canterbury Press.

Evans, R. (1994) 'The Negation Powerlessness: Maori Feminism, a Perspective', '*Hecate: Speual Aotearoa/New Zealand* 20: 2, pp. 53–65.

Fleras, A. and Spoonley, P. (1999) *Recalling Aotearoa*, Auckland: Oxford University Press.

Ginsberg, E. (ed.) (1996) *Passing and the Fictions of Identity*, Durham, NC: Duke University Press.

Graham, D. (1997) *Trick or Treaty*, Wellington: GP Publications.

Greenland, H. (1991) 'Maori Ethnicity as Ideology'. In P. Spoonley, D. Pearson and C. Macpherson, (eds.) *Nga Take: Ethnic Relations and Racism in Aotearoa/New Zealand*, Palmerston North: The Dunsmore Press.

Hoskins, T. K. C. (2000) 'In the Interests of Maori Women? Discourses of Reclamation'. In A. Jones, P. Herda and T. Suaalii (eds.) (2000), *Bitter Sweet: Indigenous Women in the Pacific*, Dunedin: University of Otago Press.

Howden-Chapman, P. (1999) 'Socioeconomic Inequalities and Health'. In P. Davis and K. Dew, (eds.) *Health and Society in Aotearoa New Zealand*, Auckland: Oxford University Press.

Jrwin, K. (1992) 'Towards Theories of Maori Feminism', in R. DuPlessis et al. (eds.) *Feminist Voices: Women's Studies Text for Aotearoan/NZ*, Auckland: Oxford University Press.

Johnson, P. and Piharma, L. (1994) 'The Marginalization of Maori Women', *Hecate*, October 1994, 20: 2. Jones, A., Herda, P. and Suaalii, T. (eds.) (2000), *Bitter Sweet: Indigenous Women in the Pacific*, Dunedin: University of Otago Press.

Jones, A. and Guy, C. (1992) 'Radical Feminism in New Zealand: From Piha to Newtown'. In R. Du Plessis et al. (eds.) *Feminist Voices*, Auckland: Oxford University Press.

Kelsey, J. (1996) 'From Flagpoles to Pine Trees: Tino Rangatiratanga and Treaty Policy Today'. In P. Spoonley, D. Pearson and C. Macpherson (eds.) *Nga Patai: Racism and Ethnic Relations in Aotearoa/New Zealand*, Palmerston North: The Dunmore Press.

Kirk, G. (1997) 'Ecofeminism and Environmental Justice: Bridges Across Gender, Race and Class', *Frontiers*, May–August, 18: 2.

Larner, W. (1996) 'Gender and Ethnicity'. In P. Spoonley, D. Pearson and C. Macpherson (eds), *Nga Patai: Racism and Ethnic Relations in Aotearoa/New Zealand*, Palmerton North: The Dunmore Press.

MacDonald, C. (ed.) (1993) *The Vote, The Pill and the Demon Drink*, Wellington: Bridget Williams Books.

Mahuika, A. (1998) 'Whakapapa is the Heart'. In K. S. Coates and P. G. McHugh, *Living Relationships: Kokiri Ngatahi: The Treaty of Waitangi in the New Millennium*, Wellington: Victoria University Press.

McArdell, P. (1993) 'Whanaupani', in R. DuPlessis et al. (eds.) *Feminist Voices: Women's Studies Text for Aotearoa/NZ*, Auckland: Oxford University Press.

McHugh, P. G. (1998) 'Aboriginal Identity and Relations in North America and Australasia', in K. S. Coates and P. G. McHugh (eds.) *Living Relationships: Kokiri: Ngatahi: The Treaty of Waitangi in the New Millennium*, Wellington: Victoria University Press.

Manatu Hauora (Ministry of Health) (2003) *Building on Strengths: A Mental Health Promotion Strategy*, Wellington: Ministry A Health.

McIntosh, T. (2001) 'Hibiscus in the Flax Bush: the Maori-Pacific Island Interface', in C. Macpherson, P. Spoonley and M. Anae (eds.) *Tangata O Te Moana Nui: The Evolving Identities of Pacific Peoples in Aotearoa/New Zealand*, Palmerston North: Dunsmore Press.

McIntosh, T. (2001a) 'Death, Every Day', in C. Bell (ed.), *Sociology of Everyday Life in New Zealand*, Palmerston North: The Dunmore Press.

Poata-Smith, E. (1996) 'He Pokeke Uenuku I Tu Ai: The Evolution of Contemporary Maori Protest', in P. Spoonley, C. Macpherson and D. Pearson (eds.) *Nga Patai: Racism and Ethnicity in Aotearoa/New Zealand*, Palmerston North: The Dunsmore Press.

Reid, P. (1999) 'Nga Mahi Whakahaehae a Te Tangata Tiriti', in P. Davis and K. Dew (eds.) *Health and Society in Aotearoa New Zealand*, Auckland: Oxford University Press.

Reilly, M. (1996) 'Te Matakite Hou O Nga Korero Nehe No Niu Tireni: Revisioning New Zealand History', in P. Spoonley, D. Pearson and C. Macpherson (eds.) *Nga Patai: Racism and Ethnic Relations in Aotearoa/New Zealand*, Palmerston North: The Dunmore Press.

Salmond C., Crapmton, P. and Sutton, F. (1998) *NZDep96 Index of Deprivation*, Wellington: Ministry of Health.

Simpkin, G. (1994) 'Women for Aotearoa: Feminism and Maori Sovereignty', *Hecate: Special Aotearoa/New Zealand Issue*, October, 20: 2.

Sollons, W. (1997) *Neither Black Nor White Yet Both: Thematic Explorations of Interracial Literature*, New York: Oxford University Press.

Spoonley, P. (1996) 'Mahi Awatea? The Racialisation of Work in Aotearoa/New Zealand', in P. Spoonley, D. Pearson and C. Macpherson (eds.) *Nga Patai: Racism and Ethnic Relations in Aotearoa/New Zealand*, Palmerston North: The Dumore Press.

Spoonley, P., Pearson, D. and Macpherson, C. (eds.) (1991) *Nga Take: Ethnic Relations and Racism in Aotearoa/New Zealand*, Palmerston North: The Dunmore Press.

Spoonley, P., Pearson, D. and Macpherson, C. (eds.) (1996), *Nga Patai: Racism and Ethnic Relations in Aotearoa/New Zealand*, Palmerston North: The Dumore Press.

Smith, L. T. (1999) *Decolonizing Methodologies: Research and Indigenous Peoples*, London: Zed Books and Dunedin: University of Otago Press.

Statistics New Zealand: Te Tari Tatau (1998) *New Zealand Official Yearbook 1998*, Wellington: GP Publications.

Statistics New Zealand: Te Tari Tatau (2001) *2001 Census Snapshot (Maori)*, Wellington: GP Publications, or www.stats.govt.nz

Szaszy M. (1993) 'Me Aro Koe kit e Ha o Hineahuone', in W. Ihimaera (ed.) *Te Ao Marama 2, Regaining Aotearoa: Maori Writers Speak Out*. Auckland: Reed Books.

Te Awekotuku, N. (1991) *Mana Wahine Maori*, Auckland: New Women's Press.

Te Puni Kokiri: Ministry of Maori Development (1999) *Titiro Hangai, Ka Marama: Maori Women in Focus*, Wellington: Te Puni Kokiri and Minitatanga Mo Nga Wahine (Ministry of Women's Affairs).

Te Puni Kokiri: Ministry of Maori Development (2000a) *Progress towards Closing Social and Economic Gaps Between Maori and Non-Maori*, Wellington: TPK.

Te Puni Kokiri: Ministry of Maori Development (2000b) *Tikanga Oranga Hauora*, Wellington: TPK

Walker, R. (1990) *Ka Whawhai Tonu Matou: Struggle Without End*, Auckland: Penguin.

Walker, R. (1996) *Nga Pepa A Ranginui: The Walker Papers*, Auckland: Penguin.

Webster, S. (1998) *Patrons of Maori Culture: Power, Theory and Ideology in the Maori Renaissance*, Dunedin: University of Otago Press.

Index